INTERNET THEORY, TECHNOLOGY AND APPLICATIONS

THE OPEN INTERNET, NET NEUTRALITY AND THE FCC

INTERNET THEORY, TECHNOLOGY AND APPLICATIONS

Additional books in this series can be found on Nova's website under the Series tab.

Additional E-books in this series can be found on Nova's website under the E-books tab.

INTERNET THEORY, TECHNOLOGY AND APPLICATIONS

THE OPEN INTERNET, NET NEUTRALITY AND THE FCC

ANDREW C. FIRTH
AND
NATALIE H. PIERSON
EDITORS

Nova Science Publishers, Inc.
New York

For permission to use material from this book please contact us:
Telephone 631-231-7269; Fax 631-231-8175
Web Site: http://www.novapublishers.com

Library of Congress Cataloging-in-Publication Data

The open Internet, net neutrality and the FCC / editors, Andrew C. Firth and Natalie H. Pierson.
p. cm.
Includes index.
ISBN 978-1-61209-983-5 (hardcover)
1. Telecommunication policy--United States. 2. Network neutrality--United States. 3. Internet--United States. I. Firth, Andrew C. II. Pierson, Natalie H.
HE7781.O64 2011
384.3'3--dc22

2011005848

Published by Nova Science Publishers, Inc. † New York

CONTENTS

Preface **vii**

Chapter 1 The FCC's Authority to Regulate Net Neutrality After *Comcast v*. FCC **1**
Kathleen Ann Ruane

Chapter 2 Preserving the Open Internet, Broadband Industry Practices **15**
Federal Communications Commission

Chapter Sources **185**

Index **187**

PREFACE

The Internet has thrived because of its freedom and openness, the absence of any gatekeeper blocking lawful uses of the network or picking winners and losers online. Consumers and innovators do not have to seek permission before they use the Internet to launch new technologies, start businesses, connect with friends or share their views. Consumers can make their own choices about what applications and services to use and are free to decide what content they want to access, create, or share with others. This openness promotes competition. This new book examines the open Internet, and the role of the FCC and their authority to regulate net neutrality.

Chapter 1- In 2007, through various experiments by the media, most notably the Associated Press, it became clear that Comcast was intermittently blocking the use of an application called BitTorrentTM and, possibly, other peer-to-peer (P2P) file sharing programs on its network. Comcast eventually admitted to the practice and agreed to cease blocking the use of the P2P applications on its network. However, Comcast maintains that its actions were reasonable network management and not in violation of the Federal Communications Commission's ("FCC" or "Commission") policy.

In response to a petition from Free Press for a declaratory ruling that Comcast's blocking of P2P applications was not "reasonable network management," the FCC conducted an investigation into Comcast's network management practices. The FCC determined that Comcast had violated the agency's Internet Policy Statement when it blocked certain applications on its network and that the practice at issue in this case was not "reasonable network management." The FCC declined to fine Comcast because its Internet Policy Statement had never previously been the basis for enforcement forfeitures. Comcast appealed this decision to the U.S. Court of Appeals for the D.C. Circuit, as did other public interest groups.

Chapter 2- Today the Commission takes an important step to preserve the Internet as an open platform for innovation, investment, job creation, economic growth, competition, and free expression. To provide greater clarity and certainty regarding the continued freedom and openness of the Internet, we adopt three basic rules that are grounded in broadly accepted Internet norms, as well as our own prior decisions:

In: The Open Internet, Net Neutrality and the FCC
Editors: Andrew C. Firth and Natalie H. Pierson
ISBN: 978-1-61209-983-5

Chapter 1

THE FCC'S AUTHORITY TO REGULATE NET NEUTRALITY AFTER *COMCAST V.* FCC

Kathleen Ann Ruane

SUMMARY

In 2007, through various experiments by the media, most notably the Associated Press, it became clear that Comcast was intermittently blocking the use of an application called BitTorrentTM and, possibly, other peer-to-peer (P2P) file sharing programs on its network. Comcast eventually admitted to the practice and agreed to cease blocking the use of the P2P applications on its network. However, Comcast maintains that its actions were reasonable network management and not in violation of the Federal Communications Commission's ("FCC" or "Commission") policy.

In response to a petition from Free Press for a declaratory ruling that Comcast's blocking of P2P applications was not "reasonable network management," the FCC conducted an investigation into Comcast's network management practices. The FCC determined that Comcast had violated the agency's Internet Policy Statement when it blocked certain applications on its network and that the practice at issue in this case was not "reasonable network management." The FCC declined to fine Comcast because its Internet Policy Statement had never previously been the basis for enforcement forfeitures. Comcast appealed this decision to the U.S. Court of Appeals for the D.C. Circuit, as did other public interest groups.

The D.C. Circuit ruled on April 6, 2010, that the FCC could not base ancillary authority to regulate cable Internet services solely upon broad policy goals contained elsewhere in the Communications Act. Whatever the merits of other jurisdictional arguments the FCC may advance, the court found that the FCC did not have jurisdiction to enforce its network management principles on the basis it had advanced in that case. The court did not address the other questions posed by the case, including whether the FCC could proceed via adjudication.

The court's ruling has thrown into doubt the FCC's authority to regulate Internet network management. The FCC had announced the possibility of reclassifying the transmission component of broadband Internet services as a telecommunications service under Title II of the Communications Act. However, in a recent statement regarding the status of the rulemaking, Chairman Genachowski announced that the agency had abandoned its proposal to reclassify broadband Internet services. In his statement, the Chairman indicated that the FCC would anchor its authority to implement the new regulations in various sections of the Communications Act. As of this writing, the order the Chairman has circulated to the other commissioners had not been released to the public, so it is unclear how the FCC's current approach differs from its previously failed attempt to assert ancillary authority. If the FCC's new proposal is adopted, the FCC's assertion of ancillary authority to regulate in this area may, again, be subject to court challenge.

Congress could act to grant the FCC the authority necessary to adopt network management rules. If a law were enacted, the FCC would not have to rely on its ancillary jurisdiction to enforce network management rules.

INTRODUCTION

Some degree of Internet traffic management is necessary for networks to function effectively. For example, in order for voice conversations to occur over the Internet, the data packets encoding the communications must arrive in rapid sequence. Long delays between the arrival of voice data packets would make voice conversations over the Internet impossible to conduct. Prioritization of voice data packets over other packets traveling simultaneously over the same network ensures clear voice transmissions, while minimally delaying other network traffic. Logically, if network managers have the power to prioritize data packets, they also have the power to subordinate them. This means network managers have the power to render the applications that depend on packet- prioritization (like voice or video applications) useless. Accordingly, there must be a line between network management that is necessary for the Internet to provide quality service to users, and network management that is anti-competitive or otherwise harmful to the free exchange of information. Questions have arisen regarding where that line is and who has the ability to draw it.

In an attempt to separate the unnecessary network management practices from the necessary, the Federal Communications Commission (FCC) issued an Internet Policy Statement. The Internet Policy Statement endeavored to ensure that broadband consumers would have access to all lawful content on the Internet and that all lawful applications could be used on networks. These rights may be limited by the needs of broadband providers to reasonably manage their networks. The Policy Statement was not a regulation carrying the force of law; therefore, violation of the Policy Statement presumably would not result in liability.

In 2007, through various experiments by the media, most notably the Associated Press, it became clear that Comcast Corporation (Comcast) was intermittently interfering actively with the use of an application called BitTorrentTM and, possibly, other peer-to-peer (P2P) file sharing programs on its network, as a method of traffic management. While initially denying the accusations, Comcast eventually admitted to the practice and agreed to cease blocking the use of the P2P applications on its network. However, Comcast maintains that its actions in relation to P2P programs were reasonable network management and not in violation of the FCC's policy.

In response to a petition from Free Press for a declaratory ruling that Comcast's blocking of P2P applications was not "reasonable network management," the FCC conducted an investigation into Comcast's network management practices. The FCC determined that Comcast had violated the agency's Internet Policy Statement when it blocked certain applications on its network and that the practice at issue in this case was not "reasonable network management." Comcast disputes the FCC's authority to issue such a ruling and appealed the decision to the U.S. Court of Appeals for the D.C. Circuit. The court held that the FCC did not make a proper argument for asserting ancillary jurisdiction over network management practices. This report will discuss these events and their legal implications in greater detail.

PROCEEDINGS AT THE FCC

FCC's Network Management Principles

Federal policy towards the Internet, as embodied in Section 240(b) of the Communications Act of 1934, as amended, is "to preserve the vibrant and competitive free market that presently exists for the Internet" and "to promote the continued development of the Internet."[1] In Section 706 of the Communications Act, Congress instructs the FCC to encourage "the deployment on a reasonable and timely basis of advanced telecommunications capability to all Americans."[2]

Basing its authority on these two provisions, the FCC issued a policy statement intended to offer guidance to network owners regarding the rights of consumers accessing the Internet through their networks.[3] The FCC acknowledged that information service providers (those who provide access to the Internet) are not governed by stringent Title II common carrier regulations, but asserted that it had jurisdiction to issue the Policy Statement pursuant to its Title I ancillary jurisdiction.[4] Title I ancillary jurisdiction permits the Commission to issue additional regulatory obligations in order to regulate interstate and foreign communications in furtherance of the Communications Act. In the FCC's assessment, Title I ancillary jurisdiction granted the FCC ample authority to take steps to ensure that broadband networks are widely deployed, open, affordable and accessible to all and to ensure that Internet services are operated in a neutral manner. Accordingly, the FCC adopted the following principles to encourage broadband deployment and to preserve and promote the open and interconnected nature of the public Internet:

- consumers are entitled to access the lawful Internet content of their choice;
- consumers are entitled to run applications and use services of their choice, subject to the needs of law enforcement;
- consumers are entitled to connect their choice of legal devices that do not harm the network; and
- consumers are entitled to competition among network providers, application and service providers, and content providers.[5]

It is also important to note that upon adopting these precepts the FCC expressly stated that it was "not adopting rules in this policy statement" and that the principles adopted were "subject to reasonable network management."[6] The Commission termed the Policy Statement to be guidance and insight into its approach to the Internet that was intended to be consistent with Congressional directives. The Commission did not put the network management principles out for public comment, nor did it publish the principles in the Code of Federal Regulations.

The Ruling Against Comcast

In 2007, the Associated Press reported the results of various tests it had conducted to investigate whether Comcast was blocking P2P applications on its network.[7] The AP concluded that Comcast "actively interfere[d] with attempts by some of its high-speed Internet subscribers to share files online."[8] The AP alleged that Comcast was specifically targeting P2P applications, such as Gnutella and BitTorrentTM, preventing anyone who wished to use these applications from being able to do so in an effective way. The Electronic Frontier Foundation conducted similar tests with similar results. Comcast admitted to interfering with P2P applications on occasions of high volume traffic, but maintained that its interferences were a reasonable network management practice.[9]

As a result, Free Press, a non-profit organization that advocates for media reform, filed a complaint against Comcast with the FCC. The complaint asked the FCC to declare "that an Internet service provider violates the [Commission's] Internet Policy Statement when it intentionally degrades a targeted Internet application."[10] Free Press also filed a petition with the Commission requesting that the agency issue a declaratory ruling that would clarify that any Internet service provider that intentionally degrades or blocks particular applications would be in violation of the FCC's Internet Policy Statement. The Commission put the petition out for public comment.[11]

After hearing comments from the public and from industry participants, the Commission determined that Comcast had violated its Internet Policy Statement, because its practice of degrading usage of P2P applications prevents consumers from using the lawful application of their choice and does not fall under the exception for reasonable network management. [12] The Commission was particularly troubled by what it determined to be Comcast's lack of transparency regarding the company's network management practices.[13] The Commission found that Comcast was less than forthcoming about its network management practices and that only after independent evidence emerged that Comcast was not being truthful did the corporation admit to its true methods of traffic management related to P2P programs.[14] The Commission noted that "[a] hallmark of whether something is reasonable is whether a provider is willing to disclose to its customers what it is doing."[15] Since Comcast, evidently, was not disclosing its practices, the Commission viewed its actions as suspect. Furthermore, the Commission found there were other effective methods for managing the heavy traffic generated by P2P programs that fell short of interfering with the applications' ability to function.[16]

Despite determining in its adjudication that Comcast had violated its Internet Policy Statement, the Commission did not issue a forfeiture order against the company. [17] The

Commission also declined to issue an injunction or a cease-and-desist order against the company. The company had already agreed to cease its objectionable practices and the Commission determined that a reasonable transition period was necessary.[18] To monitor Comcast's compliance, the Commission required Comcast submit to the Commission, within 30 days of the order: (1) the precise contours of its previous network management practices; (2) a compliance plan "with interim benchmarks that describe[d] how it intend[ed] to transition from discriminatory to nondiscriminatory network management practices [by the end of 2008]; and (3) publicly disclose its newly implemented and protocol-agnostic network management practices.[19]

Comcast filed the requested documents with the FCC on September 19, 2008.[20] Comcast also filed a certification with the FCC on January 5, 2009, affirming that the company had fulfilled its promise to move to protocol-agnostic network management practices.[21] The Commission sent a letter to Comcast on January 18, 2009 asking the company to clarify its treatment of VoIP services.[22] The Commission expressed concern that Comcast made no distinction between VoIP services in its filing, but, apparently, treats its own VoIP service offering differently than it treats other VoIP services. Furthermore, the Commission noted that if Comcast's VoIP service is a separate offering of a telephone service (distinct from the broadband offering), then it is possible that it should be classified as a "telecommunications service." Telecommunications services are subject to more stringent regulations under Title II of the Communications. The Commission, therefore, asked Comcast to explain why it omitted the effects its new network management practices would have on Comcast's VoIP service from its required filings and why Comcast's VoIP service should not be treated as a telecommunications service under Title II.

Comcast filed its answer with the Commission on January 30, 2009.[23] The company argued that Comcast's voice service is a separate service from its broadband offering. In the company's opinion, it, therefore, was not part of the ongoing discussions about Comcast's broadband network management practices and is not affected by the newly implemented management regime. Comcast also argued that the question of whether Comcast's voice service should be treated as a telecommunications service is irrelevant to the current proceedings, but, nonetheless, asserted that Comcast's voice offering is not a telecommunications service. The Commission has yet to take any action in response to Comcast's letter.

Though Comcast voluntarily ceased the network management practices that the Commission found objectionable, Comcast appealed the decision of the Commission to the D.C. Circuit.[24]

Court Opinion in Comcast v. FCC

On April 6, 2010, the D.C. Circuit vacated the FCC's order against Comcast because the FCC had failed to tie its assertion of ancillary authority to any "statutorily mandated responsibility."[25] After dispensing with the FCC's preliminary arguments against the court's jurisdiction, the panel applied the test for ancillary jurisdiction it had announced in *American Library Assn. v. FCC*,[26] and found the FCC's argument insufficient to satisfy the standards.

The Supreme Court recognizes that the FCC has so-called "ancillary authority" to regulate services that it has not been granted express authority to regulate.[27] The FCC did not claim that it had express authority to regulate cable Internet service. Rather, the agency argued that regulation of Internet services was "reasonably ancillary to the . . . effective performance of its statutorily mandated responsibilities."[28] The FCC relied primarily upon Section 230(b) of the Communications Act, which states that "it is the policy of the United States ... to promote the continued development of the Internet and other interactive computer services [and] to encourage the development of technologies which maximize user control over what information is received by individuals families and schools who use the Internet."[29] The FCC argued that this statement of policy, along with the general rulemaking authority in Title I, was sufficient to assert ancillary jurisdiction over cable Internet network management.

In *American Library Assn. v. FCC,* the D.C. Circuit recently held that the FCC may assert its ancillary authority when two conditions are met: (1) the Commission's general jurisdiction grant under Title I covers the regulated subject and (2) the regulations are reasonably ancillary to the Commission's effective performance of its *statutorily mandated responsibilities*.[30] The court agreed that condition one had been met. Cable Internet services falls within the general jurisdiction granted to the Commission under Title I. The court held, however, that the FCC had failed to satisfy the second condition because statements of policy could not be considered to be statutorily mandated responsibilities under the Communications Act.[31]

The court detailed each case heard by the Supreme Court and by the D.C. Circuit where ancillary jurisdiction was the basis for the FCC's authority to act in the case. In each case, the court found that where the FCC had ancillary authority to exercise jurisdiction, the FCC's argument for jurisdiction related to a specific grant of authority to regulate in a related area and did not rely solely on a policy statement, as the Commission had done here. The court expressed concern that if it had adopted the FCC's argument and allowed ancillary authority to rest on statements of policy in the Communications Act, the FCC's authority to regulate would have been nearly boundless and the agency could find reason to regulate in many new areas where Congress had not granted specific authority to do so.

The court also addressed the other statutory provisions upon which the FCC claimed to rely for jurisdiction.[32] Some of these statutory provisions, such as Section 706 of the Communications Act,[33] arguably might grant the FCC specific authority to regulate in an area reasonably related to the regulation of cable Internet services. In each case, however, the court found the FCC had failed in some way to properly advance the argument for jurisdiction on the basis of these other statutory provisions. Therefore, the court found that it could not hold that the FCC had ancillary authority to regulate cable Internet services based upon any of these specific grants of regulatory authority.

COMMISSION'S PROPOSALS TO ASSERT REGULATORY AUTHORITY OVER BROADBAND INTERNET SERVICES

The decision of the D.C. Circuit in *Comcast v. FCC*[34] has thrown the agency's current authority to regulate broadband Internet network managment into doubt. Broadband Internet services are currently classified as information services, to which Title I of the

Communications Act applies.[35] The FCC does not possess direct authority to regulate services classified under Title I,[36] and was unsuccessful in its initial attempt to assert ancillary authority over broadband Internet network management in the *Comcast* case. As a result, the agency announced the possibility of reclassifying the transmission component of broadband Internet services as a telecommunications service under Title II of the Communications Act.[37] The FCC hoped this potential reclassification would ground the FCC's authority to regulate broadband Internet services more firmly in the governing law. In his most recent statement addressing the issue of reclassification, Chairman Genachowski stated that the FCC has abandoned its plan to reclassify broadband Internet services, and would instead, presumably, proceed pursuant to its ancillary authority.[38] The Chairman's most recent statement is discussed below.

Background

In order to understand the uncertainty surrounding the FCC's authority over broadband Internet services, some background is needed. After the passage of the Telecommunications Act of 1996, the FCC found it necessary to determine what kind of service broadband Internet service was.[39] The agency's choices were to classify broadband Internet access as an information service,[40] over which it would have no direct authority to regulate under Title I, or as a telecommunications service,[41] over which it would have extensive authority to regulate under Title II. There was also an intermediate option. The FCC contemplated classifying the transmission component of a broadband Internet service as a telecommunications service, while classifying the processing component as an information service.[42] The FCC ultimately chose to classify broadband Internet services as information services only.[43]

At the time, in 2002, the provision of broadband Internet services arguably was still a nascent industry, and the FCC expressed a desire to avoid introducing into the developing market what it thought could be too many regulations.[44] However, this was a contentious question. The Supreme Court, in *NCTA v. Brand X*, made the final decision.[45] The question before the court was whether the FCC could define cable-modem services (i.e., cable broadband services) as information services. Opponents of that classification argued that the FCC did not have discretion to define cable modem services as an information service. The Court, however, sided with the FCC. What is important for the purposes of this discussion is that the Court did not say that cable modem services are clearly and unambiguously information services. Instead, the court said that the definitions of telecommunications services and of information services were ambiguous as they related to cable modem services, and that the FCC, as the agency with jurisdiction under the Communications Act, had the authority to interpret those definitions.[46] The Court gave deference to the FCC's determination that cable modem services should be defined as information services and determined that the FCC's classification of cable modem services in this way was reasonable.[47]

However, three Justices dissented. Justice Scalia authored the dissent, concluding that cable modem services were actually two separate services: the computing service which was an information service, and the transmission service, which was a telecommunications service.[48] The classification that these Justices believed the Communications Act clearly mandated was the classification that the FCC recently proposed to apply to broadband Internet services.[49]

Three Possible Paths to Authority Under Current Law

Chairman Genachowski announced his intention to pursue what he termed "light touch" Title II regulation of broadband services in May of 2010.[50] As explained in the statement of the FCC's General Counsel, it was the intention of the FCC to commence a rulemaking to reclassify only the transmission component of broadband access services ("Internet connectivity") as a telecommunications service, while the data processing portion of the service would remain an information service.[51] The Chairman argued that, in choosing only to reclassify the transmission component of broadband access services, the reach of the FCC's jurisdiction would have been sufficiently narrowed so as to avoid giving the agency the authority to regulate Internet content. This plan, according to the Chairman at the time, also would have avoided the imposition of regulation so pervasive as to become burdensome.[52]

In keeping with this announcement, on June 17, 2010, the FCC released a notice of inquiry (NOI) into the framework of broadband Internet services.[53] In the NOI, the agency asked for comment on a number of questions. The FCC made clear that its ultimate goal in issuing the NOI was to determine the best avenue for restoring the agency's previous understanding of its authority to regulate broadband Internet services.[54] In other words, the FCC was seeking firmer ground for its authority to continue rulemakings along the lines of the broadband network management rulemakings[55] and the order it issued in 2007 finding Comcast to be in violation of the FCC's network management policies.[56] In doing so, the FCC recognized that the D.C. Circuit's decision in *Comcast v. FCC* had thrown the agency's assertions of ancillary authority over broadband network management into considerable doubt.[57]

The NOI listed three main potential paths forward and sought comment on the feasibility of each. The first question the NOI asked was whether the FCC could find a better way to assert ancillary authority over broadband Internet services.[58] The D.C. Circuit did not foreclose on the possibility of the FCC asserting ancillary authority in other ways. It merely rejected the FCC's argument in that particular case.[59] Therefore, the FCC asked whether broadband Internet services may continue to be classified as information services while the agency asserts a different (or multiple different) statutory basis for exercising ancillary jurisdiction. There are a number of potential theories for ancillary jurisdiction for which the FCC sought comment.[60] It appears that ultimately, one of these options, or a combination thereof, will be the path the FCC will choose. Allowing broadband Internet services to remain information services will mean that the FCC may proceed straight to a network neutrality rulemaking without having to first engage in a reclassification rulemaking.

The other two potential paths towards firmer authority to regulate would have involved direct regulation under Title II of the Communications Act. Therefore, it would have been necessary to reclassify at least the Internet connectivity portion of broadband Internet services as a telecommunications service, because only telecommunications services are governed by Title II. The FCC asked for comment on how to define Internet connectivity for reclassification.[61] Assuming the FCC chose one of these two paths, this reclassification would likely have been reviewed by the courts, in light of the fact that the Supreme Court upheld the agency's previous classification of broadband Internet services as a unified information service. However, as discussed earlier, *Brand X* gave deference to the FCC's interpretation of the Communications Act in this area.[62] Furthermore, in the recent case *FCC v. Fox Television*, the Supreme Court held that when an agency issues a new (and different from its previous) interpretation of a statute it has the authority to implement, the agency "need not demonstrate to a court's satisfaction that the reasons for the new policy are better than the reasons for the old one."[63] The agency must show only that its current interpretation is reasonable, though in some circumstances a more detailed justification for the change must be made than would otherwise be necessary if the agency was rulemaking on a blank slate.[64]

Assuming that such a reclassification would have been upheld by the courts, the second potential path forward would have been to apply the full force of Title II regulation to broadband Internet connectivity (as the FCC would define it). The FCC sought comment on the potential effects of such a decision.[65] The third option was to apply limited Title II regulation to broadband and to forbear from applying the portions of Title II to broadband access services that the FCC deemed contrary to the public interest. Section 401 of the Telecommunications Act of 1996 requires the FCC to forbear from applying any regulation or provision under Title II to a provider of telecommunications services if the Commission determines that

> (1) enforcement of such regulation or provision is not necessary to ensure that the charges, practices, classifications, or regulations by, for, or in connection with that telecommunications carrier or telecommunications service are just and reasonable and are not unjustly or unreasonably discriminatory; (2) enforcement of such regulation or provision is not necessary for the protection of consumers; and (3) forbearance from applying such provision or regulation is consistent with the public interest.[66]

In their May 2010 statements, the Chairman and General Counsel argued that this provision would require forbearance from many of Title II's more onerous provisions, such as the rate regulation and tariff provisions, because applying those provisions would not be consistent with the public interest.[67]

The NOI asked for comment on this potential action.[68] It further asked for comment on the provisions on Title II from which the agency should not forbear. In particular, the NOI asked for comment on applying the provisions of Title II that the FCC had identified as likely to be needed to have adequate enforcement authority in its earlier press releases on this issue.[69] These provisions are Sections 201 (requiring service upon request and reasonable rates),[70] 202 (prohibiting unreasonable discrimination),[71] 208 (granting the FCC authority to act upon complaints),[72] 222 (protecting privacy),[73] 254 (universal service),[74] and 255[75] (access for disabled persons).[76] In the FCC's announcements, the General Counsel identified these provisions as potentially sufficient to "do the job" of providing enough authority to accomplish the FCC's goals.[77] However, the NOI asked for comment on other provisions that may have been necessary to assert jurisdiction as well.[78]

Chairman Genachowski's December 1, 2010, Statement

In a statement made on December 1, 2010, Chairman Genachowski announced that the FCC had abandoned its proposal to reclassify broadband Internet services and that they would remain classified wholly as information services.[79] In his statement, the Chairman indicated that the FCC would anchor its authority to implement the new regulations in various sections of the Communications Act. As of this writing, the order the Chairman has circulated to the other commissioners had not been released to the public, so it is unclear how the FCC's current approach differs from its previously failed attempt to assert ancillary authority. If the FCC's new proposal is adopted, the FCC's assertion of ancillary authority to regulate in this area may, again, be subject to court challenge.

In his speech, the Chairman indicated that there would be four main components to the proposed regulations. First, the agency plans to implement a "meaningful transparency obligation," to inform consumers regarding how networks are being managed. Second, the new regulations would endeavor to ensure consumers' rights to send and receive lawful material online. Third, unreasonable discrimination among lawful Internet traffic will be prohibited, so as to prevent Internet service providers from favoring their own content over other content providers. Lastly, reasonable network management will be permissible in order to aid service providers in blocking harmful Internet traffic and managing congestion.

Furthermore, the Chairman indicated that not all of these principles would immediately apply to wireless mobile broadband Internet services, as they would apply to wireline broadband Internet services. The agency plans to recognize that wireless mobile broadband is at an earlier stage of development than its wired counterpart. As a result, it appears that only a "basic no blocking rule" and a transparency rule will apply to mobile broadband, initially.[80] However, the FCC will reserve the right to monitor the industry and adjust its regulatory status as warranted.

The full details of this proposal have not yet been released to the public. Thus, it is difficult to analyze whether the FCC has sufficient grounds to assert ancillary authority or what the proposed principals will look like and mean for broadband service providers when codified into regulation. This report will be updated once the latest information regarding the proposed rules is released.

It is worth noting that both Republican FCC commissioners, Robert M. McDowell and Meredith Attwell Baker, have voiced their opposition to the Chairman's proposal to adopt this proposal at the December 21 FCC Open Meeting. Commissioner McDowell argued in his statement that "[s]uch rules would upend three decades of bipartisan and international consensus that the Internet is best able to thrive in the absence of regulation."[81] While Commissioner Baker argued that the Commission does not have authority to act and that "whether the Internet should be regulated is a decision best left to the directly elected representatives of the American people."[82]

End Notes

1 47 U.S.C. § 230(b)(2).

2 47 U.S.C. § 157 (incorporating section 706 of the Telecommunications Act of 1996, P.L. 104-104, 110 Stat. 56 (1996)).

[3] In the Matters of the Appropriate Framework for Broadband Access to the Internet over Wireline Facilities; Review of Regulatory Requirements for Incumbent LEC Broadband Telecommunications Services; Computer III Further Remand Proceedings: Bell Operating Company Provision of Enhanced Services; 1998 Biennial Regulatory Review – Review of Computer III and ONA Safeguards and Requirements; Inquiry Concerning High-Speed Access to the Internet Over Cable and Other Facilities; Internet Over Cable Declaratory Ruling; Appropriate Regulatory Treatment for Broadband Access to the Internet Over Cable Facilities, 20 FCC Rcd 14986 (2005) [hereinafter FCC's Network Management Principles].

[4] *Id.* at 14988.

[5] *Id.*

[6] *Id.* at n. 15.

[7] Peter Svensson, Comcast Blocks Some Internet Traffic, AP Testing Shows, Associated Press, Oct. 19, 2007.

[8] *Id.*

[9] Letter from Mary McManus, Senior Director of FCC and Regulatory Policy, Comcast Corporation to Kris A. Monteith, Chief, Enforcement Bureaus, File No. EB-08-OJ-1518, at 5 (Jan. 25, 2008) (Comcast Response Letter).

[10] Formal Complaint of Free Press and Public Knowledge Against Comcast Corporation for Secretly Degrading Peerto-Peer Applications, File No. EB-08-IH-1518 (Nov. 1, 2007).

[11] Broadband Industry Practices Petition of Free Press et al. for Declaratory Ruling that Degrading an Internet Application Violates the FCC's Internet Policy Statement and Does Not Meet an Exception for "Reasonable Network Management, WC Docket No. 07-52, Public Notice, 23 FCC Rcd 343 (WCB 2008).

[12] In the Matters of Formal Complaint of Free Press and Public Knowledge Against Comcast Corporation for Secretly Degrading Peer-to-Peer Applications and Broadband Industry Practices Petition of Free Press et al. for Declaratory Ruling that Degrading an Internet Application Violates the FCC's Internet Policy Statement and Does Not Meet an Exception for "Reasonable Network Management," 23 FCC Rcd 13028 (2008) [hereinafter Comcast Decision].

[13] *Id.* at para. 52.

[14] *Id.* at para. 53.

[15] *Id.*

[16] *Id.* at para. 49.

[17] *Id.* at para. 54. Because the Commission was enforcing a policy statement that had never previously been enforced, the agency did not issue a forfeiture order in this particular case. The Commission reserved the right to proceed by adjudication in the future, and believed it could issue forfeiture orders for future violations of the network management principles.

[18] *Id.*

[19] *Id.* Failure to submit the required documents and / or failure to complete its transition to protocol-agnostic network management would have resulted in further enforcement action by the Commission. *Id.* at para. 55.

[20] Letter from Kathryn A. Zachem, Vice President, Regulatory and State Legislative Affairs, Comcast to Marlene H. Dortch, Secretary, FCC, Re: In the Matters of Formal Complaint of Free Press and Public Knowledge Against Comcast Corporation for Secretly Degrading Peer-to-Peer Applications; Broadband Industry Practices: Petition of Free Press et al. for Declaratory Ruling that Degrading an Internet Application Violates the FCC's Internet Policy Statement and Does Not Meet an Exception for "Reasonable Network Management," File No. EB-08-IH-1 518, WC Docket No. 07-52 (September 19, 2008).

[21] Letter from Kathryn A. Zachem, Vice President, Regulatory and State Legislative Affairs, Comcast to Marelene Dortch, Secretary, FCC, Re: In the Matters of Formal Complaint of Free Press and Public Knowledge Against Comcast Corporation for Secretly Degrading Peer-to-Peer Applications; Broadband Industry Practices: Petition of Free Press et al. for Declaratory Ruling that Degrading an Internet Application Violates the FCC's Internet Policy Statement and Does Not Meet an Exception for "Reasonable Network Management," File No. EB-08-IH-1 518, WC Docket No. 07-52 (January 5, 2009).

[22] Letter from Dana R. Shaffer, Chief, Wireline Competition Bureau, and Matthew Berry, General Counsel, FCC, to Katherine A. Zachem, Vice President, Regulatory Affairs, Comcast Corporation, Re: In the Matters of Formal Complaint of Free Press and Public Knowledge Against Comcast Corporation for Secretly Degrading Peer-to-Peer Applications; Broadband Industry Practices: Petition of Free Press et al. for Declaratory Ruling that Degrading an Internet Application Violates the FCC's Internet Policy Statement and Does Not Meet an Exception for "Reasonable Network Management," File No. EB-08-IH-1518, WC Docket No. 07-52 (January 19, 2009).

[23] Letter from Kathryn A. Zachem, Vice President, Regulatory and State Legislative Affairs, Comcast to Dana R. Shaffer, Chief, Wireline Competition Bureau, and Matthew Berry, General Counsel, FCC Re: In the Matters of Formal Complaint of Free Press and Public Knowledge Against Comcast Corporation for Secretly Degrading Peer-to-Peer Applications; Broadband Industry Practices: Petition of Free Press et al. for Declaratory Ruling that Degrading an Internet Application Violates the FCC's Internet Policy Statement and Does Not Meet an Exception for "Reasonable Network Management," File No. EB-08-IH-1518, WC Docket No. 07-52 (January 30, 2009).

[24] Petition for Review and, in the Alternative, Notice of Appeal, Comcast Corporation v. Federal Communications Commission, (No. 08-) (D.C. Cir. 2008).

[25] Comcast v. Federal Communications Commission, No. 08-1291, 2010 U.S. App. LEXIS 7039 (D.C. Cir. April 6, 2010). The court did not address the question of whether the FCC acted appropriately in attempting to enforce the policy statement through an adjudication because the FCC did not clear its jurisdictional hurdle.

[26] 403 F. 3d 689, 69 1-92 (D.C. Cir. 2005).

[27] *See* United States v. Southwestern Cable Co., 392 U.S. 157 (1968), United States v. Midwest Video Corp., 406 U.S. 649 (1972), FCC v. Midwest Video Corp., 440 U.S. 589 (1979).

[28] Comcast v. Federal Communications Commission, No. 08-1291, 2010 U.S. App. LEXIS 7039, at *2 (D.C. Cir. April 6, 2010).

[29] *Id.* at *17.

[30] *Id.* at *7.

[31] *Id.* at *29 - 30.

[32] *Id.* at *30 – 36.

[33] Section 706 of the Communications Act states that "the Commission ... shall encourage the deployment on a reasonable and timely basis of advanced telecommunications capability to all Americans." The court agreed that this could be a direct mandate to regulate. The Commission, however, is legally bound by its previous interpretation of Section 706. The Commission had previously found that Section 706 did not constitute an independent grant of authority. In the court's opinion, the Commission could not rely on Section 706 as an independent grant of statutory authority in this case, because it had previously held that Section 706 was not an independent grant of authority and it is bound by its own interpretation of the section. *Id.* at *30 – 31. The Commission does have the option of conducting a rulemaking to reinterpret Section 706 as an independent grant of regulatory authority. The Commission would have to complete that rulemaking before asserting Section 706 as a source of ancillary authority. *See* FCC v. Fox Television Stations, Inc., 129 S.Ct. 1800, 1811 (2009).

[34] Comcast v. Federal Communications Commission, 600 F.3d 642 (D.C. Cir. 2010). (*Comcast*) CRS Report R40234, *The FCC's Authority to Regulate Net Neutrality after Comcast v. FCC* , by Kathleen Ann Ruane.

[35] *See*, Inquiry Concerning High-Speed Access to the Internet Over Cable & Other Facilities; Internet Over Cable Declaratory Ruling; Appropriate Regulatory Treatment for Broadband Access to the Internet Over Cable Facilities, 17 FCC Rcd 4798 (2002) (Cable Modem Declaratory Ruling).

[36] *Id.*

[37] Press Release, Chairman Julius Genachowski, FCC, The Third Way: A Narrowly Tailored Broadband Framework (May 6, 2010). ["Genachowski Statement"]. Press Release, Austin Schlick, FCC, A Third-Way Legal Framework for Addressing the *Comcast* Dilemma (May 6, 2010). ["Schlick Statement"].

[38] Federal Communications Commission, Chairman Julius Genachowski, Remarks on Preserving Internet Freedom and Openness (Dec. 1, 2010). Available at http://hraunfoss.fcc.gov/edocs_public/attachmatch/DOC

[39] It is worth noting that the Ninth Circuit Court of Appeals had issued a ruling declaring that cable modem Internet service was a telecommunications service, prior to the FCC's decision to implement a rulemaking on this issue. AT&T Corp. v. City of Portland, 216 F.3d 871, 877-79 (9th Cir. 2002). However, as discussed *infra*, despite the FCC reaching the opposite conclusion, the Supreme Court upheld the FCC's interpretation of the Communications Act.

[40] Information services are defined as: the offering of a capability for generating, acquiring, storing, transforming, processing, retrieving, utilizing, or making available information via telecommunications, and includes electronic publishing, but does not include any use of any such capability for the management, control or operation of a telecommunications system or the management of a telecommunications service.

47 U.S.C. § 153(20).

[41] Telecommunications services are defined as:

> the offering of telecommunications for a fee directly to the public, or to such classes of users as to be effectively available directly to the public, regardless of the facilities used.
>
> 47 U.S.C. § 153(46).

[42] The agency identified a portion of cable modem Internet services as "Internet connectivity," which is the portion the agency would seek to redefine as a telecommunications service today. See *Cable Modem Declaratory Ruling*, 17 FCC Rcd at 4809-11.

[43] *Cable Modem Declaratory Ruling*, 17 FCC Rcd at 4819.

[44] *Id.* at 14856.

[45] Nat'l Cable & Telecomms. Ass'n v. Brand X Internet Servs., 545 U.S. 967 (2005) (*Brand X*).

[46] *Id.* at 987.

[47] *Id.* at 991, 1002-03.

[48] *Id.* at 1005 (Scalia, J., dissenting).

[49] See Genachowski Statement, *supra* note 4; Schlick Statement, *supra* note 4.

[50] Genachowski Statement, *supra* note 4.

[51] Schlick Statement, *supra* note 4.

[52] Genachowski Statement, *supra* note 4.

[53] In the Matter of Framework for Broadband Internet Service, Notice of Inquiry, GN Docket No. 10-127 (2010) available at http://hraunfoss.fcc.gov/edocs_public/attachmatch/FCC-10-114A1.pdf. ["NOI"]

[54] Ibid. at ¶¶ 1-2.

[55] See Preserving the Open Internet: Broadband Industry Practices, GN Docket no. 09-19 1, WC Docket No. 07-52, Notice of Proposed Rulemaking, 24 FCC Rcd 13064 (2009).

[56] See Formal Complaint of Free Press and Public Knowledge Against Comcast Corporation for Secretly Degrading Peer-to-Peer Applications; Broadband Industry Practices et al., WC Docket No. 07-52, Memorandum Opinion and Order, 23 FCC Rcd 13028 (2008).

[57] NOI, at ¶ 1.

[58] *Id.* at ¶ 30.

[59] See CRS Report R40234, *The FCC's Authority to Regulate Net Neutrality after Comcast v. FCC* , by Kathleen Ann Ruane.

[60] NOI, at ¶¶ 32-5 1.

[61] *Id.* at ¶¶ 52-66.

[62] *Brand X*, 545 U.S. at 991.

[63] FCC v. Fox Television Stations, Inc. 129 S. Ct. 1800, 1811 (2009).

[64] *Id.*

[65] NOI, at ¶ 52.

[66] Codified at 47 U.S.C. § 160.

[67] See Genachowski Statement, *supra* note 4; Schlick Statement, *supra* note 4.

[68] NOI, at ¶ 74. The Chairman and General Counsel analogized this approach to its regulation of wireless voice communications. In 1993, Congress specified that Title II applies to wireless communications, such as cellular phone service. 47 U.S.C. § 332(c). Section 332(c) gave the FCC the discretion to determine which regulations under Title II should be inapplicable to wireless voice services; however, the FCC could not forbear from applying Sections 201, 202, or 208 to wireless voice services. *Id.* Similarly, the statement of the Chairman has pledged to apply Sections 201, 202, and 208 to broadband access services

[69] NOI, at ¶¶ 74-85.

[70] 47 U.S.C. § 201.

[71] 47 U.S.C. § 202.

[72] 47 U.S.C. § 208.

[73] 47 U.S.C. § 222.

[74] 47 U.S.C. § 254.

[75] 47 U.S.C. § 255.

[76] Genachowski Statement, *supra* note 4.

[77] Schlick Statement, *supra* note 4.

[78] NOI, at ¶¶ 86-7.

[79] Federal Communications Commission, Chairman Julius Genachowski, Remarks on Preserving Internet Freedom and Openness (Dec. 1, 2010). Available at http://hraunfoss.fcc.gov/edocs_public/attachmatch/DOC

[80] *Id.*

[81] Press Release, FCC, Statement of Commissioner Robert M. McDowell on Chairman Genachowski's Attempt to Adopt Internet Regulations, December 1, 2010, available at http://hraunfoss.fcc.gov/edocs_public/attachmatch/DOC303 128A1 .pdf.

[82] Press Release, FCC, Statement of Commissioner Meredith Attwell Baker on Inclusion of Net Neutrality on the Tentative Agenda for the Commission's December Open Meeting, December 1, 2010, available at http://hraunfoss.fcc.gov/edocs_public/attachmatch/DOC

In: The Open Internet, Net Neutrality and the FCC
Editors: Andrew C. Firth and Natalie H. Pierson
ISBN: 978-1-61209-983-5

Chapter 2

PRESERVING THE OPEN INTERNET, BROADBAND INDUSTRY PRACTICES

Federal Communications Commission

1. PRESERVING THE FREE AND OPEN INTERNET

Today the Commission takes an important step to preserve the Internet as an open platform for innovation, investment, job creation, economic growth, competition, and free expression. To provide greater clarity and certainty regarding the continued freedom and openness of the Internet, we adopt three basic rules that are grounded in broadly accepted Internet norms, as well as our own prior decisions:

i. **Transparency**. Fixed and mobile broadband providers must disclose the network management practices, performance characteristics, and terms and conditions of their broadband services;
ii. **No blocking**. Fixed broadband providers may not block lawful content, applications, services, or non-harmful devices; mobile broadband providers may not block lawful websites, or block applications that compete with their voice or video telephony services; and
iii. **No unreasonable discrimination**. Fixed broadband providers may not unreasonably discriminate in transmitting lawful network traffic.

We believe these rules, applied with the complementary principle of reasonable network management, will empower and protect consumers and innovators while helping ensure that the Internet continues to flourish, with robust private investment and rapid innovation at both the core and the edge of the network. This is consistent with the National Broadband Plan goal of broadband access that is ubiquitous and fast, promoting the global competitiveness of the United States.[1]

Just over a year ago, we launched a public process to determine whether and what actions might be necessary to preserve the characteristics that have allowed the Internet to grow into an indispensable platform supporting our nation's economy and civic life, and to foster continued investment in the physical networks that enable the Internet. Since then, more than 100,000 commenters have provided written input. Commission staff held several public workshops and convened a Technological Advisory Process with experts from industry, academia, and consumer advocacy groups to collect their views regarding key technical issues related to Internet openness.

This process has made clear that the Internet has thrived because of its freedom and openness—the absence of any gatekeeper blocking lawful uses of the network or picking winners and losers online. Consumers and innovators do not have to seek permission before they use the Internet to launch new technologies, start businesses, connect with friends, or share their views. The Internet is a level playing field. Consumers can make their own choices about what applications and services to use and are free to decide what content they want to access, create, or share with others. This openness promotes competition. It also enables a self-reinforcing cycle of investment and innovation in which new uses of the network lead to increased adoption of broadband, which drives investment and improvements in the network itself, which in turn lead to further innovative uses of the network and further investment in content, applications, services, and devices. A core goal of this Order is to foster and accelerate this cycle of investment and innovation.

The record and our economic analysis demonstrate, however, that the openness of the Internet cannot be taken for granted, and that it faces real threats. Indeed, we have seen broadband providers endanger the Internet's openness by blocking or degrading content and applications without disclosing their practices to end users and edge providers, notwithstanding the Commission's adoption of open Internet principles in 2005.[2] In light of these considerations, as well as the limited choices most consumers have for broadband service, broadband providers' financial interests in telephony and pay television services that may compete with online content and services, and the economic and civic benefits of maintaining an open and competitive platform for innovation and communication, the Commission has long recognized that certain basic standards for broadband provider conduct are necessary to ensure the Internet's continued openness. The record also establishes the widespread benefits of providing greater clarity in this area—clarity that the Internet's openness will continue, that there is a forum and procedure for resolving alleged open Internet violations, and that broadband providers may reasonably manage their networks and innovate with respect to network technologies and business models. We expect the costs of compliance with our prophylactic rules to be small, as they incorporate longstanding openness principles that are generally in line with current practices and with norms endorsed by many broadband providers. Conversely, the harms of open Internet violations may be substantial, costly, and in some cases potentially irreversible.

The rules we proposed in the Open Internet NPRM and those we adopt today follow directly from the Commission's bipartisan Internet Policy Statement, adopted unanimously in 2005 and made temporarily enforceable for certain broadband providers in 2005 and 2007;[3] openness protections the Commission established in 2007 for users of certain wireless spectrum;[4] and a notice of inquiry in 2007 that asked, among other things, whether the Commission should add a principle of nondiscrimination to the Internet Policy Statement.[5] Our rules build upon these actions, first and foremost by requiring broadband providers to be transparent in their network management practices, so that end users can make informed choices and innovators can develop, market, and maintain Internet-based offerings. The rules also prevent certain forms of blocking and discrimination with respect to content, applications, services, and devices that depend on or connect to the Internet.

An open, robust, and well-functioning Internet requires that broadband providers have the flexibility to reasonably manage their networks. Network management practices are reasonable if they are appropriate and tailored to achieving a legitimate network management purpose. Transparency and end-user control are touchstones of reasonableness.

We recognize that broadband providers may offer other services over the same last-mile connections used to provide broadband service. These "specialized services" can benefit end users and spur investment, but they may also present risks to the open Internet. We will closely monitor specialized services and their effects on broadband service to ensure, through all available mechanisms, that they supplement but do not supplant the open Internet.

Mobile broadband is at an earlier stage in its development than fixed broadband and is evolving rapidly. For that and other reasons discussed below, we conclude that it is appropriate at this time to take measured steps in this area. Accordingly, we require mobile broadband providers to comply with the transparency rule, which includes enforceable disclosure obligations regarding device and application certification and approval processes; we prohibit providers from blocking lawful websites; and we prohibit providers from blocking applications that compete with providers' voice and video telephony services. We will closely monitor the development of the mobile broadband market and will adjust the framework we adopt today as appropriate.

These rules are within our jurisdiction over interstate and foreign communications by wire and radio. Further, they implement specific statutory mandates in the Communications Act ("Act") and the Telecommunications Act of 1996 ("1996 Act"), including provisions that direct the Commission to promote Internet investment and to protect and promote voice, video, and audio communications services.

The framework we adopt aims to ensure the Internet remains an open platform— one characterized by free markets and free speech—that enables consumer choice, end-user control, competition through low barriers to entry, and the freedom to innovate without permission. The framework does so by protecting openness through high-level rules, while maintaining broadband providers' and the Commission's flexibility to adapt to changes in the market and in technology as the Internet continues to evolve.

II. The Need For Open Internet Protections

In the *Open Internet NPRM*, we sought comment on the best means for preserving and promoting a free and open Internet.[6] We noted the near-unanimous view that the Internet's openness and the transparency of its protocols have been critical to its unparalleled success.[7] Citing evidence of broadband providers covertly blocking or degrading Internet traffic, and concern that broadband providers have the incentive and ability to expand those practices in the near future, we sought comment on prophylactic rules designed to preserve the Internet's prevailing norms of openness.[8] Specifically, we sought comment on whether the Commission should codify the four principles stated in the *Internet Policy Statement*, plus proposed nondiscrimination and transparency rules, all subject to reasonable network management.[9]

Commenters agree that the open Internet is an important platform for innovation, investment, competition, and free expression, but disagree about whether there is a need for the Commission to take action to preserve its openness. Commenters who favor Commission action emphasize the risk of harmful conduct by broadband providers, and stress that failing to act could result in irreversible damage to the Internet.[10] Those who favor inaction contend that the Internet generally is open today and is likely to remain so, and express concern that rules aimed at preventing harms may themselves impose significant costs.[11] In this Part, we assess these conflicting views. We conclude that the benefits of ensuring Internet openness through enforceable, high-level, prophylactic rules outweigh the costs. The harms that could result from threats to openness are significant and likely irreversible, while the costs of compliance with our rules should be small, in large part because the rules appear to be consistent with current industry practices. The rules are carefully calibrated to preserve the benefits of the open Internet and increase certainty for all Internet stakeholders, with minimal burden on broadband providers.

A. The Internet's Openness Promotes Innovation, Investment, Competition, Free Expression, and Other National Broadband Goals

Like electricity and the computer, the Internet is a "general purpose technology" that enables new methods of production that have a major impact on the entire economy.[12] The Internet's founders intentionally built a network that is open, in the sense that it has no gatekeepers limiting innovation and communication through the network.[13] Accordingly, the Internet enables an end user to access the content and applications of her choice, without requiring permission from broadband providers. This architecture enables innovators to create and offer new applications and services without needing approval from any controlling entity, be it a network provider, equipment manufacturer, industry body, or government agency.[14] End users benefit because the Internet's openness allows new technologies to be developed and distributed by a broad range of sources, not just by the companies that operate the network. For example, Sir Tim Berners-Lee was able to invent the World Wide Web nearly two decades after engineers developed the Internet's original protocols, without needing changes to those protocols or any approval from network operators.[15] Startups and small businesses benefit because the Internet's openness enables anyone connected to the network to reach and do business with anyone else,[16] allowing even the smallest and most remotely located businesses to access national and global markets, and contribute to the economy through e-commerce[17] and online advertising.[18] Because Internet openness enables widespread innovation and allows all end users and edge providers (rather than just the significantly smaller number of broadband providers) to create and determine the success or failure of content, applications, services, and devices, it maximizes commercial and non-commercial innovations that address key national challenges—including improvements in health care, education, and energy efficiency that benefit our economy and civic life.[19]

The Internet's openness is critical to these outcomes, because it enables a virtuous circle of innovation in which new uses of the network—including new content, applications, services, and devices—lead to increased end-user demand for broadband, which drives network improvements, which in turn lead to further innovative network uses.[20] Novel, improved, or lower-cost offerings introduced by content, application, service, and device providers spur end-user demand and encourage broadband providers to expand their networks and invest in new broadband technologies.[21] Streaming video and e-commerce applications, for instance, have led to major network improvements such as fiber to the premises, VDSL, and DOCSIS 3.0.[22] These network improvements generate new opportunities for edge providers, spurring them to innovate further.[23] Each round of innovation increases the value of the Internet for broadband providers, edge providers, online businesses, and consumers. Continued operation of this virtuous circle, however, depends upon low barriers to innovation and entry by edge providers, which drive end-user demand.[24] Restricting edge providers' ability to reach end users, and limiting end users' ability to choose which edge providers to patronize, would reduce the rate of innovation at the edge and, in turn, the likely rate of improvements to network infrastructure.[25] Similarly, restricting the ability of broadband providers to put the network to innovative uses may reduce the rate of improvements to network infrastructure.[26]

Openness also is essential to the Internet's role as a platform for speech and civic engagement.[27] An informed electorate is critical to the health of a functioning democracy,[28] and Congress has recognized that the Internet "offer[s] a forum for a true diversity of political discourse, unique opportunities for cultural development, and myriad avenues for intellectual activity."[29] Due to the lack of gatekeeper control, the Internet has become a major source of news and information, which forms the basis for informed civic discourse.[30] Many Americans now turn to the Internet to obtain news,[31] and its openness makes it an unrivaled forum for free expression. Furthermore, local, state, and federal government agencies are increasingly using the Internet to communicate with the public, including to provide information about and deliver essential services.[32]

Television and radio broadcasters now provide news and other information online via their own websites, online aggregation websites such as Hulu,[33] and social networking platforms.[34] Local broadcasters are experimenting with new approaches to delivering original content, for example by creating neighborhood-focused websites; delivering news clips via online video programming aggregators, including AOL and Google's YouTube; and offering news from citizen journalists.[35] In addition, broadcast networks license their full-length entertainment programs for downloading or streaming to edge providers such as Netflix and Apple.[36] Because these sites are becoming increasingly popular with the public,[37] online distribution has a strategic value for broadcasters,[38] and is likely to provide an increasingly important source of funding for broadcast news and entertainment programming.[39]

Unimpeded access to Internet distribution likewise has allowed new video content creators to create and disseminate programs without first securing distribution from broadcasters and multichannel video programming distributors (MVPDs) such as cable and satellite television companies.[40] Online viewing of video programming content is growing rapidly.[41]

In the Open Internet NPRM, the Commission sought comment on possible implications that the proposed rules might have "on efforts to close the digital divide and encourage robust broadband adoption and participation in the Internet community by minorities and other socially and economically disadvantaged groups."[42] As we noted in the Open Internet NPRM, according to a 2009 study, broadband adoption varies significantly across demographic groups.[43] We expect that open Internet protections will help close the digital divide by maintaining relatively low barriers to entry for underrepresented groups and allowing for the development of diverse content, applications, and services.[44]

For all of these reasons, there is little dispute in this proceeding that the Internet should continue as an open platform.[45] Accordingly, we consider below whether we can be confident that the openness of the Internet will be self-perpetuating, or whether there are threats to openness that the Commission can effectively mitigate.

B. Broadband Providers Have the Incentive and Ability to Limit Internet Openness

For purposes of our analysis, we consider three types of Internet activities: providing broadband Internet access service; providing content, applications, services, and devices accessed over or connected to broadband Internet access service ("edge" products and services); and subscribing to a broadband Internet access service that allows access to edge products and services. These activities are not mutually exclusive. For example, individuals who generate and share content such as personal blogs or Facebook pages are both end users and edge providers, and a single firm could both provide broadband Internet access service and be an edge provider, as with a broadband provider that offers online video content. Nevertheless, this basic taxonomy provides a useful model for evaluating the risk and magnitude of harms from loss of openness.

The record in this proceeding reveals that broadband providers potentially face at least three types of incentives to reduce the current openness of the Internet. First, broadband providers may have economic incentives to block or otherwise disadvantage specific edge providers or classes of edge providers, for example by controlling the transmission of network traffic over a broadband connection, including the price and quality of access to end users. A broadband provider might use this power to benefit its own or affiliated offerings at the expense of unaffiliated offerings.[46]

Today, broadband providers have incentives to interfere with the operation of third-party Internet-based services that compete with the providers' revenue-generating telephony and/or pay-television services. This situation contrasts with the first decade of the public Internet, when dial-up was the primary form of consumer Internet access. Independent companies such as America Online, CompuServe, and Prodigy provided access to the Internet over telephone companies' phone lines. As broadband has replaced dial-up, however, telephone and cable companies have become the major providers of Internet access service.[47] Online content, applications, and services available from edge providers over broadband increasingly offer actual or potential competitive alternatives to broadband providers' own voice and video services, which generate substantial profits. Interconnected Voice-over-Internet-Protocol (VoIP) services, which include some over-the-top VoIP services,[48] "are increasingly being used as a substitute for traditional telephone service,"[49] and over-the-top VoIP services represent a significant share of voice-calling minutes, especially for international calls.[50] Online video is rapidly growing in popularity,[51] and MVPDs have responded to this trend by enabling their video subscribers to use the Internet to view their programming on personal computers and other Internet-enabled devices.[52] Online video aggregators such as Netflix, Hulu, YouTube, and iTunes that are unaffiliated with traditional MVPDs continue to proliferate and innovate, offering movies and television programs (including broadcast programming) on demand, and earning revenues from advertising and/or subscriptions.[53] Several MVPDs have stated publicly that they view these services as a potential competitive threat to their core video subscription service.[54] Thus, online edge services appear likely to continue gaining subscribers and market significance,[55] which will put additional competitive pressure on broadband providers' own services.[56] By interfering with the transmission of third parties' Internet-based services or raising the cost of online delivery for particular edge providers, telephone and cable companies can make those services less attractive to subscribers in comparison to their own offerings.[57]

In addition, a broadband provider may act to benefit edge providers that have paid it to exclude rivals (for example, if one online video site were to contract with a broadband provider to deny a rival video site access to the broadband provider's subscribers).[58] End users would be harmed by the inability to access desired content, and this conduct could lead to reduced innovation and fewer new services.[59] Consistent with these concerns, delivery networks that are vertically integrated with content providers, including some MVPDs, have incentives to favor their own affiliated content.[60] If broadband providers had historically favored their own affiliated businesses or those incumbent firms that paid for advantageous access to end users, some innovative edge providers that have today become major Internet businesses might not have been able to survive.[61]

Second, broadband providers may have incentives to increase revenues by charging edge providers, who already pay for their own connections to the Internet,[62] for access or prioritized access to end users.[63] Although broadband providers have not historically imposed such fees, they have argued they should be permitted to do so.[64] A broadband provider could force edge providers to pay inefficiently high fees because that broadband provider is typically an edge provider's only option for reaching a particular end user.[65] Thus broadband providers have the ability to act as gatekeepers.[66]

Broadband providers would be expected to set inefficiently high fees to edge providers because they receive the benefits of those fees but are unlikely to fully account for the detrimental impact on edge providers' ability and incentive to innovate and invest, including the possibility that some edge providers might exit or decline to enter the market.[67] The unaccounted-for harms to innovation are negative externalities,[68] and are likely to be particularly large because of the rapid pace of Internet innovation, and wide-ranging because of the role of the Internet as a general purpose technology. Moreover, fees for access or prioritized access could trigger an "arms race" within a given edge market segment.[69] If one edge provider pays for access or prioritized access to end users, subscribers may tend to favor that provider's services, and competing edge providers may feel that they must respond by paying, too.

Fees for access or prioritization to end users could reduce the potential profit that an edge provider would expect to earn from developing new offerings, and thereby reduce edge providers' incentives to invest and innovate.[70] In the rapidly innovating edge sector, moreover, many new entrants are new or small "garage entrepreneurs," not large and established firms. These emerging providers are particularly sensitive to barriers to innovation and entry,[71] and may have difficulty obtaining financing if their offerings are subject to being blocked or disadvantaged by one or more of the major broadband providers.[72] In addition, if edge providers need to negotiate access or prioritized access fees with broadband providers,[73] the resulting transaction costs could further raise the costs of introducing new products and might chill entry and expansion.[74]

Some commenters argue that an end user's ability to switch broadband providers eliminates these problems.[75] But many end users may have limited choice among broadband providers, as discussed below.[76] Moreover, those that can switch broadband providers may not benefit from switching if rival broadband providers charge edge providers similarly for access and priority transmission and prioritize each edge provider's service similarly.[77] Further, end users may not know whether charges or service levels their broadband provider is imposing on edge providers vary from those of alternative broadband providers, and even if they do have this information may find it costly to switch.[78] For these reasons, a dissatisfied end user, observing that some edge provider services are subject to low transmission quality, might not switch broadband providers (though they may switch to a rival edge provider in the hope of improving quality).

Some commenters contend that, in the absence of open Internet rules, broadband providers that earn substantial additional revenue by assessing access or prioritization charges on edge providers could avoid increasing or could reduce the rates they charge broadband subscribers, which might increase the number of subscribers to the broadband network.[79] Although this scenario is possible,[80] no broadband provider has stated in this proceeding that it actually would use any revenue from edge provider charges to offset subscriber charges.[81] In addition, these commenters fail to account for the likely detrimental effects of access and prioritization charges on the virtuous circle of innovation described above. Less content and fewer innovative offerings make the Internet less attractive for end users than would otherwise be the case. Consequently, we are unable to conclude that the possibility of reduced subscriber charges outweighs the risks of harm described herein.[82]

Third, if broadband providers can profitably charge edge providers for prioritized access to end users, they will have an incentive to degrade or decline to increase the quality of the service they provide to non-prioritized traffic.[83] This would increase the gap in quality (such as latency in transmission) between prioritized access and non-prioritized access, induce more edge providers to pay for prioritized access, and allow broadband providers to charge higher prices for prioritized access. Even more damaging, broadband providers might withhold or decline to expand capacity in order to "squeeze" non-prioritized traffic, a strategy that would increase the likelihood of network congestion[84] and confront edge providers with a choice between accepting low-quality transmission or paying fees for prioritized access to end users.

Moreover, if broadband providers could block specific content, applications, services, or devices, end users and edge providers would lose the control they currently have over whether other end users and edge providers can communicate with them through the Internet. Content, application, service, and device providers (and their investors) could no longer assume that the market for their offerings included all U.S. end users. And broadband providers might choose to implement undocumented practices for traffic differentiation that undermine the ability of developers to create generally usable applications without having to design to particular broadband providers' unique practices or business arrangements.[85]

All of the above concerns are exacerbated by broadband providers' ability to make fine-grained distinctions in their handling of network traffic as a result of increasingly sophisticated network management tools. Such tools may be used for beneficial purposes, but they also increase broadband providers' ability to act on incentives to engage in network practices that would erode Internet openness.[86]

Although these threats to Internet-enabled innovation, growth, and competition do not depend upon broadband providers having market power with respect to end users,[87] most would be exacerbated by such market power. A broadband provider's incentive to favor affiliated content or the content of unaffiliated firms that pay for it to do so, its incentive to block or degrade traffic or charge edge providers for access to end users, and its incentive to squeeze non-prioritized transmission will all be greater if end users are less able to respond by switching to rival broadband providers. The risk of market power is highest in markets with few competitors, and most residential end users today have only one or two choices for wireline broadband Internet access service.[88] As of December 2009, nearly 70 percent of households lived in census tracts where only one or two wireline or fixed wireless firms provided advertised download speeds of at least 3 Mbps and upload speeds of at least 768 Kbps[89]—the closest observable benchmark to the minimum download speed of 4 Mbps and upload speed of 1 Mbps that the Commission has used to assess broadband deployment.[90] About 20 percent of households are in census tracts with only one provider advertising at least 3 Mbps down and 768 Kbps up.[91] For Internet service with advertised download speeds of at least 10 Mbps down and upload speeds of at least 1.5 Mbps up, nearly 60 percent of households lived in census tracts served by only one wireline or fixed wireless broadband provider, while nearly 80 percent lived in census tracts served by no more than two wireline or fixed wireless broadband providers.[92]

Including mobile broadband providers does not appreciably change these numbers.[93] The roll-out of next generation mobile services is at an early stage, and the future of competition in residential broadband is unclear.[94] The record does not enable us to make a predictive judgment that the future will be more competitive than the past. Although wireless providers are increasingly offering faster broadband services,[95] we do not know, for example, how end users will value the trade-offs between the benefits of wireless service (e.g., mobility) and the benefits of fixed wireline service (e.g., higher download and upload speeds).[96] We note that the two largest mobile broadband providers also offer wireline or fixed service;[97] this could dampen their incentive to compete aggressively with wireline (or fixed) services.[98]

In addition, customers may incur significant costs in switching broadband providers[99] because of early termination fees;[100] the inconvenience of ordering, installation, and set-up, and associated deposits or fees;[101] possible difficulty returning the earlier broadband provider's equipment and the cost of replacing incompatible customer-owned equipment;[102] the risk of temporarily losing service; the risk of problems learning how to use the new service; and the possible loss of a provider-specific email address or website.[103]

C. Broadband Providers Have Acted to Limit Openness

These dangers to Internet openness are not speculative or merely theoretical. Conduct of this type has already come before the Commission in enforcement proceedings. As early as 2005, a broadband provider that was a subsidiary of a telephone company paid $15,000 to settle a Commission investigation into whether it had blocked Internet ports used for competitive VoIP applications.[104] In 2008, the Commission found that Comcast disrupted certain peer-to-peer (P2P) uploads of its subscribers, without a reasonable network management justification and without disclosing its actions.[105] Comparable practices have been observed in the provision of mobile broadband services. After entering into a contract with a company to handle online payment services, a mobile wireless provider allegedly blocked customers' attempts to use competing services to make purchases using their mobile phones.[106] A nationwide mobile provider restricted the types of lawful applications that could be accessed over its 3G mobile wireless network.[107]

There have been additional allegations of blocking, slowing, or degrading P2P traffic. We do not determine in this Order whether any of these practices violated open Internet principles, but we note that they have raised concerns among edge providers and end users, particularly regarding lack of transparency. For example, in May 2008 a major cable broadband provider acknowledged that it had managed the traffic of P2P services.[108] In July 2009, another cable broadband provider entered into a class action settlement agreement stating that it had "ceased P2P Network Management Practices,"[109] but allowing the provider to resume throttling P2P traffic.[110] There is evidence that other broadband providers have engaged in similar degradation.[111] In addition, broadband providers' terms of service commonly reserve to the provider sweeping rights to block, degrade, or favor traffic.[112] For example, one major cable provider reserves the right to engage, "without limitation," in "port blocking, . . . traffic prioritization and protocol filtering.[113] Further, a major mobile broadband provider prohibits use of its wireless service for "downloading movies using peer-to-peer file sharing services" and VoIP applications.[114] And a cable modem manufacturer recently filed a formal complaint with the Commission alleging that a major broadband Internet access service provider has violated open Internet principles through overly restrictive device approval procedures.[115]

These practices have occurred notwithstanding the Commission's adoption of open Internet principles in the Internet Policy Statement; enforcement proceedings against Madison River Communications and Comcast for their interference with VoIP and P2P traffic, respectively;[116] Commission orders that required certain broadband providers to adhere to open Internet obligations;[117] longstanding norms of Internet openness; and statements by major broadband providers that they support and are abiding by open Internet principles.[118]

D. The Benefits of Protecting the Internet's Openness Exceed the Costs

Widespread interference with the Internet's openness would likely slow or even break the virtuous cycle of innovation that the Internet enables, and would likely cause harms that may be irreversible or very costly to undo.[119] For example, edge providers could make investments in reliance upon exclusive preferential arrangements with broadband providers, and network management technologies may not be easy to change.[120] If the next revolutionary technology or business is not developed because broadband provider practices chill entry and innovation by edge providers, the missed opportunity may be significant,[121] and lost innovation, investment, and competition may be impossible to restore after the fact.[122] Moreover, because of the Internet's role as a general purpose technology, erosion of Internet openness threatens to harm innovation, investment in the core and at the edge of the network, and competition in many sectors, with a disproportionate effect on small, entering, and non-commercial edge providers that drive much of the innovation on the Internet.[123] Although harmful practices are not certain to become widespread, there are powerful reasons for immediate concern, as broadband providers have interfered with the open Internet in the past and have incentives and an increasing ability to do so in the future. Effective open Internet rules can prevent or reduce the risk of these harms, while helping to assure Americans unfettered access to diverse sources of news, information, and entertainment, as well as an array of technologies and devices that enhance health, education, and the environment.

By comparison to the benefits of these prophylactic measures, the costs associated with the open Internet rules adopted here are likely small.[124] Broadband providers generally endorse openness norms—including the transparency and no blocking principles—as beneficial and in line with current and planned business practices (though they do not uniformly support rules making them enforceable).[125] Even to the extent rules require some additional disclosure of broadband providers' practices, the costs of compliance should be modest.[126] In addition, the high-level rules we adopt carefully balance preserving the open Internet against avoiding unduly burdensome regulation. Our rules against blocking and unreasonable discrimination are subject to reasonable network management, and our rules do not prevent broadband providers from offering specialized services such as facilities-based VoIP.[127] In short, rules that reinforce the openness that has supported the growth of the Internet, and do not substantially change this highly successful status quo, should not entail significant compliance costs.

Some commenters contend that open Internet rules are likely to reduce investment in broadband deployment.[128] We disagree. There is no evidence that prior open Internet obligations have discouraged investment;[129] and numerous commenters explain that, by preserving the virtuous circle of innovation, open Internet rules will increase incentives to invest in broadband infrastructure.[130] Moreover, if permitted to deny access, or charge edge providers for prioritized access to end users, broadband providers may have incentives to allow congestion rather than invest in expanding network capacity.[131] And as described in Part 0, below, our rules allow broadband providers sufficient flexibility to address legitimate congestion concerns and other network management considerations. Nor is there any persuasive reason to believe that in the absence of open Internet rules broadband providers would lower charges to broadband end users,[132] or otherwise change their practices in ways that benefit innovation, investment, competition, or end users.[133]

The magnitude and character of the risks we identify make it appropriate to adopt prophylactic rules now to preserve the openness of the Internet, rather than waiting for substantial, pervasive, and potentially irreversible harms to occur before taking any action.[134] The Supreme Court has recognized that even if the Commission cannot "predict with certainty" the future course of a regulated market, it may "plan in advance of foreseeable events, instead of waiting to react to them."[135] Moreover, as the Commission found in another context, "[e]xclusive reliance on a series of individual complaints," without underlying rules, "would prevent the Commission from obtaining a clear picture of the evolving structure of the entire market, and addressing competitive concerns as they arise. . . . Therefore, if the Commission exclusively relied on individual complaints, it would only become aware of specific . . . problems if and when the individual complainant's interests coincided with those of the interest of the overall 'public.'"[136]

Finally, we note that there is currently significant uncertainty regarding the future enforcement of open Internet principles and what constitutes appropriate network management, particularly in the wake of the court of appeals' vacatur of the Comcast Network Management Practices Order. A number of commenters, including leading broadband providers, recognize the benefits of greater predictability regarding open Internet protections.[137] Broadband providers benefit from increased certainty that they can reasonably manage their networks and innovate with respect to network technologies and business models.[138] For those who communicate and innovate on the Internet,[139] and for investors in edge technologies,[140] there is great value in having confidence that the Internet will remain open, and that there will be a forum available to bring complaints about violations of open Internet standards.[141] End users also stand to benefit from assurances that services on which they depend "won't suddenly be pulled out from under them, held ransom to extra payments either from the sites or from them."[142] Providing clear yet flexible rules of the road that enable the Internet to continue to flourish is the central goal of the action we take today.[143]

III. Open Internet Rules

To preserve the Internet's openness and broadband providers' ability to manage and expand their networks, we adopt high-level rules embodying four core principles: transparency, no blocking, no unreasonable discrimination, and reasonable network management. These rules are generally consistent with, and should not require significant changes to, broadband providers' current practices, and are also consistent with the common understanding of broadband Internet access service as a service that enables one to go where one wants on the Internet and communicate with anyone else online.[144]

A. Scope of the Rules

We find that open Internet rules should apply to "broadband Internet access service," which we define as:

> *A mass-market retail service by wire or radio that provides the capability to transmit data to and receive data from all or substantially all Internet endpoints, including any capabilities that are incidental to and enable the operation of the communications service, but excluding dial-up Internet access service. This term also encompasses any service that the Commission finds to be providing a functional equivalent of the service described in the previous sentence, or that is used to evade the protections set forth in this Part.*

The term "broadband Internet access service" includes services provided over any technology platform, including but not limited to wire, terrestrial wireless (including fixed and mobile wireless services using licensed or unlicensed spectrum), and satellite.[145]

"Mass market" means a service marketed and sold on a standardized basis to residential customers, small businesses, and other end-user customers such as schools and libraries.[146] For purposes of this definition, "mass market" also includes broadband Internet access services purchased with the support of the E-rate program that may be customized or individually negotiated. The term does not include enterprise service offerings, which are typically offered to larger organizations through customized or individually negotiated arrangements.[147]

"Broadband Internet access service" encompasses services that "provide the capability to transmit data to and receive data from all or substantially all Internet endpoints." To ensure the efficacy of our rules in this dynamic market, we also treat as a "broadband Internet access service" any service the Commission finds to be providing a functional equivalent of the service described in the previous sentence, or that is used to evade the protections set forth in these rules.

A key factor in determining whether a service is used to evade the scope of the rules is whether the service is used as a substitute for broadband Internet access service. For example, an Internet access service that provides access to a substantial subset of Internet endpoints based on end users preference to avoid certain content, applications, or services;[148] Internet access services that allow some uses of the Internet (such as access to the World Wide Web) but not others (such as e-mail); or a "Best of the Web" Internet access service that provides access to 100 top websites could not be used to evade the open Internet rules applicable to "broadband Internet access service." Moreover, a broadband provider may not evade these rules simply by blocking end users' access to some Internet endpoints. Broadband Internet access service likely does not include services offering connectivity to one or a small number of Internet endpoints for a particular device, e.g., connectivity bundled with e-readers, heart monitors, or energy consumption sensors, to the extent the service relates to the functionality of the device.[149] Nor does broadband Internet access service include virtual private network services, content delivery network services, multichannel video programming services, hosting or data storage services, or Internet backbone services (if those services are separate from broadband Internet access service). These services typically are not mass market services and/or do not provide the capability to transmit data to and receive data from all or substantially all Internet endpoints.[150]

Although one purpose of our open Internet rules is to prevent blocking or unreasonable discrimination in transmitting online traffic for applications and services that compete with traditional voice and video services, we determine that open Internet rules applicable to fixed broadband providers should protect all types of Internet traffic, not just voice or video Internet traffic. This reflects, among other things, our view that it is generally preferable to neither require nor encourage broadband providers to examine Internet traffic in order to discern which traffic is subject to the rules. Even if we were to limit our rules to voice or video traffic, moreover, it is unlikely that broadband providers could reliably identify such traffic in all circumstances, particularly if the voice or video traffic originated from new services using uncommon protocols.[151] Indeed, limiting our rules to voice and video traffic alone could spark a costly and wasteful cat-and-mouse game in which edge providers and end users seeking to obtain the protection of our rules could disguise their traffic as protected communications.[152]

We recognize that there is one Internet (although it is comprised of a multitude of different networks), and that it should remain open and interconnected regardless of the technologies and services end users rely on to access it. However, for reasons discussed in Part 0 below related to mobile broadband—including the fact that it is at an earlier stage and more rapidly evolving—we apply open Internet rules somewhat differently to mobile broadband than to fixed broadband at this time. We define "fixed broadband Internet access service" as a broadband Internet access service that serves end users primarily at fixed endpoints using stationary equipment, such as the modem that connects an end user's home router, computer, or other Internet access device to the network. This term encompasses fixed wireless broadband services (including services using unlicensed spectrum) and fixed satellite broadband services. We define "mobile broadband Internet access service" as a broadband Internet access service that serves end users primarily using mobile stations.[153] Mobile broadband Internet access includes services that use smartphones as the primary endpoints for connection to the Internet.[154] The discussion in this Part applies to both fixed and mobile broadband, unless specifically noted. Part 0 further discusses application of open Internet rules to mobile broadband.

For a number of reasons, these rules apply only to the provision of broadband Internet access service and not to edge provider activities, such as the provision of content or applications over the Internet.[155] First, the Communications Act particularly directs us to prevent harms related to the utilization of networks and spectrum to provide communication by wire and radio.[156] Second, these rules are an outgrowth of the Commission's Internet Policy Statement.[157] The Statement was issued in 2005 when the Commission removed key regulatory protections from DSL service, and was intended to protect against the harms to the open Internet that might result from broadband providers' subsequent conduct.[158] The Commission has always understood those principles to apply to broadband Internet access service only, as have most private-sector stakeholders.[159] Thus, insofar as these rules translate existing Commission principles into codified rules, it is appropriate to limit the application of the rules to broadband Internet access service. Third, broadband providers control access to the Internet for their subscribers and for anyone wishing to reach those subscribers.[160] They are therefore capable of blocking, degrading, or favoring any Internet traffic that flows to or from a particular subscriber.

We also do not apply these rules to dial-up Internet access service because telephone service has historically provided the easy ability to switch among competing dial-up Internet access services. Moreover, the underlying dial-up Internet access service is subject to protections under Title II of the Communications Act. The Commission's interpretation of those protections has resulted in a market for dial-up Internet access that does not present the same concerns as the market for broadband Internet access.[161] No commenters suggested extending open Internet rules to dial-up Internet access service.

Finally, we decline to apply our rules directly to coffee shops, bookstores, airlines, and other entities when they acquire Internet service from a broadband provider to enable their patrons to access the Internet from their establishments (we refer to these entities as "premise operators").[162] These services are typically offered by the premise operator as an ancillary benefit to patrons. However, to protect end users, we include within our rules broadband Internet access services provided to premise operators for purposes of making service available to their patrons.[163] Although broadband providers that offer such services are subject to open Internet rules, we note that addressing traffic unwanted by a premise operator is a legitimate network management purpose.[164]

B. Transparency

Promoting competition throughout the Internet ecosystem is a central purpose of these rules. Effective disclosure of broadband providers' network management practices and the performance and commercial terms of their services promotes competition—as well as innovation, investment, end-user choice, and broadband adoption—in at least five ways. First, disclosure ensures that end users can make informed choices regarding the purchase and use of broadband service, which promotes a more competitive market for broadband services and can thereby reduce broadband providers' incentives and ability to violate open Internet principles.[165] Second, and relatedly, as end users' confidence in broadband providers' practices increases, so too should end users' adoption of broadband services—leading in turn to additional investment in Internet infrastructure as contemplated by Section 706 of the 1996 Act and other provisions of the communications laws.[166] Third, disclosure supports innovation, investment, and competition by ensuring that startups and other edge providers have the technical information necessary to create and maintain online content, applications, services, and devices, and to assess the risks and benefits of embarking on new projects.[167] Fourth, disclosure increases the likelihood that broadband providers will abide by open Internet principles, and that the Internet community will identify problematic conduct and suggest fixes.[168] Transparency thereby increases the chances that harmful practices will not occur in the first place and that, if they do, they will be quickly remedied, whether privately or through Commission oversight. Fifth, disclosure will enable the Commission to collect information necessary to assess, report on, and enforce the other open Internet rules.[169] For all of these reasons, most commenters agree that informing end users, edge providers, and the Commission about the network management practices, performance, and commercial terms of broadband Internet access service is a necessary and appropriate step to help preserve an open Internet.[170]

The Open Internet NPRM sought comment on what end users and edge providers need to know about broadband service, how this information should be disclosed, when disclosure should occur, and where information should be available.[171] The resulting record supports adoption of the following rule:

> *A person engaged in the provision of broadband Internet access service shall publicly disclose accurate information regarding the network management practices, performance, and commercial terms of its broadband Internet access services sufficient for consumers to make informed choices regarding use of such services and for content, application, service, and device providers to develop, market, and maintain Internet offerings.*[172]

The rule does not require public disclosure of competitively sensitive information or information that would compromise network security or undermine the efficacy of reasonable network management practices.[173] For example, a broadband provider need not publicly disclose information regarding measures it employs to prevent spam practices at a level of detail that would enable a spammer to defeat those measures.

Despite broad agreement that broadband providers should disclose information sufficient to enable end users and edge providers to understand the capabilities of broadband services, commenters disagree about the appropriate level of detail required to achieve this goal.[174] We believe that at this time the best approach is to allow flexibility in implementation of the transparency rule, while providing guidance regarding effective disclosure models. We expect that effective disclosures will likely include some or all of the following types of information, timely and prominently disclosed in plain language accessible to current and prospective end users and edge providers, the Commission, and third parties who wish to monitor network management practices for potential violations of open Internet principles:[175]

Network Practices[176]

- *Congestion Management*: If applicable, descriptions of congestion management practices; types of traffic subject to practices; purposes served by practices; practices' effects on end users' experience; criteria used in practices, such as indicators of congestion that trigger a practice, and the typical frequency of congestion; usage limits and the consequences of exceeding them; and references to engineering standards, where appropriate.[177]
- *Application-Specific Behavior*: If applicable, whether and why the provider blocks or rate-controls specific protocols or protocol ports, modifies protocol fields in ways not prescribed by the protocol standard, or otherwise inhibits or favors certain applications or classes of applications.[178]
- *Device Attachment Rules*: If applicable, any restrictions on the types of devices and any approval procedures for devices to connect to the network. (For further discussion of required disclosures regarding device and application approval procedures for mobile broadband providers, see paragraph 0, *infra.*)
- *Security*: If applicable, practices used to ensure end-user security or security of the network, including types of triggering conditions that cause a mechanism to be invoked (but excluding information that could reasonably be used to circumvent network security).

Performance Characteristics[179]

- *Service Description*: A general description of the service, including the service technology, expected and actual access speed and latency, and the suitability of the service for real-time applications.
- *Impact of Specialized Services*: If applicable, what specialized services, if any, are offered to end users, and whether and how any specialized services may affect the last-mile capacity available for, and the performance of, broadband Internet access service.

Commercial Terms[180]

- *Pricing*: For example, monthly prices, usage-based fees, and fees for early termination or additional network services.
- *Privacy Policies*: For example, whether network management practices entail inspection of network traffic, and whether traffic information is stored, provided to third parties, or used by the carrier for non-network management purposes.
- *Redress Options*: Practices for resolving end-user and edge provider complaints and questions.

We emphasize that this list is not necessarily exhaustive, nor is it a safe harbor—there may be additional information, not included above, that should be disclosed for a particular broadband service to comply with the rule in light of relevant circumstances. Broadband providers should examine their network management practices and current disclosures to determine what additional information, if any, should be disclosed to comply with the rule.

In the Open Internet NPRM, we proposed that broadband providers publicly disclose their practices on their websites and in promotional materials.[181] Most commenters agree that a provider's website is a natural place for end users and edge providers to find disclosures,[182] and several contend that a broadband provider's only obligation should be to post its practices on its website.[183] Others assert that disclosures should also be displayed prominently at the point-of-sale, in bill inserts, and in the service contract.[184] We agree that broadband providers must, at a minimum, prominently display or provide links to disclosures on a publicly available, easily accessible website that is available to current and prospective end users and edge providers as well as to the Commission, and must disclose relevant information at the point of sale. Current end users must be able to easily identify which disclosures apply to their service offering. Broadband providers' online disclosures shall be considered disclosed to the Commission for purposes of monitoring and enforcement. We may require additional disclosures directly to the Commission.[185]

We anticipate that broadband providers may be able to satisfy the transparency rule through a single disclosure, and therefore do not at this time require multiple disclosures targeted at different audiences.[186] We also decline to adopt a specific format for disclosures, and instead require that disclosure be sufficiently clear and accessible to meet the requirements of the rule.[187] We will, however, continue to monitor compliance with this rule, and may require adherence to a particular set of best practices in the future.[188]

Although some commenters assert that a disclosure rule will impose significant burdens on broadband providers, no commenter cites any particular source of increased costs, or attempts to estimate costs of compliance.[189] For a number of reasons, we believe that the costs of the disclosure rule we adopt today are outweighed by the benefits of empowering end users and edge providers to make informed choices and of facilitating the enforcement of the other open Internet rules. First, we require only that providers post disclosures on their websites and provide disclosure at the point of sale, not that they bear the cost of printing and distributing bill inserts or other paper documents to all existing customers.[190] Second, although we may subsequently determine that it is appropriate to require that specific information be disclosed in particular ways, the transparency rule we adopt today gives broadband providers some flexibility to determine what information to disclose and how to disclose it. We also expressly exclude from the rule competitively sensitive information, information that would compromise network security, and information that would undermine the efficacy of reasonable network management practices. Third, as discussed below, by setting the effective date of these rules 60 days after notice in the Federal Register announcing the decision of the Office of Management and Budget regarding its mandatory approval of the information collection requirements contained in the rules, we give broadband providers adequate time to develop cost effective methods of compliance.

A key purpose of the transparency rule is to enable third-party experts such as independent engineers and consumer watchdogs to monitor and evaluate network management practices, in order to surface concerns regarding potential open Internet violations. We also note the existence of free software tools that enable Internet end users and edge providers to monitor and detect blocking and discrimination by broadband providers.[191] Although current tools cannot detect all instances of blocking or discrimination and cannot substitute for disclosure of network management policies, such tools may help supplement the transparency rule we adopt today.[192]

Although transparency is essential for preserving Internet openness, we disagree with commenters that suggest it is alone sufficient to prevent open Internet violations.[193] The record does not convince us that a transparency requirement by itself will adequately constrain problematic conduct,[194] and we therefore adopt two additional rules, as discussed below.

C. No Blocking and No Unreasonable Discrimination

1. No Blocking

The freedom to send and receive lawful content and to use and provide applications and services without fear of blocking is essential to the Internet's openness and to competition in adjacent markets such as voice communications and video and audio programming.[195] Similarly, the ability to connect and use any lawful devices that do not harm the network helps ensure that end users can enjoy the competition and innovation that result when device manufacturers can depend on networks' openness.[196] Moreover, the no-blocking principle has been broadly accepted since its inclusion in the Commission's Internet Policy Statement. Major broadband providers represent that they currently operate consistent with this principle and are committed to continuing to do so.[197]

In the Open Internet NPRM, the Commission proposed codifying the original three Internet Policy Statement principles that addressed blocking of content, applications and services, and devices.[198] After consideration of the record, we consolidate the proposed rules into a single rule for fixed broadband providers:[199]

> A person engaged in the provision of fixed broadband Internet access service, insofar as such person is so engaged, shall not block lawful content, applications, services, or non-harmful devices, subject to reasonable network management.

The phrase "content, applications, services" refers to all traffic transmitted to or from end users of a broadband Internet access service, including traffic that may not fit cleanly into any of these categories.[200] The rule protects only transmissions of lawful content, and does not prevent or restrict a broadband provider from refusing to transmit unlawful material such as child pornography.[201]

We also note that the rule entitles end users to both connect and use any lawful device of their choice, provided such device does not harm the network.[202] A broadband provider may require that devices conform to widely accepted and publicly-available standards applicable to its services.[203]

We make clear that the no-blocking rule bars broadband providers from impairing or degrading particular content, applications, services, or non-harmful devices so as to render them effectively unusable (subject to reasonable network management).[204] Such a prohibition is consistent with the observation of a number of commenters that degrading traffic can have the same effects as outright blocking,[205] and that such an approach is consistent with the traditional interpretation of the Internet Policy Statement.[206] The Commission has recognized that in some circumstances the distinction between blocking and degrading (such as by delaying) traffic is merely "semantic."[207]

Some concerns have been expressed that broadband providers may seek to charge edge providers simply for delivering traffic to or carrying traffic from the broadband provider's end-user customers.[208] To the extent that a content, application, or service provider could avoid being blocked only by paying a fee, charging such a fee would not be permissible under these rules.[209]

2. No Unreasonable Discrimination

Based on our findings that fixed broadband providers have incentives and the ability to discriminate in their handling of network traffic in ways that can harm innovation, investment, competition, end users, and free expression,[210] we adopt the following rule:

> A person engaged in the provision of fixed broadband Internet access service, insofar as such person is so engaged, shall not unreasonably discriminate in transmitting lawful network traffic over a consumer's broadband Internet access service. Reasonable network management shall not constitute unreasonable discrimination.[211]

The rule strikes an appropriate balance between restricting harmful conduct and permitting beneficial forms of differential treatment. As the rule specifically provides, and as discussed below, discrimination by a broadband provider that constitutes "reasonable network management" is "reasonable" discrimination.[212] We provide further guidance regarding distinguishing reasonable from unreasonable discrimination:

Transparency. Differential treatment of traffic is more likely to be reasonable the more transparent to the end user that treatment is. The Commission has previously found broadband provider practices to violate open Internet principles in part because they were not disclosed to end users.[213] Transparency is particularly important with respect to the discriminatory treatment of traffic as it is often difficult for end users to determine the causes of slow or poor performance of content, applications, services, or devices.[214]

End-User Control. Maximizing end-user control is a policy goal Congress recognized in Section 230(b) of the Communications Act, and end-user choice and control are touchstones in evaluating the reasonableness of discrimination.[215] As one commenter observes, "letting users choose how they want to use the network enables them to use the Internet in a way that creates more value for them (and for society) than if network providers made this choice," and "is an important part of the mechanism that produces innovation under uncertainty."[216] Thus, enabling end users to choose among different broadband offerings based on such factors as assured data rates and reliability, or to select quality-of-service enhancements on their own connections for traffic of their choosing, would be unlikely to violate the no unreasonable discrimination rule, provided the broadband provider's offerings were fully disclosed and were not harmful to competition or end users.[217] We recognize that there is not a binary distinction between end-user controlled and broadband-provider controlled practices, but rather a spectrum of practices ranging from more end-user controlled to more broadband provider-controlled.[218] And we do not suggest that practices controlled entirely by broadband providers are by definition unreasonable.

Some commenters suggest that open Internet protections would prohibit broadband providers from offering their subscribers different tiers of service or from charging their subscribers based on bandwidth consumed.[219] We are, of course, always concerned about anti-consumer or anticompetitive practices, and we remain so here. However, prohibiting tiered or usage-based pricing and requiring all subscribers to pay the same amount for broadband service, regardless of the performance or usage of the service, would force lighter end users of the network to subsidize heavier end users. It would also foreclose practices that may appropriately align incentives to encourage efficient use of networks.[220] The framework we adopt today does not prevent broadband providers from asking subscribers who use the network less to pay less, and subscribers who use the network more to pay more.

Use-Agnostic Discrimination. Differential treatment of traffic that does not discriminate among specific uses of the network or classes of uses is likely reasonable. For example, during periods of congestion a broadband provider could provide more bandwidth to subscribers that have used the network less over some preceding period of time than to heavier users.[221] Use-agnostic discrimination (sometimes referred to as application-agnostic discrimination) is consistent with Internet openness because it does not interfere with end users' choices about which content, applications, services, or devices to use. Nor does it distort competition among edge providers.[222]

Standard Practices. The conformity or lack of conformity of a practice with best practices and technical standards adopted by open, broadly representative, and independent Internet engineering, governance initiatives, or standards-setting organizations is another factor to be considered in evaluating reasonableness. Recognizing the important role of such groups is consistent with Congress's intent that our rules in the Internet area should not "fetter[]" the free market with unnecessary regulation,[223] and is consistent with broadband providers' historic reliance on such groups.[224] We make clear, however, that we are not delegating authority to interpret or implement our rules to outside bodies.[225]

In evaluating unreasonable discrimination, the types of practices we would be concerned about include, but are not limited to, discrimination that harms an actual or potential competitor to the broadband provider (such as by degrading VoIP applications or services when the broadband provider offers telephone service),[226] that harms end users (such as by inhibiting end users from accessing the content, applications, services, or devices of their choice),[227] or that impairs free expression (such as by slowing traffic from a particular blog because the broadband provider disagrees with the blogger's message).[228]

For a number of reasons, including those discussed above in Part 0, a commercial arrangement between a broadband provider and a third party to directly or indirectly favor some traffic over other traffic in the broadband Internet access service connection to a subscriber of the broadband provider (i.e., "pay for priority") would raise significant cause for concern.[229] First, pay for priority would represent a significant departure from historical and current practice. Since the beginning of the Internet, Internet access providers have typically not charged particular content or application providers fees to reach the providers' retail service end users or struck pay-for-priority deals, and the record does not contain evidence that U.S. broadband providers currently engage in such arrangements. Second this departure from longstanding norms could cause great harm to innovation and investment in and on the Internet. As discussed above, pay-for-priority arrangements could raise barriers to entry on the Internet by requiring fees from edge providers, as well as transaction costs arising from the need to reach agreements with one or more broadband providers to access a critical mass of potential end users.[230] Fees imposed on edge providers may be excessive because few edge providers have the ability to bargain for lesser fees, and because no broadband provider internalizes the full costs of reduced innovation and the exit of edge providers from the market.[231] Third, pay-for-priority arrangements may particularly harm non-commercial end users, including individual bloggers, libraries, schools, advocacy organizations, and other speakers,[232] especially those who communicate through video or other content sensitive to network congestion. Even open Internet skeptics acknowledge that pay for priority may disadvantage non-commercial uses of the network, which are typically less able to pay for priority, and for which the Internet is a uniquely important platform.[233] Fourth, broadband providers that sought to offer pay-for-priority services would have an incentive to limit the quality of service provided to non-prioritized traffic.[234] In light of each of these concerns, as a general matter, it is unlikely that pay for priority would satisfy the "no unreasonable discrimination" standard. The practice of a broadband Internet access service provider prioritizing its own content, applications, or services, or those of its affiliates, would raise the same significant concerns and would be subject to the same standards and considerations in evaluating reasonableness as third-party pay-for-priority arrangements.[235]

Because we agree with the diverse group of commenters who argue that any nondiscrimination rule should prohibit only unreasonable discrimination, we decline to adopt the more rigid nondiscrimination rule proposed in the Open Internet NPRM.[236] A strict nondiscrimination rule would be in tension with our recognition that some forms of discrimination, including end-user controlled discrimination, can be beneficial. The rule we adopt provides broadband providers' sufficient flexibility to develop service offerings and pricing plans, and to effectively and reasonably manage their networks.[237] We disagree with commenters who argue that a standard based on "reasonableness" or "unreasonableness" is too vague to give broadband providers fair notice of what is expected of them.[238] This is not so. "Reasonableness" is a well-established standard for regulatee conduct.[239] As other commenters have pointed out, the term "reasonable" is "both administrable and indispensable to the sound administration of the nation's telecommunications laws."[240]

We also reject the argument that only "anticompetitive" discrimination yielding "substantial consumer harm" should be prohibited by our rules.[241] We are persuaded those proposed limiting terms are unduly narrow and could allow discriminatory conduct that is contrary to the public interest.[242] The broad purposes of this rule—to encourage competition and remove impediments to infrastructure investment while protecting consumer choice, free expression, end-user control, and the ability to innovate without permission[243]—cannot be achieved by preventing only those practices that are demonstrably anticompetitive or harmful to consumers. Rather, the rule rests on the general proposition that broadband providers should not pick winners and losers on the Internet—even for reasons that may be independent of providers' competitive interests[244] or that may not immediately or demonstrably cause substantial consumer harm.[245]

We disagree with commenters who argue that a rule against unreasonable discrimination violates section 3(51) of the Communications Act for those broadband providers that are telecommunications carriers but do not provide their broadband Internet access service as a telecommunications service.[246] Section 3(51) provides that a "telecommunications carrier shall be treated as a common carrier under this Act only to the extent that it is engaged in providing telecommunications services."[247] This limitation is not relevant to the Commission's actions here.[248] The hallmark of common carriage is an "undertak[ing] to carry for all people indifferently."[249] An entity "will not be a common carrier where its practice is to make individualized decisions, in particular cases, whether and on what terms to deal" with potential customers.[250] The customers at issue here are the end users who subscribe to broadband Internet access services.[251] With respect to those customers, a broadband provider may make individualized decisions. A broadband provider that chooses not to offer its broadband Internet access service on a common carriage basis can, for instance, decide on a case-by-case basis whether to serve a particular end user, what connection speed(s) to offer, and at what price. The open Internet rules become effective only after such a provider has voluntarily entered into a mutually satisfactory arrangement with the end user, which may be tailored to that user. Even then, as discussed above, the allowance for reasonable disparities permits customized service features such as those that enhance end user control over what Internet content is received. This flexibility to customize service arrangements for a particular customer is the hallmark of private carriage, which is the antithesis of common carriage.[252]

D. Reasonable Network Management

Since at least 2005, when the Commission adopted the Internet Policy Statement, we have recognized that a flourishing and open Internet requires robust, well-functioning broadband networks, and accordingly that open Internet protections require broadband providers to be able to reasonably manage their networks. The open Internet rules we adopt today expressly provide for and define "reasonable network management" in order to provide greater clarity to broadband providers, network equipment providers, and Internet end users and edge providers regarding the types of network management practices that are consistent with open Internet protections.

In the Open Internet NPRM, the Commission proposed that open Internet rules be subject to reasonable network management, consisting of "reasonable practices employed by a provider of broadband Internet access service to: (1) reduce or mitigate the effects of congestion on its network or to address quality-of-service concerns; (2) address traffic that is unwanted by users or harmful; (3) prevent the transfer of unlawful content; or (4) prevent the unlawful transfer of content."[253] The proposed definition also stated that reasonable network management consists of "other reasonable network management practices."[254]

Upon reviewing the record, we conclude that the definition of reasonable network management should provide greater clarity regarding the standard used to gauge reasonableness, expressly account for technological differences among networks that may affect reasonable network management, and omit elements that do not relate directly to network management functions and are therefore better handled elsewhere in the rules—for example, measures to prevent the transfer of unlawful content.[255] We therefore adopt the following definition of reasonable network management:

> A network management practice is reasonable if it is appropriate and tailored to achieving a legitimate network management purpose, taking into account the particular network architecture and technology of the broadband Internet access service.

Legitimate network management purposes include: ensuring network security and integrity, including by addressing traffic that is harmful to the network;[256] addressing traffic that is unwanted by end users (including by premise operators), such as by providing services or capabilities consistent with an end user's choices regarding parental controls or security capabilities;[257] and reducing or mitigating the effects of congestion on the network.[258] The term "particular network architecture and technology" refers to the differences across access platforms such as cable, DSL, satellite, and fixed wireless.

As proposed in the Open Internet NPRM, we will further develop the scope of reasonable network management on a case-by-case basis, as complaints about broadband providers' actual practices arise.[259] The novelty of Internet access and traffic management questions, the complex nature of the Internet, and a general policy of restraint in setting policy for Internet access service providers weigh in favor of a case-by-case approach.[260]

In taking this approach, we recognize the need to balance clarity with flexibility.[261] We discuss below certain principles and considerations that will inform the Commission's case-by-case analysis. Further, although broadband providers are not required to seek permission from the Commission before deploying a network management practice, they or others are free to do so, for example by seeking a declaratory ruling.[262]

We reject proposals to define reasonable network management practices more expansively[263] or more narrowly than stated above.[264] We agree with commenters that the Commission should not adopt the "narrowly or carefully tailored" standard discussed in the Comcast Network Management Practices Order.[265] We find that this standard is unnecessarily restrictive and may overly constrain network engineering decisions.[266] Moreover, the "narrowly tailored" language could be read to import strict scrutiny doctrine from constitutional law, which we are not persuaded would be helpful here. Broadband providers may employ network management practices that are appropriate and tailored to the network management purpose they seek to achieve, but they need not necessarily employ the most narrowly tailored practice theoretically available to them.

We also acknowledge that reasonable network management practices may differ across platforms. For example, practices needed to manage congestion on a fixed satellite network may be inappropriate for a fiber-to-the-home network.[267] We also recognize the unique network management challenges facing broadband providers that use unlicensed spectrum to deliver service to end users.[268] Unlicensed spectrum is shared among multiple users and technologies and no single user can control or assure access to the spectrum. We believe the concept of reasonable network management is sufficiently flexible to afford such providers the latitude they need to effectively manage their networks.[269]

The principles guiding case-by-case evaluations of network management practices are much the same as those that guide assessments of "no unreasonable discrimination," and include transparency,[270] end-user control,[271] and use- (or application-) agnostic treatment.[272] We also offer guidance in the specific context of the legitimate network management purposes listed above.

Network Security or Integrity and Traffic Unwanted by End Users. Broadband providers may implement reasonable practices to ensure network security and integrity, including by addressing traffic that is harmful to the network.[273] Many commenters strongly support allowing broadband providers to implement such network management practices.[274] Some commenters, however, express concern that providers might implement anticompetitive or otherwise problematic practices in the name of protecting network security.[275] We make clear that, for the singling out of any specific application for blocking or degradation based on harm to the network to be a reasonable network management practice, a broadband provider should be prepared to provide a substantive explanation for concluding that the particular traffic is harmful to the network, such as traffic that constitutes a denial-of-service attack on specific network infrastructure elements or exploits a particular security vulnerability.

Broadband providers also may implement reasonable practices to address traffic that a particular end user chooses not to receive. Thus, for example, a broadband provider could provide services or capabilities consistent with an end user's choices regarding parental controls,[276] or allow end users to choose a service that provides access to the Internet but not to pornographic websites.[277] Likewise, a broadband provider serving a premise operator could restrict traffic unwanted by that entity,[278] though such restrictions should be disclosed. Our rule will not impose liability on a broadband provider where such liability is prohibited by section 230(c)(2) of the Act.[279]

We note that, in some cases, mechanisms that reduce or eliminate some forms of harmful or unwanted traffic may also interfere with legitimate network traffic. Such mechanisms must be appropriate and tailored to the threat; should be evaluated periodically as to their continued necessity; and should allow end users to opt-in or opt-out if possible.[280] Disclosures of network management practices used to address network security or traffic a particular end user does not want to receive should clearly state the objective of the mechanism and, if applicable, how an end user can opt in or out of the practice.

Network Congestion. Numerous commenters support permitting the use of reasonable network management practices to address the effects of congestion, and we agree that congestion management may be a legitimate network management purpose.[281] For example, broadband providers may need to take reasonable steps to ensure that heavy users do not crowd out others. What constitutes congestion and what measures are reasonable to address it may vary depending on the technology platform for a particular broadband Internet access service. For example, if cable modem subscribers in a particular neighborhood are experiencing congestion, it may be reasonable for a broadband provider to temporarily limit the bandwidth available to individual end users in that neighborhood who are using a substantially disproportionate amount of bandwidth.[282]

We emphasize that reasonable network management practices are not limited to the categories described here, and that broadband providers may take other reasonable steps to maintain the proper functioning of their networks, consistent with the definition of reasonable network management we adopt. As we stated in the Open Internet NPRM, "we do not presume to know now everything that providers may need to do to provide robust, safe, and secure Internet access to their subscribers, much less everything they may need to do as technologies and usage patterns change in the future."[283] Broadband providers should have flexibility to experiment, innovate, and reasonably manage their networks.

E. Mobile Broadband

There is one Internet, which should remain open for consumers and innovators alike, although it may be accessed through different technologies and services. The record demonstrates the importance of freedom and openness for mobile broadband networks,[284] and the rationales for adopting high-level open Internet rules, discussed above, are for the most part as applicable to mobile broadband as they are to fixed broadband. Consumer choice, freedom of expression, end-user control, competition, and the freedom to innovate without permission are as important when end users are accessing the Internet via mobile broadband as via fixed. And there have been instances of mobile providers blocking certain third-party applications, particularly applications that compete with the provider's own offerings; relatedly, concerns have been raised about inadequate transparency regarding network management practices.[285] We also note that some mobile broadband providers affirmatively state they do not oppose the application of openness rules to mobile broadband.[286]

However, as explained in the Open Internet NPRM and subsequent Public Notice,[287] mobile broadband presents special considerations that suggest differences in how and when open Internet protections should apply. Mobile broadband is an earlier-stage platform than fixed broadband, and it is rapidly evolving. For most of the history of the Internet, access has been predominantly through fixed platforms—first dial-up, then cable modem and DSL services. As of a few years ago, most consumers used their mobile phones primarily to make phone calls and send text messages, and most mobile providers offered Internet access only via "walled gardens" or stripped down websites.[288] Today, however, mobile broadband is an important Internet access platform that is helping drive broadband adoption,[289] and data usage is growing rapidly.[290] The mobile ecosystem is experiencing very rapid innovation and change, including an expanding array of smartphones, aircard modems, and other devices that enable Internet access; the emergence and rapid growth of dedicated-purpose mobile devices like e-readers; the development of mobile application ("app") stores and hundreds of thousands of mobile apps; and the evolution of new business models for mobile broadband providers, including usage-based pricing.[291]

Moreover, most consumers have more choices for mobile broadband than for fixed (particularly fixed wireline) broadband.[292] Mobile broadband speeds, capacity, and penetration are typically much lower than for fixed broadband,[293] though some providers have begun offering 4G service that will enable offerings with higher speeds and capacity and lower latency than previous generations of mobile service.[294] In addition, existing mobile networks present operational constraints that fixed broadband networks do not typically encounter.[295] This puts greater pressure on the concept of "reasonable network management" for mobile providers,[296] and creates additional challenges in applying a broader set of rules to mobile at this time. Further, we recognize that there have been meaningful recent moves toward openness in and on mobile broadband networks, including the introduction of third-party devices and applications on a number of mobile broadband networks, and more open mobile devices. In addition, we anticipate soon seeing the effects on the market of the openness conditions we imposed on mobile providers that operate on upper 700 MHz C Block ("C Block") spectrum,[297] which includes Verizon Wireless, one of the largest mobile wireless carriers in the U.S.[298]

In light of these considerations, we conclude it is appropriate to take measured steps at this time to protect the openness of the Internet when accessed through mobile broadband. We apply certain of the open Internet rules, requiring compliance with the transparency rule and a basic no-blocking rule.[299]

1. Application of Openness Principles to Mobile Broadband

a. Transparency

The wide array of commenters who support a disclosure requirement generally agree that all broadband providers, including mobile broadband providers, should be required to disclose their network management practices.[300] Although some mobile broadband providers argue that the dynamic nature of mobile network management makes meaningful disclosure difficult,[301] we conclude that end users need a clear understanding of network management practices, performance, and commercial terms, regardless of the broadband platform they use to access the Internet. Although a number of mobile broadband providers have adopted voluntary codes of conduct regarding disclosure, we believe that a uniform rule applicable to all mobile broadband providers will best preserve Internet openness by ensuring that end users have sufficient information to make informed choices regarding use of the network; and that content, application, service, and device providers have the information needed to develop, market, and maintain Internet offerings. The transparency rule will also aid the Commission in monitoring the evolution of mobile broadband and adjusting, as appropriate, the framework adopted today.

Therefore, as stated above,[302] we require mobile broadband providers to follow the same transparency rule applicable to fixed broadband providers. Further, although we do not require mobile broadband providers to allow third-party devices or all third-party applications on their networks, we nonetheless require mobile broadband providers to disclose their third-party device and application certification procedures, if any; to clearly explain their criteria for any restrictions on use of their network; and to expeditiously inform device and application providers of any decisions to deny access to the network or of a failure to approve their particular devices or applications. With respect to the types of disclosures required to satisfy the rule, we direct mobile broadband providers to the discussion in Part 0, above. Additionally, mobile broadband providers should follow the guidance the Commission provided to licensees of the upper 700 MHz C Block spectrum regarding compliance with their disclosure obligations, particularly regarding disclosure to third-party application developers and device manufacturers of criteria and approval procedures (to the extent applicable).[303] For example, these disclosures include, to the extent applicable, establishing a transparent and efficient approval process for third parties, as set forth in Rule 27.16(d).[304]

b. No Blocking

We adopt a no blocking rule that guarantees end users' access to the web and protects against mobile broadband providers' blocking applications that compete with their other primary service offering—voice and video telephony—while ensuring that mobile broadband providers can engage in reasonable network management:

> A person engaged in the provision of mobile broadband Internet access service, insofar as such person is so engaged, shall not block consumers from accessing lawful websites, subject to reasonable network management; nor shall such person block applications that compete with the provider's voice or video telephony services, subject to reasonable network management.

We understand a "provider's voice or video telephony services" to include a voice or video telephony service provided by any entity in which the provider has an attributable interest.[305] We emphasize that the rule protects any and all applications that compete with a mobile broadband provider's voice or video telephony services. Further, degrading a particular website or an application that competes with the provider's voice or video telephony services so as to render the website or application effectively unusable would be considered tantamount to blocking (subject to reasonable network management).[306]

End users expect to be able to access any lawful website through their broadband service, whether fixed or mobile. Web browsing continues to generate the largest amount of mobile data traffic,[307] and applications and services are increasingly being provisioned and used entirely through the web, without requiring a standalone application to be downloaded to a device. Given that the mobile web is well-developed relative to other mobile applications and services, and enjoys similar expectations of openness that characterize web use through fixed broadband, we find it appropriate to act here. We also recognize that accessing a website typically does not present the same network management issues that downloading and running an app on a device may present. At this time, a prohibition on blocking access to lawful websites (including any related traffic transmitted or received by any plug-in, scripting language, or other browser extension) appropriately balances protection for the ability of end users to access content, applications, and services through the web and assurance that mobile broadband providers can effectively manage their mobile broadband networks.

Situations have arisen in which mobile wireless providers have blocked third-party applications that arguably compete with their telephony offerings.[308] This type of blocking confirms that mobile broadband providers may have strong incentives to limit Internet openness when confronted with third-party applications that compete with their telephony services.[309] Some commenters express concern that wireless providers could favor their own applications over the applications of unaffiliated developers, under the guise of reasonable network management.[310] A number of commenters assert that blocking or hindering the delivery of services that compete with those offered by the mobile broadband provider, such as over-the-top VoIP, should be prohibited.[311] According to Skype, for example, there is "a consensus that at a minimum, a 'no blocking' rule should apply to voice and video applications that compete with broadband network operators' own service offerings."[312] Clearwire argues that the Commission should restrict only practices that appear to have an element of anticompetitive intent.[313] Although some commenters support a broader no-blocking rule,[314] we believe that a targeted prophylactic rule is appropriate at this time,[315] and necessary to deter this type of behavior in the future.

The prohibition on blocking applications that compete with a broadband provider's voice or video telephony services does not apply to a broadband provider's operation of application stores or their functional equivalent. In operating app stores, broadband providers compete directly with other types of entities, including device manufacturers and operating system developers,[316] and we do not intend to limit mobile broadband providers' flexibility to curate their app stores similar to app store operators that are not subject to these rules.[317]

As indicated in Part 0 above, the reasonable network management definition takes into account the particular network architecture and technology of the broadband Internet access service. Thus, in determining whether a network management practice is reasonable, the Commission will consider technical, operational, and other differences between wireless and other broadband Internet access platforms, including differences relating to efficient use of spectrum. We anticipate that conditions in mobile broadband networks may necessitate network management practices that would not be necessary in most fixed networks, but conclude that our definition of reasonable network management is flexible enough to accommodate such differences.

2. Ongoing Monitoring

Although some commenters support applying the no unreasonable discrimination rule to mobile broadband,[318] for the reasons discussed above, we decline to do so, preferring at this time to put in place basic openness protections and monitor the development of the mobile broadband marketplace. We emphasize that our decision to proceed incrementally with respect to mobile broadband at this time should not suggest that we implicitly approve of any provider behavior that runs counter to general open Internet principles. Beyond those practices expressly prohibited by our rules, other conduct by mobile broadband providers, particularly conduct that would violate our rules for fixed broadband, may not necessarily be consistent with Internet openness and the public interest.

We are taking measured steps to protect openness for mobile broadband at this time in part because we want to better understand how the mobile broadband market is developing before determining whether adjustments to this framework are necessary. To that end, we will closely monitor developments in the mobile broadband market, with a particular focus on the following issues: (1) the effects of these rules, the C Block conditions, and market developments related to the openness of the Internet as accessed through mobile broadband; (2) any conduct by mobile broadband providers that harms innovation, investment, competition, end users, free expression or the achievement of national broadband goals; (3) the extent to which differences between fixed and mobile rules affect fixed and mobile broadband markets, including competition among fixed and mobile broadband providers; and (4) the extent to which differences between fixed and mobile rules affect end users for whom mobile broadband is their only or primary Internet access platform.[319] We will investigate and evaluate concerns as they arise. We also will adjust our rules as appropriate. To aid the Commission in these tasks, we will create an Open Internet Advisory Committee, as discussed below in paragraph 162, with a mandate that includes monitoring and regularly reporting on the state of Internet openness for mobile broadband.

Further, we reaffirm our commitment to enforcing the open platform requirements applicable to upper 700 MHz C Block licensees.[320] The first networks using this spectrum are now becoming operational.[321]

F. Other Laws and Considerations

Open Internet rules are not intended to expand or contract broadband providers' rights or obligations with respect to other laws or safety and security considerations, including the needs of emergency communications and law enforcement, public safety, and national security authorities. Similarly, open Internet rules protect only lawful content, and are not intended to inhibit efforts by broadband providers to address unlawful transfers of content. For example, there should be no doubt that broadband providers can prioritize communications from emergency responders, or block transfers of child pornography. To make clear that open Internet protections can and must coexist with these other legal frameworks, we adopt the following clarifying provisions:

> Nothing in this part supersedes any obligation or authorization a provider of broadband Internet access service may have to address the needs of emergency communications or law

enforcement, public safety, or national security authorities, consistent with or as permitted by applicable law, or limits the provider's ability to do so.

Nothing in this part prohibits reasonable efforts by a provider of broadband Internet access service to address copyright infringement or other unlawful activity.

1. Emergency Communications and Safety and Security Authorities

Commenters are broadly supportive of our proposal to state that open Internet rules do not supersede any obligation a broadband provider may have—or limit its ability—to address the needs of emergency communications or law enforcement, public safety, or homeland or national security authorities (together, "safety and security authorities").[322] Broadband providers have obligations under statutes such as the Communications Assistance for Law Enforcement Act,[323] the Foreign Intelligence Surveillance Act,[324] and the Electronic Communications Privacy Act[325] that could in some circumstances intersect with open Internet protections, and most commenters recognize the benefits of clarifying that these obligations are not inconsistent with open Internet rules. Likewise, in connection with an emergency, there may be federal, state, tribal, and local public safety entities; homeland security personnel; and other authorities that need guaranteed or prioritized access to the Internet in order to coordinate disaster relief and other emergency response efforts, or for other emergency communications.[326] In the Open Internet NPRM we proposed to address the needs of law enforcement in one rule and the needs of emergency communications and public safety, national, and homeland security authorities in a separate rule.[327] We are persuaded by the record that these rules should be combined, as the interests at issue are substantially similar.[328] We also agree that the rule should focus on the needs of "law enforcement . . . authorities" rather than the needs of "law enforcement."[329] The purpose of the safety and security provision is first to ensure that open Internet rules do not restrict broadband providers in addressing the needs of law enforcement authorities, and second to ensure that broadband providers do not use the safety and security provision without the imprimatur of a law enforcement authority, as a loophole to the rules.[330] As such, application of the safety and security rule should be tied to invocation by relevant authorities rather than to a broadband provider's independent notion of law enforcement.

Some commenters urge us to limit the scope of the safety and security rule, or argue that it is unnecessary because other statutes give broadband providers the ability and responsibility to assist law enforcement.[331] Several commenters urge the Commission to revise its proposal to clarify that broadband providers may not take any voluntary steps that would be inconsistent with open Internet principles, beyond those steps required by law.[332] They argue, for example, that a broad exception for voluntary efforts could swallow open Internet rules by allowing broadband providers to cloak discriminatory practices under the guise of protecting safety and security.[333]

We agree with commenters that the safety and security rule should be tailored to avoid the possibility of broadband providers using their discretion to mask improper practices. But it would be a mistake to limit the rule to situations in which broadband providers have an obligation to assist safety and security personnel. For example, such a limitation would prevent broadband providers from implementing the Cellular Priority Access Service (also known as the Wireless Priority Service (WPS)), which allows for but does not legally require the prioritization of public safety communications on wireless networks.[334] We do not think it necessary or advisable to provide for pre-deployment review by the Commission, particularly because time may be of the essence in meeting safety and security needs.[335]

2. Transfers of Unlawful Content and Unlawful Transfers of Content

In the NPRM, we proposed to treat as reasonable network management "reasonable practices to . . . prevent the transfer of unlawful content; or . . . prevent the unlawful transfer of content." For reasons explained above we decline to include these practices within the scope of "reasonable network management." However, we conclude that a clear statement that open Internet rules do not prohibit broadband providers from making reasonable efforts to address the transfer of unlawful content or unlawful transfers of content is helpful to ensure that open Internet rules are not used as a shield to enable unlawful activity or to deter prompt action against such activity. For example, open Internet rules should not be invoked to protect copyright infringement, which has adverse consequences for the economy, nor should they protect child pornography. We emphasize that open Internet rules do not alter copyright laws and are not intended to prohibit or discourage voluntary practices undertaken to address or mitigate the occurrence of copyright infringement.[336]

G. Specialized Services

In the Open Internet NPRM, the Commission recognized that broadband providers offer services that share capacity with broadband Internet access service over providers' last-mile facilities, and may develop and offer other such services in the future.[337] These "specialized services," such as some broadband providers' existing facilities-based VoIP and Internet Protocol-video offerings, differ from broadband Internet access service and may drive additional private investment in broadband networks and provide end users valued services, supplementing the benefits of the open Internet.[338] At the same time, specialized services may raise concerns regarding bypassing open Internet protections, supplanting the open Internet, and enabling anticompetitive conduct.[339] For example, open Internet protections may be weakened if broadband providers offer specialized services that are substantially similar to, but do not meet the definition of, broadband Internet access service, and if consumer protections do not apply to such services.[340] In addition, broadband providers may constrict or fail to continue expanding network capacity allocated to broadband Internet access service to provide more capacity for specialized services. If this occurs, and particularly to the extent specialized services grow as substitutes for the delivery of content, applications, and services over broadband Internet access service, the Internet may wither as an open platform for competition, innovation, and free expression.[341] These concerns may be exacerbated by consumers' limited choices for broadband providers, which may leave some end users unable to effectively exercise their preferences for broadband Internet access service (or content, applications, or services available through broadband Internet access service) over specialized services.[342]

We agree with the many commenters who advocate that the Commission exercise its authority to closely monitor and proceed incrementally with respect to specialized services,[343] rather than adopting policies specific to such services at this time.[344] We will carefully observe market developments to verify that specialized services promote investment, innovation, competition, and end-user benefits without undermining or threatening the open Internet.[345] We note also that our rules define broadband Internet access service to encompass "any service that the Commission finds to be providing a functional equivalent of [broadband Internet access service], or that is used to evade the protections set forth in these rules."[346]

We will closely monitor the robustness and affordability of broadband Internet access services, with a particular focus on any signs that specialized services are in any way retarding the growth of or constricting capacity available for broadband Internet access service. We fully expect that broadband providers will increase capacity offered for broadband Internet access service if they expand network capacity to accommodate specialized services. We would be concerned if capacity for broadband Internet access service did not keep pace. We also expect broadband providers to disclose information about specialized services' impact, if any, on last-mile capacity available for, and the performance of, broadband Internet access service. We may consider additional disclosure requirements in this area in our related proceeding regarding consumer transparency and disclosure.[347] We would also be concerned by any marketing, advertising, or other messaging by broadband providers suggesting that one or more specialized services, taken alone or together, and not provided in accordance with our open Internet rules, is "Internet" service or a substitute for broadband Internet access service. Finally, we will monitor the potential for anticompetitive or otherwise harmful effects from specialized services, including from any arrangements a broadband provider may seek to enter into with third parties to offer such services.[348] The Open Internet Advisory Committee will aid us in monitoring these issues.

IV. THE COMMISSION'S AUTHORITY TO ADOPT OPEN INTERNET RULES

Congress created the Commission "[f]or the purpose of regulating interstate and foreign commerce in communication by wire and radio so as to make available, so far as possible, to all people of the United States . . . a rapid, efficient, Nation-wide, and world-wide wire and radio communication service with adequate facilities at reasonable charges, for the purpose of the national defense, [and] for the purpose of promoting safety of life and property through the use of wire and radio communication."[349] Section 2 of the Communications Act grants the Commission jurisdiction over "all interstate and foreign communication by wire or radio."[350] As the Supreme Court explained in the radio context, Congress charged the Commission with "regulating a field of enterprise the dominant characteristic of which was the rapid pace of its unfolding" and therefore intended to give the Commission sufficiently "broad" authority to address new issues that arise with respect to "fluid and dynamic" communications technologies.[351] Broadband Internet access services are clearly within the Commission's subject matter jurisdiction[352] and historically have been supervised by the Commission. Furthermore, as explained below, our adoption of basic rules of the road for broadband providers implements specific statutory mandates in the Communications Act and the Telecommunications Act of 1996.

Congress has demonstrated its awareness of the importance of the Internet and advanced services to modern interstate communications. In Section 230 of the Act, for example, Congress announced "the policy of the United States" concerning the Internet, which includes "promot[ing] the continued development of the Internet" and "encourag[ing] the development of technologies which maximize user control over what information is received by individuals, families, and schools who use the Internet," while also "preserv[ing] the vibrant and competitive free market that presently exists for the Internet and other interactive computer services" and avoiding unnecessary regulation.[353] Other statements of congressional policy further confirm the Commission's statutory authority. In Section 254 of the Act, for example, Congress charged the Commission with designing a federal universal program that has as one of several objectives making "[a]ccess to advanced telecommunications and information services" available "in all regions of the Nation," and particularly to schools, libraries, and health care providers.[354] To the same end, in Section 706 of the 1996 Act, Congress instructed the Commission to "encourage the deployment on a reasonable and timely basis of advanced telecommunications capability to all Americans (including, in particular, elementary and secondary schools and classrooms)" and, if it finds that advanced telecommunications capability is not being deployed to all Americans "on a reasonable and timely basis," to "take immediate action to accelerate deployment of such capability."[355] This mandate provides the Commission both "authority" and "discretion" "to settle on the best regulatory or deregulatory approach to broadband."[356] As the legislative history of the 1996 Act confirms, Congress believed that the laws it drafted would compel the Commission to protect and promote the Internet, while allowing the agency sufficient flexibility to decide how to do so.[357] As explained in detail below, Congress did not limit its instructions to the Commission to one section of the communications laws. Rather, it expressed its instructions in multiple sections which, viewed as a whole, provide broad authority to promote competition, investment, transparency, and an open Internet through the rules we adopt today.

A. Section 706 of the 1996 Act Provides Authority for the Open Internet Rules

As noted, Section 706 of the 1996 Act directs the Commission (along with state commissions) to take actions that encourage the deployment of "advanced telecommunications capability."[358] "[A]dvanced telecommunications capability," as defined in the statute, includes broadband Internet access.[359] Under Section 706(a), the Commission must encourage the deployment of such capability by "utilizing, in a manner consistent with the public interest, convenience, and necessity," various tools including "measures that promote competition in the local telecommunications market, or other regulating methods that remove barriers to infrastructure investment."[360] For the reasons stated in Parts II.A, II.D and III.B, above, our open Internet rules will have precisely that effect.

In Comcast, the D.C. Circuit identified Section 706(a) as a provision that "at least arguably . . . delegate[s] regulatory authority to the Commission," and in fact "contain[s] a direct mandate—the Commission 'shall encourage.'"[361] The court, however, regarded the Commission as "bound by" a prior order[362] that, in the court of appeals' understanding, had held that Section 706(a) is not a grant of authority.[363] In the Advanced Services Order, to which the court referred, the Commission held that Section 706(a) did not permit it to encourage advanced services deployment through the mechanism of forbearance without complying with the specific requirements for forbearance set forth in Section 10 of the

Communications Act.[364] The issue presented in the 1998 proceeding was whether the Commission could rely on the broad terms of Section 706(a) to trump those specific requirements. In the Advanced Services Order, the Commission ruled that it could not do so, noting that it would be "unreasonable" to conclude that Congress intended Section 706(a) to "allow the Commission to eviscerate [specified] forbearance exclusions after having expressly singled out [those exclusions] for different treatment in section 10."[365] The Commission accordingly concluded that Section 706(a) did not give it independent authority—in other words, authority over and above what it otherwise possessed[366]—to forbear from applying other provisions of the Act.[367] The Commission's holding thus honored the interpretive canon that "[a] specific provision . . . controls one[] of more general application."[368]

While disavowing a reading of Section 706(a) that would allow the agency to trump specific mandates of the Communications Act, the Commission nonetheless affirmed in the Advanced Services Order that Section 706(a) "gives this Commission an affirmative obligation to encourage the deployment of advanced services" using its existing rulemaking, forbearance and adjudicatory powers, and stressed that "this obligation has substance."[369] The Advanced Services Order is, therefore, consistent with our present understanding that Section 706(a) authorizes the Commission (along with state commissions) to take actions, within their subject matter jurisdiction and not inconsistent with other provisions of law, that encourage the deployment of advanced telecommunications capability by any of the means listed in the provision.[370]

In directing the Commission to "encourage the deployment on a reasonable and timely basis of advanced telecommunications capability to all Americans . . . by utilizing . . . price cap regulation, regulatory forbearance, measures that promote competition in the local telecommunications market, or other regulating methods that remove barriers to infrastructure investment,"[371] Congress necessarily invested the Commission with the statutory authority to carry out those acts. Indeed, the relevant Senate Report explained that the provisions of Section 706 are "intended to ensure that one of the primary objectives of the [1996 Act]—to accelerate deployment of advanced telecommunications capability—is achieved," and stressed that these provisions are "a necessary fail-safe" to guarantee that Congress's objective is reached.[372] It would be odd indeed to characterize Section 706(a) as a "fail-safe" that "ensures" the Commission's ability to promote advanced services if it conferred no actual authority. Here, under our reading, Section 706(a) authorizes the Commission to address practices, such as blocking VoIP communications, degrading or raising the cost of online video, or denying end users material information about their broadband service, that have the potential to stifle overall investment in Internet infrastructure and limit competition in telecommunications markets.

This reading of Section 706(a) obviates the concern of some commenters that our jurisdiction under the provision could be "limitless" or "unbounded."[373] To the contrary, our Section 706(a) authority is limited in three critical respects. First, our mandate under Section 706(a) must be read consistently with Sections 1 and 2 of the Act, which define the Commission's subject matter jurisdiction over "interstate and foreign commerce in communication by wire and radio."[374] As a result, our authority under Section 706(a) does not, in our view, extend beyond our subject matter jurisdiction under the Communications Act. Second, the Commission's actions under Section 706(a) must "encourage the deployment on a reasonable and timely basis of advanced telecommunications capability to all Americans."[375] Third, the activity undertaken to encourage such deployment must "utilize[e], in a manner consistent with the public interest, convenience, and necessity," one (or more) of various specified methods.[376] These include: "price cap regulation, regulatory forbearance, measures that promote competition in the local telecommunications market, or other regulating methods that remove barriers to infrastructure investment."[377] Actions that do not fall within those categories are not authorized by Section 706(a). Thus, as the D.C. Circuit has noted, while the statutory authority granted by Section 706(a) is broad, it is "not unfettered."[378]

Section 706(a) accordingly provides the Commission a specific delegation of legislative authority to promote the deployment of advanced services, including by means of the open Internet rules adopted today. Our understanding of Section 706(a) is, moreover, harmonious with other statutory provisions that confer a broad mandate on the Commission. Section 706(a)'s directive to "encourage the deployment [of advanced telecommunications capability] on a reasonable and timely basis" using the methods specified in the statute is, for example, no broader than other provisions of the Commission's authorizing statutes that command the agency to ensure "just" and "reasonable" rates and practices, or to regulate services in the "public interest."[379] Indeed, our authority under Section 706(a) is generally consistent with—albeit narrower than—the understanding of ancillary jurisdiction under which this Commission operated for decades before the Comcast decision.[380] The similarities between the two in fact explain why the Commission has not heretofore had occasion to describe Section 706(a) in this way: In the particular proceedings prior to Comcast, setting out the understanding of Section 706(a) that we articulate in this Order would not meaningfully have increased the authority that we understood the Commission already to possess.[381]

Section 706(b) of the 1996 Act[382] provides additional authority to take actions such as enforcing open Internet principles. It directs the Commission to undertake annual inquiries concerning the availability of advanced telecommunications capability to all Americans and requires that, if the Commission finds that such capability is not being deployed in a reasonable and timely fashion, it "shall take immediate action to accelerate deployment of such capability by removing barriers to infrastructure investment and by promoting competition in the telecommunications market."[383] In July 2010, the Commission "conclude[d] that broadband deployment to all Americans is not reasonable and timely" and noted that "[a]s a consequence of that conclusion," Section 706(b) was triggered.[384] Section 706(b) therefore provides express authority for the pro-investment, pro-competition rules we adopt today.

B. Authority to Promote Competition and Investment In, and Protect End Users of, Voice, Video, and Audio Services

The Commission also has authority under the Communications Act to adopt the open Internet rules in order to promote competition and investment in voice, video, and audio services. Furthermore, for the reasons stated in Part II, above, even if statutory provisions related to voice, video, and audio communications were the only sources of authority for the open Internet rules (which is not the case), it would not be sound policy to attempt to implement rules concerning only voice, video, or audio transmissions over the Internet.[385]

1. The Commission Has Authority to Adopt Open Internet Rules to Further Its Responsibilities Under Title II of the Act

Section 201 of the Act delegates to the Commission "express and expansive authority"[386] to ensure that the "charges [and] practices . . . in connection with" telecommunications services are "just and reasonable."[387] As described in Part II.B, interconnected VoIP services, which include some over-the-top VoIP services, "are increasingly being used as a substitute for traditional telephone service."[388] Over-the-top services therefore do, or will, contribute to the marketplace discipline of voice telecommunications services regulated under Section 201.[389] Furthermore, companies that provide both voice communications and broadband Internet access services (for example, telephone companies that are broadband providers) have the incentive and ability to block, degrade, or otherwise disadvantage the services of their online voice competitors.[390] Because the Commission may enlist market forces to fulfill its Section 201 responsibilities,[391] we possess authority to prevent these anticompetitive practices through open Internet rules.[392]

Section 251(a)(1) of the Act imposes a duty on all telecommunications carriers "to interconnect directly or indirectly with the facilities of other telecommunications carriers."[393] Many over-the-top VoIP services allow end users to receive calls from and/or place calls to traditional phone networks operated by telecommunications carriers.[394] The Commission has not determined whether any such VoIP providers are telecommunications carriers. To the extent that VoIP services are information services (rather than telecommunications services), any blocking or degrading of a call from a traditional telephone customer to a customer of a VoIP provider, or vice-versa, would deny the traditional telephone customer the intended benefits of telecommunications interconnection under Section 251(a)(1). Over-the-top VoIP customers account for a growing share of telephone usage.[395] If calls to and from these VoIP customers were not delivered efficiently and reliably by broadband providers, all users of the public switched telephone network would be limited in their ability to communicate, and Congress's goal of "efficient, Nation-wide, and world-wide" communications[396] across interconnected networks would be frustrated. To the extent that VoIP services are telecommunications services, a broadband provider's interference with traffic exchanged between a provider of VoIP telecommunications services and another telecommunications carrier would interfere with interconnection between two telecommunications carriers under Section 251(a)(1).[397]

2. The Commission Has Authority to Adopt Open Internet Rules to Further Its Responsibilities Under Titles III and VI of the Act

"The Commission has been charged with broad responsibilities for the orderly development of an appropriate system of local television broadcasting,"[398] which arise from the Commission's more general public interest obligation to "ensure the larger and more effective use of radio."[399] Similarly, the Commission has broad jurisdiction to oversee MVPD services, including direct-broadcast satellite (DBS).[400] Consistent with these mandates, our jurisdiction over video and audio services under Titles III and VI of the Communications Act provides additional authority for open Internet rules.[401]

First, such rules are necessary to the effective performance of our Title III responsibilities to ensure the "orderly development . . . of local television broadcasting"[402] and the "more effective use of radio."[403] As discussed in Parts II.A and II.B, Internet video distribution is increasingly important to all video programming services, including local television broadcast service.[404] Radio stations also are providing audio and video content on the Internet.[405] At the same time, broadband providers—many of which are also MVPDs—have the incentive and ability to engage in self-interested practices that may include blocking or degrading the quality of online programming content, including broadcast content, or charging unreasonable additional fees for faster delivery of such content. Absent the rules we adopt today, such practices jeopardize broadcasters' ability to offer news (including local news) and other programming over the Internet, and, in turn, threaten to impair their ability to offer high-quality broadcast content.[406]

The Commission likewise has authority under Title VI of the Act to adopt open Internet rules that protect competition in the provision of MVPD services. A cable or telephone company's interference with the online transmission of programming by DBS operators or stand-alone online video programming aggregators that may function as competitive alternatives to traditional MVPDs[407] would frustrate Congress's stated goals in enacting Section 628 of the Act, which include promoting "competition and diversity in the multichannel video programming market"; "increase[ing] the availability of satellite cable programming and satellite broadcast programming to persons in rural and other areas not currently able to receive such programming"; and "spur[ring] the development of communications technologies."[408]

When Congress enacted Section 628 in 1992, it was specifically concerned about the incentive and ability of cable operators to use their control of video programming to impede competition from the then-nascent DBS industry.[409] Since that time, the Internet has opened a new competitive arena in which MVPDs that offer broadband service have the opportunity and incentive to impede DBS providers and other competing MVPDs—and the statute reaches this analogous arena as well. Section 628(b) prohibits cable operators from engaging in "unfair or deceptive acts or practices the purpose or effect of which is to prevent or hinder significantly the ability of an MVPD to deliver satellite cable programming or satellite broadcast programming to consumers."[410] An "unfair method of competition or unfair act or practice" under Section 628(b) includes acts that can be anticompetitive.[411] Thus, Section 628(b) proscribes practices by cable operators that (i) can impede competition, and (ii) have the purpose or effect of preventing or significantly hindering other MVPDs from providing consumers their satellite-delivered programming (i.e., programming transmitted to MVPDs via satellite for retransmission to subscribers).[412] Section 628(c)(1), in turn, directs the Commission to adopt rules proscribing unfair practices by cable operators and their affiliated satellite cable programming vendors.[413] Section 628(j) provides that telephone companies offering video programming services are subject to the same rules as cable operators.[414]

The open Internet rules directly further our mandate under Section 628. Cable operators, telephone companies, and DBS operators alike are seeking to keep and win customers by expanding their MVPD offerings to include online access to their programming.[415] For example, in providing its MVPD service, DISH (one of the nation's two DBS providers) relies significantly on online dissemination of programming, including video-on-demand and other programming, that competes with similar offerings by cable operators.[416] As DISH explains, "[a]s more and more video consumption moves online, the competitive viability of stand-alone MVPDs depends on their ability to offer an online video experience of the same quality as the online video offerings of integrated broadband providers."[417] The open Internet rules will prevent practices by cable operators and telephone companies, in their role as broadband providers, that have the purpose or effect of significantly hindering (or altogether preventing) delivery of video programming protected under Section 628(b).[418] The Commission therefore is authorized to adopt open Internet rules under Section 628(b), (c)(1), and (j).[419]

Similarly, open Internet rules enable us to carry out our responsibilities under Section 616(a) of the Act,[420] which confers additional express statutory authority to combat discriminatory network management practices by broadband providers. Section 616(a) directs the Commission to adopt regulations governing program carriage agreements "and related practices" between cable operators or other MVPDs and video programming vendors.[421] The program carriage regulations must include provisions that prevent MVPDs from "unreasonably restrain[ing] the ability of an unaffiliated video programming vendor to compete fairly by discriminating in video programming distribution," on the basis of a vendor's affiliation or lack of affiliation with the MVPD, in the selection, terms, or conditions of carriage of the vendor's programming.[422] MVPD practices that discriminatorily impede competing video programming vendors' online delivery of programming to consumers affect the vendors' ability to "compete fairly" for viewers,[423] just as surely as MVPDs' discriminatory selection of video programming for carriage on cable systems has this effect. We find that discriminatory practices by MVPDs in their capacity as broadband providers, such as blocking or charging fees for termination of online video programming to end users, are "related" to program carriage agreements and within our mandate to adopt regulations under Section 616(a).[424]

C. Authority to Protect the Public Interest Through Spectrum Licensing

Open Internet rules for wireless services are further supported by our authority, under Title III of the Communications Act, to protect the public interest through spectrum licensing.[425] Congress has entrusted the Commission with "maintain[ing] the control of the United States over all the channels of radio transmission."[426] Licensees hold Commission-granted authorizations to use that spectrum subject to conditions the Commission imposes on that use.[427] In considering whether to grant a license to use spectrum, therefore, the Commission must "determine . . . whether the public interest, convenience, and necessity will be served by the granting of such application."[428] Likewise, when identifying classes of licenses to be awarded by auction and the characteristics of those licenses, the Commission "shall include safeguards to protect the public interest" and must seek to promote a number of goals, including "the development and rapid deployment of new technologies, products, and services."[429] Even after licenses are awarded, the Commission may change the license terms "if in the judgment of the Commission such action will promote the public interest, convenience, and necessity."[430] The Commission may exercise this authority on a license-by-license basis or through a rulemaking,[431] even if the affected licenses were awarded at auction.[432]

The Commission previously has required wireless licensees to comply with open Internet principles, as appropriate in the particular situation before it. In 2007, when it modified the service rules for the 700 MHz band, the Commission took "a measured step to encourage additional innovation and consumer choice at this critical stage in the evolution of wireless broadband services."[433] Specifically, the Commission required C block licensees "to allow customers, device manufacturers, third-party application developers, and others to use or develop the devices and applications of their choosing in C Block networks, so long as they meet all applicable regulatory requirements and comply with reasonable conditions related to management of the wireless network (i.e., do not cause harm to the network)."[434] The open Internet conditions we adopt today likewise are necessary to advance the public interest in innovation and investment.[435]

AT&T contends that the Commission cannot apply "neutrality" regulations to wireless broadband services outside the upper 700 MHz C Block spectrum because any such regulations "would unlawfully rescind critical rulings in the Commission's 700 MHz Second Report and Order on which providers relied in making multi-billion dollar investments,"[436] and that adopting these regulations more broadly to all mobile providers would violate the Administrative Procedure Act.[437] We disagree. As explained above, the Commission retains the statutory authority to impose new requirements on existing licenses beyond those that were in place at the time of grant, whether the licenses were assigned by auction[438] or by other means.[439] In this case, parties were made well aware that the agency might extend openness requirements beyond the C Block, diminishing any reliance interest they might assert.[440] To the extent that AT&T argues that application of openness principles reduced auction bids on the C Block spectrum,[441] we find that the reasons for the price differences between the C Block and other 700 MHz spectrum blocks are far more complex. A number of factors, including unique auction dynamics and significant differences between the C Block spectrum and other blocks of 700 MHz spectrum[442] contributed to these price differences. In balancing the public interest factors we are required to consider, we have determined that adopting a targeted set of rules that apply to all mobile broadband providers is necessary at this time.[443]

D. Authority to Collect Information to Enable the Commission to Perform Its Reporting Obligations to Congress

Additional sections of the Communications Act provide authority for our transparency requirement in particular. Section 4(k) provides for an annual report to Congress that "shall contain . . . such information and data collected by the Commission as may be considered of value in the determination of questions connected with the regulation of interstate . . . wire and radio communication" and provide "recommendations to Congress as to additional legislation which the Commission deems necessary or desirable."[444] The Commission has previously relied on Section 4(k), among other provisions, as a basis for its authority to gather information.[445] The Comcast court, moreover, "readily accept[ed]" that "certain assertions of Commission authority could be 'reasonably ancillary' to the Commission's statutory responsibility to issue a report to Congress. For example, the Commission might impose disclosure requirements on regulated entities in order to gather data needed for such a report."[446] We adopt such disclosure requirements here.

Finally, the Commission has broad authority under Section 218 of the Act to obtain "full and complete information" from common carriers and their affiliates.[447] To the extent broadband providers are affiliated with communications common carriers, Section 218 allows the Commission to require the provision of information such as that covered by the transparency rule we adopt today.[448] We believe that these disclosure requirements will assist us in carrying out our reporting obligations to Congress.

E. Constitutional Issues

Some commenters contend that open Internet rules violate the First Amendment and amount to an unconstitutional taking under the Fifth Amendment. We examine these constitutional arguments below, and find them unfounded.

1. First Amendment

Several broadband providers argue that open Internet rules are inconsistent with the free speech guarantee of the First Amendment.[449] These commenters generally contend that because broadband providers distribute their own and third-party content to customers, they are speakers entitled to First Amendment protections.[450] Therefore, they argue, rules that prevent broadband providers from favoring the transmission of some content over other content violate their free speech rights. Other commenters contend that none of the proposed rules implicate the First Amendment, because providing broadband service is conduct that is not correctly understood as speech.[451]

In arguing that broadband service is protected by the First Amendment, AT&T compares its provision of broadband service to the operation of a cable television system, and points out that the Supreme Court has determined that cable programmers and cable operators engage in speech protected by the First Amendment.[452] The analogy is inapt. When the Supreme Court held in Turner I that cable operators were protected by the First Amendment, the critical factor that made cable operators "speakers" was their production of programming and their exercise of "editorial discretion over which programs and stations to include" (and thus which to exclude).[453]

Unlike cable television operators, broadband providers typically are best described not as "speakers," but rather as conduits for speech. The broadband Internet access service at issue here does not involve an exercise of editorial discretion that is comparable to cable companies' choice of which stations or programs to include in their service. In this proceeding broadband providers have not, for instance, shown that they market their services as benefiting from an editorial presence.[454] To the contrary, Internet end users expect that they can obtain access to all or substantially all content that is available on the Internet, without the editorial intervention of their broadband provider.[455]

Consistent with that understanding, broadband providers maintain that they qualify for statutory immunity from liability for copyright violations or the distribution of offensive material precisely because they lack control over what end users transmit and receive.[456] In addition, when defending themselves against subpoenas in litigation involving alleged copyright violations, broadband providers typically take the position that they are simply conduits of information provided by others.[457]

To be sure, broadband providers engage in network management practices designed to protect their Internet services against spam and malicious content, but that practice bears little resemblance to an editor's choosing which programs, among a range of programs, to carry.[458]

Furthermore, this Order does not limit broadband providers' ability to modify their own webpages, or transmit any lawful message that they wish, just like any other speaker. Broadband providers are also free under this Order to offer a wide range of "edited" services. If, for example, a broadband provider wanted to offer a service limited to "family friendly" materials to end users who desire only such content, it could do so under the rules we promulgate today.[459]

AT&T and NCTA argue that open Internet rules interfere with the speech rights of content and application providers to the extent they are prevented from paying broadband providers for higher quality service.[460] Purchasing a higher quality of termination service for one's own Internet traffic, though, is not speech—just as providing the underlying transmission service is not. Telephone common carriers, for instance, transmit users' speech for hire, but no court has ever suggested that regulation of common carriage arrangements triggers First Amendment scrutiny.[461]

Even if open Internet rules did implicate expressive activity, they would not violate the First Amendment. Because the rules are based on the characteristics of broadband Internet access service, independent of content or viewpoint, they would be subject to intermediate First Amendment scrutiny.[462] The regulations in this Order are triggered by a broadband provider offering broadband Internet access, not by the message of any provider. Indeed, the point of open Internet rules is to protect traffic regardless of its content. Verizon's argument that such regulation is presumptively suspect because it makes speaker-based distinctions[463] likewise lacks merit: Our action is based on the transmission service provided by broadband providers rather than on what providers have to say. In any event, speaker-based distinctions are permissible so long as they are "'justified by some special characteristic of' the particular medium being regulated"[464]—here the ability of broadband providers to favor or disfavor Internet traffic to the detriment of innovation, investment, competition, public discourse, and end users.

Under intermediate scrutiny, a content-neutral regulation will be sustained if "it furthers an important or substantial government interest . . . unrelated to the suppression of free expression," and if "the means chosen" to achieve that interest "do not burden substantially more speech than is necessary."[465] The government interests underlying this Order—preserving an open Internet to encourage competition and remove impediments to infrastructure investment while enabling consumer choice, end-user control, free expression, and the freedom to innovate without permission—ensure the public's access to a multiplicity of information sources and maximize the Internet's potential to further the public interest. As a result, these interests satisfy the intermediate-scrutiny standard.[466] Indeed, the interest in keeping the Internet open to a wide range of information sources is an important free speech interest in its own right. As Turner I affirmed, "assuring that the public has access to a multiplicity of information sources is a governmental purpose of the highest order, for it promotes values central to the First Amendment."[467] This Order protects the speech interests of all Internet speakers.

Time Warner and Verizon contend that the government lacks important or substantial interests because the harms from prohibited practices supposedly are speculative.[468] This ignores actual instances of harmful practices by broadband providers, as discussed in Part II.B. In any event, the Commission is not required to stay its hand until substantial harms already have occurred. On the contrary, the Commission's predictive judgments as to the development of a problem and likely injury to the public interest are entitled to great deference.[469]

In sum, the rules we adopt are narrowly tailored to advance the important government interests at stake. The rules apply only to that portion of the end user's link to the Internet over which the end user's broadband provider has control. They forbid only those actions that could unfairly impede the public's use of this important resource. Broadband providers are left with ample opportunities to transmit their own content, to maintain their own websites, and to engage in reasonable network management. In addition, they can offer edited services to their end users. The rules are narrowly tailored because they address the problem at hand, and go no farther.[470]

2. Fifth Amendment Takings

Contrary to the claims of some broadband providers,[471] open Internet rules pose no issue under the Fifth Amendment's Takings Clause. Our rules do not compel new services or limit broadband providers' flexibility in setting prices for their broadband Internet access services, but simply require transparency and prevent broadband providers—when they voluntarily carry Internet traffic—from blocking or unreasonably discriminating in their treatment of that traffic. Moreover, this Order involves setting policies for communications networks, an activity that has been one of this Commission's central duties since it was established in 1934.

Absent compelled permanent physical occupations of property,[472] takings analysis involves "essentially ad hoc, factual inquiries" regarding such factors as the degree of interference with "investment-backed expectations," the "economic impact of the regulation" and "the character of the government action."[473] In this regard, takings law makes clear that property owners cannot, as a general matter, expect that existing legal requirements regarding their property will remain entirely unchanged.[474] As discussed in Part II, the history of broadband Internet access services offers no basis for reasonable reliance on a policy regime in which providers are free to conceal or discriminate without limit, and the rules we adopt today should not impose substantial new costs on broadband providers.[475] Accordingly, our Order does not raise constitutional concerns under regulatory takings analysis.

V. ENFORCEMENT

Prompt and effective enforcement of the rules adopted in this Order is crucial to preserving an open Internet and providing clear guidance to stakeholders. We anticipate that many of the disputes that will arise regarding alleged open Internet violations—particularly those centered on engineering-focused questions—will be resolvable by the parties without Commission involvement. We thus encourage parties to endeavor to resolve disputes through direct negotiation focused on relevant technical issues, and to consult with independent technical bodies. Many commenters endorse this approach.[476]

Should issues develop that are not resolved through private processes, the Commission will provide backstop mechanisms to address such disputes.[477] In the Open Internet NPRM, the Commission proposed to enforce open Internet rules through case-by-case adjudication, a proposal that met with almost universal support among commenters.[478] The Commission also sought comment on whether it should adopt complaint procedures specifically governing alleged violations of open Internet rules, and whether any of the Commission's existing rules provide a suitable model.[479]

A. Informal Complaints

Many commenters urge the Commission to adopt informal complaint procedures that equip end users and edge providers with a simple and cost-effective option for calling attention to open Internet rule violations.[480] We agree that end users, edge providers, and others should have an efficient vehicle to bring potential open Internet violations to the Commission, and indeed, such a vehicle is already available. Parties may submit complaints to the Commission pursuant to Section 1.41 of the Commission's rules.[481] Unlike formal complaints, no filing fee is required. We recommend that end users and edge providers submit any complaints through the Commission's website, at http://esupport.fcc.gov/complaints.htm. The Consumer and Governmental Affairs Bureau will also make available resources explaining these rules and facilitating the filing of informal complaints. Although individual informal complaints will not typically result in written Commission orders, the Enforcement Bureau will examine trends or patterns in complaints to identify potential targets for investigation and enforcement action.[482]

B. Formal Complaints

Many commenters propose that the Commission adopt formal complaint procedures to address open Internet disputes.[483] We agree that such procedures should be available in the event an open Internet dispute cannot be resolved through other means. Formal complaint processes permit anyone—including individual end users and edge providers—to file a claim alleging that another party has violated a statute or rule, and asking the Commission to rule on the dispute. A number of commenters suggest that existing Commission procedural rules could readily be utilized to govern open Internet complaints.[484]

We conclude that adopting a set of procedures based on our Part 76 cable access complaint rules will best suit the needs of open Internet disputes that may arise.[485] Although similar to the complaint rules under section 208, we find that the Part 76 rules are more streamlined and thus preferable.[486]

Under the rules we adopt today, any person may file a formal complaint.[487] Before filing a complaint, a complainant must first notify the defendant in writing that it intends to file a complaint with the Commission for violation of rules adopted in this Order.[488] After the complaint has been filed, the defendant must submit an answer, and the complainant may submit a reply.[489] In some cases, the facts might be uncontested, and the proceeding can be completed based on the pleadings. In other cases, a thorough analysis of the challenged conduct might require further factual development and briefing.[490] Based on the record developed, Commission staff (or the Commission itself) will issue an order determining the lawfulness of the challenged practice.

As in other contexts, complainants in open Internet proceedings will ultimately bear the burden of proof to demonstrate by a preponderance of the evidence that an alleged violation of the rules has occurred.[491] A number of commenters propose, however, that once a complainant makes a prima facie showing that an open Internet rule has been violated, the burden should shift to the broadband provider to demonstrate that the challenged practice is reasonable.[492] This approach is appropriate in the context of certain open Internet complaints, when the evidence necessary to apply the open Internet rules is predominantly in the possession of the broadband provider. Accordingly, we require a complainant alleging a violation of the open Internet rules to plead fully and with specificity the basis of its claims and to provide facts, supported when possible by documentation or affidavit, sufficient to establish a prima facie case of an open Internet violation. In turn, the broadband provider must answer each claim with particularity and furnish facts, supported by documentation or affidavit, demonstrating the reasonableness of the challenged practice. At that point, the complainant will have the opportunity to demonstrate that the practice is not reasonable. Should experience reveal the need to adjust the burden of proof in open Internet disputes, we will do so as appropriate.

Several commenters urge the Commission to adopt timelines for the complaint process.[493] We recognize the need to resolve alleged violations swiftly, and accordingly will allow requests for expedited treatment of open Internet complaints under the Enforcement Bureau's Accelerated Docket procedures.[494]

In resolving formal complaints, the Commission will draw on resources from across the agency—including engineering, economic, and legal experts—to resolve open Internet complaints in a timely manner. In addition, we will take into account standards and best practices adopted by relevant standard-setting organizations, and such organizations and outside advisory groups also may provide valuable technical assistance in resolving disputes. Further, in order to facilitate prompt decision-making, when possible we will resolve open Internet formal complaints at the bureau level, rather than the Commission level.[495]

C. FCC Initiated Actions

As noted above, in addition to ruling on complaints, the Commission has the authority to initiate enforcement actions on its own motion. For instance, section 403 of the Act permits the Commission to initiate an inquiry concerning any question arising under the Act, and section 503(b) authorizes us to issue citations and impose forfeiture penalties for violations of our rules. Should the Commission find that a broadband Internet provider is engaging in activity that violates the open Internet rules, we will take appropriate enforcement action, including the issuance of forfeitures.[496]

VI. Effective Date, Open Internet Advisory Committee, and Commission Review

As described below in Part 0.B, some of the rules adopted in this Order contain new information collection requirements subject to the Paperwork Reduction Act (PRA). Our rules addressing transparency are among those requiring PRA approval. The disclosure rule is essential to the proper functioning of our open Internet framework, and we therefore make all the rules we adopt in this Order effective 60 days after the date of Federal Register notice announcing the decision of the Office of Management and Budget regarding approval of the information collection requirements.

To assist the Commission in monitoring the state of Internet openness and the effects of our rules, we intend to create an Open Internet Advisory Committee. The Committee, to be created in consultation with the General Services Administration pursuant to the Federal Advisory Committee Act, will be an inclusive and transparent body that will hold public meetings. It will be comprised of a balanced group including consumer advocates; Internet engineering experts; content, application, and service providers; network equipment and end-user-device manufacturers and suppliers; investors; broadband service providers; and other parties the Commission may deem appropriate. The Committee will aid the Commission in tracking developments with respect to the freedom and openness of the Internet, in particular with respect to issues discussed in this Order, including technical standards and issues relating to mobile broadband and specialized services.[497] The Committee will report to the Commission and make recommendations it deems appropriate concerning our open Internet framework.

In light of the pace of change of technologies and the market for broadband Internet access service, and to evaluate the efficacy of the framework adopted today for preserving Internet openness, the Commission will review all of the rules in this Order no later than two years from their effective date, and will adjust its open Internet framework as appropriate.

VII. PROCEDURAL MATTERS

A. Final Regulatory Flexibility Analysis

As required by the Regulatory Flexibility Act (RFA),[498] an Initial Regulatory Flexibility Analysis (IRFA) was incorporated into the Open Internet NPRM.[499] The Commission sought written public comment on the possible significant economic impact on small entities regarding the proposals addressed in the Open Internet NPRM, including comments on the IRFA. Pursuant to the RFA, a Final Regulatory Flexibility Analysis is set forth in Appendix D.

B. Paperwork Reduction Act of 1995 Analysis

This document contains new information collection requirements subject to the Paperwork Reduction Act of 1995 (PRA), Public Law 104-13. It will be submitted to the Office of Management and Budget (OMB) for review under Section 3507(d) of the PRA. OMB, the general public, and other federal agencies are invited to comment on the new information collection requirements contained in this proceeding. In addition, we note that pursuant to the Small Business Paperwork Relief Act of 2002, Public Law 107-198, see 44 U.S.C. 3506(c)(4), we previously sought specific comment on how the Commission might further reduce the information collection burden for small business concerns with fewer than 25 employees.

In this present document, we require broadband Internet access service providers to publicly disclose accurate information regarding the commercial terms, performance, and network management practices of their broadband Internet access services sufficient for end users to make informed choices regarding use of such services and for content, application, service, and device providers to develop, market, and maintain Internet offerings. We have assessed the effects of this rule and find that any burden on small businesses will be minimal because (1) the rule gives broadband Internet access service providers flexibility in how to implement the disclosure rule, and (2) the rule gives providers adequate time to develop cost-effective methods of compliance.

C. Congressional Review Act

The Commission will send a copy of this Report and Order to Congress and the Government Accountability Office pursuant to the Congressional Review Act, *see* 5 U.S.C. § 801(a)(1)(A).

D. Data Quality Act

The Commission certifies that it has complied with the Office of Management and Budget Final Information Quality Bulletin for Peer Review, 70 Fed. Reg. 2664 (2005), and the Data Quality Act, Pub. L. No. 106-554 (2001), codified at 44 U.S.C. § 3516 note, with regard to its reliance on influential scientific information in the Report and Order in GN Docket No. 09-191 and WC Docket No. 07-52.[500]

E. Accessible Formats

To request materials in accessible formats for people with disabilities (braille, large print, electronic files, audio format), send an e-mail to fcc504@fcc.gov or call the Consumer & Governmental Affairs Bureau at 202-418-0530 (voice), 202-418-0432 (tty). Contact the FCC to request reasonable accommodations for filing comments (accessible format documents, sign language interpreters, CARTS, *etc.*) by e-mail: FCC504@fcc.gov; phone: (202) 418-0530 (voice), (202) 418-0432 (TTY).

VIII. Ordering Clauses

Accordingly, IT IS ORDERED that, pursuant to sections 1, 2, 3, 4, 201, 218, 230, 251, 254, 256, 257, 301, 303, 304, 307, 309, 316, 332, 403, 503, 602, 616, and 628, of the Communications Act of 1934, as amended, and section 706 of the Telecommunications Act of 1996, as amended, 47 U.S.C. §§ 151, 152, 153, 154, 201, 218, 230, 251, 254, 256, 257,

301, 303, 304, 307, 309, 316, 332, 403, 503, 522, 536, 548, 1302, this Report and Order IS ADOPTED.

IT IS FURTHER ORDERED that Part 0 of the Commission's rules IS AMENDED as set forth in Appendix B.

IT IS FURTHER ORDERED that Part 8 of the Commission's Rules, 47 C.F.R. Part 8, IS ADDED as set forth in Appendix A and B.

IT IS FURTHER ORDERED that this Report and Order shall become effective 60 days after the date of Federal Register notice announcing the decision of the Office of Management and Budget regarding approval of the information collection requirements contained in the rules contained in Appendix A.

IT IS FURTHER ORDERED that the Commission's Consumer and Governmental Affairs Bureau, Reference Information Center, SHALL SEND a copy of this Report and Order, including the Final Regulatory Flexibility Analysis, to the Chief Counsel for Advocacy of the Small Business Administration.

FEDERAL COMMUNICATIONS
COMMISSION

Marlene H. Dortch
Secretary

Appendix A. Substantive Rules

Part 8 of Title 47 of the Code of Federal Regulations is added as follows:

Part 8 – Preserving the Open Internet

Sec.
8.1 Purpose.
8.3 Transparency.
8.5 No Blocking.
8.7 No Unreasonable Discrimination.
8.9 Other Laws and Considerations.
8.11 Definitions.

AUTHORITY: 47 U.S.C. §§ 151, 152, 153, 154, 201, 218, 230, 251, 254, 256, 257, 301, 303, 304, 307, 309, 316, 332, 403, 503, 522, 536, 548, 1302

§ 8.1 Purpose

The purpose of this Part is to preserve the Internet as an open platform enabling consumer choice, freedom of expression, end-user control, competition, and the freedom to innovate without permission.

§ 8.3. *Transparency*

A person engaged in the provision of broadband Internet access service shall publicly disclose accurate information regarding the network management practices, performance, and commercial terms of its broadband Internet access services sufficient for consumers to make informed choices regarding use of such services and for content, application, service, and device providers to develop, market, and maintain Internet offerings.

§ 8.5. *No Blocking*

A person engaged in the provision of fixed broadband Internet access service, insofar as such person is so engaged, shall not block lawful content, applications, services, or non-harmful devices, subject to reasonable network management.

A person engaged in the provision of mobile broadband Internet access service, insofar as such person is so engaged, shall not block consumers from accessing lawful websites, subject to reasonable network management; nor shall such person block applications that compete with the provider's voice or video telephony services, subject to reasonable network management.

§ 8.7. *No Unreasonable Discrimination*

A person engaged in the provision of fixed broadband Internet access service, insofar as such person is so engaged, shall not unreasonably discriminate in transmitting lawful network traffic over a consumer's broadband Internet access service. Reasonable network management shall not constitute unreasonable discrimination.

§ 8.9. *Other Laws and Considerations*

Nothing in this part supersedes any obligation or authorization a provider of broadband Internet access service may have to address the needs of emergency communications or law enforcement, public safety, or national security authorities, consistent with or as permitted by applicable law, or limits the provider's ability to do so.

Nothing in this part prohibits reasonable efforts by a provider of broadband Internet access service to address copyright infringement or other unlawful activity.

§ 8.11. *Definitions*

(a) *Broadband Internet access service.* A mass-market retail service by wire or radio that provides the capability to transmit data to and receive data from all or substantially all Internet endpoints, including any capabilities that are incidental to and enable the operation of the communications service, but excluding dial-up Internet access service. This term also encompasses any service that the Commission finds to be providing a functional equivalent of the service described in the previous sentence, or that is used to evade the protections set forth in this Part.

(b) *Fixed broadband Internet access service.* A broadband Internet access service that serves end users primarily at fixed endpoints using stationary equipment. Fixed broadband Internet access service includes fixed wireless services (including fixed unlicensed wireless services), and fixed satellite services.

(c) *Mobile broadband Internet access service.* A broadband Internet access service that serves end users primarily using mobile stations.
(d) *Reasonable network management.* A network management practice is reasonable if it is appropriate and tailored to achieving a legitimate network management purpose, taking into account the particular network architecture and technology of the broadband Internet access service.

Appendix B. Procedural Rules

AUTHORITY: 47 U.S.C. §§ 151, 152, 153, 154, 201, 218, 230, 251, 254, 256, 257, 301, 303, 304, 307, 309, 316, 332, 403, 503, 522, 536, 548, 1302

§ 0.111. Functions of the Bureau

Amend § 0.111(a) of the rules to add subsection (24) as follows: Resolve complaints alleging violations of the open Internet rules.

Formal Complaints

§ 8.12. Formal Complaints

Any person may file a formal complaint alleging a violation of the rules in this part.

§ 8.13. General pleading requirements.

(a) General pleading requirements. All written submissions, both substantive and procedural, must conform to the following standards:
  (1) A pleading must be clear, concise, and explicit. All matters concerning a claim, defense or requested remedy should be pleaded fully and with specificity.
  (2) Pleadings must contain facts that, if true, are sufficient to warrant a grant of the relief requested.
  (3) Facts must be supported by relevant documentation or affidavit.
  (4) The original of all pleadings and submissions by any party shall be signed by that party, or by the party's attorney. Complaints must be signed by the complainant. The signing party shall state his or her address and telephone number and the date on which the document was signed. Copies should be conformed to the original. Each submission must contain a written verification that the signatory has read the submission and to the best of his or her knowledge, information and belief formed after reasonable inquiry, it is well grounded in fact and is warranted by existing law or a good faith argument for the extension, modification or reversal of existing law; and that it is not interposed for any improper purpose. If any pleading or other submission is

signed in violation of this provision, the Commission shall upon motion or upon its own initiative impose appropriate sanctions.

(5) Legal arguments must be supported by appropriate judicial, Commission, or statutory authority. Opposing authorities must be distinguished. Copies must be provided of all non-Commission authorities relied upon which are not routinely available in national reporting systems, such as unpublished decisions or slip opinions of courts or administrative agencies.

(6) Parties are responsible for the continuing accuracy and completeness of all information and supporting authority furnished in a pending complaint proceeding. Information submitted, as well as relevant legal authorities, must be current and updated as necessary and in a timely manner at any time before a decision is rendered on the merits of the complaint.

(7) Parties seeking expedited resolution of their complaint may request acceptance on the Enforcement Bureau's Accelerated Docket pursuant to the procedures at section 1.730 of the Commission's rules.

(b) Copies to be Filed. The complainant shall file an original copy of the complaint, accompanied by the correct fee, in accordance with part 1, subpart G (*see* § 1.1106) and, on the same day:

(1) File three copies of the complaint with the Office of the Commission Secretary;

(2) Serve two copies on the Market Disputes Resolution Division, Enforcement Bureau;

(3) Serve the complaint by hand delivery on either the named defendant or one of the named defendant's registered agents for service of process, if available, on the same date that the complaint is filed with the Commission.

(c) Prefiling notice required. Any person intending to file a complaint under this section must first notify the potential defendant in writing that it intends to file a complaint with the Commission based on actions alleged to violate one or more of the provisions contained in this part. The notice must be sufficiently detailed so that its recipient(s) can determine the specific nature of the potential complaint. The potential complainant must allow a minimum of ten (10) days for the potential defendant(s) to respond before filing a complaint with the Commission.

(d) Frivolous pleadings. It shall be unlawful for any party to file a frivolous pleading with the Commission. Any violation of this paragraph shall constitute an abuse of process subject to appropriate sanctions.

§ 8.14. General formal complaint procedures.

(a) Complaints. In addition to the general pleading requirements, complaints must adhere to the following requirements:

(1) Certificate of service. Complaints shall be accompanied by a certificate of service on any defendant.

(2) Statement of relief requested.

(i) The complaint shall state the relief requested. It shall state fully and precisely all pertinent facts and considerations relied on to demonstrate the need for the relief requested and to support a determination that a grant of such relief would serve the public interest.

(ii) The complaint shall set forth all steps taken by the parties to resolve the problem.

(iii) A complaint may, on request of the filing party, be dismissed without prejudice as a matter of right prior to the adoption date of any final action taken by the Commission with respect to the petition or complaint. A request for the return of an initiating document will be regarded as a request for dismissal.

(3) Failure to prosecute. Failure to prosecute a complaint, or failure to respond to official correspondence or request for additional information, will be cause for dismissal. Such dismissal will be without prejudice if it occurs prior to the adoption date of any final action taken by the Commission with respect to the initiating pleading.

(b) Answers to complaints. Unless otherwise directed by the Commission, any party who is served with a complaint shall file an answer in accordance with the following requirements:

(1) The answer shall be filed within 20 days of service of the complaint.

(2) The answer shall advise the parties and the Commission fully and completely of the nature of any and all defenses, and shall respond specifically to all material allegations of the complaint. Collateral or immaterial issues shall be avoided in answers and every effort should be made to narrow the issues. Any party against whom a complaint is filed failing to file and serve an answer within the time and in the manner prescribed by these rules may be deemed in default and an order may be entered against defendant in accordance with the allegations contained in the complaint.

(3) Facts must be supported by relevant documentation or affidavit.

(4) The answer shall admit or deny the averments on which the adverse party relies. If the defendant is without knowledge or information sufficient to form a belief as to the truth of an averment, the defendant shall so state and this has the effect of a denial. When a defendant intends in good faith to deny only part of an averment, the answer shall specify so much of it as is true and shall deny only the remainder, and state in detail the basis of that denial.

(5) Averments in a complaint are deemed to be admitted when not denied in the answer.

(c) Reply. In addition to the general pleading requirements, replies must adhere to the following requirements:

(1) The complainant may file a reply to a responsive pleading that shall be served on the defendant and shall also contain a detailed full showing, supported by affidavit, of any additional facts or considerations relied on. Unless expressly permitted by the Commission, replies shall not contain new matters.

(2) Failure to reply will not be deemed an admission of any allegations contained in the responsive pleading, except with respect to any affirmative defense set forth therein.

(3) Unless otherwise directed by the Commission, replies must be filed within ten (10) days after submission of the responsive pleading.

(d) Motions. Except as provided in this section, or upon a showing of extraordinary circumstances, additional motions or pleadings by any party will not be accepted.

(e) Additional procedures and written submissions.

(1) The Commission may specify other procedures, such as oral argument or evidentiary hearing directed to particular aspects, as it deems appropriate. In the event that an evidentiary hearing is required, the Commission will determine, on the basis of the pleadings and such other procedures as it may specify, whether temporary relief should be afforded any party pending the hearing and the nature of any such temporary relief.

(2) The Commission may require the parties to submit any additional information it deems appropriate for a full, fair, and expeditious resolution of the proceeding, including copies of all contracts and documents reflecting arrangements and understandings alleged to violate the requirements set forth in the Communications Act and in this part, as well as affidavits and exhibits.

(3) The Commission may, in its discretion, require the parties to file briefs summarizing the facts and issues presented in the pleadings and other record evidence.

(i) These briefs shall contain the findings of fact and conclusions of law which that party is urging the Commission to adopt, with specific citations to the record, and supported by relevant authority and analysis.

(ii) The schedule for filing any briefs shall be at the discretion of the Commission. Unless ordered otherwise by the Commission, such briefs shall not exceed fifty (50) pages.

(iii) Reply briefs may be submitted at the discretion of the Commission. Unless ordered otherwise by the Commission, reply briefs shall not exceed thirty (30) pages.

(f) Discovery.

(1) The Commission may in its discretion order discovery limited to the issues specified by the Commission. Such discovery may include answers to written interrogatories, depositions, document production, or requests for admissions.

(2) The Commission may in its discretion direct the parties to submit discovery proposals, together with a memorandum in support of the discovery requested. Such discovery requests may include answers to written interrogatories, admissions, document production, or depositions. The Commission may hold a status conference with the parties, pursuant to § 8.15 of this part, to determine the scope of discovery, or direct the parties regarding the scope of discovery. If the Commission determines that extensive discovery is required or that depositions are warranted, the Commission may advise the parties that the proceeding will be referred to an administrative law judge in accordance with paragraph (g) of this section.

(g) Referral to administrative law judge.

(1) After reviewing the pleadings, and at any stage of the proceeding thereafter, the Commission may, in its discretion, designate any proceeding or discrete issues arising out of any proceeding for an adjudicatory hearing before an administrative law judge.

(2) Before designation for hearing, the Commission shall notify, either orally or in writing, the parties to the proceeding of its intent to so designate, and the parties shall be given a period of ten (10) days to elect to resolve the dispute through

alternative dispute resolution procedures, or to proceed with an adjudicatory hearing. Such election shall be submitted in writing to the Commission.

(3) Unless otherwise directed by the Commission, or upon motion by the Enforcement Bureau Chief, the Enforcement Bureau Chief shall not be deemed to be a party to a proceeding designated for a hearing before an administrative law judge pursuant to this paragraph (g).

(h) Commission ruling. The Commission (or the Enforcement Bureau on delegated authority), after consideration of the pleadings, shall issue an order ruling on the complaint.

§ 8.15. Status Conference

(a) In any proceeding subject to the part 8 rules, the Commission may in its discretion direct the attorneys and/or the parties to appear for a conference to consider:

(1) Simplification or narrowing of the issues;

(2) The necessity for or desirability of amendments to the pleadings, additional pleadings, or other evidentiary submissions;

(3) Obtaining admissions of fact or stipulations between the parties as to any or all of the matters in controversy;

(4) Settlement of the matters in controversy by agreement of the parties;

(5) The necessity for and extent of discovery, including objections to interrogatories or requests for written documents;

(6) The need and schedule for filing briefs, and the date for any further conferences; and

(7) Such other matters that may aid in the disposition of the proceeding.

(b) Any party may request that a conference be held at any time after an initiating document has been filed.

(c) Conferences will be scheduled by the Commission at such time and place as it may designate, to be conducted in person or by telephone conference call.

(d) The failure of any attorney or party, following advance notice with an opportunity to be present, to appear at a scheduled conference will be deemed a waiver and will not preclude the Commission from conferring with those parties or counsel present.

(e) During a status conference, the Commission may issue oral rulings pertaining to a variety of matters relevant to the conduct of the proceeding including, inter alia, procedural matters, discovery, and the submission of briefs or other evidentiary materials. These rulings will be promptly memorialized in writing and served on the parties. When such rulings require a party to take affirmative action, such action will be required within ten (10) days from the date of the written memorialization unless otherwise directed by the Commission.

§ 8.16. Confidentiality of proprietary information

(a) Any materials filed in the course of a proceeding under this part may be designated as proprietary by that party if the party believes in good faith that the materials fall within an exemption to disclosure contained in the Freedom of Information Act (FOIA), 5 U.S.C. 552(b). Any party asserting confidentiality for such materials shall so indicate by clearly marking each page, or portion thereof, for which a proprietary designation is claimed. If a proprietary designation is challenged, the party claiming confidentiality will have the burden of demonstrating, by a preponderance of the evidence, that the material designated as proprietary falls under the standards for nondisclosure enunciated in FOIA.

(b) Submissions containing information claimed to be proprietary under this section shall be submitted to the Commission in confidence pursuant to the requirements of § 0.459 of this chapter and clearly marked "Not for Public Inspection." An edited version removing all proprietary data shall be filed with the Commission for inclusion in the public file within five (5) days from the date the unedited reply is submitted, and shall be served on the opposing parties.

(c) Except as provided in paragraph (d) of this section, materials marked as proprietary may be disclosed solely to the following persons, only for use in the proceeding, and only to the extent necessary to assist in the prosecution or defense of the case:
  (1) Counsel of record representing the parties in the proceeding and any support personnel employed by such attorneys;
  (2) Officers or employees of the parties in the proceeding who are named by another party as being directly involved in the proceeding;
  (3) Consultants or expert witnesses retained by the parties;
  (4) The Commission and its staff; and
  (5) Court reporters and stenographers in accordance with the terms and conditions of this section.

(d) The Commission will entertain, subject to a proper showing, a party's request to further restrict access to proprietary information as specified by the party. The other parties will have an opportunity to respond to such requests.

(e) The persons designated in paragraphs (c) and (d) of this section shall not disclose information designated as proprietary to any person who is not authorized under this section to receive such information, and shall not use the information in any activity or function other than the prosecution or defense of the case before the Commission. Each individual who is provided access to the information by the opposing party shall sign a notarized statement affirmatively stating, or shall certify under penalty of perjury, that the individual has personally reviewed the Commission's rules and understands the limitations they impose on the signing party.

(f) No copies of materials marked proprietary may be made except copies to be used by persons designated in paragraphs (c) and (d) of this section. Each party shall maintain a log recording the number of copies made of all proprietary material and the persons to whom the copies have been provided.

(g) Upon termination of the complaint proceeding, including all appeals and petitions, all originals and reproductions of any proprietary materials, along with the log recording persons who received copies of such materials, shall be provided to the producing party. In addition, upon final termination of the proceeding, any notes or other work product derived in whole or in part from the proprietary materials of an opposing or third party shall be destroyed.

§ 8.17. Review

(a) Interlocutory review.

  (1) Except as provided below, no party may seek review of interlocutory rulings until a decision on the merits has been issued by the Commission's staff, including an administrative law judge.

  (2) Rulings listed in this paragraph are reviewable as a matter of right. An application for review of such ruling may not be deferred and raised as an exception to a decision on the merits.

    (i) If the staff's ruling denies or terminates the right of any person to participate as a party to the proceeding, such person, as a matter of right, may file an application for review of that ruling.

    (ii) If the staff's ruling requires production of documents or other written evidence, over objection based on a claim of privilege, the ruling on the claim of privilege is reviewable as a matter of right.

    (iii) If the staff's ruling denies a motion to disqualify a staff person from participating in the proceeding, the ruling is reviewable as a matter of right.

(b) Petitions for reconsideration. Petitions for reconsideration of interlocutory actions by the Commission's staff or by an administrative law judge will not be entertained. Petitions for reconsideration of a decision on the merits made by the Commission's staff should be filed in accordance with §§ 1.104 through 1.106 of this chapter.

(c) Application for review.

  (1) Any party to a part 8 proceeding aggrieved by any decision on the merits issued by the staff pursuant to delegated authority may file an application for review by the Commission in accordance with § 1.115 of this chapter.

  (2) Any party to a part 8 proceeding aggrieved by any decision on the merits by an administrative law judge may file an appeal of the decision directly with the Commission, in accordance with §§ 1.276(a) and 1.277(a) through (c) of this chapter.

APPENDIX C. LIST OF COMMENTERS

NPRM Comments[501]

Commenter	Abbreviation
100 Black Men of America et al. (filed by Sylvia Aguilera)	100 Black Men of America et al.
2Wire, Inc. (filed by Jonathan Symonds)	2Wire
4Info, Inc.	4Info
ACT 1 Group et al. (filed as World WideTechnology, Inc)	ACT 1 Group et al.
Adam Candeub and Daniel John McCartney	Candeub/McCartney
The Ad Hoc Telecommunications Users Committee	Ad Hoc
ADTRAN, Inc.	ADTRAN
Adventia Innovative Systems (filed by Dino Rodwell)	Adventia
African American Chamber of Commerce - Milwaukee	AACC
African Methodist Episcopal Church	AMEC
Akamai Technologies, Inc.	Akamai
Alabama State Conference of the NAACP	Alabama State NAACP
Alcatel-Lucent	ALU
Alliance for Digital Equality (filed by Julius Hollis)	ADE
Alliance for Telecommunications Industry Solutions	ATIS
Amazon.com	Amazon
American Arab Chamber of Commerce (filed by Ahmed Chebbani)	American Arab CC
American Association of People with Disabilities	AAPD
American Business Media	ABM
American Cable Association	ACA
American Center for Law and Justice	ACLJ
American Civil Rights Union	ACRU
American Consumer Institute CCR	ACI
American Council of the Blind	ACB
American Federation of Television & Radio Artists, Directors Guild of America, International Alliance of Theatrical Stage Employees, Screen Actors Guild	AFTRA *et al.*
American Homeowners Grassroots Alliance	AHGA
American Indian Chamber of Commerce of Wisconsin	AICCW
American Legislative Exchange Council	ALEC
American Library Association	ALA
Americans for Prosperity	AFP
Americans for Tax Reform and Media Freedom Project (filed by Christopher Butler)	ATR
Americans for Technology Leadership (filed by Randy Skoglund)	ATL
Annie McGrady	Annie McGrady
Anti-Defamation League	ALD
Arts+Labs	Arts+Labs
Asian American Justice Center (filed by Karen K. Narasaki)	AAJC
Assemblywoman Debbie Smith	Assemblywoman Smith
Association for Competitive Technology	ACT
Association of Research Libraries, EDUCAUSE, Internet2, NYSERNet, and ACUTA	ARL *et al.*
AT&T Inc.	AT&T
Automation Alley (filed by Ken Rogers)	Automation Alley
Ball State University Center for Information and Communications Science	Ball State University Center
Barbara S. Esbin, Senior Fellow and Director of the Center for Communications	Barbara S. Esbin,

Table. (Continued)

Commenter	Abbreviation
The Berroteran Group	The Berroteran Group
Big Brothers Big Sisters of Will and Grundy Counties	Big Brothers
Bright House Networks, LLC	Bright House
BroadBand Institute of California and the Broadband Regulatory Clinic (filed by Prof. Allen S. Hammond, IV)	BBIC/BRC
Broadcast Music, Inc.	BMI
BT Americas Inc.	BT Americas
Camiant, Inc.	Camiant
Career Link Inc.	Career Link
Connecticut Association for United Spanish Action, Inc.	CAUSA
CDMA Development Group, Inc.	CDG
Center for Democracy & Technology	CDT
Center for Individual Freedom	CFIF
Center for Rural Strategies	Center for Rural Strategies
Central Washington Hispanic Chamber of Commerce	CWHCC
CenturyLink	CenturyLink
Chamber of Commerce of St. Joseph County	St. Joseph Chamber of Commerce
Charter Communications	Charter
Christopher Sacca	Christopher Sacca
Cincinnati Bell Wireless LLC	CBW
Cisco Systems, Inc.	Cisco
City of Philadelphia	Philadelphia
Clearwire Corporation	Clearwire
Coalition of Minority Chambers	Coalition of Minority Chambers
ColorOfChange.org	ColorOfChange
Comcast Corporation	Comcast
Communications Workers of America	CWA
Competitive Enterprise Institute	CEI
COMPTEL	COMPTEL
CompTIA	CompTIA
Computer & Communications Industry Association	CCIA
Computer Communications Industry Association, Consumer Electronics Association	CCIA/CEA
Computing Technology Industry Association (filed by Mike Wendy)	CompTIA
CONNECT	CONNECT
Connecticut Technology Council (filed by Matthew Nemerson)	Conn. Tech. Council
Consumer Policy Solutions	Consumer Policy Solutions
Corning Incorporated	Corning
Corporation for National Research Initiatives	CNRI
Council of Baptist Pastors of Detroit & Vicinity, Inc.	Council of Baptist Pastors
Covad Communications Company	Covad
Cox Communications, Inc	Cox
Craig Settles (Successful.com)	Craig Settles
Cricket Communications, Inc.	Cricket
CTIA - The Wireless Association	CTIA
CWA Indiana State Council	CWA Indiana
CWA Local 4900	CWA Local 4900
Damian Kulash	Damian Kulash
Data Foundry, Inc.	Data Foundry
David D.F. Uran, Mayor, City of Crown Point, Indiana	Uran
Deborah Turner	Deborah Turner
Debra Brown	Debra Brown

Table. (Continued)

Commenter	Abbreviation
Derek Leebaert	Derek Leebaert
Digital Education Coalition	Digital Education Coalition
Dickinson Area Partnership	Dickinson Area Partnership
The Disability Network (filed by Mike Zelley)	Disability Network
DISH Network L.L.C.	DISH
Distributed Computing Industry Association	DCIA
Downtown Springfield, Inc.	Downtown Springfield
Eastern Kentucky's Youth Association for the Arts, Inc.	EKYAA
Economic Development Council of Livingston County (filed by Fred Dillingham)	Livingston EDC
Eight Mile Boulevard Association	8MBA
El Centro	El Centro
Electronic Frontier Foundation	EFF
Elgin Area Chamber	Elgin Area Chamber
Elizabeth A. Dooley, Ed. D	Elizabeth A. Dooley, Ed. D
Entertainment Software Association	ESA
Ericsson Inc.	Ericsson
Erie Neighborhood House	Erie Neighborhood House
Fiber-to-the-Home Council	FTTH Council
Free Press	Free Press
The Free State Foundation	Free State Foundation
Future of Privacy Forum	FPF
George Ou	George Ou
Genesee Regional Chamber of Commerce (filed by Tim Herman)	Genesee Regional Chamber of Commerce
Georgetown/Scott County Kentucky Chamber of Commerce	Georgetown/Scott County Chamber of Commerce
Georgia Minority Supplier Development Council	GMSDC
Global Crossing North America, Inc.	Global Crossing
Global Intellectual Property Center	Global Intellectual Property Center
Google Inc.	Google
Great River Economic Development Foundation	Great River
The Greater Centralia Chamber of Commerce & Tourism Office	Greater Centralia
Greater Kokomo Economic Development Alliance	Greater Kokomo Economic Development Alliance
The Greenlining Institute	Greenlining
GSM Association	GSM
GVNW Consulting, Inc.	GVNW
Hamilton County Alliance	Hamilton County Alliance
Hannah Miller	Hannah Miller
HB Clark	HB Clark
Hispanic Leadership Fund	Hispanic Leadership Fund
Hispanic Technology and Telecommunications Partnership	HTTP
Hmong/American Friendship Association, Inc.	Hmong/American Friendship
Illinois Hispanic Chamber of Commerce	Illinois Hispanic Chamber
Independent Creator Organizations	Independent Creator Organizations
Independent Film & Television Alliance	IFTA
Independent Telephone & Telecommunications Alliance	ITTA
Indiana Secretary of State (filed by Todd Rokita)	Indiana Secretary of State
Indianapolis Urban League	Indianapolis Urban League
Information and Communications Manufacturers and Service Providers (filed by Paul Brunato, 2Wire, Inc.)	Information and Communications Manufacturers
Information Technology and Innovation Foundation	ITIF

Table. (Continued)

Commenter	Abbreviation
Information Technology Industry Council	ITIC
Institute for Emerging Leaders, Inc.	IEL
Institute for Policy Innovation	IPI
Internet Freedom Coalition	Internet Freedom Coalition
Internet Society	ISOC
Intrado Inc. and Intrado Communications Inc.	Intrado
Jared Morris	Jared Morris
Jeanne K. Magill, Pabst Farms Development Inc.	Jeanne K. Magill
Joe Armstrong, Tennessee State Representative	Joe Armstrong
Joe Homnick	Joe Homnick
John Staurulakis, Inc.	John Staurulakis
Johnson County Board of Commissioners	Johnson County
Joliet Region Chamber of Commerce & Industry	Joliet Chamber
Kankakee County Farm Bureau	Kankakee
Karen Maples	Karen Maples
Chairman Kenneth D. Koehler, McHenry County Board	Kenneth D. Koehler
Kentucky Commission on the Deaf and Hard of Hearing	Kentucky Commission on the Deaf
Lake Superior Community Partnership	LSCP
Lakewood Chamber of Commerce (filed by Patty Ryan)	Lakewood Chamber
Latin American Chamber of Commerce of Charlotte	LACCC
Latin Chamber of Commerce of Nevada	Latin Chamber of Nevada
Laurence Brett Glass, d/b/a LARIAT	LARIAT
Lawrence County Economic Growth Council	Lawrence County Economic Growth Council
Lawrence Morrow	Lawrence Morrow
Leadership East Kentucky	Leadership East Kentucky
Leap Wireless International, Inc. and Cricket Communications, Inc.	Leap
Level 3 Communications LLC	Level 3
Links Technology Solutions, Inc.	Links
Lisa Marie Hanlon, TelTech Communications LLC	Lisa Marie Hanlon
Maneesh Pangasa	Maneesh Pangasa
Mary-Anne Wolf	Mary-Anne Wolf
Matthew J. Cybulski	Matthew J. Cybulski
Mayor Brad Stephens	Mayor Brad Stephens
Mayor Leon Rockingham, Jr.	Mayor Leon Rockingham, Jr.
Mayor Rudolph Clay, Gary, Indiana	Mayor Rudolph Clay
McAllen Solutions	McAllen Solutions
Media Action Grassroots Network, ColorOfChange.org, Presente.org, Applied Research Center, Afro-Netizen, National Association of Hispanic Journalists, Native Public Media, and Rural Broadband Policy Group	MAG-Net
Messaging Anti-Abuse Working Group	MAAWG
MetroPCS Communications, Inc.	MetroPCS
Michele Hodges, Troy Chamber	Michele Hodges
Mid-Atlantic Community Papers Association, on behalf of Association of Free Community Papers, Community Papers of Michigan, Free Community Papers of New York, Community Papers of Florida, Midwest Free Community Papers, Community Papers of Ohio and West Virginia, Southeastern Advertising Publishers Association, Wisconsin Community Papers (filed by Jim Haigh)	Community Papers Commenters
Mississippi Center for Education Innovation	Mississippi Center for Education Innovation
Mississippi Center for Justice	Mississippi Center for Justice

Table. (Continued)

Commenter	Abbreviation
MLB Advanced Media, L.P.	MLBAM
Mobile Future	Mobile Future
Motion Picture Association of America, Inc.	MPAA
Motorola, Inc.	Motorola
National Association for the Advancement of Colored People	NAACP
Nacional Records	Nacional Records
Nate Zolman	Nate Zolman
National Association of Manufacturers	NAM
National Association of Realtors	NAR
National Association of State Utility Consumer Advocates	NASUCA
National Black Chamber of Commerce	NBCC
National Cable & Telecommunications Association	NCTA
National Council of La Raza	NCLR
National Exchange Carrier Association, Inc.	NECA
National Farmers Union	NFU
National Foundation for Women Legislators High Speed Internet Caucus (filed by Robin Read)	NFWL High Speed Caucus
National Hispanic Media Coalition	NHMC
National Organization of Black Elected Legislative Women	NOBEL Women
National Organizations	National Organizations
National Rural Health Association	NRHA
National Spinal Cord Injury Association (filed by K. Eric Larson)	NSCIA
National Taxpayers Union	NTU
National Telecommunications Cooperative Association	NTCA
National Urban League	National Urban League
National Association of Telecommunications Office & Advisors	NATOA
National Emergency Number Association	NENA
The Nebraska Rural Independent Companies	Nebraska Companies
Netflix, Inc	Netflix
Network 2010	Network 2010
New America Foundation	New America Foundation
New Jersey Rate Counsel	NJRC
New York State Office of Chief Information Officer/Office for Technology (CIO/OFT) (filed by David Salway)	NY CIO/OFT
Nickolaus E. Leggett	Leggett
Nokia Siemens Networks US LLC	NSN
Northern Nevada Black Cultural Awareness Society	Northern Nevada Black Cultural Awareness Society
Nippon Telegraph and Telephone Corporation	NTT
Office of the Mayor, City of Peru	City of Peru
Older Adults Technology Services, Inc.	OATS
Operation Action U.P. (filed by John Marshall)	Operation Action
Organization for the Promotion & Advancement of Small Telecommunication Companies	OPASTCO
Open Internet Coalition	OIC
Open Media and Information Companies Initiative	Open MIC
Oregon State Grange	Oregon State Grange
Mayor George Pabey, City of East Chicago, Indiana	Mayor Pabey
PAETEC Holding Corp.	PAETEC
Patricia Dye	Patricia Dye
Prof. Barbara A. Cherry	Prof. Barbara A. Cherry
David Clark, William Lehr, and Steve Bauer (filed by William Lehr)	David Clark et al.

Table. (Continued)

Commenter	Abbreviation
Professor Scott Jordan	Professor Scott Jordan
Property Rights Alliance	PRA
Public Interest Advocates	Public Interest Advocates
Public Interest Commenters (filed by Public Knowledge et al.)	PIC
QUALCOMM Incorporated	QUALCOMM
Qwest Communications International Inc.	Qwest
R. L. Barnes	R. L. Barnes
Rainbow PUSH Coalition	Rainbow PUSH
Recording Industry Association of America	RIAA
Red Hat, Inc.	Red Hat
Rev. W.L.T. Littleton	Rev. W.L.T. Littleton
Richmond Chamber of Commerce	Richmond Chamber of Commerce
RNK Communications	RNK
Robert K. McEwen dba PowerView Systems	Robert K. McEwen
Robert Steele, Cook County Commissioner	Robert Steele
Rural Cellular Association	RCA
Safe Internet Alliance (filed by Linda Criddle)	Safe Internet Alliance
Saint Xavier University (filed by Maureen Connor Kelly)	St. Xavier Univ.
Sandvine Incorporated	Sandvine
Satellite Broadband Commenters	Satellite Broadband
SavetheInternet.com	SavetheInternet.com
Scott Cleland	Scott Cleland
Sean Sowell	Sean Sowell
The Senior Alliance (filed by Bob Brown)	Senior Alliance
Seth Johnson	Seth Johnson
Shelby County Development Corporation	Shelby County
Skype Communications S.A.R.L.	Skype
Sling Media, Inc.	Sling
Karen Kerrigan, President & CEO, Small Business & Entrepreneurship Council	SBE Council
Smithville Telephone Company	Smithville
Software & Information Industry Association	SIIA
Songwriters Guild of America	SGA
Sony Electronics Inc.	Sony
Southern Wayne County Regional Chamber of Commerce	SWCRCC
Sprint Nextel Corporation	Sprint
Steve Forte, Chief Strategy Officer, Telerik	Steve Forte
St. Louis Society for the Blind and Visually Impaired (filed by David C. Ekin)	St. Louis Society
SureWest Communications	SureWest
TDS Telecommunications Corp.	TDS Telecom
Telecom Italia, S.P.A.	Telecom Italia
Telecom Manufacturer Coalition	Telecom Manufacturer Coalition
Telecommunications Industry Association	TIA
TeleDimensions, Inc.	TeleDimensions
Telefonica S.A.	Telefonica
Telephone Association of Maine	TAM
Texas Office of Public Utility Counsel	TxOPC
Texas Public Policy Foundation	TPPF
Texas Statewide Telephone Cooperative, Inc.	TSTCI
Thomas C. Poorman, President, Zanesville-Muskingum County Chamber of Commerce	Thomas C. Poorman

Table. (Continued)

Commenter	Abbreviation
Thomas D. Sydnor II, Senior Fellow and Director, Center for the Study of Digital Property at the Progress & Freedom Foundation	Thomas D. Sydnor II
Thomas Richard Reinsel, Executive in Residence, Sewickley Oak Capital	Thomas Richard Reinsel
Tim Wu, Professor at Columbia Law School	Tim Wu
Time Warner Cable Inc.	Time Warner
T-Mobile USA, Inc.	T-Mobile
U.S. Chamber of Commerce	U.S. Chamber
Union Square Ventures (filed by Brad Burnham)	Union Square
United Service Organizations of Illinois	USC of Illinois
United States Telecom Association	USTelecom
UNITY: Journalists of Color, Inc.	UNITY
Upper Peninsula Economic Development Alliance (filed by Joel Schultz)	UPEDA
Upper Peninsula Health Plan	UPHP
Urban League of Metropolitan Seattle	Urban League of Metropolitan Seattle
Verizon and Verizon Wireless	Verizon
Verizon, Google	Verizon, Google
Village of Maywood	Village of Maywood
Vincent Watts of the Greater Stark County Urban League	Vincent Watts
Voice on the Net Coalition	VON Coalition
Vonage Holdings Corp.	Vonage
Voto Latino	Voto Latino
Washington State Grange	Washington State Grange
Wayne Brough, James Gattuso, Hance Haney, Ryan Radia, and James Lakely	Wayne Brough et al.
Wireless Communications Association International, Inc.	WCAI
Wireless Internet Service Providers Association	WISPA
Writers Guild of America, East AFL-CIO	WGAE
XO Communications, LLC	XO
YWCA of St. Joseph County	St. Joseph YWCA

NPRM Reply Comments

Reply Commenter	Abbreviation
Aircell LLC	Aircell
Akamai Technologies, Inc.	Akamai
Alarm Industry Communications Committee	AICC
Alcatel-Lucent	ALU
Alliance for Digital Equality	ADE
American Association of Independent Music	A2IM
American Cable Association	ACA
American Homeowners Grassroots Alliance	AHGA
American Legislative Exchange Council	ALEC
American Federation of Television & Radio Artists, Directors Guild of America, International Alliance of Theatrical Stage Employees, Screen Actors Guild	AFTRA et al.
Americans for Tax Reform Digital Liberty Project	ATR Digital Liberty Project
AOL Inc.	AOL
Association for Competitive Technology	ACT
AT&T Inc.	AT&T

Table. (Continued)

Reply Commenter	Abbreviation
Black Leadership Forum, Inc.	BLF
Bret Swanson, President, Entropy Economics LLC	Bret Swanson
Bright House Networks, LLC	Bright House
Broadband Institute of California and Broadband Regulatory Clinic	BBIC & BRC
Broadcast Music, Inc. et al.	BMI et al.
Cablevision Systems Corporation	Cablevision
California Consumers for Net Neutrality	CCNN
California Public Utilities Commission	CPUC
Carbon Disclosure Project	CDP
Center for Democracy & Technology	CDT
Center for Individual Freedom	CFIF
Center for Media Justice, Consumers Union, Media Access Project, and New America	Center for Media Justice et al.
Charter Communications	Charter
ColorOfChange.org (filed by James Rucker)	ColorOfChange.org
Comcast Corporation	Comcast
Communications Workers of America	CWA
Communications Workers of America—District 2 in West Virginia	CWA: D2WV
Communications Workers of America—Local 3806	CWA: 3806
Communications Workers of America—Local 4900	CWA: 4900
COMPTEL	COMPTEL
Computer & Communications Industry Association	CCIA
CREDO Action	CREDO
CTIA—The Wireless Association	CTIA
Daniel Lyons, Professor, Boston College Law School	Lyons
Digital Entrepreneurs	Digital Entrepreneurs
Digital Society	Digital Society
DISH Network L.L.C.	DISH
EarthLink, Inc.	EarthLink
Electronic Frontier Foundation	EFF
Free Press	Free Press
Future of Privacy Forum	FPF
George Ou	George Ou
Google Inc.	Google
The Greenlining Institute	Greenlining
GSM Association	GSM
Hance Haney	Hance Haney
The Heartland Institute	Heartland Institute
Independent Telephone & Telecommunications Alliance	ITTA
Information Technology and Innovation Foundation	ITIF
Information Technology Industry Council	ITIC
Institute for Liberty	IFL
Institute for Policy Integrity	IPI
Intellectual Property and Communications Law Program at Michigan State University College of Law, filed by Daniel John McCartney, Fellow	MSU IPCLP
International Documentary Association, Film Independent, and others	International Documentary Association et al.
Internet Freedom Coalition	Internet Freedom Coalition
Internet Innovation Alliance	IIA
Joint Center for Political and Economic Studies	Joint Center
Karen Kerrigan, President & CEO, Small Business & Entrepreneurship Council	SBE Council

Table. (Continued)

Reply Commenter	Abbreviation
Labor Council for Latin American Advancement	LCLAA
Latinos in Information Sciences & Technology Association	LISTA
Laurence Brett Glass, d/b/a LARIAT	LARIAT
Lawerence E. Denney, Speaker of the House, State of Idaho	Representative Denney
League of United Latin American Citizens	League of United Latin American Citizens
Leap Wireless International, Inc. and Cricket Communications, Inc.	Leap
Maneesh Pangasa	Maneesh Pangasa
Media Action Grassroots Network, ColorOfChange.org, Presente.org, Applied Research Center, Afro-Netizen, National Association of Hispanic Journalists, Native Public Media, and Rural Broadband Policy Group	MAG-Net et al.
Microsoft Corp.	Microsoft
Ministerial Alliance Against the Digital Divide	MAADD
Mobile Future	Mobile Future
Mobile Internet Content Coalition	MICC
Motion Picture Association of America, Inc.	MPAA
National Association for the Advancement of Colored People	NAACP
National Association of Manufacturers	NAM
National Association of State Utility Consumer Advocates	NASUCA
National Cable & Telecommunications Association	NCTA
National Farmers Union	NFU
National Hispanic Caucus of State Legislators (filed by Jason Llorenz)	NHCSL
National Hispanic Media Coalition	NHMC
National Organizations	National Organizations
National Organization of Black Elected Legislative Women et al. (filed by Alma Morales Rojas, MANA—A National Latina Organization)	NOBELW et al.
National Taxpayers Union	NTU
National Telecommunications Cooperative Association	NTCA
Nicholas Bramble, Information Society Project at Yale Law School	Nicholas Bramble
Office of the Attorney General of Virginia	Virginia Attorney General
Open Internet Coalition	OIC
PAETEC Holding Corp.	PAETEC
Performing Arts Alliance	Performing Arts Alliance
Phil Kerpen, Vice President, Americans for Prosperity	Phil Kerpen
Professor Barbara A. Cherry, Indiana University	Prof. Barbara A. Cherry
Professor Catherine Sandoval and Broadband Institute of California	Prof. Catherine Sandoval
Professor Christopher S. Yoo, Professor and Founding Director, Center for Technology, Innovation, and Competition, University of Pennsylvania	Yoo
Public Knowledge	Public Knowledge
Qwest Communications International, Inc.	Qwest
Recording Industry Association of America	RIAA
Rural Cellular Association	RCA
Sandvine Inc.	Sandvine
SavetheInternet.com	SavetheInternet.com
Sean Kraft	Sean Kraft
Skype Communications S.A.R.L.	Skype
Songwriters Guild of America	SGA
Sony Electronics Inc.	Sony
Sprint Nextel Corp.	Sprint
Stephen Beck, Professor of music technology and digital media at Louisiana State University	Stephen Beck
stic.man of Dead Prez	stic.man of Dead Prez

Table. (Continued)

Reply Commenter	Abbreviation
TDS Telecommunications Corp.	TDS Telecom
Tech Council of Maryland	TCM
TechAmerica	TechAmerica
Telecom Manufacturer Coalition	Telecom Manufacturer Coalition
Telecommunications Industry Association	TIA
Thomas W. Hazlett, Professor at George Mason University	Thomas W. Hazlett
Time Warner Cable Inc.	TWC
T-Mobile USA, Inc.	T-Mobile
tw telecom, inc.	TWTC
U.S. Chamber of Commerce	U.S. Chamber
United States Hispanic Chamber of Commerce	USHCC
United States Telecom Association	USTelecom
Verizon and Verizon Wireless	Verizon
Via Christi Health System eCare-ICU, filed by Elizabeth Cowboy on March 9, 2010	Via Christi
Vonage Holdings Corp.	Vonage
Winston-Salem Urban League	Winston-Salem Urban League
Writers Guild of America, West, Inc.	WGAW
World Institute on Disability et al. (filed by The Advanced Communications Law & Policy Institute at New York Law School)	World Institute on Disability et al.
XO Communications, LLC	XO

Public Notice Comments

Commenter	Abbreviation
4G Americas, LLC	4G
ADTRAN, Inc.	ADTRAN
Alarm Industry Communications Committee	AICC
Alcatel-Lucent	ALU
American Association of Independent Music	A2IM
American Consumer Institute CCR	ACI
American Federation of Television & Radio Artists, Directors Guild of America, International Alliance of Theatrical Stage Employees, Screen Actors Guild	AFTRA et al.
American Library Association, Association of Research Libraries, EDUCAUSE	ALA et al.
Americans for Tax Reform Digital Liberty Project	ATR Digital Liberty Project
Association for Competitive Technology	ACT
AT&T Inc.	AT&T
Bright House Networks, LLC	Bright House
BT Americas Inc.	BT Americas
CDMA Development Group, Inc.	CDG
Center for Democracy & Technology	CDT
Center for Individual Freedom	CFIF
Center for Social Media, filed by Jessica Clark	Center for Social Media
CenturyLink	CenturyLink
Charter Communications	Charter
Clearwire Corporation	Clearwire
Communications Workers of America	CWA
Competitive Enterprise Institute	CEI
Computer & Communications Industry Association	CCIA

Table. (Continued)

Commenter	Abbreviation
Cricket Communications, Inc.	Cricket
CTIA—The Wireless Association	CTIA
DISH Network L.L.C.	DISH
Ericsson Inc.	Ericsson
Fiber-to-the-Home Council	FTTH Council
Free Press	Free Press
The Free State Foundation	Free State Foundation
Frontier Communications	Frontier
Future of Music Coalition	FMC
G. Baeslack	G. Baeslack
GSM Association	GSM
Hance Haney	Hance Haney
Hispanic Technology & Telecommunications Partnership (filed by Jason Llorenz)	HTTP
Hughes Network Systems, LLC	Hughes
Independent Film & Television Alliance	IFTA
Information Technology Industry Council	ITIC
Information Technology and Innovation Foundation	ITIF
Internet Innovation Alliance	IIA
Ionary Consulting	Ionary
Karen Kerrigan, President & CEO, Small Business & Entrepreneurship Council	SBE Council
Latinos for Internet Freedom and Media Action Grassroots Network	Latinos for Internet Freedom
M3X Media, Inc.	M3X Media
Mabuhay Alliance	Mabuhay Alliance
MetroPCS Communications, Inc.	MetroPCS
Mike Riley	Mike Riley
Mobile Future	Mobile Future
Mobile Internet Content Coalition	MICC
National Cable & Telecommunications Association	NCTA
National Coalition on Black Civic Participation	NCBCP
National Organizations	National Organizations
National Exchange Carrier Association, Inc., National Telecommunications Cooperative Association, Organization for the Promotion & Advancement of Small Telecommunication Companies, Eastern Rural Telecom Association, Western Telecommunications Alliance	NECA et al.
Netflix, Inc	Netflix
Open Internet Coalition	OIC
PAETEC Holding Corp.	PAETEC
Professor Scott Jordan	Professor Scott Jordan
Public Interest Commenters (filed by Benton Foundation et al.)	PIC
QUALCOMM Incorporated	Qualcomm
Qwest Communications International Inc.	Qwest
Smartcomm, LLC	Smartcomm
Southern Company Services, Inc.	Southern
Sprint Nextel Corporation	Sprint
SureWest Communications	SureWest
Telecommunications Industry Association	TIA
Time Warner Cable Inc.	TWC
T-Mobile USA, Inc.	T-Mobile
tw telecom inc.	TWTC
United States Telecom Association	USTelecom
Verizon and Verizon Wireless	Verizon

Table. (Continued)

Commenter	Abbreviation
Vonage Holdings Corp.	Vonage
Wireless Communications Association International, Inc.	WCAI
Windstream Communications, Inc.	Windstream
Writers Guild of America, East AFL-CIO	WGAE
Writers Guild of America, West, Inc.	WGAW

Public Notice Reply Comments

Reply Commenter	Abbreviation
Akamai Technologies, Inc.	Akamai
Allbritton Communications Company	Allbritton
Alliance for Digital Equality	ADE
American Cable Association	ACA
American Library Association	ALA
Americans for Tax Reform Digital Liberty Project	ATR Digital Liberty Project
Association for Competitive Technology	ACT
Association of Research Libraries	ARL
AT&T Inc.	AT&T
California Consumers for Net Neutrality	CCNN
CenturyLink	CenturyLink
Computer & Communications Industry Association	CCIA
CONNECT	CONNECT
Cricket Communications, Inc.	Cricket
CTIA - The Wireless Association	CTIA
DISH Network L.L.C.	DISH
Free Press	Free Press
General Communication, Inc.	GCI
Harris Corporation	Harris
Institute for Policy Integrity	Institute for Policy Integrity
Information Technology and Innovation Foundation	ITIF
Internet Innovation Alliance	IIA
MegaPath, Inc. and Covad Communications Company	MegaPath/Covad
Mobile Future	Mobile Future
Motion Picture Association of America, Inc.	MPAA
National Association of State Utility Consumer Advocates	NASUCA
National Cable & Telecommunications Association	NCTA
National Medical Association	NMA
Nicholas Bramble, Information Society Project at Yale Law School	Nicholas Bramble
Open Internet Coalition	OIC
John Palfrey	Palfrey
Public Knowledge	Public Knowledge
Public Interest Commenters (filed by Public Knowledge et al.)	PIC
Qwest Communications International Inc.	Qwest
Skype Communications S.A.R.L.	Skype
Susan Jacobi	Susan Jacobi

Table. (Continued).

Reply Commenter	Abbreviation
TDS Telecommunications Corp.	TDS Telecom
TechAmerica	TechAmerica
Time Warner Cable Inc.	Time Warner
T-Mobile USA, Inc.	T-Mobile
Various Advocates for the Open Internet	Various Advocates for the Open Internet
Verizon and Verizon Wireless	Verizon
Vonage Holdings Corp.	Vonage
Christopher S. Yoo	Yoo

Appendix D. Final Regulatory Flexibility Analysis

As required by the Regulatory Flexibility Act of 1980, as amended (RFA),[502] an Initial Regulatory Flexibility Analysis (IRFA) was included in the Open Internet NPRM in GN Docket No. 09-191 and WC Docket No. 07-52.[503] The Commission sought written public comment on the proposals in these dockets, including comment on the IRFA. This Final Regulatory Flexibility Analysis (FRFA) conforms to the RFA.[504]

A. Need for, and Objectives of, the Rules

Today the Commission takes an important step to preserve the Internet as an open platform for innovation, investment, job creation, economic growth, competition, and free expression. To provide greater clarity and certainty regarding the continued freedom and openness of the Internet, we adopt three basic rules that are grounded in broadly accepted Internet norms, as well as our own prior decisions:

i. **Transparency**. Fixed and mobile broadband providers must disclose the network management practices, performance characteristics, and terms and conditions of their broadband services;
ii. **No blocking**. Fixed broadband providers may not block lawful content, applications, services, or non-harmful devices; mobile broadband providers may not block lawful websites, or block applications that compete with their voice or video telephony services; and
iii. **No unreasonable discrimination**. Fixed broadband providers may not unreasonably discriminate in transmitting lawful network traffic.

We believe these rules, applied with the complementary principle of reasonable network management, will empower and protect consumers and innovators while helping ensure that the Internet continues to flourish, with robust private investment and rapid innovation at both the core and the edge of the network. This is consistent with the National Broadband Plan goal of broadband access that is ubiquitous and fast, promoting the global competitiveness of the United States.[505]

Just over a year ago, we launched a public process to determine whether and what actions might be necessary to preserve the characteristics that have allowed the Internet to grow into an indispensable platform supporting our nation's economy and civic life, and to foster continued investment in the physical networks that enable the Internet. Since then, more than 100,000 commenters have provided written input. Commission staff held several public workshops and convened a Technological Advisory Process with experts from industry, academia, and consumer advocacy groups to collect their views regarding key technical issues related to Internet openness.

This process has made clear that the Internet has thrived because of its freedom and openness—the absence of any gatekeeper blocking lawful uses of the network or picking winners and losers online. Consumers and innovators do not have to seek permission before they use the Internet to launch new technologies, start businesses, connect with friends, or share their views. The Internet is a level playing field. Consumers can make their own choices about what applications and services to use and are free to decide what content they want to access, create, or share with others. This openness promotes competition. It also enables a self-reinforcing cycle of investment and innovation in which new uses of the network lead to increased adoption of broadband, which drives investment and improvements in the network itself, which in turn lead to further innovative uses of the network and further investment in content, applications, services, and devices. A core goal of this Order is to foster and accelerate this cycle of investment and innovation.

The record and our economic analysis demonstrate, however, that the openness of the Internet cannot be taken for granted, and that it faces real threats. Indeed, we have seen broadband providers endanger the Internet's openness by blocking or degrading content and applications without disclosing their practices to end users and edge providers, notwithstanding the Commission's adoption of open Internet principles in 2005. In light of these considerations, as well as the limited choices most consumers have for broadband service, broadband providers' financial interests in telephony and pay television services that may compete with online content and services, and the economic and civic benefits of maintaining an open and competitive platform for innovation and communication, the Commission has long recognized that certain basic standards for broadband provider conduct are necessary to ensure the Internet's continued openness. The record also establishes the widespread benefits of providing greater clarity in this area—clarity that the Internet's openness will continue; that there is a forum and procedure for resolving alleged open Internet violations; and that broadband providers may reasonably manage their networks and innovate with respect to network technologies and business models. We expect the costs of compliance with our prophylactic rules to be small, as they incorporate longstanding openness principles that are generally in line with current practices and with norms endorsed by many broadband providers. Conversely, the harms of open Internet violations may be substantial, costly, and in some cases potentially irreversible.

The rules we proposed in the Open Internet NPRM and those we adopt today follow directly from the Commission's bipartisan Internet Policy Statement, adopted unanimously in 2005 and made temporarily enforceable for certain providers in 2005 and 2006;[506] openness protections the Commission established in 2007 for users of certain wireless spectrum;[507] and a notice of inquiry in 2007 that asked, among other things, whether the Commission should add a principle of nondiscrimination to the Internet Policy Statement.[508] Our rules build upon these actions, first and foremost by requiring broadband providers to be transparent in their network management practices, so that end users can make informed choices and innovators can develop, market, and maintain Internet-based offerings. The rules also prevent certain forms of blocking and discrimination with respect to content, applications, services, and devices that depend on or connect to the Internet.

An open, robust, and well-functioning Internet requires that broadband providers have the flexibility to reasonably manage their networks. Network management practices are reasonable if they are appropriate and tailored to achieving a legitimate network management purpose. Transparency and end-user control are touchstones of reasonableness.

We recognize that broadband providers may offer other services over the same last-mile connections used to provide broadband service. These "specialized services" can benefit end users and spur investment, but they may also present risks to the open Internet. We will closely monitor specialized services and their effects on broadband service to ensure, through all available mechanisms, that they supplement but do not supplant the open Internet.

Mobile broadband is at an earlier stage in its development than fixed broadband and is evolving rapidly. For that and other reasons discussed below, we conclude that it is appropriate at this time to take measured steps in this area. Accordingly, we require mobile providers to comply with the transparency rule, which includes enforceable disclosure obligations regarding device and application certification and approval processes; we prohibit providers from blocking lawful websites; and we prohibit providers from blocking applications that compete with providers' voice and video telephony services. We will closely monitor the development of the mobile broadband market and will adjust the framework we adopt today as appropriate.

These rules are within our jurisdiction over interstate and foreign communications by wire and radio. Further, they implement specific statutory mandates in the Communications Act ("Act") and the Telecommunications Act of 1996 ("1996 Act"), including provisions that direct the Commission to promote Internet investment and to protect and promote voice, video, and audio communications services.

The framework we adopt today aims to ensure the Internet remains an open platform—one characterized by free markets and free speech—that enables consumer choice, end-user control, competition through low barriers to entry, and the freedom to innovate without permission. The framework does so by protecting openness through high-level rules, while maintaining broadband providers' and the Commission's flexibility to adapt to changes in the market and in technology as the Internet continues to evolve.

B. Summary of the Significant Issues Raised by the Public Comments in Response to the IRFA and Summary of the Assessment of the Agency of Such Issues

A few commenters discussed the IRFA from the Open Internet NPRM. The Center for Regulatory Effectiveness (CRE) argued that the Open Internet NPRM's IRFA was defective because it ineffectively followed 5 U.S.C. §§ 603(a) ("Such analysis shall describe the impact of the proposed rule on small entities.") and 603(c) ("Each initial regulatory flexibility analysis shall also contain a description of any significant alternatives to the proposed rule which accomplish the stated objectives of applicable statutes and which minimize any significant economic impact of the proposed rule on small entities.").[509] CRE does not provide any case law to support its interpretation that the Commission is in violation of these aspects of the statute, nor does CRE attempt to argue that SBEs have actually or theoretically been harmed.[510] Rather, CRE is concerned that by not following its reading of these parts of the law, the Commission is being hypocritical by not being transparent enough. CRE recommends that the Commission publish a revised IRFA for public comment.[511] We disagree: we believe that the IRFA was adequate and that the opportunity for SBEs to comment in a publicly accessible docket should remove any potential harm to openness that CRE is concerned with,[512] as well as any harms to SBEs that could occur by not following CRE's interpretation of the law.

The Smithville Telephone Company (Smithville) notes that many ILECs have vastly fewer employees than the 1500 or less that is required to be recognized as a small business under the SBA. For instance, Smithville states that it has seven employees.[513] Smithville also observes that some other small ILECs in Mississippi have staffs of 8, 4, 2, 3, and 21. Smithville argues that companies of this size do not have the resources to fully analyze issues and participate in Commission proceedings. Smithville would like the Commission to use the data that it regularly receives from carriers to set a carrier size where exemptions from proposed rules and less complex reporting requirements can be set. In the present case, however, we determine that this is not necessary. We expect the costs of compliance with these rules to be small, as the high-level rules incorporate longstanding openness principles that appear to be generally in line with most broadband providers' current practices. We note that Smithville does not cite any particular source of increased costs, or attempt to estimate costs of compliance.[514] Nonetheless, the Commission attempts to ease any burden that the transparency rule may cause by only requiring disclosure on a website and at the point of sale, making the transparency rule flexible. In addition, by setting the effective date of these rules 60 days after notice in the Federal Register announcing the decision of the Office of Management and Budget regarding approval of the information collection requirements contained in the rules, the Order gives broadband providers adequate time to develop cost-effective methods of compliance. Finally, to the extent that the transparency rule imposes a new obligation on small businesses, we find that the flexibility built into the rule addresses any compliance concerns.[515]

The American Cable Association (ACA) notes that the Commission has an obligation to "include in the FRFA a comprehensive discussion of the economic impact its actions will have on small cable operators."[516] The ACA cites its other comments, which ask the Commission to clarify that the codified principles would not obligate broadband service providers to (1) "employ specific network management practices," (2) "impose affirmative obligations dealing with unlawful content or the unlawful transfer of content," (3) "accommodate lawful devices that are not supported by a broadband provider's network," and (4) "provide information regarding a company's network management practices through any reporting, recordkeeping, or means other than through a company's website or webpage."[517] Addressing ACA's arguments with regard to cable operators, and fixed broadband providers in particular, (1), the Commission is not requiring specific network management practices. The Commission only requires that any network management be reasonable; the Commission does not require that any specific practice be employed. Regarding (2), the rules do not impose affirmative obligations dealing with unlawful content or the unlawful transfer of content. We state that the "no blocking" rule does not prevent or restrict a broadband provider from refusing to transmit material such as child pornography. In response to (3), the Order clarifies that the "no blocking" rule protects only devices that do not harm the network and only requires fixed broadband service providers to allow devices that conform to publicly available industry standards applicable to the providers' services. Directly addressing ACA's concern, the Order notes that a DOCSIS-based provider is not required to support a DSL modem. In response to (4), the disclosure requirement in today's Order does not require additional forms of disclosure, other than, at a minimum, requiring broadband providers to prominently display or provide links to disclosures on a publicly available, easily accessible website that is available to current and prospective end users and edge providers as well as to the Commission, and disclosing relevant information at the point of sale.

C. Description and Estimate of the Number of Small Entities to Which the Rules Apply

The RFA directs agencies to provide a description of, and, where feasible, an estimate of, the number of small entities that may be affected by the rules adopted herein.[518] The RFA generally defines the term "small entity" as having the same meaning as the terms "small business," "small organization," and "small governmental jurisdiction."[519] In addition, the term "small business" has the same meaning as the term "small business concern" under the Small Business Act.[520] A "small business concern" is one which: (1) is independently owned and operated; (2) is not dominant in its field of operation; and (3) satisfies any additional criteria established by the Small Business Administration (SBA).[521]

1. Total Small Entities

Our action may, over time, affect small entities that are not easily categorized at present. We therefore describe here, at the outset, three comprehensive, statutory small entity size standards.[522] First, nationwide, there are a total of approximately 27.2 million small businesses, according to the SBA.[523] In addition, a "small organization" is generally "any not-for-profit enterprise which is independently owned and operated and is not dominant in its field."[524] Nationwide, as of 2002, there were approximately 1.6 million small organizations.[225] Finally, the term "small governmental jurisdiction" is defined generally as "governments of cities, towns, townships, villages, school districts, or special districts, with a population of less than fifty thousand."[526] Census Bureau data for 2002 indicate that there were 87,525 local governmental jurisdictions in the United States.[527] We estimate that, of this total, 84,377 entities were "small governmental jurisdictions."[528] Thus, we estimate that most governmental jurisdictions are small.

2. Internet Access Service Providers

Internet Service Providers. The 2007 Economic Census places these firms, whose services might include voice over Internet Protocol (VoIP), in either of two categories, depending on whether the service is provided over the provider's own telecommunications facilities (*e.g.*, cable and DSL ISPs), or over client-supplied telecommunications connections (*e.g.*, dial-up ISPs). The former are within the category of Wired Telecommunications Carriers,[529] which has an SBA small business size standard of 1,500 or fewer employees.[530]

These are also labeled "broadband." The latter are within the category of All Other Telecommunications,[531] which has a size standard of annual receipts of $25 million or less.[532] These are labeled non-broadband. The most current Economic Census data for all such firms are 2007 data, which are detailed specifically for ISPs within the categories above. For the first category, the data show that 396 firms operated for the entire year, of which 159 had nine or fewer employees.[533] For the second category, the data show that 1,682 firms operated for the entire year.[534] Of those, 1,675 had annual receipts below $25 million per year, and an additional two had receipts of between $25 million and $ 49,999,999. Consequently, we estimate that the majority of ISP firms are small entities.

The ISP industry has changed since 2007. The 2007 data cited above may therefore include entities that no longer provide Internet access service and may exclude entities that now provide such service. To ensure that this FRFA describes the universe of small entities that our action might affect, we discuss in turn several different types of entities that might be providing Internet access service.

3. Wireline Providers

Incumbent Local Exchange Carriers (Incumbent LECs). Neither the Commission nor the SBA has developed a small business size standard specifically for incumbent local exchange services. The appropriate size standard under SBA rules is for the category Wired Telecommunications Carriers. Under that size standard, such a business is small if it has 1,500 or fewer employees.[535] According to Commission data,[536] 1,311 carriers have reported that they are engaged in the provision of incumbent local exchange services. Of these 1,311 carriers, an estimated 1,024 have 1,500 or fewer employees and 287 have more than 1,500 employees. Consequently, the Commission estimates that most providers of incumbent local exchange service are small businesses that may be affected by our proposed action.

Competitive Local Exchange Carriers (Competitive LECs), Competitive Access Providers (CAPs), Shared-Tenant Service Providers, and Other Local Service Providers. Neither the Commission nor the SBA has developed a small business size standard specifically for these service providers. The appropriate size standard under SBA rules is for the category Wired Telecommunications Carriers. Under that size standard, such a business is small if it has 1,500 or fewer employees.[537] According to Commission data,[538] 1005 carriers have reported that they are engaged in the provision of either competitive access provider services or competitive local exchange carrier services. Of these 1005 carriers, an estimated 918 have 1,500 or fewer employees and 87 have more than 1,500 employees. In addition, 16 carriers have reported that they are "Shared-Tenant Service Providers," and all 16 are estimated to have 1,500 or fewer employees. In addition, 89 carriers have reported that they are "Other Local Service Providers." Of the 89, all have 1,500 or fewer employees. Consequently, the Commission estimates that most providers of competitive local exchange service, competitive access providers, Shared-Tenant Service Providers, and other local service providers are small entities that may be affected by our action.

We have included small incumbent LECs in this present RFA analysis. As noted above, a "small business" under the RFA is one that, inter alia, meets the pertinent small business size standard (e.g., a telephone communications business having 1,500 or fewer employees), and "is not dominant in its field of operation."[539] The SBA's Office of Advocacy contends that, for RFA purposes, small incumbent LECs are not dominant in their field of operation because any such dominance is not "national" in scope.[540] We have therefore included small incumbent LECs in this RFA analysis, although we emphasize that this RFA action has no effect on Commission analyses and determinations in other, non-RFA contexts.

Interexchange Carriers. Neither the Commission nor the SBA has developed a small business size standard specifically for providers of interexchange services. The appropriate size standard under SBA rules is for the category Wired Telecommunications Carriers. Under that size standard, such a business is small if it has 1,500 or fewer employees.[541] According to Commission data,[542] 300 carriers have reported that they are engaged in the provision of interexchange service. Of these, an estimated 268 have 1,500 or fewer employees and 32 have more than 1,500 employees. Consequently, the Commission estimates that the majority of IXCs are small entities that may be affected by our action.

Operator Service Providers (OSPs). Neither the Commission nor the SBA has developed a small business size standard specifically for operator service providers. The appropriate size standard under SBA rules is for the category Wired Telecommunications Carriers. Under that size standard, such a business is small if it has 1,500 or fewer employees.[543] According to Commission data, 33 carriers have reported that they are engaged in the provision of operator services. Of these, an estimated 31 have 1,500 or fewer employees and 2 has more than 1,500 employees.[544] Consequently, the Commission estimates that the majority of OSPs are small entities that may be affected by our proposed action.

4. Wireless Providers – Fixed and Mobile

For reasons discussed above in the text of the Order, the Commission has distinguished wireless fixed broadband Internet access service from wireless mobile broadband Internet access service. Specifically, the Commission decided that fixed broadband Internet access service providers, whether wireline or wireless, must disclose their network management practices and the performance characteristics and commercial terms of their broadband services; may not block lawful content, applications, services or non-harmful devices; and may not unreasonably discriminate in transmitting lawful network traffic. Also for the reasons discussed above, the Commission decided that wireless mobile broadband Internet access service providers must disclose their network management practices and performance characteristics and commercial terms of their broadband service and may not block lawful websites or block applications that compete with their voice or video telephony service. Thus, to the extent the wireless services listed below are used by wireless firms for fixed and mobile broadband Internet access services, today's actions may have an impact on those small businesses as set forth above and further below. In addition, for those services subject to auctions, we note that, as a general matter, the number of winning bidders that claim to qualify as small businesses at the close of an auction does not necessarily represent the number of small businesses currently in service. Also, the Commission does not generally track subsequent business size unless, in the context of assignments and transfers or reportable eligibility events, unjust enrichment issues are implicated.

Wireless Telecommunications Carriers (except Satellite). Since 2007, the Census Bureau has placed wireless firms within this new, broad, economic census category.[545] Prior to that time, such firms were within the now-superseded categories of "Paging" and "Cellular and Other Wireless Telecommunications."[546] Under the present and prior categories, the SBA has deemed a wireless business to be small if it has 1,500 or fewer employees.[547] For the category of Wireless Telecommunications Carriers (except Satellite), preliminary data for 2007 show that there were 11,927 firms operating that year.[548] While the Census Bureau has not released data on the establishments broken down by number of employees, we note that the Census Bureau lists total employment for all firms in that sector at 281,262.[549] Since all firms with fewer than 1,500 employees are considered small, given the total employment in the sector, we estimate that the vast majority of wireless firms are small.

Wireless Communications Services. This service can be used for fixed, mobile, radiolocation, and digital audio broadcasting satellite uses. The Commission defined "small business" for the wireless communications services (WCS) auction as an entity with average gross revenues of $40 million for each of the three preceding years, and a "very small business" as an entity with average gross revenues of $15 million for each of the three preceding years.[550] The SBA has approved these definitions.[551] The Commission auctioned geographic area licenses in the WCS service. In the auction, which commenced on April 15, 1997 and closed on April 25, 1997, seven bidders won 31 licenses that qualified as very small business entities, and one bidder won one license that qualified as a small business entity.

1670–1675 MHz Services. This service can be used for fixed and mobile uses, except aeronautical mobile.[552] An auction for one license in the 1670–1675 MHz band commenced on April 30, 2003 and closed the same day. One license was awarded. The winning bidder was not a small entity.

Wireless Telephony. Wireless telephony includes cellular, personal communications services, and specialized mobile radio telephony carriers. As noted, the SBA has developed a small business size standard for Wireless Telecommunications Carriers (except Satellite).[553] Under the SBA small business size standard, a business is small if it has 1,500 or fewer employees.[554] According to Trends in Telephone Service data, 413 carriers reported that they were engaged in wireless telephony.[555] Of these, an estimated 261 have 1,500 or fewer employees and 152 have more than 1,500 employees.[556] Therefore, more than half of these entities can be considered small.

Broadband Personal Communications Service. The broadband personal communications services (PCS) spectrum is divided into six frequency blocks designated A through F, and the Commission has held auctions for each block. The Commission initially defined a "small business" for C- and F-Block licenses as an entity that has average gross revenues of $40 million or less in the three previous calendar years.[557] For F-Block licenses, an additional small business size standard for "very small business" was added and is defined as an entity that, together with its affiliates, has average gross revenues of not more than $15 million for the preceding three calendar years.[558] These small business size standards, in the context of broadband PCS auctions, have been approved by the SBA.[559] No small businesses within the SBA-approved small business size standards bid successfully for licenses in Blocks A and B. There were 90 winning bidders that claimed small business status in the first two C-Block auctions. A total of 93 bidders that claimed small business status won approximately 40 percent of the 1,479 licenses in the first auction for the D, E, and F Blocks.[560] On April 15, 1999, the Commission completed the reauction of 347 C-, D-, E-, and F-Block licenses in Auction No. 22.[561] Of the 57 winning bidders in that auction, 48 claimed small business status and won 277 licenses.

On January 26, 2001, the Commission completed the auction of 422 C and F Block Broadband PCS licenses in Auction No. 35. Of the 35 winning bidders in that auction, 29 claimed small business status.[562] Subsequent events concerning Auction 35, including judicial and agency determinations, resulted in a total of 163 C and F Block licenses being available for grant. On February 15, 2005, the Commission completed an auction of 242 C-, D-, E-, and

F-Block licenses in Auction No. 58. Of the 24 winning bidders in that auction, 16 claimed small business status and won 156 licenses.[563] On May 21, 2007, the Commission completed an auction of 33 licenses in the A, C, and F Blocks in Auction No. 71.[564] Of the 12 winning bidders in that auction, five claimed small business status and won 18 licenses.[565] On August 20, 2008, the Commission completed the auction of 20 C-, D-, E-, and F-Block Broadband PCS licenses in Auction No. 78.[566] Of the eight winning bidders for Broadband PCS licenses in that auction, six claimed small business status and won 14 licenses.[567]

Specialized Mobile Radio Licenses. The Commission awards "small entity" bidding credits in auctions for Specialized Mobile Radio (SMR) geographic area licenses in the 800 MHz and 900 MHz bands to firms that had revenues of no more than $15 million in each of the three previous calendar years.[568] The Commission awards "very small entity" bidding credits to firms that had revenues of no more than $3 million in each of the three previous calendar years.[569] The SBA has approved these small business size standards for the 900 MHz Service.[570] The Commission has held auctions for geographic area licenses in the 800 MHz and 900 MHz bands. The 900 MHz SMR auction began on December 5, 1995, and closed on April 15, 1996. Sixty bidders claiming that they qualified as small businesses under the $15 million size standard won 263 geographic area licenses in the 900 MHz SMR band. The 800 MHz SMR auction for the upper 200 channels began on October 28, 1997, and was completed on December 8, 1997. Ten bidders claiming that they qualified as small businesses under the $15 million size standard won 38 geographic area licenses for the upper 200 channels in the 800 MHz SMR band.[571] A second auction for the 800 MHz band was held on January 10, 2002 and closed on January 17, 2002 and included 23 BEA licenses. One bidder claiming small business status won five licenses.[572]

The auction of the 1,053 800 MHz SMR geographic area licenses for the General Category channels began on August 16, 2000, and was completed on September 1, 2000. Eleven bidders won 108 geographic area licenses for the General Category channels in the 800 MHz SMR band and qualified as small businesses under the $15 million size standard.[573] In an auction completed on December 5, 2000, a total of 2,800 Economic Area licenses in the lower 80 channels of the 800 MHz SMR service were awarded.[574] Of the 22 winning bidders, 19 claimed small business status and won 129 licenses. Thus, combining all four auctions, 41 winning bidders for geographic licenses in the 800 MHz SMR band claimed status as small businesses.

In addition, there are numerous incumbent site-by-site SMR licenses and licensees with extended implementation authorizations in the 800 and 900 MHz bands. We do not know how many firms provide 800 MHz or 900 MHz geographic area SMR service pursuant to extended implementation authorizations, nor how many of these providers have annual revenues of no more than $15 million. In addition, we do not know how many of these firms have 1,500 or fewer employees, which is the SBA-determined size standard.[575] We assume, for purposes of this analysis, that all of the remaining extended implementation authorizations are held by small entities, as defined by the SBA.

Lower 700 MHz Band Licenses. The Commission previously adopted criteria for defining three groups of small businesses for purposes of determining their eligibility for special provisions such as bidding credits.[576] The Commission defined a "small business" as an entity that, together with its affiliates and controlling principals, has average gross revenues not exceeding $40 million for the preceding three years.[577] A "very small business" is defined as an entity that, together with its affiliates and controlling principals, has average gross revenues that are not more than $15 million for the preceding three years.[578] Additionally, the lower 700 MHz Service had a third category of small business status for Metropolitan/Rural Service Area (MSA/RSA) licenses—"entrepreneur"—which is defined as an entity that, together with its affiliates and controlling principals, has average gross revenues that are not more than $3 million for the preceding three years.[579] The SBA approved these small size standards.[580] An auction of 740 licenses (one license in each of the 734 MSAs/RSAs and one license in each of the six Economic Area Groupings (EAGs)) commenced on August 27, 2002, and closed on September 18, 2002. Of the 740 licenses available for auction, 484 licenses were won by 102 winning bidders. Seventy-two of the winning bidders claimed small business, very small business or entrepreneur status and won a total of 329 licenses.[581] A second auction commenced on May 28, 2003, closed on June 13, 2003, and included 256 licenses: 5 EAG licenses and 476 Cellular Market Area licenses.[582] Seventeen winning bidders claimed small or very small business status and won 60 licenses, and nine winning bidders claimed entrepreneur status and won 154 licenses.[583] On July 26, 2005, the Commission completed an auction of 5 licenses in the Lower 700 MHz band (Auction No. 60). There were three winning bidders for five licenses. All three winning bidders claimed small business status.

In 2007, the Commission reexamined its rules governing the 700 MHz band in the 700 MHz Second Report and Order.[584] An auction of 700 MHz licenses commenced January 24, 2008 and closed on March 18, 2008, which included, 176 Economic Area licenses in the A Block, 734 Cellular Market Area licenses in the B Block, and 176 EA licenses in the E Block.[585] Twenty winning bidders, claiming small business status (those with attributable average annual gross revenues that exceed $15 million and do not exceed $40 million for the preceding three years) won 49 licenses. Thirty three winning bidders claiming very small business status (those with attributable average annual gross revenues that do not exceed $15 million for the preceding three years) won 325 licenses.

Upper 700 MHz Band Licenses. In the 700 MHz Second Report and Order, the Commission revised its rules regarding Upper 700 MHz licenses.[586] On January 24, 2008, the Commission commenced Auction 73 in which several licenses in the Upper 700 MHz band were available for licensing: 12 Regional Economic Area Grouping licenses in the C Block, and one nationwide license in the D Block.[587] The auction concluded on March 18, 2008, with 3 winning bidders claiming very small business status (those with attributable average annual gross revenues that do not exceed $15 million for the preceding three years) and winning five licenses.

700 MHz Guard Band Licensees. In 2000, in the 700 MHz Guard Band Order, the Commission adopted size standards for "small businesses" and "very small businesses" for purposes of determining their eligibility for special provisions such as bidding credits and installment payments.[588] A small business in this service is an entity that, together with its affiliates and controlling principals, has average gross revenues not exceeding $40 million for the preceding three years.[589] Additionally, a very small business is an entity that, together with its affiliates and controlling principals, has average gross revenues that are not more than $15 million for the preceding three years.[590] SBA approval of these definitions is not required.[591] An auction of 52 Major Economic Area licenses commenced on September 6, 2000, and closed on September 21, 2000.[592] Of the 104 licenses auctioned, 96 licenses were sold to nine bidders. Five of these bidders were small businesses that won a total of 26 licenses. A second auction of 700 MHz Guard Band licenses commenced on February 13,

2001, and closed on February 21, 2001. All eight of the licenses auctioned were sold to three bidders. One of these bidders was a small business that won a total of two licenses.[593]

Air-Ground Radiotelephone Service. The Commission has previously used the SBA's small business size standard applicable to Wireless Telecommunications Carriers (except Satellite), i.e., an entity employing no more than 1,500 persons.[594] There are fewer than 10 licensees in the Air-Ground Radiotelephone Service, and under that definition, we estimate that almost all of them qualify as small entities under the SBA definition. For purposes of assigning Air-Ground Radiotelephone Service licenses through competitive bidding, the Commission has defined "small business" as an entity that, together with controlling interests and affiliates, has average annual gross revenues for the preceding three years not exceeding $40 million.[595] A "very small business" is defined as an entity that, together with controlling interests and affiliates, has average annual gross revenues for the preceding three years not exceeding $15 million.[596] These definitions were approved by the SBA.[597] In May 2006, the Commission completed an auction of nationwide commercial Air-Ground Radiotelephone Service licenses in the 800 MHz band (Auction No. 65). On June 2, 2006, the auction closed with two winning bidders winning two Air-Ground Radiotelephone Services licenses. Neither of the winning bidders claimed small business status.

AWS Services (1710–1755 MHz and 2110–2155 MHz bands (AWS-1); 1915–1920 MHz, 1995–2000 MHz, 2020–2025 MHz and 2175–2180 MHz bands (AWS-2); 2155–2175 MHz band (AWS-3)). For the AWS-1 bands, the Commission has defined a "small business" as an entity with average annual gross revenues for the preceding three years not exceeding $40 million, and a "very small business" as an entity with average annual gross revenues for the preceding three years not exceeding $15 million.[598] For AWS-2 and AWS-3, although we do not know for certain which entities are likely to apply for these frequencies, we note that the AWS-1 bands are comparable to those used for cellular service and personal communications service. The Commission has not yet adopted size standards for the AWS-2 or AWS-3 bands but proposes to treat both AWS-2 and AWS-3 similarly to broadband PCS service and AWS-1 service due to the comparable capital requirements and other factors, such as issues involved in relocating incumbents and developing markets, technologies, and services.[599]

3650–3700 MHz band. In March 2005, the Commission released a Report and Order and Memorandum Opinion and Order that provides for nationwide, non-exclusive licensing of terrestrial operations, utilizing contention-based technologies, in the 3650 MHz band (i.e., 3650–3700 MHz).[600] As of April 2010, more than 1270 licenses have been granted and more than 7433 sites have been registered. The Commission has not developed a definition of small entities applicable to 3650–3700 MHz band nationwide, non-exclusive licensees. However, we estimate that the majority of these licensees are Internet Access Service Providers (ISPs) and that most of those licensees are small businesses.

Fixed Microwave Services. Microwave services include common carrier,[601] private-operational fixed,[602] and broadcast auxiliary radio services.[603] They also include the Local Multipoint Distribution Service (LMDS),[604] the Digital Electronic Message Service (DEMS),[605] and the 24 GHz Service,[606] where licensees can choose between common carrier and non-common carrier status.[607] At present, there are approximately 31,428 common carrier fixed licensees and 79,732 private operational-fixed licensees and broadcast auxiliary radio licensees in the microwave services. There are approximately 120 LMDS licensees, three DEMS licensees, and three 24 GHz licensees. The Commission has not yet defined a small business with respect to microwave services. For purposes of the IRFA, we will use the

SBA's definition applicable to Wireless Telecommunications Carriers (except satellite)—i.e., an entity with no more than 1,500 persons.[608] Under the present and prior categories, the SBA has deemed a wireless business to be small if it has 1,500 or fewer employees.[609] For the category of Wireless Telecommunications Carriers (except Satellite), preliminary data for 2007 show that there were 11,927 firms operating that year.[610] While the Census Bureau has not released data on the establishments broken down by number of employees, we note that the Census Bureau lists total employment for all firms in that sector at 281,262.[611] Since all firms with fewer than 1,500 employees are considered small, given the total employment in the sector, we estimate that the vast majority of firms using microwave services are small. We note that the number of firms does not necessarily track the number of licensees. We estimate that virtually all of the Fixed Microwave licensees (excluding broadcast auxiliary licensees) would qualify as small entities under the SBA definition.

Broadband Radio Service and Educational Broadband Service. Broadband Radio Service systems, previously referred to as Multipoint Distribution Service (MDS) and Multichannel Multipoint Distribution Service (MMDS) systems, and "wireless cable," transmit video programming to subscribers and provide two-way high speed data operations using the microwave frequencies of the Broadband Radio Service (BRS) and Educational Broadband Service (EBS) (previously referred to as the Instructional Television Fixed Service (ITFS)).[612] In connection with the 1996 BRS auction, the Commission established a small business size standard as an entity that had annual average gross revenues of no more than $40 million in the previous three calendar years.[613] The BRS auctions resulted in 67 successful bidders obtaining licensing opportunities for 493 Basic Trading Areas (BTAs). Of the 67 auction winners, 61 met the definition of a small business. BRS also includes licensees of stations authorized prior to the auction. At this time, we estimate that of the 61 small business BRS auction winners, 48 remain small business licensees. In addition to the 48 small businesses that hold BTA authorizations, there are approximately 392 incumbent BRS licensees that are considered small entities.[614] After adding the number of small business auction licensees to the number of incumbent licensees not already counted, we find that there are currently approximately 440 BRS licensees that are defined as small businesses under either the SBA or the Commission's rules. In 2009, the Commission conducted Auction 86, the sale of 78 licenses in the BRS areas.[615] The Commission offered three levels of bidding credits: (i) a bidder with attributed average annual gross revenues that exceed $15 million and do not exceed $40 million for the preceding three years (small business) will receive a 15 percent discount on its winning bid; (ii) a bidder with attributed average annual gross revenues that exceed $3 million and do not exceed $15 million for the preceding three years (very small business) will receive a 25 percent discount on its winning bid; and (iii) a bidder with attributed average annual gross revenues that do not exceed $3 million for the preceding three years (entrepreneur) will receive a 35 percent discount on its winning bid.[616] Auction 86 concluded in 2009 with the sale of 61 licenses.[617] Of the ten winning bidders, two bidders that claimed small business status won 4 licenses; one bidder that claimed very small business status won three licenses; and two bidders that claimed entrepreneur status won six licenses.

In addition, the SBA's Cable Television Distribution Services small business size standard is applicable to EBS. There are presently 2,032 EBS licensees. All but 100 of these licenses are held by educational institutions. Educational institutions are included in this analysis as small entities.[618] Thus, we estimate that at least 1,932 licensees are small businesses. Since 2007, Cable Television Distribution Services have been defined within the broad economic census category of Wired Telecommunications Carriers; that category is defined as follows: "This industry comprises establishments primarily engaged in operating and/or providing access to transmission facilities and infrastructure that they own and/or lease for the transmission of voice, data, text, sound, and video using wired telecommunications networks. Transmission facilities may be based on a single technology or a combination of technologies."[619] The SBA has developed a small business size standard for this category, which is: all such firms having 1,500 or fewer employees. To gauge small business prevalence for these cable services we must, however, use the most current census data that are based on the previous category of Cable and Other Program Distribution and its associated size standard; that size standard was: all such firms having $13.5 million or less in annual receipts.[620] According to Census Bureau data for 2002, there were a total of 1,191 firms in this previous category that operated for the entire year.[621] Of this total, 1,087 firms had annual receipts of under $10 million, and 43 firms had receipts of $10 million or more but less than $25 million.[622] Thus, the majority of these firms can be considered small.

5. Satellite Service Providers

Satellite Telecommunications Providers. Two economic census categories address the satellite industry. The first category has a small business size standard of $15 million or less in average annual receipts, under SBA rules.[623] The second has a size standard of $25 million or less in annual receipts.[624] The most current Census Bureau data in this context, however, are from the (last) economic census of 2002, and we will use those figures to gauge the prevalence of small businesses in these categories.[625]

The category of Satellite Telecommunications "comprises establishments primarily engaged in providing telecommunications services to other establishments in the telecommunications and broadcasting industries by forwarding and receiving communications signals via a system of satellites or reselling satellite telecommunications."[626] For this category, Census Bureau data for 2002 show that there were a total of 371 firms that operated for the entire year.[627] Of this total, 307 firms had annual receipts of under $10 million, and 26 firms had receipts of $10 million to $24,999,999.[628] Consequently, we estimate that the majority of Satellite Telecommunications firms are small entities that might be affected by our action.

The second category of All Other Telecommunications comprises, inter alia, "establishments primarily engaged in providing specialized telecommunications services, such as satellite tracking, communications telemetry, and radar station operation. This industry also includes establishments primarily engaged in providing satellite terminal stations and associated facilities connected with one or more terrestrial systems and capable of transmitting telecommunications to, and receiving telecommunications from, satellite systems."[629] For this category, Census Bureau data for 2002 show that there were a total of 332 firms that operated for the entire year.[630] Of this total, 303 firms had annual receipts of under $10 million and 15 firms had annual receipts of $10 million to $24,999,999.[631] Consequently, we estimate that the majority of All Other Telecommunications firms are small entities that might be affected by our action.

6. Cable Service Providers

Because section 706 requires us to monitor the deployment of broadband regardless of technology or transmission media employed, we anticipate that some broadband service providers may not provide telephone service. Accordingly, we describe below other types of firms that may provide broadband services, including cable companies, MDS providers, and utilities, among others.

Cable and Other Program Distributors. Since 2007, these services have been defined within the broad economic census category of Wired Telecommunications Carriers; that category is defined as follows: "This industry comprises establishments primarily engaged in operating and/or providing access to transmission facilities and infrastructure that they own and/or lease for the transmission of voice, data, text, sound, and video using wired telecommunications networks. Transmission facilities may be based on a single technology or a combination of technologies."[632] The SBA has developed a small business size standard for this category, which is: all such firms having 1,500 or fewer employees. To gauge small business prevalence for these cable services we must, however, use current census data that are based on the previous category of Cable and Other Program Distribution and its associated size standard; that size standard was: all such firms having $13.5 million or less in annual receipts.[633] According to Census Bureau data for 2002, there were a total of 1,191 firms in this previous category that operated for the entire year.[634] Of this total, 1,087 firms had annual receipts of under $10 million, and 43 firms had receipts of $10 million or more but less than $25 million.[635] Thus, the majority of these firms can be considered small.

Cable Companies and Systems. The Commission has also developed its own small business size standards, for the purpose of cable rate regulation. Under the Commission's rules, a "small cable company" is one serving 400,000 or fewer subscribers, nationwide.[636] Industry data indicate that, of 1,076 cable operators nationwide, all but eleven are small under this size standard.[637] In addition, under the Commission's rules, a "small system" is a cable system serving 15,000 or fewer subscribers.[638] Industry data indicate that, of 7,208 systems nationwide, 6,139 systems have under 10,000 subscribers, and an additional 379 systems have 10,000–19,999 subscribers.[639] Thus, under this second size standard, most cable systems are small.

Cable System Operators. The Communications Act of 1934, as amended, also contains a size standard for small cable system operators, which is "a cable operator that, directly or through an affiliate, serves in the aggregate fewer than 1 percent of all subscribers in the United States and is not affiliated with any entity or entities whose gross annual revenues in the aggregate exceed $250,000,000."[640] The Commission has determined that an operator serving fewer than 677,000 subscribers shall be deemed a small operator, if its annual revenues, when combined with the total annual revenues of all its affiliates, do not exceed $250 million in the aggregate.[641] Industry data indicate that, of 1,076 cable operators nationwide, all but ten are small under this size standard.[642] We note that the Commission neither requests nor collects information on whether cable system operators are affiliated with entities whose gross annual revenues exceed $250 million,[643] and therefore we are unable to estimate more accurately the number of cable system operators that would qualify as small under this size standard.

7. Electric Power Generators, Transmitters, and Distributors

Electric Power Generators, Transmitters, and Distributors. The Census Bureau defines an industry group comprised of "establishments, primarily engaged in generating, transmitting, and/or distributing electric power. Establishments in this industry group may perform one or more of the following activities: (1) operate generation facilities that produce electric energy; (2) operate transmission systems that convey the electricity from the generation facility to the distribution system; and (3) operate distribution systems that convey electric power received from the generation facility or the transmission system to the final consumer."[644] The SBA has developed a small business size standard for firms in this category: "A firm is small if, including its affiliates, it is primarily engaged in the generation, transmission, and/or distribution of electric energy for sale and its total electric output for the preceding fiscal year did not exceed 4 million megawatt hours."[645] According to Census Bureau data for 2002, there were 1,644 firms in this category that operated for the entire year.[646] Census data do not track electric output and we have not determined how many of these firms fit the SBA size standard for small, with no more than 4 million megawatt hours of electric output. Consequently, we estimate that 1,644 or fewer firms may be considered small under the SBA small business size standard.

D. Description of Projected Reporting, Recordkeeping, and Other Compliance Requirements for Small Entities

As indicated above, the Internet's legacy of openness and transparency has been critical to its success as an engine for creativity, innovation, and economic development. To help preserve this fundamental character of the Internet, the Order requires that broadband providers must, at a minimum, prominently display or provide links to disclosures on a publicly available, easily accessible website that is available to current and prospective end users and edge providers as well as to the Commission, and at the point of sale. Providers should ensure that all website disclosures are accessible by persons with disabilities. We do not require additional forms of disclosure. Broadband providers' disclosures to the public include disclosure to the Commission; that is, the Commission will monitor public disclosures and may require additional disclosures directly to the Commission. We anticipate that broadband providers may be able to satisfy the transparency rule through a single disclosure, and therefore do not require multiple disclosures targeted at different audiences. This affects all classes of small entities mentioned in Appendix D, part C, *supra*, and requires professional skills of entering information onto a webpage and an understanding of the entities' network practices, both of which are easily managed by staff of these types of small entities.

E. Steps Taken to Minimize the Significant Economic Impact on Small Entities, and Significant Alternatives Considered

The RFA requires an agency to describe any significant alternatives that it has considered in reaching its proposed approach, which may include (among others) the following four alternatives: (1) the establishment of differing compliance or reporting requirements or timetables that take into account the resources available to small entities; (2) the clarification, consolidation, or simplification of compliance or reporting requirements under the rule for small entities; (3) the use of performance, rather than design, standards; and (4) an exemption from coverage of the rule, or any part thereof, for small entities.[647]

The rules adopted in this Order are generally consistent with current industry practices, so the costs of compliance should be small. Although some commenters assert that a disclosure rule will impose significant burdens on broadband providers, no commenter cites any particular source of increased costs, or attempts to estimate costs of compliance. For a number of reasons, we believe that the costs of the disclosure rule we adopt today are outweighed by the benefits of empowering end users to make informed choices and of facilitating the enforcement of the other open Internet rules. First, we require only that providers post disclosures on their websites and at the point of sale, not that they bear the cost of printing and distributing bill inserts or other paper documents to all existing customers. Second, although we may subsequently determine that it is appropriate to require that specific information be disclosed in particular ways, the transparency rule we adopt today gives broadband providers flexibility to determine what information to disclose and how to disclose it. We also expressly exclude from the rule competitively sensitive information, information that would compromise network security, and information that would undermine the efficacy of reasonable network management practices. Third, by setting the effective date of these rules 60 days after notice in the Federal Register announcing the decision of the Office of Management and Budget regarding approval of the information collection requirements contained in the rules, we give broadband providers adequate time to develop cost effective methods of compliance. Thus, the rule gives broadband providers—including small entities—sufficient time and flexibility to implement the rules in a cost-effective manner. Finally, these rules provide certainty and clarity that are beneficial both to broadband providers and to their customers.

F. Report to Congress

The Commission will send a copy of the Order, including this FRFA, in a report to be sent to Congress and the Government Accountability Office pursuant to the Congressional Review Act.[648] In addition, the Commission will send a copy of the Order, including this FRFA, to the Chief Counsel for Advocacy of the SBA. A copy of the Order and FRFA (or summaries thereof) will also be published in the Federal Register.[649]

STATEMENT OF CHAIRMAN JULIUS GENACHOWSKI

Re: *Preserving the Open Internet*, GN Docket No. 09-191, *Broadband Industry Practices,* WC Docket No. 07-52

Let me start with a quote: "The Web as we know it [is] being threatened." That's Tim Berners-Lee, the inventor of the World Wide Web, in a recent article. He continued, "A neutral communications medium is the basis of a fair, competitive market economy, of democracy, and of science. Although the Internet and the Web generally thrive on lack of regulation, some basic values have to be legally preserved."

Today, for the first time, the FCC is adopting rules to preserve basic Internet values. While the Commission had in the past pursued bipartisan enforcement of Open Internet principles, we have not had properly adopted rules. Now, for the first time, we'll have enforceable, high-level rules of the road to preserve Internet freedom and openness.

As we stand here now, the freedom and openness of the Internet are unprotected. No rules on the books to protect basic Internet values. No process for monitoring Internet openness as technology and business models evolve. No recourse for innovators, consumers, or speakers harmed by improper practices. And no predictability for Internet service providers, so that they can effectively manage and invest in broadband networks. That will change once we vote to approve this strong and balanced order.

The vote on this order comes after many months of debate – which has often produced more heat than light. Almost everyone says that they agree that the openness of the Internet is essential – that openness has unleashed an enormous wave of innovation, economic growth, job creation, small business generation, and vibrant free expression.

But despite a shared allegiance to the Internet as an open platform, there has been intense disagreement about the role of government in preserving Internet freedom and openness. On one end of the spectrum, there are those who say government should do nothing at all on open Internet. On the other end are those who would adopt extensive, detailed and rigid regulations. Both sides impose tests of ideological purity. To some, unless their test is met, open Internet rules are "fake net neutrality." To others, unless their test is met, open internet rules are "a government takeover of the Internet."

For myself, I reject both extremes in favor of a strong and sensible, non-ideological framework – one that protects Internet freedom and openness and promotes robust innovation and investment throughout the broadband ecosystem. Because none of these goals are abstractions. They live or die not in ideology or theory, but in practice – in the hard work of grappling with technology, business, and real-world consumer experiences.

Now, in this issue we encounter familiar arguments – we've heard some today – the kind trotted out to oppose almost any government action. We are told by some, for example, not to try to fix what isn't broken, and that rules of the road protecting Internet freedom would discourage innovation and investment. But countless innovators, investors and business executives say just the opposite, including many who generally oppose government action.

Over the course of this proceeding we have heard from so many entrepreneurs, engineers, venture capitalists, CEOs and others working daily to invent and distribute new Internet products and thereby maintain U.S. leadership in innovation. Their message has been clear: the next decade of innovation in this sector is at risk without sensible FCC rules of the road. As one leading early stage investor put it, in thoughts echoed in a letter we receiving from 30 prominent venture capitalists: "the lack of basic 'rules of the road' for what network providers and others can and can't do is starting to hamper innovation and growth." And as we heard in a letter from more than two dozen leading technology CEOs: "Common sense baseline rules are critical to ensuring that the Internet remains a key engine of economic growth, innovation, and global competitiveness."

The innovators, entrepreneurs, and tech leaders recognize, as I do, the vital need for massive investment in broadband infrastructure. Based on their in-market experience – they also tell us that broadband providers have natural business incentives to leverage their positions as gatekeepers of the Internet in ways that would stifle innovation and limit the benefits of the Internet. They point out that, even after the Commission on a bipartisan basis announced open Internet principles in 2005, we have seen clear and troubling deviations from open practices.

Given the importance of an open Internet to our economic future, given the potentially irreversible nature of some harmful practices, and given the competition issues among broadband providers, it is essential that the FCC fulfill its historic role as a cop on the beat to ensure the vitality of our communications networks and to empower and protect consumers of those networks. Now at the same time, government must not overreach by imposing rules that are overly restrictive or that assume perfect knowledge about this dynamic and rapidly changing marketplace.

We know that – to meet our broadband speed and deployment goals for the country – broadband providers must have the business incentives to invest many billions of dollars to build out their networks, the ability to run their networks effectively, and the flexibility to experiment with new business models to further drive private investment.

Today, we are adopting a set of high-level rules of the road that strikes the right balance between the imperatives. We're adopting a framework that will increase certainty for businesses, investors, and entrepreneurs.

In key respects, the interests of edge innovators – the entrepreneurs creating Internet content, services, and applications – broadband providers, and American consumers are aligned. Innovation at the edge catalyzes consumer demand for broadband. Consumer demand spurs private investment in faster broadband networks. And faster networks spark ever-cooler innovation at the edge.

I believe our action today will foster an ongoing cycle of massive investment, innovation and consumer demand both at the edge and in the core of our broadband networks. Our action will strengthen the Internet job-creation engine. Our action will advance our goal of having America's broadband networks be the freest and fastest in the world. Our action will ensure Internet freedom at home, a necessary foundation to fight for Internet freedom around the world.

The crux of the order we are adopting – which is based on a strong and sound legal framework – is straightforward. Here are the key principles it enshrines, and the key rules designed to preserve Internet freedom and openness:

First, consumers and innovators have a right to know the basic performance characteristics of their Internet access and how their network is being managed. The transparency rule we adopt today will give consumers and innovators the clear and simple information they need to make informed choices in choosing networks or designing the next killer app. Shining a light on network management practices will also have an important deterrent effect on bad conduct.

Second, consumers and innovators have a right to send and receive lawful traffic – to go where they want, say what they want, experiment with ideas – commercial and social, and use the devices of their choice. The rules thus prohibit the blocking of lawful content, apps, services, and the connection of devices to the network.

Third, consumers and innovators have a right to a level playing field. No central authority, public or private, should have the power to pick winners and losers on the Internet; that's the role of the commercial market and the marketplace of ideas. So we are adopting a ban on unreasonable discrimination. And we are making clear that we are not approving so-called "pay for priority" arrangements involving fast lanes for some companies but not others. The order states that as a general rule such arrangements won't satisfy the no-unreasonable-discrimination standard – because it simply isn't consistent with an open Internet for broadband providers to skew the marketplace by favoring one idea or application or service over another by selectively prioritizing Internet traffic.

Fourth, the rules recognize that broadband providers need meaningful flexibility to manage their networks to deal with congestion, security, and other issues. And we also recognize the importance and value of business-model experimentation, such as tiered pricing. These are practical necessities, and will help promote investment in, and expansion of, high-speed broadband networks. So, for example, the order rules make clear that broadband providers can engage in "reasonable network management".

Fifth, the principle of Internet openness applies to mobile broadband. There is one Internet, and it must remain an open platform, however consumers and innovators access it. And so today we are adopting, for the first time, broadly applicable rules requiring transparency for mobile broadband providers, and prohibiting them from blocking websites or blocking certain competitive applications.

As I have said for many months, as many innovators and entrepreneurs have told us, and as the facts and record bear out, there are differences between mobile and fixed broadband that are relevant in determining what action government should take for mobile at this time. Among the differences: unique technical issues involving spectrum and mobile networks, the stage and rate of innovation in mobile broadband; and market structure. Also, one of the largest mobile broadband providers has just begun providing 4G service using wireless spectrum subject to openness conditions adopted in connection with the auction of that spectrum.

Importantly, our order makes clear that we are not endorsing or approving practices that the order doesn't prohibit, particularly conduct that is barred for fixed broadband. And we affirm our commitment to an ongoing process to ensure the continued evolution of mobile broadband in a way that's consistent with Internet freedom and openness. Any reduction in mobile Internet openness would be a cause for concern—as would any reduction in innovation and investment in mobile broadband applications, devices, or networks that depend on Internet openness.

Sixth, and finally, today's order recognizes the importance of vigilance – vigilance in promptly enforcing the rules we are adopting and vigilance in monitoring developments in areas such as mobile and the market for specialized services, which may affect Internet openness. That's why I'm pleased that we've committed to create an Open Internet Advisory Committee that will assist the Commission in monitoring the state of Internet openness and the effects of our rules.

We're also launching an Open Internet Apps Challenge on challenge.gov that will foster private-sector development of applications to empower consumers with information about their own broadband connections, which will also help protect Internet openness.

The rules of the road we adopt today are rooted in ideas first articulated by Republican Chairmen Michael Powell and Kevin Martin, and endorsed in a unanimous FCC policy statement in 2005. And they are grounded in the record we have developed over the last 14 months, including more than 100,000 public comments, numerous public workshops, and hundreds of meetings with stakeholders ranging across the spectrum.

I am proud of this process, which has been one of the most transparent in FCC history. And I am proud of the result, which has already garnered broad support – from the technology industry, including TechNet, the Information Technology Industry Council, the Internet Innovation Alliance and the hundreds of technology companies those groups represent, as well as many other technology companies; support from investors of all sizes, including some of the nation's preeminent venture capitalists and angel investors.

Our framework has also drawn support from key consumer, labor, and civil rights groups, a list that includes the Consumer Federation of America, Consumers Union, the Center for Democracy and Technology, and the Communications Workers of America. I thank them and the other groups that have worked on this issue. And our framework has been supported by a number of broadband providers as well, who recognize the sensible balance of our action and the value of bringing a level of certainty to this fraught issue.

Our action today culminates recent efforts to find common ground on this challenging issue – here at the FCC, as well by private parties, and in Congress. I thank each of those who took their time over the last several months to take on these difficult issues, seeking to bridge gaps and find solutions, and who supported us in our efforts.

I want to praise and thank my colleagues Commissioners Copps and Clyburn particularly, for their vision and constancy in pushing this Commission to focus on the interest of consumers. Their work has certainly improved our rules and order. As Commissioner McDowell and Commissioner Baker pointed out, virtually all of our decisions are bipartisan or unanimous, and I look forward to working together on a series of items to serve the public and grow the economy. And I can't express enough appreciation to the remarkable staff of the FCC, who have worked so hard – and so well – to wrestle with difficult issues and turn complex ideas into simple rules. This includes many offices and bureaus at the FCC, including the Office of General Counsel, the Office of Strategic Planning, the Office Engineering and Technology, and the Wireline, Wireless, Media, Consumer, Enforcement, and International Bureaus. Thank you all. And thank you to all the staff on the 8th floor, and in particular to the extraordinary team I'm lucky to have in the Chairman's office. Eddie Lazarus, Zac Katz, Rick Kaplan, Josh Gottheimer, Jen Howard, Daniel Ornstein, and Maria Gaglio – you've each gone well above and beyond the call of duty. I apologize to your families. But I know they join me in honoring your service. Thanks to the work of these incredible public servants, today a strengthened FCC is adopting rules to ensure that the Internet remains a powerful platform for innovation and job creation; to empower consumers and entrepreneurs; and protect free expression.

These rules will increase certainty in the marketplace; spur investment both at the edge and in the core of our broadband networks, and contribute to a 21st century job-creation engine in the United States. Finally, these rules fulfill many promises, including a promise to the future – a promise to the companies that don't yet exist, and the entrepreneurs who haven't yet started work in their dorm rooms or garages. For all that, I am proud to cast my vote.

CONCURRING STATEMENT OF COMMISSIONER MICHAEL J. COPPS

Re: *Preserving the Open Internet,* GN Docket No. 09-191, *Broadband Industry Practices,* WC Docket No. 07-52

In years to come, I hope we can look back on this day as an important turning point in the struggle to ensure the continued openness of the Internet against powerful gatekeeper control. On numerous fronts in the *Open Internet Order* before us today, the Commission is taking strides forward. On others, I pray that our timidity will not undermine the spirit of the Order that we are adopting. The Internet was born on openness, thrived on openness and will achieve its full potential only through continued openness. It is my fervent desire that, with this Order, we start to write the next chapter in the great Internet success story—one of continued openness, innovation without needing permission from anyone, and expanded access for all Americans. We cannot afford to permit special interests to relegate the awesome opportunity-creating power of the open Internet into the sad history of "what might have beens."

Allowing gigantic corporations—in many cases, monopoly or duopoly broadband Internet access service providers—to exercise unfettered control over Americans' access to the Internet not only creates risks to technological innovation and economic growth, but it poses a real threat to freedom of speech and the future of our democracy. Increasingly our national conversation, our source for news and information, our knowledge of one another, will depend upon the Internet. Our future town square will be paved with broadband bricks. It must be accessible to all—not handed over to a handful of gatekeepers who can control our access. As I have long argued—and as many students of the medium have written—previous telecommunications and media technologies, also conceived in openness, eventually fell victim to consolidated control by a few powerful interests, speculative mania by investors, and mistaken government policies which assumed that wise public policy was no public policy. We're supposed to learn from history; too often we don't. Increasingly, the private interests who control our Twenty-first century information infrastructure resemble those who seized the master switch, as Tim Wu's new book calls it, of the last century's communications networks.

In 2003, I cautioned, somewhat dramatically perhaps—but not inaccurately—that the "Internet may be dying . . . because entrenched interests [were] positioning themselves to control the Internet's choke-points." I called then—as I have repeatedly since—for clear rules to maintain openness and freedom on the Internet and to fight discrimination over ideas, content and technologies. Two years later, I was able to convince my colleagues to—at a minimum—adopt an *Internet Policy Statement* that contained the basic rights of Internet end-users to access lawful content, run applications and services, connect devices to the network and enjoy the benefits of competition. Now, at long last, we adopt at least some concrete rules to prevent gatekeepers from circumventing the openness that made the Internet the Internet and from stifling innovation, investment and job creation.

All we need to do is look at our history at the FCC as a cautionary tale. It wasn't all that long ago (well, at least, when you're my age) that one network—AT&T—ran the whole show. AT&T had the power to decide how the network would be used. When innovators showed up at the door with ideas and new technologies, they were often greeted with a courteous but quick "go away." For a long time, the FCC fully supported this type of network, and in fact served as its protector. It was thought that only through comprehensive control by a single company could the quality, safety and scale economies of the network be guaranteed. Bigger was better, and uniformity and stability were thought to be worth the price of lost opportunities for innovation and consumer benefits.

All of this began to change in the late 1960s when an innovator called Carter Electronics Corporation developed a device that connected mobile radio-telephone systems to the wireline network. This device, called the Carterfone, had a cradle into which a regular handset was placed. It converted voice signals to radio signals without the need for a direct electrical connection. But the entrenched incumbent claimed that allowing this innovative and foreign attachment would bring down its entire system. Why? Because the entrenched incumbent didn't build it, sell it and control it. Sound familiar?

Over the complaints of a powerful special interest, the Commission worked up enough courage to change tack, stand up to the network gate-keeper and do the right thing, requiring the network operator to permit attachment of this new application into the existing network. In spite of all the monopolist's alarm bells that this decision meant the end of network quality and the end of reliable service as we knew it, just the opposite came to pass. The idea of having a network that couldn't discriminate against innovators who wanted to improve it finally began to break the choke-hold that the gatekeeper had on the system.

Years after the *Carterfone* decision, as we entered the early days of the Internet age, the Commission reaffirmed its policy of openness and competition by protecting freedom on both the access layer and the architectural layer of the network. In the *Computer Inquiries*, earlier Commissions mandated that common carriers that own transmission pipes used to access the Internet must offer those pipes on non-discriminatory terms to independent Internet Service Providers, among others. Through these decisions the Commission fostered competition by ensuring that customers could reach independent providers. Congress then moved, in provisions of the Telecommunications Act of 1996, to protect the architectural layer. Congress said that local telephone companies with choke-point control of physical infrastructures would have to unbundle their transmission networks.

Sadly, both of these policies were, in fairly short order, decimated by the two Commissions that served between 2001 and 2009. Over my strenuous objections—and those of my colleague Jonathan Adelstein—the FCC took American consumers on a dangerous deregulatory ride, moving the transmission component of broadband outside of the statutory framework that applies to telecommunications carriers. When those Commissions stopped treating advanced telecommunications as telecommunications, they relegated American competitiveness to the sidelines. I don't like to see my country on the sidelines. Neither do most Americans. And remember, this was a major flip-flop from the historic—and successful—approach of requiring nondiscrimination in our communications networks. Because of the errors of those previous Commissions, a court told us earlier this year that the legal framework upon which the FCC built its action against Comcast for disrupting peer-to-peer traffic was inadequate.

Since the decision in *Comcast*, the "Good Ship FCC" has found itself adrift without the tools needed to keep even the most basic consumer protections afloat in today's communications networks. Today, we finally try to patch the hole left by the *Comcast* decision by adopting certain rules to preserve the openness of the Internet. To be clear, we do not anchor ourselves on what I believe to be the best legal framework. Nor have we crafted rules as strong as I would have liked. But, with today's action, we do nonetheless appear to steer ourselves back toward a better course.

I had hoped that we would move full-throttle to restore the kind of policies that had worked in the past. I wanted to put those eight years of public policy aberration—some, me included, dare call them years of abdication—totally behind us. So I pushed—pushed as hard as I could—to get broadband telecommunications back where they belonged, under Title II of our enabling statute, where hard-won consumer-friendly protections that had been built up over many years provided a framework under which business could do its job of building and managing this great communications enterprise—making handsome profits in the process—while operating within a public policy framework giving them certainty and giving consumers the protections they needed and deserved. I wanted to go back to that balancing act that had generally worked, for so many years, for the common good. So, yes, I continue to believe that a reassertion of our Title II authority would have provided the surest foundation for future Commission action. And I note with interest that the Commission's *Reclassification* docket will remain open.

There is more that I would have liked in this Order. I would have preferred a general ban to discourage broadband providers from engaging in "pay for priority"—prioritizing the traffic of those with deep pockets while consigning the rest of us to a slower, second-class Internet. I also believe we should have done more to strip loopholes from the definition of "broadband Internet access service" to prevent companies falsely claiming they are not broadband companies from slipping through. We've made some improvements on the definition, but I still have some worries. I also argued for real parity between fixed and mobile—read wireline and wireless—technologies. After all, the Internet ***is*** the Internet, no matter how you access it, and the millions of citizens going mobile nowadays for their Internet and the entrepreneurs creating innovative wireless content, applications and services should have the same freedoms and protections as those in the wired context. I had other areas of concern about something less than a bright-line nondiscrimination rule, keeping "reasonable network management" within bounds, and the substitution of monitoring for the certainty of enforcement in too many areas.

So, in my book, today's action could—and should—have gone further. Going as far as I would have liked was not, however, in the cards. The simpler and easier course for me at that point would have been dissent—and I considered that very, very seriously. But it became ever more clear to me that without some action today, the wheels of network neutrality would grind to a screeching halt for at least the next two years. So, reserving the right to dissent throughout, I spent the past three weeks in intensive discussions—with all interested parties—about how we might be able to do something to ensure the continued openness of the Internet and to put consumers—not Big Phone or Big Cable—in control of their online experiences. In the end, I believe we made some progress. Not nearly so much as I had hoped, but more, I think, than many people expected. The language in the Order that we will hopefully approve today moves the item, in my mind, from unacceptable to something in which I can concur. That is what I intend to do.

Among the many improvements to the Order we achieved, we now at least conclude that "pay for priority" arrangements would generally violate our "no unreasonable discrimination" rule. We have also explicitly changed the text of the definition of "broadband Internet access service" to close a loophole that, while protecting residential customers, would have jeopardized the open Internet rights of small businesses, educational institutions and libraries.

We insisted on providing greater context to the definition so that broadband companies cannot easily evade the open Internet protections. We have expanded our transparency requirements to give consumers the information they need to make an informed choice by requiring disclosure on the broadband provider's website and also at the point of sale. In discussing the "no unreasonable discrimination" standard, we put particular emphasis on keeping control in the hands of users and preserving an application-blind network—a key part of making the Internet the innovative platform it is today. Given the importance of preserving the open Internet, we have also provided for "rocket docket" expedited treatment to address consumer complaints. Rules on the books are simply a tool waiting to be wielded unless the Commission makes a priority of enforcing them.

While it is no secret that I would have liked to see much more in the mobile section of today's Order, I believe the improvements we have made can start us on a path toward full parity with fixed broadband. After all, we clearly recognize today that "[t]here is one Internet, which should remain open for consumers and innovators alike, although it may be accessed through different technologies and services." More narrowly, we have managed to better refine the actions we do take today. For example, we clarify that a wireless broadband provider cannot block applications that compete with not only its own competitive voice and video telephony applications, but also with those in which it has an attributable interest.

Separate and apart from today's Order, we as a Commission must recognize that we have much urgent business to address to ensure a truly competitive mobile broadband environment—including resolving the pending proceedings related to early termination fees (ETFs), handset exclusivity arrangements, interoperability in the 700 MHz band, and data roaming, to name some of the pending decisions this Commission needs to make.

It is not the job of just the FCC or government writ large, or just consumers ands citizens, or just innovators and entrepreneurs to keep our information infrastructure open and dynamic. It is the job of all of us. Why is this important? Because we have in our grasp now the most powerful and promising communications technology in all of history. If we allow this opportunity-creating technology the freedom and openness it needs to reach its full potential, we can prepare our kids for a future that our country is finding more and more challenging. We will give our schools powerful new tools to educate us, young and old. We will be able to deploy these tools to improve our health, decrease our energy dependence, and create opportunities for whole communities that are being left behind in this new century—rural communities, the inner cities, minorities, Indian country, and those with disabilities. The Internet has be accessible to all, responsive to all, and affordable to all. That's what this country worked for—and largely achieved—in building out electricity and plain old telephone service to all our citizens. It is what we now need to work for with our Twenty-first century broadband infrastructure.

If vigilantly and vigorously implemented by the Commission—and if upheld by the courts—today's Order could represent an important milestone in the ongoing struggle to safeguard the awesome opportunity-creating power of the open Internet. While I cannot vote wholeheartedly to approve the order, I will not block it by voting against it. It is a first step in the right direction—not that first sturdy step I hope my newest grandchild will take, but at least forward, if somewhat hesitant, movement.

Today's majority was crafted by discussion, respectful consideration of one another's thoughts, and give-and-take. I would have welcomed a little more "give," but I suppose the Chairman might see it differently. In any event, I thank him for his engagement and his commitment. I want to pay special tribute to my colleague Commissioner Mignon Clyburn. We shared many of the same concerns, I think it is fair to say, and her thoughtful and creative work, along with her heartfelt commitment to make this item work for consumers—***all*** consumers—had a lot to do with making this a better Order.

Finally, I want to express a deep sense of gratitude to staff. Mine was great in every aspect of this endeavor. John Giusti and Margaret McCarthy worked creatively and tirelessly into the wee hours of many nights and through some awfully long weekends. So, too, Commissioner Clyburn's excellent team, Dave Grimaldi and Angie Kronenberg. I know many folks in the Chairman's office sacrificed similarly, especially Rick Kaplan, Zac Katz and Eddie Lazarus. Literally dozens of people in the Bureaus have worked mightily here, too. I thank them all.

Thanks apart, our job doesn't end today. We haven't finished any race here. We haven't guaranteed an open Internet going forward. We will have, I suspect, a lot of new roads to build—and some other roads, even ones that we lay out in today's Order, that may require repaving and repair before long. If that happens, I hope we will be fast off the mark to do whatever needs to be done. So better than lapsing into a year of post-game armchair analysis, impugning motivations and all the rest, let's instead get to work on the huge job at-hand. Our challenge is nothing short of historic—it is to ensure that the liberating potential of our Twenty-first century communications tools are used to provide the opportunities our citizens—***all*** our citizens—require to be fully productive citizens of a fully productive country.

Thank you.

DISSENTING STATEMENT OF COMMISSIONER ROBERT M. MCDOWELL

Re: *Preserving the Open Internet,* GN Docket No. 09-191, *Broadband Industry Practices,* WC Docket No. 07-52

Thank you, Mr. Chairman. And thank you for your solicitousness throughout this proceeding. In the spirit of the holidays, with good will toward all, I will present a condensed version of a more in-depth statement, the entirety of which I respectfully request be included in this Report and Order.

At the outset, I would like to thank the selfless and tireless work of all of the career public servants here at the Commission who have worked long hours on this project. Although I strongly disagree with this Order, all of us should recognize and appreciate that you have spent time away from your families as you have worked through weekends, the holidays of Thanksgiving and Chanukah, as well as deep into the Christmas season. Such hours take their toll on family life, and I thank you for the sacrifices made by you and your loved ones.

For those who might be tuning in to the FCC for the first time, please know that over 90 percent of our actions are not only bipartisan, but unanimous. I challenge anyone to find another policy making body in Washington with a more consistent record of consensus. We agree that the Internet is, and should remain, open and freedom enhancing. It is, and always has been so, under existing law. Beyond that, we disagree. The contrasts between our perspectives could not be sharper. My colleagues and I will deliver our statements and cast our votes. Then I am confident that we will move on to other issues where we can find common ground once again. I look forward to working on public policy that is more positive and constructive for American economic growth and consumer choice.

William Shakespeare taught us in *The Tempest,* "What's past is prologue." That time-tested axiom applies to today's Commission action. In 2008, the FCC tried to reach beyond its legal authority to regulate the Internet, and it was slapped back by an appellate court only eight short months ago. Today, the Commission is choosing to ignore the recent past as it attempts the same act. In so doing, the FCC is not only defying a court, but it is circumventing the will of a large, bipartisan majority of Congress as well. More than 300 Members have warned the agency against exceeding its legal authority. The FCC is not Congress. We cannot make laws. Legislating is the sole domain of the directly *elected* representatives of the American people. Yet the majority is determined to ignore the growing chorus of voices emanating from Capitol Hill in what appears to some as an obsessive quest to regulate at all costs. Some are saying that, instead of acting as a "cop on the beat," the FCC looks more like a regulatory vigilante. Moreover, the agency is further angering Congress by ignoring increasing calls for a cessation of its actions and choosing, instead, to move ahead just as Members leave town. As a result, the FCC has provocatively charted a collision course with the legislative branch.

Furthermore, on the night of Friday, December 10, just two business days before the public would be prohibited by law from communicating further with us about this proceeding, the Commission dumped nearly 2,000 pages of documents into the record. As if that weren't enough, the FCC unloaded an additional 1,000 pages into the record less than 24 hours before the end of the public comment period. All of these extreme measures, defying the D.C. Circuit, Congress, and undermining the public comment process, have been deployed to deliver on a misguided campaign promise.

Not only is today the winter solstice, the darkest day of the year, but it marks one of the darkest days in recent FCC history. I am disappointed in these "ends-justify-the-means" tactics and the doubts they have created about this agency. The FCC is capable of better. Today is not its finest hour.

Using these new rules as a weapon, politically favored companies will be able to pressure three political appointees to regulate their rivals to gain competitive advantages. Litigation will supplant innovation. Instead of investing in tomorrow's technologies, precious capital will be diverted to pay lawyers' fees. The era of Internet regulatory arbitrage has dawned.

And to say that today's rules don't regulate the Internet is like saying that regulating highway on-ramps, off-ramps, and its pavement doesn't equate to regulating the highways themselves.

What had been bottom-up, non-governmental, and grassroots based Internet governance will become politicized. Today, the United States is abandoning the long-standing bipartisan and international consensus to insulate the Internet from state meddling in favor of a preference for top-down control by unelected political appointees, three of whom will decide what constitutes "reasonable" behavior. Through its actions, the majority is inviting countries around the globe to do the same thing. "Reasonable" is a subjective term. Not only is it perhaps the most litigated word in American history, its definition varies radically from country to country. The precedent has now been set for the Internet to be subjected to state interpretations of "reasonable" by governments of all stripes. In fact, at the United Nations just last Wednesday, a renewed effort by representatives from countries such as China and Saudi Arabia is calling for what one press account says is, "an international body made up of Government representatives that would attempt to create global standards for policing the internet."[650] By not just sanctioning, but *encouraging* more state intrusion into the Internet's affairs, the majority is fueling a global Internet regulatory pandemic. Internet freedom will not be enhanced, it will suffer.

My dissent is based on four primary concerns:

1) Nothing is broken in the Internet access market that needs fixing;
2) The FCC does not have the legal authority to issue these rules;
3) The proposed rules are likely to cause irreparable harm; and
4) Existing law and Internet governance structures provide ample consumer protection in the event a systemic market failure occurs.

Before I go further, however, I apologize if my statement does not address some important issues raised by the Order, but we received the current draft at 11:42 p.m. last night and my team is still combing through it.

I. Nothing Is Broken in the Internet Access Market That Needs Fixing

All levels of the Internet supply chain are thriving due to robust competition and low market entry barriers. The Internet has flourished because it was privatized in 1994.[651] Since then, it has migrated further away from government control. Its success was the result of bottom-up collaboration, not top-down regulation. No one needs permission to start a website or navigate the Web freely. To suggest otherwise is nothing short of fear mongering.

Myriad suppliers of Internet related devices, applications, online services and connectivity are driving productivity and job growth in our country. About eighty percent of Americans own a personal computer.[652] Most are connected to the Internet. In the meantime, the Internet is going mobile. By this time next year, consumers will see more smartphones in the U.S. market than feature phones.[653] In addition to countless applications used on PCs, growth in the number of mobile applications available to consumers has gone from nearly zero in 2007 to half a million just three years later.[654] Mobile app downloads are growing at an annual rate of 92 percent, with an estimated 50 billion applications expected to be downloaded in 2012.[655]

Fixed and mobile broadband Internet access is the fastest penetrating disruptive technology in history. In 2003, only 15 percent of Americans had access to broadband. Just seven years later, 95 percent do.[656] Eight announced national broadband providers are building out facilities in addition to the construction work of scores more local and regional providers. More competition is on the way as providers light up recently auctioned spectrum. Furthermore, the Commission's work to make unlicensed use of the television "white spaces" available to consumers will create even more competition and consumer choice.

In short, competition, investment, innovation, productivity, and job growth are healthy and dynamic in the Internet sector thanks to bipartisan, deregulatory policies that have spanned four decades. The Internet has blossomed under *current law*.

Policies that promote abundance and competition, rather than the rationing and unintended consequences that come with regulation, are the best antidotes to the potential anticompetitive behavior feared by the rules' proponents. But don't take my word for it. Every time the government has examined the broadband market, its experts have concluded that no evidence of concentrations or abuses of market power exists. The Federal Trade Commission (FTC), one of the premier antitrust authorities in government, not only concluded that the broadband market was competitive, but it also warned that regulators should be "wary" of network management rules because of the unknown "net effects on consumers."[657] The FTC rendered that unanimous and bipartisan conclusion in 2007. As I discussed earlier, the broadband market has become only more competitive since then.

More recently, the Department of Justice's Antitrust Division reached a similar conclusion when it filed comments with us earlier this year.[658] While it sounded optimistic regarding the prospects for broadband competition, it also warned against the temptation to regulate "to avoid stifling the infrastructure investments needed to expand broadband access."[659]

Disturbingly, the Commission is taking its radical step today without conducting even a rudimentary market analysis. Perhaps that is because a market study would not support the Order's predetermined conclusion.

II. THE FCC DOES NOT HAVE THE LEGAL AUTHORITY TO ISSUE THESE RULES

Time does not allow me to refute all of the legal arguments in the Order used to justify its claim of authority to regulate the Internet. I have included a more thorough analysis in the supplemental section of this statement, however. Nonetheless, I will touch on a few of the legal arguments endorsed by the majority.

Overall, the Order is designed to circumvent the D.C. Circuit's *Comcast* decision,[660] but this new effort will fail in court as well. The Order makes a first-time claim that somehow, through the *de*regulatory bent of Section 706, in 1996 Congress gave the Commission *direct* authority to regulate the Internet. The Order admits that its rationale requires the Commission to reverse its longstanding interpretation that this section conveys no additional authority beyond what is already provided elsewhere in the Act.[661] This new conclusion, however, is suddenly convenient for the majority while it grasps for a foundation for its predetermined outcome. Instead of "*remov*[*ing*] barriers to infrastructure investment," as Section 706 encourages, the Order fashions a legal fiction to construct *additional* barriers. This move is arbitrary and capricious and is not supported by the evidence in the record or a change of law.[662] The Commission's gamesmanship with Section 706 throughout the year is reminiscent of what was attempted with the contortions of the so-called "70/70 rule" three years ago. I objected to such factual and legal manipulations then, and I object to them now.

Furthermore, the Order desperately scours the Act to find a tether to moor its alleged Title I ancillary authority. As expected, the Order's legal analysis ignores the fundamental teaching of the *Comcast* case: Titles II, III, and VI of the Communications Act give the FCC the power to regulate specific, recognized classes of electronic communications services, which consist of common carriage telephony, broadcasting and other licensed wireless services, and multichannel video programming services.[663] Despite the desires of some, Congress has *not* established a new title of the Act to police Internet network management, not even implicitly. The absence of statutory authority is perhaps why Members of Congress introduced legislation to give the FCC such powers. In other words, if the Act already gave the Commission the legal tether it seeks, why was legislation needed in the first place? I'm afraid that this leaky ship of an Order is attempting to sail through a regulatory fog without the necessary ballast of factual or legal substance. The courts will easily sink it.

In another act of legal sleight of hand, the Order claims that it does not attempt to classify broadband services as Title II common carrier services. Yet functionally, that is precisely what the majority is attempting to do to Title I information services, Title III licensed wireless services, and Title VI video services by subjecting them to nondiscrimination obligations in the absence of a congressional mandate. What we have before us today is a Title II Order dressed in a threadbare Title I disguise. Thankfully, the courts have seen this bait-and-switch maneuver by the FCC before – and they have struck it down each time.[664]

The Order's expansive grasp for jurisdictional power here is likely to alarm any reviewing court because the effort appears to have no limiting principle.[665] If we were to accept the Order's argument, "it would virtually free the Commission from its congressional tether."[666] "As the [Supreme] Court explained in *Midwest Video II*, 'without reference to the provisions of the Act' expressly granting regulatory authority, 'the Commission's [ancillary] jurisdiction would be unbounded.'"[667] I am relieved, however, that in the Order, the Commission is explicitly refraining from regulating coffee shops.[668]

In short, if this Order stands, there is no end in sight to the Commission's powers.

I also have concerns regarding the constitutional implications of the Order, especially its trampling on the First and Fifth Amendments. But in the observance of time, those thoughts are contained in my extended written remarks.

III. The Commission's Rules Will Cause Irreparable Harm to Broadband Investment and Consumers

DOJ's cogent observation from last January regarding the competitive nature of the broadband market raises the important issue of the likely irreparable harm to be brought about by these new rules. In addition to government agencies, investors, investment analysts, and broadband companies themselves have told us that network management rules would create uncertainty to the point where crucial investment capital will become harder to find. This point was made over and over again at the FCC's Capital Formation Workshop on October 1, 2009. A diverse gathering of investors and analysts told us that even rules emanating from Title I would create uncertainty. Other evidence suggests that Internet management rules could not only make it difficult for companies to "predict their revenues and cash flow," but a new regime could "have the perverse effect of raising prices to all users" as well.[669]

Additionally, today's Order implies that the FCC has price regulation authority over broadband. In fact, the D.C. Circuit noted in its *Comcast* decision last spring that the

Commission's attorneys openly asserted at January's oral argument that "the Commission could someday subject [broadband] service to pervasive rate regulation to ensure that [a broadband] company provides the service at 'reasonable charges.'"[670] Nothing indicates that the Commission has changed its mind since then. In fact, the Order appears to support both indirect and direct price regulation of broadband services.[671]

Moreover, as lobbying groups accept this Order's invitation to file complaints asking the government to distort the market further the Commission will be under increasing pressure from political interest groups to expand its power and influence over the broadband Internet market. In fact, some of my colleagues today are complaining that the Order doesn't go far enough. Each complaint filed will create more uncertainty as the enforcement process becomes a *de facto* rulemaking circus, just as the Commission attempted in the ill-fated *Comcast/BitTorrent* case.[672] How does this framework create regulatory certainty?[673] the European Commission recognized the harm such rules could cause to the capital markets when it decided last month *not* to impose measures similar to these.[674]

Part of the argument in favor of new rules alleges that "giant corporations" will serve as hostile "gatekeepers" to the Internet. First, in the almost nine years since those fears were first sewn, net regulation lobbyists can point to fewer than a handful of cases of alleged misconduct, out of an infinite number of Internet communications. *All* of those cases were resolved in favor of consumers under *current* law.

More importantly, however, many broadband providers are not large companies. Many are small businesses. Take, for example, LARIAT, a fixed wireless Internet service provider serving rural communities in Wyoming. LARIAT has told the Commission that the imposition of network management rules will impede its ability to obtain investment capital and will limit the company's "ability to deploy new service to currently unserved and underserved areas."[675] Furthermore, LARIAT echoes the views of many others by asserting that, "[t]he imposition of regulations that would drive up costs or hamper innovation would further deter future outside investment in our company and others like it."[676] Additionally, "[t]o mandate overly [burdensome] network management policies would foster lower quality of service, raise operating costs (which in turn would raise prices for all subscribers), and/or create a large backlog of adjudicative proceedings at the Commission (in which it would be prohibitively expensive for *small and competitive ISPs* to participate)".[677] LARIAT also notes that the imposition of net neutrality rules would cause immediate harm such that "[d]ue to immediate deleterious impacts upon investment, these damaging effects would be likely to occur even if the Commission's Order was later invalidated, nullified, or effectively modified by a court challenge or Congressional action."[678] Other small businesses have echoed these concerns.[679]

Less investment. Less innovation. Increased business costs. Increased prices for consumers. Disadvantages to smaller ISPs. Jobs lost. And all of this is in the name of promoting the exact opposite? The evidence in the record simply does not support the majority's outcome driven conclusions.

In short, the Commission's action today runs directly counter to the laudable broadband deployment and adoption goals of the National Broadband Plan. No government has ever succeeded in mandating investment and innovation. And nothing has been holding back Internet investment and innovation, until now.

IV. Existing Law Provides Ample Consumer Protection

To reiterate, the Order fails to put forth either a factual or legal basis for regulatory intervention. Repeated government economic analyses have reached the same conclusion: no concentrations or abuses of market power exist in the broadband space. If market failure were to occur, however, America's antitrust and consumer protection laws stand at the ready. Both the Department of Justice and the Federal Trade Commission are well equipped to cure any market ills.[680] In fact, the Antitrust Law Section of the American Bar Association agrees.[681] Nowhere does the Order attempt to explain why these laws are insufficient in its quest for more regulation.

Moreover, for several years now, I have been advocating a potentially effective approach that won't get overturned on appeal. In lieu of new rules, which will be tied up in court for years, the FCC could create a new role for itself by partnering with already established, non-governmental Internet governance groups, engineers, consumer groups, academics, economists, antitrust experts, consumer protection agencies, industry associations, and others to spotlight allegations of anticompetitive conduct in the broadband market, and work *together* to resolve them. Since it was privatized, Internet governance has always been based on a foundation of bottom-up collaboration and cooperation rather than top-down regulation. This truly "light touch" approach has created a near-perfect track record of resolving Internet management conflicts without government intervention.

Unfortunately, the majority has not even considered this idea for a moment. But once today's Order is overturned in court, it is still my hope that the FCC will consider and adopt this constructive proposal.

In sum, what's past is indeed prologue. Where we left the saga of the FCC's last net neutrality order before was with a spectacular failure in the appellate courts. Today, the FCC seems determined to make the same mistake instead of learning from it. The only illness apparent from this Order is regulatory hubris. Fortunately, cures for this malady are obtainable in court. For all of the foregoing reasons, I respectfully dissent.

Extended Legal Analysis: The Commission Lacks Authority To Impose

Network Management Mandates on Broadband Networks

The Order is designed to circumvent the effect of the D.C. Circuit's *Comcast* decision,[682] but that effort will fail. Careful consideration of the Order shows that its legal analysis ignores the fundamental teaching of *Comcast*: Titles II, III, and VI of the Communications Act regulate specific, recognized classes of electronic communications services, which consist of common carriage telephony, broadcasting and other licensed wireless services, and multichannel video programming services.[683] Despite any policy desires to the contrary, Congress has not yet established a new title of the Act to govern some or all parts of the Internet – which includes the operation, or "management," of the networks that support the Internet's functioning as a new and highly complex communications platform for diverse and interactive data, voice, and video services. Until such time as lawmakers may act, the Commission has no power to regulate Internet network management.

As detailed below, the provisions of existing law upon which the Order relies afford the Commission neither direct nor ancillary authority here. The tortured logic needed to support the Order's conclusion requires that the agency either reverse its own interpretation of its statutorily granted express powers or rely on sweeping pronunciations of ancillary authority that lack any "congressional tether" to specific provisions of the Act.[684] Either path will fail in court.

Instead, the judicial panel that ends up reviewing the inevitable challenges is highly likely to recognize this effort for what it is. While ostensibly eschewing reclassification of broadband networks as Title II platforms, the Order imposes the most basic of all common carriage mandates: nondiscrimination, albeit with a vague "we'll know it when we see it" caveat for "reasonable" network management. This may be only a pale version of common carriage (at least for now), but it is still quite discernible even to the untrained eye.

A. Reversal of the Commission's Interpretation of Section 706 Cannot Provide Direct Authority for Network Management Rules

Less than one year ago, the Commission in attempting to defend its *Comcast/BitTorrent* decision at the D.C. Circuit "[a]cknowledged that it has no express statutory authority over [an Internet service provider's network management] practices."[685] The Commission was right then, and the Order is wrong now. Congress has never contemplated, much less enacted, a regulatory scheme for broadband network management, notwithstanding the significant revision of the Communications Act undertaken through the Telecommunications Act of 1996 (1996 Act).[686] It is an exercise in legal fiction to contend otherwise.

Any analysis of an arguable basis for the Commission's power to act in this area must begin with the recognition that broadband Internet access service remains an unregulated "information service" under Title I of the Communications Act.[687] Overtly, the Order does not purport to change this legal classification.[688] Yet a reviewing court will look beyond the Order's characterization of the Commission's action to scrutinize what the new codified rules – and the directives and warnings set forth in the text – actually do.[689] Dispassionate analysis will lead to the conclusion that the Order attempts to relegate this type of information service to common carriage by effectively applying major Title II obligations to it. The Title I disguise will not be convincing.

The threadbare nature of the disguise becomes clear with scrutiny of the Order's claims for a legal basis for the new regulations. The Order's only serious effort to assert direct authority is based on Section 706.[690] The Order glosses over the key point that no language within Section 706 – or anywhere else in the Act, for that matter – bestows the FCC with explicit authority to regulate Internet network management. Rather, Section 706's explicit focus is on "deployment" and "availability" of broadband network facilities.[691] So what precisely is the nexus between Section 706's focus on broadband deployment and availability and the Order's focus on network management once the facilities *have been* deployed and the service *is* available? The Order seems to imply that Section 706 somehow provides the Commission with network management authority because if the government lacks such power, some American might have less access to the Internet. This rationale is contrary to the provision's language and illogical on its face. Imposing new regulations on network providers in the business of deploying broadband[692] will have the opposite effect of what Section 706 seeks to do. Instead, the imposition of network management rules will likely depress investment in deployment of broadband throughout our nation.[693] This outcome will prove true not simply for the large providers tracked by Wall Street analysts but for the small businesses that supply vital and competitive broadband options to consumers in many locales across the nation.[694]

A closer reading of the statutory text bears out this assessment. Turning specifically to the language of Section 706(a), the provision opens with a policy pronouncement that the Commission "shall encourage the deployment on a reasonable and timely basis of advanced telecommunications capability to all Americans."[695] As *Comcast* already has pointed out, "under Supreme Court and D.C. Circuit case law statements of policy, by themselves, do not create 'statutorily mandated responsibilities.'"[696] Rather, "[p]olicy statements are just that – statements of policy. They are not delegations of regulatory authority."[697] The same holds true for congressional statements of policy, such as the opening of Section 706, as it does for any agency's policy pronouncements.

The Order makes a strenuous effort to argue that Section 706 is not limited to deregulatory actions, a herculean task taken on because the Order rests nearly all of its heavy weight on this thin foundation.[698] Section 706 does refer to one specific regulatory provision – price cap regulation.[699] Readers should keep in mind, however, that at the time Section 706 was enacted, 1996, price cap regulation of incumbent local exchange carriers was considered to be *deregulatory* when compared to the legacy alternative: rate-of-return regulation. The provision's remaining language is even more broad and deregulatory. For instance, the end of section 706(a) states that the FCC should explore "*other* regulating methods that *remove barriers to infrastructure investment*."[700] Additionally, its counterpart subsection, Section 706(b), states that if the FCC's annual inquiry determines that advanced telecommunications is not "being deployed to all Americans in a reasonable and timely fashion" the FCC shall take action to "*remove[e] barriers to infrastructure investment* and ... promot[e] competition in the telecommunications market."[701] As discussed above, the Order's actions will have the opposite effect.

Moreover, the Order's new interpretation of Section 706(a) is self serving and outcome determinative. The Order admits that its rationale requires reversing the Commission's longstanding interpretation of that subsection as conveying no authority beyond that already provided elsewhere in the Act.[702] This arbitrary and capricious move is not supported by evidence in the record or a change in law.[703] The Order offers the excuse that "[i]n the particular proceedings prior to *Comcast*, setting out the understanding of Section 706(a) that we articulate in this Order would not meaningfully have increased the authority that we understood the Commission already to possess."[704] In other words, apparently, the agency's confused understanding of the limits of its ancillary authority meant that the Commission then did not have to rest on Section 706(a) in order to overreach by "pursu[ing] a stand-alone policy objective" not moored to "a specifically delegated power."[705]

The Order's reliance on Section 706(b) as providing a statutory foundation for network management regulations is similarly flawed. That subsection requires that the FCC determine on an annual basis whether "advanced telecommunications capability is being deployed to all Americans in a reasonable and timely fashion."[706] Congress then further directed the

Commission, if the agency's determination were negative, to "take immediate action to accelerate deployment of such capability by *removing barriers to infrastructure investment* and by promoting competition in the telecommunications market" (emphasis added).[707]

To justify its use of this trigger, the Order points to the fact that approximately six months ago, the Commission on a divided 3-2 vote issued a report finding – for the first time in history – that "broadband deployment to all Americans is not reasonable and timely."[708] This determination, in conflict with all previous reports dating back to 1999, was both perplexing and unsettling. It ignored the impressive strides the nation has made in developing and deploying broadband infrastructure and services since issuance of the first 706 Report. Amazingly enough, the most recent 706 Report managed to find failure even while pointing to data (first made public in the National Broadband Plan) showing that "95% of the U.S. population lives in housing units with access to terrestrial, fixed broadband infrastructure capable of supporting actual download speeds of at least 4 Mbps."[709] In fact, only 15 percent of Americans had access to residential broadband services in 2003.[710] Only seven years later, 95 percent enjoyed access, making broadband the fastest penetrating disruptive technology in history.[711] At the time that I dissented from the 706 Report, I expressed concern that its findings could be a pretext for justifying additional regulation, rather than "removing barriers to infrastructure investment."[712] Unfortunately, this Order reveals that my fears were well founded.

One is left to wonder where this assertion of power, if left unchecked, may lead next.[713] As for the Order itself, the short-term path is clear: It will be challenged in court. Once there, the Commission must struggle with the fact that the empirical evidence in this docket demonstrates "no relationship whatever" between the plain meaning of Section 706 and the network management rules being adopted.[714]

B. Efforts to Advance New Arguments for Exercising Ancillary Authority Will Not Survive Court Review

In spite of the D.C. Circuit's decision in *Comcast*, the Order attempts to continue to assert ancillary authority as another basis for its imposition of network management rules. To bolster the Commission's case this time, the Order points to some provisions of the Act that it failed to cite the first time around. Its arguments for new and putatively better bases for network management rules fall victim largely to the same weaknesses the court identified before.

Efforts to defend a valid exercise of the agency's ancillary powers are subject to a two-part test – and the "central issue," as the D.C. Circuit already has explained, is whether the Commission can satisfy the second prong of the test.[715] Under it, "[t]he Commission may exercise this 'ancillary' authority only if it demonstrates that its action ... is 'reasonably ancillary to the ... effective performance of its statutorily mandated responsibilities.'"[716]

Those "statutorily mandated responsibilities" must be concrete and readily identifiable. As the Supreme Court instructed in *NARUC II* and the D.C. Circuit reiterated in *Comcast*, "the Commission's ancillary authority 'is really incidental to, and contingent upon, *specifically delegated powers under the Act*.'"[717] For the ancillary authority arguments to prevail here, the Order must identify specific subsections within Title II, III or VI that provide the ancillary hook, and then show how the Commission's assertion of power will advance the regulated services directly subject to those particular provisions. Existing court precedent shows that sweeping generalizations are not sufficient.[718] Nor may the general framework of one title of the Act – such as common carriage obligations – be grafted upon services subject to another title that does not include the same obligations.[719] And long descriptions of services delivered via broadband networks do not substitute for hard legal analysis.[720]

Moreover, arguments must be advanced on "a case-by-case basis" for each specific assertion of jurisdiction.[721] *Comcast* explains that the Commission must "independently justif[y]" any action resting on ancillary authority by demonstrating in each and every instance how the action at issue advances the services actually regulated by specific provisions of the Act.[722] The D.C. Circuit apparently was concerned about the Commission's ability to grasp this point, for the opinion makes it repeatedly.[723] In doing so, the court directed the Commission to more closely study the agency's failures in *NARUC II* and *Midwest Video II* to comprehend the limits of its ancillary reach.[724]

The Order's claim of ancillary jurisdiction is not convincing with respect to Title II because, *inter alia*, it invokes only Section 201 in support of its nondiscrimination mandate.[725] Yet in a glaring omission, Section 201 does not reference nondiscrimination – that concept is under the purview of Section 202, which appears not to be invoked in the Order.[726] (By this omission, it appears that the Order may be attempting an end run around the most explicit Title II mandates because of other considerations.) Nor are the arguments successful with respect to the Title III and VI provisions cited in the Order because those statutory mandates address services that are not subject to common carriage-style nondiscrimination obligations absent explicit application of statutory directives.[727]

In addition, the Order's expansive grasp for jurisdictional power here is likely to alarm any reviewing court because the effort appears to have no limiting principle.[728] The D.C. Circuit's warning in *Comcast* against one form of overreaching – the misreading of policy statements as blanket extensions of power – applies here as well:

> Not only is this argument flatly inconsistent with *Southwestern Cable*, *Midwest Video I*, *Midwest Video II*, and *NARUC II*, but if accepted it would virtually free the Commission from its congressional tether. As the Court explained in *Midwest Video II*, "without reference to the provisions of the Act" expressly granting regulatory authority, "the Commission's [ancillary] jurisdiction ... would be unbounded." Indeed, Commission counsel told us at oral argument that just as the Order seeks to make Comcast's Internet service more "rapid" and "efficient," the Commission could someday subject Comcast's Internet service to pervasive rate regulation to ensure that the company provides the service at "reasonable charges." *Were we to accept that theory of ancillary authority, we see no reason why the Commission would have to stop there, for we can think of few examples of regulations that apply to Title II common carrier services, Title III broadcast services, or Title VI cable services that the Commission, relying on the broad policies articulated in section 230(b) and section 1, would be unable to impose upon Internet service providers.* If in *Midwest Video I* the Commission "strain[ed] the outer limits of even the open-ended and pervasive jurisdiction that has evolved by decisions of the Commission and the courts," and if in *NARUC II* and *Midwest Video II* it exceeded those limits, then here it seeks to shatter them entirely.[729]

Some of the Order's most noteworthy flaws are addressed below.

1. The Order's patchwork citation of Title II provisions does not provide the necessary support for extending common carriage obligations to broadband Internet access providers

Comcast instructs the Commission that the invocation of any Title II citation as a basis for ancillary jurisdiction must be shown to be "integral to telephone communication."[730] The Order's efforts to meet this legal requirement are thin and unconvincing – and in some instances downright perplexing. For example, it points to Section 201 in arguing that it provides the Commission with "express and expansive authority"[731] to ensure that the "charges [and] practices in connection with"[732] telecommunications services are "just and reasonable".[733] The Order contends that the use of interconnected VoIP services via broadband is becoming a substitute service for traditional telephone service and therefore certain broadband service providers might have an incentive to block VoIP calls originating on competitors' networks. The Order then stretches Section 201's language concerning "charges" and "practices" to try to bolster the claim that it provides a sufficient nexus for ancillary jurisdiction over potential behavior by nonregulated service providers that conceptually would best be characterized as "discrimination."[734] There are at least two obvious weaknesses in this rationale. First, the Order ignores the D.C. Circuit's instruction that the Commission has "expansive authority" only when it is "regulating common carrier services, including landline telephony."[735] Yet broadband Internet access providers are not common carriers and the Order purposely avoids declaring them to be so. Second, the Order seems to pretend that the plain meaning of Section 201's text is synonymous with that of Section 202, which does address "discrimination" but is not directly invoked here.

The Order's reliance on Section 251(a)(1) is flawed for similar reasons. That provision imposes a duty on telecommunications carriers "to interconnect directly or indirectly with the facilities of other telecommunications carriers."[736] The Order notes that an increasing number of customers use VoIP services and posits that if a broadband Internet service provider were to block certain calls via VoIP, it would ultimately harm users of the public switched telephone network. All policy aspirations aside, this jurisdictional argument fails as a legal matter. As the Order admits, VoIP services have never been classified as "telecommunications services," *i.e.*, common carriage services, under Title II of the Act.[737] Therefore, as a corollary matter, broadband Internet service providers are not "telecommunications carriers" – or at least the Commission has never declared them to be so. The effect of the Order is to do indirectly what the Commission is reluctant to do explicitly.

2. The language of Title III and VI provisions cannot be wrenched out of context to impose common carriage obligations on non-common carriage services

The Order makes a rather breathtaking attempt to find a basis for ancillary authority to impose nondiscrimination and other common carriage mandates in statutory schemes that since their inception have been distinguished from common carriage. This effort, too, will fail in court, for it flouts Supreme Court precedent on valid exercises of ancillary authority, as reviewed in detail in *Comcast*. If the "derivative nature of ancillary jurisdiction"[738] has any objectively discernible boundaries, it must bar the Commission from taking obligations explicitly set forth in one statutory scheme established in the Act – such as the nondiscrimination mandates of Title II – and grafting them into different statutory schemes set forth in other sections of Act, such as Title III and Title VI, that either directly or indirectly *eschew* such obligations. Here, the Act itself explicitly distinguishes between broadcasting and common carriage.[739] And the Supreme Court long ago drew the line between Title VI video services and Title II-style mandates by forbidding the Commission to "relegate[] cable systems ... to common-carrier status".[740]

The Order's effort to search high and low through provisions of the Communications Act to find hooks for ancillary jurisdiction may be at its most risible in the broadcasting context. The attempt here seems hardly serious, given that the legal discussion is limited to a one-paragraph discussion that cites to no specific section within Title III.[741] Rather, it stands its ground on the observation that TV and radio broadcasters now distribute content through their own websites – coupled with the hypothetical contention that some possible future "self-interested" act by broadband providers could potentially have a negative effect on the emerging business models that may provide important support for the broadcast of local news and other programming.[742]

This is far from the kind of tight ancillary nexus that the Supreme Court upheld in *Southwestern Cable* and *Midwest Video I*,[743] and it is even more attenuated than the jurisdictional stretch that the Court rejected in *Midwest Video II*.[744] One wonders how far this new theory for an ancillary reach could possibly extend. Many broadcasters for years have benefitted through the sales of tapes and DVDs of their programming marketed through paper catalogs. Does the rationale here mean that the Commission has power to regulate the management of that communications platform, too?

The equally generalized Title III arguments based on "spectrum licensing" apparently are intended to support jurisdiction over the many point-to-point wireless services that are not point-to-multipoint broadcasting. They, too, appear off-point.[745] For example, the Order's recitation of a long array of Title III provisions (*e.g.*, maintenance of control over radio transmissions in the U.S., imposition of conditions on the use of spectrum) seems misplaced. If this overview is intended to serve as analysis, it contains a logical flaw: Most of the rules adopted today are not being applied – yet – to mobile broadband Internet access service.[746] Certainly the Commission need not depend on the full sweep of Title III authority to impose the "transparency" rule; it need only act in our pending "Truth-in-Billing" docket.[747] Similarly, with regard to the "no blocking" rule, the Order need only rest on the provisions of Title III discussed in the *700 MHz Second Report and Order*, where this rule was originally adopted.[748]

With respect to the asserted Title VI bases for ancillary jurisdiction, the Order actually does point to three specific provisions, but none provides a firm foundation for extending the Commission's authority to encompass Internet network management. The Order first cites Section 628, which is designed to promote competition among the multichannel video programming distributors (MVPDs) regulated under Title VI, such as cable operators and satellite TV providers. The best-known elements of this provision authorize our program access rules, but the Commission recently has strayed – over my dissent – beyond the plain meaning of the statutory language to read away explicit constraints on our power in this area.[749] Apparently the Commission is about to make a bad habit of doing this.

Of course, Section 628 does not explicitly refer to the Internet, much less the management of its operation. The Congressional framers of the Cable Consumer Protection and Competition Act of 1992, of which Section 628 was a part, were concerned about, and specifically referenced, video services regulated under Title VI.[750] Yet the Order employs a general statutory reference to "unfair methods of competition or unfair or deceptive acts or practices" as a hook for a broad exercise of ancillary jurisdiction over an unregulated network of networks.[751] This time the theory rests largely on the contention that, absent network management regulation, network providers might improperly interfere with the delivery of "over the top" (OTT) video programming that may compete for viewer attention with the platform providers' own MVPD services.[752] The Order cites to no actual instances of such behavior, however, nor does it grapple with the implications of the market forces that are driving MVPDs in the opposite direction – to add Internet connectivity to their multichannel video offerings.[753]

The second Title VI provision upon which the Order stakes a claim for ancillary jurisdiction is Section 616, which regulates the terms of program carriage agreements.[754] The specific text and statutory design of this provision make plain that it addresses independently produced content carried by contract as part of a transmission platform provider's Title VI MVPD service, and not a situation in which there is no privity of contract and the service is Internet access. The Order attempts to make much of Section 616's rather broad definition "video programming vendor" without grappling with the incongruities created when one tries to shove the provision's explicit directives about carriage contract terms into the Internet context.[755] In fact, the application of Section 616 here is only comprehensible if one conceives of it as a new flavor of common carriage, with all the key contract terms supplied by statute.[756] Such a reading, however, would be in considerable conflict with the rationale of *Midwest Video II,*[757] as the D.C. Circuit in *Comcast* already has noted.[758]

In short, the Order's efforts to find a solid grounding for exercising ancillary power here – and thereby imposing sweeping new common carriage-style obligations on an unregulated service – strain credulity. Policy concerns cannot overcome the limits of the agency's current statutory authority. The Commission should heed the closing admonition of *Comcast*:

> [N]otwithstanding the "difficult regulatory problem of rapid technological change" posed by the communications industry, "the allowance of wide latitude in the exercise of delegated powers is not the equivalent of untrammeled freedom to regulate activities over which the statute fails to confer ... Commission authority." Because the Commission has failed to tie its assertion of ancillary authority over Comcast's Internet service to any "statutorily mandated responsibility," we ... vacate the Order.[759]

The same fate awaits this new rulemaking decision.

C. The Order Will Face Serious Constitutional Challenges

It is reasonable to assume that broadband Internet service providers will challenge the FCC ruling on constitutional grounds as well.[760] Contrary to the Order's thinly supported assertions, broadband ISPs are speakers for First Amendment purposes – and therefore challenges on that basis should not be so lightly dismissed. There are several reasons for being concerned about legal infirmities here.

First, the Order is too quick to rely on simplistic service labels of the past in brushing off First Amendment arguments. For example, while it ostensibly avoids classifying broadband providers as Title II common carriers, it still indirectly alludes to old case law concerning the speech rights of common carriers by dismissing broadband ISPs as mere "conduits for speech" undeserving of First Amendment consideration.[761] There is good reason today to call into question well-worn conventional wisdom dating from the era of government-sanctioned monopolies about common carriers' freedom of speech, particularly in the context of a competitive marketplace.[762] Indeed, at least two sitting Justices have signaled a willingness to wrestle with the implications of the issue of common carriers' First Amendment protections.[763]

Similarly, the Order offhandedly rejects the analogies drawn to First Amendment precedent concerning cable operators and broadcasters, based only on the unremarkable observation that cable operators and broadcasters exercise a noteworthy degree of editorial control over the content they transmit via their legacy services.[764] In so doing, the Order disregards the fact that at least two federal district courts have concluded that broadband providers, whether they originated as telephone companies or cable companies, have speech rights.[765] Although the Order acknowledges the cases in today's Order, it makes no effort to distinguish or challenge them. Instead, the Order simply "disagree[s] with the reasoning of those decisions."[766]

Second, I question the Order's breezy assertion that broadband ISPs perform no editorial function worthy of constitutional recognition. The Order rests the weight of its argument here on the fact that broadband ISPs voluntarily devote the vast majority of their capacity to uses by independent speakers with very little editorial invention by the platform provider beyond "network management practices designed to protect their Internet services against spam and malicious content."[767] But what are acts such as providing quality of service (QoS) management and content filters if not editorial functions?[768]

And the mere act of opening one's platform to a large multiplicity of independent voices does not divest the platform owner of its First Amendment rights.[769] The Order cites no legal precedent for determining how much "editorial discretion" must be exercised before a speaker can merit First Amendment protection. Newspapers provide other speakers access to their print "platforms" in the form of classified and display advertising, letters to the editor, and, more recently, reader comments posted in response to online news stories. Advertising historically has filled 60 percent or more of the space in daily newspapers,[770] and publishers rarely turn away ads in these difficult economic times[771]– though they still may exercise some minor degree of "editorial discretion" to screen out "malicious" content deemed inappropriate for family consumption. Under the Order's rationale, would newspaper publishers therefore be deemed to have relinquished rights to free speech protection?

Third, it is undisputed that broadband ISPs merit First Amendment protection when using their own platforms to provide multichannel video programming services and similar offerings. The Order acknowledges as much but simply asserts that the new regulations will leave broadband ISPs sufficient room to speak in this fashion[772]– unless, of course, hints elsewhere in the document concerning capacity usage come to pass.[773] So while the Order concedes, as it must, that network management regulation could well be subject to heightened First Amendment review, it disregards the most significant hurdle posed by even the intermediate scrutiny standard.[774] The Order devotes all of its sparse discussion to the first prong of the intermediate scrutiny test, the "substantial" government interest,[775] while wholly failing to address the second and typically most difficult prong for the government to satisfy: demonstrating that the regulatory means chosen does not "burden substantially more speech than is necessary."[776] And what is the burden here? One need look no further than the Order's discussion of specialized services to find it. It announces an "expectation" that network providers will limit their use of their own capacity for speech in order to make room for others – an expectation that may rise to the level of effectively requiring the platform provider to pay extra, in the form of capacity build-outs, before exercising its own right to speak.[777] Such a vague expectation creates a chilling effect of the type that courts are well placed to recognize.[778]

Yet the Order makes *no* effort, as First Amendment precedent requires, to weigh this burden against the putative benefit.[779] Instead, Broadband ISP speakers are left in the dark to grope their way through this regulatory fog. Before speaking via their own broadband platforms, they must either: (1) guess and hope that they have left enough capacity for third party speech, or (2) go hat in hand to the government for pre-clearance of their speech plans.

Finally, it should be noted one of the underlying policy rationales for imposing Internet network management regulations effectively turns the First Amendment on its head. The Founders crafted the Bill of Rights, and the First Amendment in particular, to act as a bulwark against state attempts to trample on the rights of individuals. (Given that they had just won a war against government tyranny, they were wary of recreating the very ills that had sparked the Revolution – and which so many new Americans had sacrificed much to overcome.) More than 200 years later, our daily challenges may be different but the constitutional principles remain the same. The First Amendment begins with the phrase "Congress shall make no law" for a reason. Its restraint on government power ensures that we continue to enjoy all of the vigorous discourse, conversation and debate that we, along with the rest of the world, now think of as quintessentially American.

Conclusion

For the foregoing reasons, I respectfully dissent.

Attachment A

Letter of FCC Commissioner Robert M. McDowell to the Hon. Henry A. Waxman, Chairman, Committee on Energy and Commerce, U.S. House of Representatives (May 5, 2010)

Office of Commissioner Robert M. McDowell
Federal Communications Commission
Washington, D.C. 20554
May 5, 2010

The Honorable Henry A. Waxman
Chairman
Committee on Energy and Commerce
United States House of Representatives
Washington, DC 20515

Dear Chairman Waxman:

Thank you for the opportunity to testify before you and your colleagues on the Subcommittee on Communications, Technology and the Internet on March 25 regarding the National Broadband Plan.[780] As I testified at the hearing, the Commission has never classified broadband Internet access services as "telecommunications services" under Title II of the Communications Act. In support of that assertion, I respectfully submit to you the instant summary of the history of the regulatory classification of broadband Internet access services.

In the wake of the privatization of the Internet in 1994, Congress overwhelmingly passed the landmark Telecommunications Act of 1996 (1996 Act) and President Clinton signed it into law. Prior to this time, the Commission had never regulated "information services" or "Internet access services" as common carriage under Title II. Instead, such services were classified as "enhanced services" under Title I. To the extent that regulated common carriers offered their own enhanced services, using their own transmission facilities, the FCC required the underlying, local transmission component to be offered on a common carrier basis.[781] No provider of retail information services was ever required to tariff such service. With the 1996 Act, Congress had the opportunity to reverse the Commission and regulate information services, including Internet access services, as traditional common carriers, but chose not to do so. Instead, Congress codified the Commission's existing classification of "enhanced sevices" as "information services" under Title I.

Two years after the 1996 Act was signed into law, Congress directed the Commission to report on its interpretation of various parts of the statute, including the definition of "information service."[782] In response, on April 10,1998, under the Clinton-era leadership of Chairman William Kennard, the Commission issued a *Report to Congress* finding that "Internet access services are appropriately classed as information, rather than telecommunications, services."[783] The Commission reasoned as follows:

> The provision of Internet access service ... offers end users *information-service capabilities inextricably intertwined with data transport. As such, we conclude that it is appropriately classed as an "information service"*[784]

In reaching this conclusion, the Commission reasoned that treating Internet access services as telecommunications services would lead to "negative policy consequences."[785]

To be clear, the FCC consistently held that any provider of information services could do so pursuant to Title I.[786] No distinction was made in the way that retail providers of Internet access service offered that information service to the public. The only distinction of note was under the Commission's *Computer Inquiry* rules, which required common carriers that were also providing information services to offer the transmission component of the information service as a separate, tariffed telecommunications service. But again, this requirement had no effect on the classification of retail Internet access service as an information service.

In the meantime, during the waning days of the Clinton Administration in 2000, the Commission initiated a Notice of Inquiry (NOI) to examine formalizing the regulatory classification of cable modem services as information services.[787] As a result of the *Cable Modem NOI,* on March 14, 2002, the Commission issued a declaratory ruling classifying cable modem service as an information service.[788] In the Commission's *Cable Modem Declaratory Ruling,* it pointed out that "[t]o date ... the Commission has declined to determine a regulatory classification for, or to regulate, cable modem service on an industry-wide basis."[789] Only one month earlier, on February 14, 2002, in its Notice of Proposed Rulemaking[790] regarding the classification of broadband Internet access services provided over wireline facilities, the Commission underscored its view that information services integrated with telecommunications services cannot simultaneously be deemed to contain a telecommunications service, even though the combined offering has telecommunications components.

On June 27,2005, the Supreme Court upheld the Commission's determination that cable modem services should be classified as information services.[791] The Court, in upholding the Commission's *Cable Modem Order,* explained the Commission's historical regulatory treatment of "enhanced" or "information" services:

> By contrast to basic service, the Commission decided not to subject providers of enhanced service, *even enhanced service offered **via** transmission wires,* to Title II common-carrier regulation. The Commission explained that it was unwise to subject enhanced service to common-carrier regulation given the "fast-moving, competitive market" in which they were offered.[792]

Subsequent to the Supreme Court upholding the Commission's classification of cable modem service as an information service in its *Brand X* decision, the Commission *without dissent* issued a series of orders classifying all broadband services as information services: wireline (2005)[793], powerline (2006)[794] * and wireless (2007).[795] Consistent with the Court's characterization, the Commission made these classifications to catch up to market developments, to treat similar services alike and to provide certainty to those entities provisioning broadband services, or contemplating doing so. Prior to these rulings, however, such services were never classified as telecommunications services under Title II.

Again, I thank you for providing the opportunity to testify before your Committee and to provide this analysis regarding the regulatory classification of broadband Internet access services. I look forward to working with you and your colleagues as we continue to find ways to encourage broadband deployment and adoption throughout our nation.

Sincerely,

Robert M. McDowell

cc: The Honorable Joe Barton
The Honorable Rick Boucher The
Honorable Cliff Steams

APPROVING IN PART, CONCURRING IN PART STATEMENT OF COMMISSIONER MIGNON L. CLYBURN

Re: *Preserving the Open Internet*, GN Docket No. 09-191, *Broadband Industry Practices,*
WC Docket No. 07-52.

A few weeks ago, I discussed the importance of collaboration in tackling the important, yet difficult policy issues before us today. I want to thank the thousands of stakeholders who engaged with us over the past 16 months in crafting a framework that gives both broadband providers and consumers clear guidance about what provider behavior is and is not acceptable. It was a result of all of your engagement—from the filings you made to the many meetings we had—that we have been able to get to this point today. Your dedication to the process and that of those whom you represent should be commended.

Of course, as we all know, compromises typically must be made as many different interests collaborate on critical and significant issues. As a result of such compromise, it is often the case that one cannot be completely satisfied with the result. Nonetheless, it is my belief that we have made real progress in this proceeding, and through this Order, we are ensuring that the Internet will remain open for the benefit of many consumers. After all, *they* are the ultimate beneficiaries of an open Internet.

Left to my own devices, there are several issues I would have tackled differently. As such, I am approving in part and concurring in part to today's Order. While I appreciate the Chairman's recognition of some of my concerns, and the adjustments made in the Order to allay those concerns, there are several areas in the Order I would have strengthened so that more consumers would benefit from the protections we are adopting.

First, I would have extended all of the fixed rules to mobile, so that those consumers who heavily or exclusively rely upon mobile broadband would be fully protected. There is evidence in our record that some communities, namely African American and Hispanic, use and rely upon mobile Internet access much more than other socio-economic groups. While this Order does not go as far as I would like in protecting mobile consumers, I am pleased that it is quite clear that we are not pre-approving any actions by mobile providers that would violate the fixed rules and the general principles of Internet openness. Moreover, the Order provides for the ongoing monitoring of the mobile broadband marketplace, including the Commission's intention to create an Open Internet Advisory Committee. That body's specific mission will be to assess and report to the Commission new developments and concerns in the mobile broadband industry. I expect that the Committee will closely observe the effects disparate rules for fixed and mobile providers will have on consumers who have chosen to cut the broadband cord and the effects on intermodal competition. To that end, the Commission will stand ready to protect mobile consumers from any actions by providers that are inconsistent with an open Internet.

Second, I would have prohibited pay for priority arrangements altogether. The Order stresses the various harmful effects of these arrangements, including the serious threat to innovation on the Internet. I believe that prohibiting such arrangements would be more appropriate based on the evidence before us. Nevertheless, should providers enter such arrangements, and they are subsequently challenged at the Commission, providers will have to demonstrate that the pay for priority arrangement is not harmful and is consistent with the public interest.

Third, an open Internet should be available to *all* end users—residential, enterprise, for-profit, or not. This Order goes a long way toward protecting an open Internet for residents, small businesses, schools, libraries, patrons of coffee shops, bookstores, and the like, but I worry that those who may not fit into these categories will have to negotiate for access to the open Internet, and they may be denied such access. We should carefully monitor whether an open Internet truly is available to *all* end users and correct course, if needed. I also hope that the aforementioned Open Internet Advisory Committee can track any harmful effects for those end users who do not currently qualify for the protections adopted today and recommend Commission action as necessary.

Finally, earlier this year I stated my preference for the Commission's legal authority over broadband Internet access service. While the route taken here is not the one I originally preferred, I believe that it is appropriate for the Commission to act to protect an open Internet. I know there will be many lawyers studying the legal authority cited in this Order in the weeks, months and perhaps years ahead, and judicial review ultimately will determine the fate of this Order. I sincerely hope that the Commission's authority to protect consumers' access to an open Internet is upheld.

Today, the Internet is as critical to the nation for communicating as our legacy telephone, broadcast, and mobile phone systems. As described more fully in the Order, without an open Internet, consumers will have fewer choices and opportunities, which has the potential to impact many aspects of their lives—their ability to obtain an education, telecommute, look for a job, search information online, shop, make investment decisions, communicate with friends, family and colleagues, obtain news, and I could go on and on. Accordingly, I believe that it is necessary and appropriate that broadband providers operate pursuant to a legal and policy framework that ensures the Internet remains open under the Commission's watchful eye.

DISSENTING STATEMENT OF COMMISSIONER MEREDITH ATTWELL BAKER

Re: *Preserving the Open Internet,* GN Docket No. 09-191, *Broadband Industry Practices,* WC Docket No. 07-52

Preserving the open Internet is non-negotiable: it is a bedrock principle shared by all in the Internet economy, a building block on which we can all agree. And, the Internet is open today. The evidentiary record in our proceeding has reaffirmed that government action is not necessary to preserve it. Yet the majority acts, and acts decisively, to adopt Net Neutrality rules, imposing the heavy hand of government into how broadband networks will be managed and operated. The data most certainly does not drive us to this result. In the final analysis, the Commission intervenes to regulate the Internet because it wants to, not because it needs to.

I cannot support this decision. It is not a consumer-driven or engineering-focused decision. It is not motivated by a tangible competitive harm or market failure. The majority bypasses a market power analysis altogether, and acts on speculative harms alone. The majority is unable to identify a single ongoing practice of a single broadband provider that it finds problematic upon which to base this action. In the end, the Internet will be no more open tomorrow than it is today.

Further, the majority regulates an entire sector of the Internet without any legitimate legal authority to do so. The D.C. Circuit only months ago rejected our attempt to enforce Net Neutrality principles.[796] The Commission will return to court with the same basic infirmities: no explicit statutory authority to support its action, and a legal theory that would give the Commission an unbounded right to adopt any policies it desires to promote its particular vision of the Internet.

The majority does all of this without any apparent appreciation of the regulatory costs and distortive effect of government micromanagement of broadband networks. Did the Commission kill the future of the Internet today? Of course not. But, in this dynamic industry, the majority also has no rational means by which to estimate the real damage it does to the future development of business models, network management techniques, and core networks. The Commission puts its thumb on the scale as to where innovation in the Internet economy will be focused, and how future networks will be financed. The Order repeatedly expresses concerns about the significant consequences to Internet edge companies if their incentive to innovate, invest, and compete is chilled. The majority ignores the same grave consequences of government action chilling the networks' analogous incentives to innovate, invest, and compete. It is regrettable the majority did not take a more holistic view of the Internet economy.

I keep returning to what should be a threshold question: why do we intervene in the one sector of the economy that is working so well to create high-paying jobs, untold consumer choice, and entrepreneurial opportunity? Pick any statistic, the story is one of success.

Our competition-focused regulatory approach has attracted over half a trillion dollars to build network infrastructure this decade.[797] Billions more have been invested in devices and applications that ride on those networks. Tablets and smartphones will fill stockings this holiday season, straining the capacity of even the most advanced networks. Over 95 percent of American households have access to a robust terrestrial broadband offering.[798] Eighty percent of those households have choice of at least two providers.[799] This time next year, the continued deployment of 4G wireless offerings promise even greater broadband competition and amazing new functionalities. Each day, consumers benefit from new services, faster connections, and the latest and greatest applications. The Commission's own surveys reveal that 93 percent of broadband subscribers are happy with their service.[800]

The facts, the law, and the policy cannot support this decision. So again, why do we act? The only plausible reason left is to deliver on one of the President's campaign promises. I must respectfully dissent.

I have seven principal objections to this decision. First, the factual record does not support government intervention. Second, the majority's claim that consumers will benefit from this government overreach is unsupported and deeply flawed. Third, the majority's focus on preserving network operators' current conditions will distort tomorrow's Internet. Fourth, the majority puts the Commission in the unworkable role of Internet referee. Fifth, the majority fails to marshal a sustainable legal foundation. Sixth, the majority's decision to act a legislator, not regulator, is a mistake that may undermine our agency's mission. And, lastly, opportunity cost. By that I mean, we have squandered months on this effort, diverting resources and political capital away from real problems that lie within our core competencies, like universal service and spectrum reform.

The Importance of Regulatory Certainty

Before I address those concerns directly, I would like to touch on the question of regulatory certainty. The Net Neutrality and the Title II proceedings have been an economic drag on operators for over a year. While Net Neutrality has been bantered about as a policy issue since at least 2002, it was not until the Title II debate this Spring that this uncertainty triggered considerable real world consequences.[801] It has affected jobs, investment, and innovation. I empathize with businesses that desperately need certainty to help jump start efforts to invest and recover economically. It was our stable regulatory foundation that gave investors and innovators the confidence to pump billions into the Internet economy for much of the last decade, and I share the desire to find a new stable footing to move forward.

I object, however, to the majority suggesting that its action is premised on providing regulatory certainty.[802] At best, the majority solves a problem of its own making. They initiated the immediate proceeding and the highly controversial Title II docket in June, igniting a crisis across much of the industry and investment community. By some accounts, the majority has used this self-generated uncertainty as leverage in the negotiations leading up to this decision, a tactic I have reservations about the government using to manufacture support. I also have some apprehension that our legally precarious action today cannot provide the certainty promised, and that our decision may unfortunately add to the uncertainty. By avoiding definitions of key terms, questioning but not banning practices, couching decisions as "at this time" repeatedly, and inviting both case-by-case complaints and declaratory rulings, this action—in too many ways—is a first step, not a last step.[803]

There is no Factual Basis to Support Government Intervention

Five years ago, in adopting the Internet Policy Statement, FCC Chairman Kevin Martin noted that "competition has ensured consumers have the[] rights [outlined in the Policy Statement] to date, and I remain confident that it will continue to do so."[804] It has. The Federal Trade Commission ("FTC") in its 2007 Net Neutrality report concluded that there was "no significant market failure of demonstrated consumer harm" to support Net Neutrality.[805] Our review revealed the same. Competition and consumer demand have ensured that the Internet remains open, and the majority offers no record evidence to suggest otherwise. The FTC accurately found that consumers "have a powerful collective voice [and] a strong preference for the current open access to Internet content and applications."[806]

The majority has resorted to metaphor: there are cracks in the infrastructure. But, our record does not support a conclusion of any structural failing. At best, there is a burned-out bulb in the Christmas lights. We endeavor to replace the entire electrical system to fix it. There is no systemic problem—no crisis of magnitude—to justify the majority's overreach.

The majority's repeated fallback is that network operators have incentives to act badly. Throughout the decision, the majority presumes a malign intent on the part of broadband providers for which there is no factual foundation. The language is consistently hypothetical—the word "could" alone appears over 60 times. The majority's rationale is flatly inconsistent with a decade of actual industry practice, which is devoid of any such global misconduct. The Order also fails to explain why other parts of the Internet community do not have similar incentives, or how such incentives alone could justify such sweeping action.

If the incentives and ability for misconduct are so strong, one would assume the evidentiary record would include widespread examples of anti-competitive conduct resulting in consumer harm. There is no such evidence. The Order provides only the same handful of dated examples of past conduct. There is no attempt to portray any of those isolated incidents as representative of bigger issues, and, tellingly, no examples of any ongoing misconduct are offered. The courts have clearly stated that rules cannot be based on claims that would "ameliorate[] a real industry problem" where an agency "cite[es] no evidence [of] an industry problem."[807]

From an economist's perspective, incentives alone are an inadequate basis to support this decision. Drs. Sidak and Teece explain that, "there is no empirical evidence or support in economic theory that such incentives exist or are sufficiently strong as to outweigh countervailing incentives."[808] The majority ignores those countervailing incentives as well as the empirical evidence on the record, relying only on speculative harms. They do not find market power on the part of network operators, asserting no need to do so. The majority sidesteps our own analysis that demonstrates that competition is strong and growing. Almost two-thirds of broadband customers find switching to be easy, and over a third of households have switched in the past three years.[809]

Given the nonexistent factual record of consumer harm, the majority is left to grandiose declarations about the Internet as an "indispensable platform supporting our nation's economy and civic life" to mask the clear deficiencies in its analysis. In doing so, they ignore the FTC's Net Neutrality Report's caution that regulators "should be wary of enacting regulation solely to prevent prospective harm."[810] The FTC was especially concerned with "adverse effects on consumer welfare" and "product and service innovation."[811] I share the FTC's concerns. By regulating in anticipation of speculative harms, the majority cannot evaluate properly the regulatory costs of its actions, or target its actions to diminish any unintended consequences. The Commission has failed to take the approach I would have preferred: to focus any action on narrowly tailored solutions to address documented industry-wide abuses.

Consumers Will Not Benefit From Net Neutrality

The majority repeatedly couches this as a pro-consumer or consumer-driven approach. They try to frame this as big business gatekeeper versus the consumer. This contention cannot withstand scrutiny. Upon closer inspection, the Order is focused on promoting the edge—Internet applications and services—over networks and consumers.

In the short-term, consumers will receive the same broadband service they do today and benefit from the same open Internet. In the mid- and long-term, consumers may well be worse off as government micromanagement will distort the future development of broadband networks and services. Deployment efforts to ensure that all Americans have access to broadband will be put at risk. Broadband adoption efforts to attract the third of American households that do not subscribe will be challenged. Affordability concerns will be magnified by forcing more of the cost of network investment onto consumers. And both consumers and entrepreneurs will be adversely affected if network upgrades and improvements are delayed or forgone, frustrating the ability to create or to use the next great application or service. Forgive me if I do not view these potential developments as pro-consumer.

The Order's analysis of the new rules also contradicts any declared consumer focus. With respect to paid prioritization, the majority concludes that prioritization arrangements with consumers "would be unlikely to violate" the nondiscrimination requirement. In stark contrast, prioritization arrangements with third party Internet companies "would raise significant cause for concern." In other words, the majority suggests that charging end-user customers is fine, but charging Internet companies may be problematic. While the majority is careful not to outlaw charging Internet companies, the apparent discouragement of such practices is misplaced. It sweeps too broadly and may foreclose current and future developments that could be pro-competitive and pro-consumer. It also may create workability issues under which a future quality-of-service commitment to the end-user consumer cannot be satisfied without a corresponding business relationship with the edge company. Economic theory is clear that there is potential value in two-sided markets, which could promote innovative business models and services, and reduce the costs of service to end-users, potentially increasing broadband adoption.[812] By seeking to carve out application providers from future compensation models, the practical effect of this decision may be that the bulk of the costs of building out next-generation networks—estimated to be $182 billion by 2015—will be borne by consumers.[812]

A similar preference for edge companies over consumers is reflected in the majority's approach to transparency.[814] Transparency should be about giving consumers the basic tools to make an informed decision. We should be working across the Internet economy towards standardized disclosures to inform consumer choice, and shed sunlight—both good and bad—on practices of networks, applications, and devices. That is not the approach the majority takes. The language in the Order is exceedingly prescriptive, and the all-encompassing approach seemingly prejudices Commission consideration of these matters in pending proceedings.[815], the majority seeks to micromanage how information is conveyed to broadband consumers about their service. In my experience, government involvement in consumer disclosures is not a recipe for clarity. By doing so, the Order sets up a transparency regime that may be so detailed and engineering-focused, only Internet companies and special interest groups could find them useful. The average consumer will be no better off.

The majority's repeated spotlight on protecting Internet companies represents an apparent preference for the Internet edge over networks and consumers.[816] This is a fatal error, because no choice was necessary. In this instance, having your cake and eating it too was an actual option. The Commission should have sought to maintain an environment in which companies across the Internet economy continue to have the incentives to invest and innovate. In the majority's quest to address the unsubstantiated allegation that broadband providers may try to pick winners and losers, the government has picked its own winners. By promoting the edge over networks, we render the future development of networks a secondary matter. This is the antithesis of the virtuous cycle of Internet investment the majority espouses.

The Order May Inhibit the Development of Tomorrow's Internet

One of my primary misgivings with this Order is that it fails to confront in a forthright manner the substantial risk that this action may distort the future of the Internet. The Order's focus is on maintaining the "status quo" and "current practices" in how networks are managed and operated. Given the dynamic nature of the Internet, this is the wrong objective. The Internet is not a mature market. There continues to be a great amount of experimentation in business models, business relationships, customer usage patterns and expectations. The majority's approach will inhibit the ability of networks to freely evolve and experiment, and to seek out the differentiation that breeds opportunity and consumer choice. The threat of government censure will unmistakably chill new developments, including those that would be pro-consumer and pro-competition. Innovate at your own risk is the wrong message to send.

The stakes are heightened because networks cannot stand still. Estimates project that by 2014 the Internet will be four times the size it was last year, and mobile data will double each and every year.[817] The growing prevalence of real-time applications and bandwidth-intensive applications like HD television will only intensify the challenges faced by network operators. CITI estimates that the bulk of the $182 billion to be invested in the next five years will be focused on "increasing broadband capacity and speed in currently served areas."[818] The capacity required to meet the escalating demands of existing users—let alone new users—will strain the resources of all operators, and test network management practices.

To give some context to the challenge, I pose this basic question: would you be happy to have your Internet connection (*e.g.*, speed, latency, and features) from 2005? I know I would not. When we look back in 2015, how will we answer that question about today? How much of the 2010 network did we just lock in for our future selves? There are too many variables for us to make a reliable prediction, which underscores that the Commission should act with more humility and in much more targeted ways when faced with industry shaping decisions.

The measuring stick for if, and how far, we have fallen behind will increasingly be networks overseas. The majority has taken a far more interventionist approach to Net Neutrality than other global regulators. The European Commission's Neelie Kroes has consistently called on regulators to "avoid over-hasty regulatory intervention," and to steer clear of "unnecessary measures which may hinder new efficient business models from emerging."[819] As a result, operators overseas from Europe and Asia – free from prescriptive rules and ominous warnings – will be the ones innovating, and creating value for consumers and businesses. As a result, the United States may cede its role as experimenter, innovator, and market leader in Internet networks and technologies. The economic implications of that for this nation could be stark for our overall global competitiveness and for job creation.

The majority also fails to account properly for a prominent Wall Street analyst's recent observation that "[b]uilding networks is hard. Earning a return on them is even harder."[820] By the majority's action, the Commission may have further increased the degree of difficulty. I am troubled by the negative treatment so many vital components of our modern broadband networks receive in this Order. We have turned paid prioritization into a dirty word, a dangerous tool. To me, it is about quality of service, and optimizing services for real-time applications. I reject that such measures are anti-competitive on their face. In fact, 4G wireless networks have prioritization built into the standard to provide optimized service across classes of offerings.[821] The record contains evidence of other services and offerings under which prioritization is offered today in a pro-consumer, pro-competitive manner, typically in commercial settings.

Specialized services—a term the Commission created in this docket—receives no better handling. Specialized services have been one of the primary drivers of greater voice and video competition in the United States. They have also been fundamental in justifying the huge cost necessary to build-out today's Internet, and will be central to the analysis in raising additional risk capital to improve existing networks and deploy new networks. Relatedly, specialized services have also helped to offset the costs of broadband to consumers. The Commission should be promoting specialized services to help spark greater broadband deployment.

Network management is similarly characterized as a potential loophole for misconduct, not an engineering marvel that enables services to operate, mitigate congestion, thwart threats both domestic and foreign, and block unwanted materials. These are not dumb pipes for which network management is used for only nefarious purposes.

I do not think the majority believes any of these services or functionalities to be inherently problematic, but the overwhelming focus on the potential for wrongdoing is misplaced. It is fair to highlight potential areas of concerns, but only in the context of a more balanced and neutral presentation that outlines the different dimensions of today and tomorrow's networks more objectively. I care about how these issues are presented because even if the rules are silent about many of these issues, the text and tone of the Order will inform operators' assessment of the potential risks of governmental rebuke in determining whether to approve an engineer's proposal for a new approach, a new practice, or a new business model to serve consumers better.

The Commission is Miscast as the Internet's Referee

The genius of the Internet is that there is no central command, no unitary authority to dictate how innovation is to occur. No one must ask for permission. The majority has altered fundamentally that winning formula, forcing the Commission into the role of judging how the Internet and broadband networks will evolve. By adopting rules that will require significant interpretation, by creating new undefined terms, and by muddling its analysis with warnings and cautionary notes, the majority has ensured that new innovation and new practices will be subject to its approval, and the corresponding delay and uncertainty. As networks, devices, and applications continue to evolve and converge, the majority's artificial line-drawing of imposing regulatory costs only on networks will necessarily plunge this agency into a definitional quagmire. As it does, I fear the government will assume too prominent a role in shaping tomorrow's Internet.

I have related administrative concerns with our ability to administer the regime established today.[822] The majority has now given the Commission a significant responsibility to manage a space as dynamic as the Internet. Government will be hard pressed to manage the next-generation of the Internet as well as competition and consumer demand has done for the previous generations. We will need to address issues that arise in a timely, thoughtful, and technical manner. Non-governmental groups like the Broadband Internet Technical Advisory Group (BITAG) should be the primary forum for disputes, and the Commission would be wise to rely on such expert resources.[823] These groups have the ability to craft engineering-based solutions in a more flexible, responsive, and efficient manner.

The Commission Lacks Authority to Adopt Net Neutrality Rules

"The FCC, like other federal agencies, 'literally has no power to act . . . unless and until Congress confers power upon it.'"[824] The Supreme Court has cautioned that "the Commission's estimations of desirable policy cannot alter the meaning of the federal Communications Act."[825] Congress has never given the Commission authority to regulate Internet network management, a fact validated by the court in *Comcast.* Lacking any statutory authority to act in this area, the Commission's effort to establish Net Neutrality rules should have been a non-starter.[826] To paraphrase the D.C. Circuit, I "find nothing in the statute, its legislative history, the applicable case law, or agency practice indicating that Congress meant to provide the sweeping authority the FCC now claims…the agency's strained and implausible interpretations of the definitional provisions … do not lend credence to its position."[827]

The majority, however, tries the everything-but-the-kitchen-sink defense – 24 different claimed statutory bases. The majority elects sheer quantity to make up for quality, and, in doing so, contorts the letter and spirit of the Act to try to justify rules adopted in a result-orientated process. The bulk of the legal support is based on ancillary authority grounds. The majority has swapped in a different set of statutory provisions from the ones the *Comcast* court rejected, but these provisions share the same inherent infirmity. The courts have long required any regulation to be "reasonably ancillary to the effective performance of the Commission's various responsibilities."[828] Ancillary authority has developed as a gap filler to provide the Commission with the tools to conduct the tasks explicitly directed by Congress. The majority's intent here is to regulate broadband platforms, not protect traditional voice, video, broadcast or audio services. The references to direct authority are a pretext to try to aggregate the desired authority, which would be far greater than any gap filling exercise. In the end, these ancillary authority claims are indistinguishable from the ones rejected by the court in *Comcast.*

I will, therefore, focus on section 706(a), which receives the bulk of the majority's analysis. I am not persuaded by the majority's attempt to twist a 14-year old deregulatory policy statement into a grant of direct authority. The majority's view of section 706(a) is inconsistent with a plain reading of the statute, sound notions of statutory interpretation, and over a decade of consistent Commission and judicial precedent.

As the Commission has explained repeatedly, section 706(a) "gives this Commission an affirmative obligation to encourage the deployment of advanced services, relying on our authority established elsewhere in the Act."[829] Our decisions are "informed" by section 706.[830] It is a guidepost as to how to use our statutorily mandated responsibilities. The Commission held long ago that the "most logical statutory interpretation is that section 706 does not constitute an independent grant of authority."[831] And that is precisely how the Commission has successfully incorporated section 706 into its decision-making for over a decade. The Commission has repeatedly explained that "the directives of section 706 require that we ensure that our broadband policies promote infrastructure investment, consistent with our other obligations under the Act."[832]

The majority effectively attempts to rewrite this straightforward provision and its clear-cut history. This is ultimately an unsuccessful gamble. The core of the majority's analysis is its mischaracterization of the 1998 *Advanced Services Order*. Under the majority's view, the Commission has only interpreted a single clause from section 706(a)—regulatory forbearance—not the section as a whole.[833] The Commission raised this identical argument to the *Comcast* court, and it was appropriately rejected.[834] In June, subsequent to the *Comcast* decision, in the Title II proceeding, the Commission seemingly abandoned this theory by asking if it should "change[] its conclusion that section 706(a) is not an independent grant of authority."[835] In doing so, the Commission suggested no caveat or limitation tied to the forbearance authority. The court this April and the agency this June got it right: the Commission should not deviate from its historic understanding of section 706(a) as a policy statement.[836] Pursuing this strained reading of section 706(a) to serve as the cornerstone of the majority's legal authority to regulate the Internet is unsound.

Even if section 706 were a grant of authority, that provision could not support today's prescriptive and investment-chilling action that erects, not removes, barriers to broadband network infrastructure investment. The text of section 706(a) is clear: it is about "encourag[ing]" broadband "deployment," with clear deregulatory focus on "remov[ing] barriers to infrastructure investment."[837] The D.C. Circuit has held "section 706(a) identifies one of the Act's goals namely, removing barriers to infrastructure investment."[838] The Commission itself has repeatedly held the same.[839] Section 706 is about deployment of broadband network infrastructure, and the Commission has no authority to erect obstacles in the name of removing them. The majority attempts to muddle the issue, referring to "overall investment in Internet infrastructure." It strains all credibility to contend that imposing Net Neutrality obligations would do anything to promote broadband deployment.[840] Investment in other parts of the Internet—in applications and devices—is not relevant to a section 706 analysis.

By reading out of the provision any deregulatory focus, the explicit broadband deployment purpose, and the removal of barrier limitation, the Commission has given itself plenary authority to regulate the Internet. Anything that promotes the "virtuous cycle" in the Internet ecosystem could be regulated under this analysis. This is my biggest concern with the majority's section 706(a) analysis. In essence, the majority has replaced an unbounded ancillary authority rejected by the *Comcast* court with an equally unbounded direct authority under section 706(a).

The majority is quite candid that this was its intent: it sought a power as broad as its pre-*Comcast* understanding of its ancillary authority. The Order explains that "our authority under Section 706(a) is generally consistent with... ancillary jurisdiction before the *Comcast* decision." The *Comcast* court had significant concerns with the Commission's legal theories under which "if accepted it would virtually free the Commission from its congressional tether."[841] The same fundamental concern applies here with equal force: trading one unlimited power for another is far from comforting to me, or the courts. I also have to believe a court will be skeptical of the timing and manner in which the majority has discovered section 706(a) to be a superpower, unlocked only after an adverse court opinion and political pressure to find some legal foundation to justify Net Neutrality rules.

To that end, it is also instructive where in the Act section 706 was located. Congress placed this provision – the provision the majority would make the centerpiece of all broadband and Internet regulation going forward – in a footnote to a non-substantive regulatory requirement.[842] I am "confident that Congress could not have intended to delegate a decision of such economic and political significance to an agency in so cryptic a fashion."[843] I agree with the Supreme Court's analysis that "we must be guided to a degree by common sense as to the manner in which Congress is likely to delegate a policy decision of such economic and political magnitude to an administrative agency."[844] The Commission lacks authority to adopt Net Neutrality rules under any of the legal theories put forth in the Order.

The Commission Acts Improperly as a Quasi-Legislative Body

The Commission adopts rules that are almost word-for-word a draft bill under consideration in Congress. We are a creature of Congress, not Congress itself. Using a legislative proposal to base our action underscores that the majority acts beyond the appropriate role of an independent agency. The majority does what Congress could not, or would not do. They adopt legislation and the implementing order all in one step. By definition, the majority does much more than the proposed draft bill by exercising its own discretion and judgment. The draft bill would have given the Commission very specific responsibilities and powers. In contrast, by doing it themselves, the majority has created a sweeping Internet policy without any jurisdictional limits. When the Federal Communications Commission feels compelled to explicitly "decline to apply our rules directly to coffee shops, bookstores, [and] airlines," it illustrates the broad scope of these rules, and the lack of any ascertainable outer limits to our claimed authority.

By this action, the majority has blurred the line between legislator and regulator. In doing so, this decision raises broader concerns about our agency's institutional credibility. The long-term concern is that a pattern of action to seek out perceived harms beyond our core competencies may erode the trust in the Commission to be an expert agency on those things for which Congress has given us clear statutorily mandated responsibilities. This is not meant to be alarmist: the vast majority of our portfolio is done on a consensus and bipartisan basis well within our delegated authority. The bad news is that big decisions garner far more attention, and can affect our standing in a disproportionate manner. Institutionally, we must resist the desire to stretch our authority beyond its breaking point to capture some real or perceived concern. Here, given the lack of any record evidence of an immediate crisis to resolve, the appropriate approach should have been to allow Congress to deliberate on the proper means to address network management concerns. The Supreme Court has stressed that if a statute "falls short of providing [authority for an agency to adopt] safeguards desirable or necessary to protect the public interest, that is a problem for Congress, and not the [agency] or the courts, to address."[845]

When the Commission makes political decisions and takes actions best left to elected officials, our proceedings inevitably turn more partisan and more controversial. This agency lacks the institutional capability of handling divisive issues of this import. Indeed, issues of this magnitude, with such significant long-term consequences, are decisions that should be left to Congress. That is particularly true here given the clear interest of Congress in the subject matter. Over 300 members of Congress have expressed concern with the Commission's approach to regulating the Internet,[846] and a vocal minority has offered its support for the majority's approach.[847] Last week, 29 U.S. Senators "strongly urge[d the Commission] to abandon [its] decision to impose new restrictions on" broadband services.[848] In their view, "this is an unjustified and unnecessary expansion of government control," and the resulting "cost of th[is] action will be measured in investment foregone, innovation stifled, and most importantly, jobs lost."[849] The incoming leadership of the House Energy and Commerce Committee last week wrote noting that this "is likely the most controversial item the FCC has had before it in at least a decade. It holds huge implications for the future of the Internet, investment, innovation, and jobs."[850] Taken as a whole, the only appropriate course of action was to defer to Congress.

The Commission Has Strayed from a Pro-Jobs Consensus Agenda

Regrettably, this proceeding has led me to question our priorities. The Commission repeatedly moved Net Neutrality to the top of our to-do list, an issue that is the cause célèbre of the institutional left. But, from a legal and factual perspective, it remains a solution in search of a problem. In contrast, action languishes in other areas where there is bipartisan support and objective evidence of real problems necessitating prompt government action. The Commission unanimously adopted a *Joint Statement on Broadband* this Spring that called for action on the nation's core communications challenges: broadband deployment and adoption; spectrum reform; universal service and intercarrier compensation reform; and a public safety network.[851] Our focus belongs on that agenda, an actual pro-growth, pro-jobs game plan focused appropriately on infrastructure and private investment as recommended by the National Broadband Plan.

Starting today, we should redouble our efforts to craft policies to create the incentives and regulatory environment necessary to attract the billions in risk capital necessary to expand and improve our broadband infrastructure. That capital is the critical first step in the formation of new high-paying jobs laying the fiber and building the towers. Central to those policies should be spectrum reform. The majority's concerns about potential gatekeepers would be best addressed by building more roads: 4G and next generation wireless offerings can be the third, fourth, fifth, and sixth broadband choice for consumers. That is why a spectrum policy focused on 4G is critical, and the need for a clear roadmap to industry about future spectrum availability is paramount to help enable greater broadband competition and consumer choice.

I fear that today's action is not the end of this debate because of its significant consequences for the Internet, for the jurisdictional authority of this agency, and for the proper role of the FCC. This debate may well move to different fora, but I fear it will continue to take up too much of the oxygen in our community.

That said, I remain always the optimist. When we work together, there is so much good we can do. I hope the New Year brings a fresh perspective on our nation's communications challenges and a renewed focus on working collaboratively together.

End Notes

[1] National Broadband Plan at xi, 3–5.

[2] In this Order we use "broadband" and "broadband Internet access service" interchangeably, and "broadband provider" and "broadband Internet access provider" interchangeably. "End user" refers to any individual or entity that uses a broadband Internet access service; we sometimes use "subscriber" or "consumer" to refer to those end users that subscribe to a particular broadband Internet access service. *Cf. infra* note 172 (defining "consumer" and "person"). We use "edge provider" to refer to content, application, service, and device providers, because they generally operate at the edge rather than the core of the network. These terms are not mutually exclusive. *See infra* para. 0.

[3] *See Appropriate Framework for Broadband Access to the Internet Over Wireline Facilities et al.*, Policy Statement, 20 FCC Rcd 14986 (2005) (*Internet Policy Statement*); *SBC Commc'ns, Inc. and AT&T Corp. Applications for Approval of Transfer of Control*, Memorandum Opinion and Order, 20 FCC Rcd 18290, 18392, para. 211 (2005); *Verizon Commc'ns Inc. and MCI, Inc. Applications for Approval of Transfer of Control*, Memorandum Opinion and Order, 20 FCC Rcd 18433, 18537, para. 221 (2005); *AT&T Inc. and BellSouth Corp. Application for Transfer of Control*, Memorandum Opinion and Order, 22 FCC Rcd 5662, 5663, para. 2 (2007).

[4] *Service Rules for the 698–746, 747–762 and 777–792 MHz Bands et al.*, Second Report and Order, 22 FCC Rcd 15289 (2007) (*700 MHz Second Report and Order*); 47 C.F.R. § 27.16.

[5] *Broadband Industry Practices*, Notice of Inquiry, 22 FCC Rcd 7894, 7896, para. 8 (2007).

[6] *See Preserving the Open Internet et al.*, Notice of Proposed Rulemaking, 24 FCC Rcd 13064, 13067–68, paras. 10, 16 (2009) (*Open Internet NPRM*).

[7] *Id.* at 13065, 13069–71, paras. 3, 17–23.

[8] *Id.* at 13084, 13087–97, paras. 50, 57–80.

[9] *Id.* at 13068, 13100–115, paras. 16, 88–141. The *Open Internet NPRM* recast the *Internet Policy Statement* principles as rules rather than consumer entitlements, but did not change the fact that protecting and empowering end users is a central purpose of open Internet protections.

[10] *See, e.g.*, Google Comments at i–ii; Netflix Comments at 3–7; Skype Comments at 1–5; Vonage Comments at 1–10; Institute for Policy Integrity (IPI) Reply at 1–7.

[11] *See, e.g.*, Comcast Comments at 27–29; Time Warner Cable (TWC) Comments at 1–2; AT&T Reply at 1–5; Verizon Reply at 1–8.

[12] Letter from Wireline Competition Bureau, FCC, to Marlene Dortch, Secretary, FCC (filed Dec. 10, 2010) (WCB Letter 12/10/10), Attach. at 1–26, Timothy F. Bresnahan & M. Trajtenberg, *General Purpose Technologies: Engines of Growth'?*, 65 J. OF ECONOMETRICS 83–108 (1995); WCB Letter 12/10/10, Attach. at 156–159, RICHARD G. LIPSEY ET AL., ECONOMIC TRANSFORMATIONS: GENERAL PURPOSE TECHNOLOGIES AND LONG TERM ECONOMIC GROWTH 132 (2005); *see also* Google Comments at 15; Free Press PN Reply at 9.

[13] The Internet's openness is supported by an "end-to-end" network architecture that was formulated and debated in standard-setting organizations and foundational documents. *See, e.g.*, WCB Letter 12/10/10, Attach. at 17–29, Vinton G. Cerf & Robert E. Kahn, *A Protocol for Packet Network Interconnection*, COM-22 *IEEE TRANSACTIONS OF COMMC'NS TECH. 637–48* (1974); WCB Letter 12/10/10, Attach. at 30–39, J.H. Saltzer et al., *End to End Arguments in System Design*, Second Int'l Conf. on Distributed Computing Systems, 509–12 (1981); WCB Letter 12/10/10, Attach. at 49–55, B. Carpenter, Internet Engineering Task Force ("IETF"), *Architectural Principles of the Internet*, RFC 1958, 1–8 (June 1996), www.ietf.org/rfc/rfc1958.txt; Lawrence Roberts, *Multiple Computer Networks and Intercomputer Communication*, ACM Symposium on Operation System Principles (1967). Under the end-to-end principle, devices in the middle of the network are not optimized for the handling of any particular application, while devices at network endpoints perform the functions necessary to support networked applications and services. *See generally* WCB Letter 12/10/10, Attach. at 40–48, J. Kempf & R. Austein, IETF, *The Rise of the Middle and the Future of End-to-End: Reflections on the Evolution of the Internet Architecture*, RFC 3724, 1–14 (March 2004), ftp://ftp.rfc-editor.org/in-notes/rfc3724.txt.

[14] *See* Google Comments at 13 ("[T]he end-to-end, open architectural principles underlying the Internet are its true genius, and the source of its unparalleled power."); Clearwire Comments at 3; CDT Comments at 7; Free Press Comments at 44; Open Internet Coalition (OIC) Comments at i; Vonage Comments at 2, 18.

[15] *See* WCB Letter 12/10/10, Attach. at 27–29, TIM BERNERS-LEE, WEAVING THE WEB 16 (2000).

[16] *See, e.g.*, Google Comments at 5–7; OIC Comments at i, 3–12; Vonage Comments at 4; XO Comments at 13–14; *see also* National Broadband Plan at 284 ("Broadband and the Internet make it possible for small businesses to reach new markets and improve their business processes.").

[17] Business-to-consumer e-commerce was estimated to total $135 billion in 2009. *See* WCB Letter 12/10/10, Attach. at 81–180, Robert D. Atkinson et al., *The Internet Economy 25 Years After .com*, INFO. TECH. & INNOVATION FOUND., at 24 (March 2010), *available at* www.itif.org/files/2010-25-years.pdf.

[18] The advertising-supported Internet sustains about $300 billion of U.S. GDP. *See* Google Comments at 7.

[19] *See* National Broadband Plan at 199–217, 225–40, 247–59, 272–73 (discussing the benefits of broadband-enabled telework); American Library Association (ALA) Comments at 1; Google Comments at 8–11; Public Interest Advocates (PIA) Comments at 5; XO Comments at 9.

[20] *See, e.g.*, Skype Reply at 14; SONY Reply at 6; MetroPCS Comments at 16 (the Internet "is the model of the virtuous cycle: innovators are creating content and application products that consumers desire, which drives consumers to purchase from service and equipment providers, which in turn drives investment in infrastructure and new technology in response to consumer demand"); *see also* Clearwire Comments at 7; Google Comments at 5–8, 17; OIC Comments at 23–27; Letter from Access Humboldt et al., to Chairman Genachowski et al., GN Docket No. 09-191 (filed Dec. 1, 2010) at 1–2 (asserting that the "best way to promote broadband adoption is through programs that result in a new generation of content creators and innovators," and urging Commission "to protect our local economies [and] community-based innovation" through open Internet rules).

[21] We note that broadband providers can also be edge providers. *See infra* para. 0.

[22] *See, e.g.,* Comcast Comments at 2, 8; MetroPCS Comments at 16; SONY Comments at 5; Qwest Comments, Factual Record Appendix at 6–10; Bright House Networks PN Comments at 7.

[23] For example, the increasing availability of multimedia applications on the World Wide Web during the 1990s was one factor that helped create demand for residential broadband services. Internet service providers responded by adopting new network infrastructure, modem technologies, and network protocols, and marketed broadband to residential customers. *See, e.g.*, WCB Letter 12/13/10, Attach. at 250–72, Chetan Sharma, *Managing Growth and Profits in the Yottabyte Era* (2009), www.chetansharma.com/yottabyteera.htm (Yottabyte). By the late 1990s, a residential end user could download content at speeds not achievable even on the Internet backbone during the 1980s. *See, e.g.*, WCB Letter 12/13/10, Attach. at 226–32, Susan Harris & Elise Gerich, *The NSFNET Backbone Service: Chronicling the End of an Era*, 10 CONNEXIONS (April 1996), *available at* www.merit.edu/networkresearch/projecthistory/nsfnet/nsfnet_article.php. Higher speeds and broadband's "always on" capability, in turn, stimulated more innovation in applications, from gaming to video streaming, which in turn encouraged broadband providers to increase network speeds. WCB Letter 12/13/10, Attach. at 233–34, Link Hoewing, *Twitter, Broadband and Innovation*, POLICYBLOG, Dec. 4, 2010, policyblog.verizon.com/BlogPost/626/TwitterBroadbandandInnovation.aspx.

[24] *See, e.g.*, OIC Comments at 34; Vonage Comments at 2.

[25] *See, e.g.*, Google Comments at 34–36; Public Interest Commenters (PIC) Comments at 28–30; *see also* WCB Letter 12/10/10, Attach. at 81–130, Joseph Farrell & Philip J. Weiser, *Modularity, Vertical Integration, and Open Access Policies: Toward a Convergence of Antitrust and Regulation in the Internet Age*, 17 HARV. J. L. & TECH. 85, 95 (2003) (an open industry architecture "can facilitate innovation in individual components, spur market entry, and result in lower prices").

[26] *See infra* para. 0. *Cf.* Part 0.

[27] *See, e.g.*, OIC Comments at ii; PIA Comments at 4–6; Vonage Comments at 1–2.

[28] *See Buckley v. Valeo*, 424 U.S. 1, 49 n.55 (1976).

[29] 47 U.S.C. § 230(a)(3); *see also Reno v. ACLU*, 521 U.S. 844, 853 (1997) ("No single organization controls any membership in the Web, nor is there any single centralized point from which individual Web sites or services can be blocked from the Web.") (citation omitted).

[30] *Cf. Turner Broad. Sys. v. FCC*, 512 U.S. 622, 648, 663-64 (1994) (discussing value of "diverse and antagonistic" sources of information).

[31] *See* WCB Letter 12/10/10, Attach. at 133–41, PEW RESEARCH CTR. FOR PEOPLE AND THE PRESS, AMERICANS SPEND MORE TIME FOLLOWING THE NEWS; IDEOLOGICAL NEWS SOURCES: WHO WATCHES AND WHY 17, 22 (Sept. 12, 2010), people-press.org/report/652/ (stating that "44% of Americans say they got news through one or more internet or mobile digital source yesterday"); WCB Letter 12/10/10, Attach. at 131–32, TVB LOCAL MEDIA MARKETING SOLUTIONS, LOCAL NEWS: LOCAL TV STATIONS ARE THE TOP DAILY NEWS SOURCE, www.tvb.org/planning_buying/120562 (estimating that 61% of Americans get news from the Internet) ("*TVB*"). However, according to the Pew Project for Excellence in Journalism, the majority of news that people access online originates from legacy media. *See* PEW PROJECT FOR EXCELLENCE IN JOURNALISM, THE STATE OF THE NEWS MEDIA: AN ANNUAL REPORT ON AMERICAN JOURNALISM (2010), www.stateofthemedia.org/2010/overview_key_findings.php ("Of news sites with half a million visitors a month (or the top 199 news sites once consulting, government and information data bases are removed), 67% are from legacy media, most of them (48%) newspapers.").

[32] *See, e.g.*, Google Comments at 9; OIC Comments at 2; Letter from Emily Sheketoff to Comm'r Copps, FCC, GN Docket No. 09-191, Attach. at 5 (filed Aug. 13, 2010); *see also Open Internet NPRM*, 24 FCC Rcd at 13095–96, paras. 75–76; National Broadband Plan at 317–28.

[33] WCB Letter 12/13/10, Attach. at 240–43, Hulu, *Media Info*, www.hulu.com/about; WCB Letter 12/13/10, Attach. at 244–45, Hulu, *News and Information*, www.hulu.com/channels/News-and-Information#kind=shows&sort=popular_today. Hulu aggregates television programs and is a joint venture of Providence Equity Partners and Disney, NBC Universal, and News Corp, which operate the ABC, NBC, and Fox broadcast networks, respectively. *See* Hulu, *Media Info*, www.hulu.com/about.

[34] *See* AT&T Comments at 81; Telecom Manufacturer Coalition Comments at 7; Metro PCS Comments at 12; Motorola Comments at 5; Motion Picture Association of America (MPAA) Comments at 5–6; Vonage Comments at 13–14; National Cable and Telecommunications Association (NCTA) PN Reply at 2; Traci Patterson, CEDMAGAZINE.COM, *Fox offers Web VOD play to broadcast affiliates* (Mar. 1, 2007), www.cedmagazine.com/fox-offers-web-vod-play-to-broadcast.aspx; WCB Letter 12/10/10, Attach. at 17–71, Radio Television Digital News Association May 10, 2010 Comments, GN Docket No. 10-25, at 6–9 (RTDNA 10-25 Comments); *see also* sources cited *infra*, note 35. We use the term "broadcasters" to refer to broadcast networks as well as local stations, many of which air broadcast television network programming. The major English- and Spanish-language television broadcast networks own approximately 130 local stations serving a substantial portion of the nation's population. *See* WCB Letter 12/10/10, Attach. at 278–86, Paige Albiniak, *B&C's Top 25 Station Groups 2010*, BROADCASTING & CABLE (Apr. 12, 2010), www.broadcastingcable.com/article/451325-B_C_s_Top_25_Station_Groups_2010.php.

[35] *See* WCB Letter 12/10/10, Attach. at 3–4, Press Release, PR Newswire, Raycom and Datasphere to Launch Hundreds of Neighborhood Websites in 35 Cities Across the U.S. (Mar. 3, 2010), *available at* www.prnewswire.com/news-releases/raycom-and-datasphere-to-launch-hundreds-of-neighborhood-websites-in-35-cities-across-the-us-86187412.html; WCB Letter 12/10/10, Attach. at 5–12, Erik Schonfeld, *Syndicaster Adds AOL, Brightcove, and YouTube Distribution for Local TV News Clips*, TECHCRUNCH, Apr. 14, 2009, techcrunch.com/2009/04/14/syndicaster-adds-aol-brightcove-and-youtube-distribution-for-local-tv-news-clips; WCB Letter 12/10/10, Attach. at 72–73, Press Release, Broadcast Interactive Media, Belo Corp Launches YouNews™ Social Media Platform on 16 Websites (Jan. 20, 2010), *available at* www.broadcast-interactive.com/news/82170542.html; RTDNA 10-25 Comments at 6–7.

[36] *See* WCB Letter 12/13/10, Attach. at 90–92, Stephen Cavendish, *How to Drop the Box (and Survive)*, CHICAGO TRIBUNE, Sept. 30, 2010, at C1; WCB Letter 12/10/10, Attach. at 77–78, Claire Atkinson, *Primetime Netflix*, N.Y. POST, Dec. 2, 2010, www.nypost.com/p/news/business/primetime_netflix_OMIP3b4KmH8odXiLSickCN; WCB Letter 12/13/10, Attach. at 83–85, Paul Bond, *Studios Lick Their Lips Over New-Look Netflix*, REUTERS, Aug. 16, 2010, www.reuters.com/article/idUSTRE6792T920100816.

[37] Motorola Comments at 5; MPAA Comments at 5–6; *see also* WCB Letter 12/10/10, Attach. at 79–81, Press Release, comScore, Inc., ComScore Releases October 2010 U.S. Online Video Rankings (Nov. 1, 2010), available at www.comscore.com/Press_Events/Press_Releases/2010/11/comScore_Releases_October_2010_U.S._Online_Video_Rankings (showing Hulu and broadcast networks in the top ten online video sources ranked by unique users and advertisements viewed); WCB Letter 12/13/10, Attach. at 316–19, Jed Williams, *Roku's Channel Store Brings OTT Option to Local TV*, BIA KELSEY (Dec. 1, 2010), www.blog.bia.com/bia/2010/12/01/rokus-channel-store-brings-ott-option-to-local-tv/ (discussing consumers' interest in viewing local television online).

[38] WCB Letter 12/10/10, Attach. at 13–16, Diana Marszalek, *TV & Papers Ramp Up Similar Strategies*, NETNEWSCHECK, Sept. 13, 2010, www.netnewscheck.com/article/2010/09/13/5774/tv--papers-ramp-up-similar-strategies; WCB Letter 12/13/10, Attach. at 86–88, Bridget Carey & Glenn Garvin, *Showtime for Univision*, THE MIAMI HERALD, Oct. 18, 2010, at G14.

[39] *See* WCB Letter 12/10/10, Attach. at 84–117, BORRELL ASSOCIATES INC., BENCHMARKING: TV WEB SALES DEFY GRAVITY, GAIN 10%; TV WEB REVENUES & ONLINE AD SPENDING PROJECTIONS FOR 211 MARKETS (Apr. 2010) at 5, 7 www.tvb.org/media/file/TVB_FF_TV_Basics.pdf (online revenues projected to increase 21% between 2009 and 2010); WCB Letter 12/10/10, Attach. at 118–20, Press Release, BIA/Kelsey, BIA/Kesley Raises Its Outlook for Television Station Revenues in 2010, as Industry Benefits from Primary Elections and Advertisers Returning to Local TV (June 20, 2010), *available at* www.bia.com/pr100630-IITV2.asp (estimating 25% growth in television stations' online revenues between 2009 and 2010); WCB Letter 12/13/10, Attach. at 293–97, Brian Steinberg, *Fox to Use Hulu Inventory for Advertisers 'Make-Goods,'* ADVERTISING AGE, Nov. 23, 2010, www.adage.com/mediaworks/article?article_id=147256 (discussing the sale of advertising time based on TV networks' combined television and online viewership). Americans rely heavily on broadcast television and radio for news, *see TVB*, *supra* note 31(on a typical day 78% of Americans get news from a local TV station, 73% from a broadcast network, and 54% from a radio news program), and broadcast network programming, as the most-watched programming on TV, is highly valuable as a source of funding for networks and local affiliates alike. WCB Letter 12/10/10, Attach. at 1–19, TELEVISION BUREAU OF ADVERTISING, INC., TV BASICS 11 (updated Oct. 2010), www.tvb.org/media/file/TVB_FF_TV_Basics.pdf, www.tvb.org/facts_and_figures/95487 (broadcast networks aired 98 of the 100 top-rated shows in the 2009–2010 season).

[40] *See* MPAA PN Reply at 7; WCB Letter 12/13/10, Attach. at 326–623, FCC Open Internet Workshop: Speech, Democratic Engagement, and the Open Internet, Dec. 15, 2009 ("Dec. 15, 2009 Workshop Tr."), *video available at* www.openinternet.gov/workshops/speech-democratic-engagement-and-the-open-internet.html; Dec. 15, 2009 Workshop Tr. at 52–60 (remarks of Ruth Livier, YLSE); WCB Letter 12/13/10, Attach. at 322–25, Ylse, www.ylse.net/about (distributing studio-quality videos online); Dec. 15, 2009 Workshop Tr. at 40–43 (remarks of Jonathan Moore, Rowdy Orbit IPTV, LLC); WCB Letter 12/13/10, Attach. at 320–21, Rowdy Orbit, www.rowdyorbit.com (aggregating shows not carried on cable or broadcast television), *See also*

Writer's Guild of America, West (WGAW) Reply at 5 (open Internet necessary to promote content competition and diversity); Independent Film & Television Alliance (IFTA) PN Comments at 1–2 (same); Writer's Guild of America, East (WGAE) PN Comments at 1–2 (same).

[41] *See* Google Comments at 28; Motorola Comments at 5; MPAA Comments at 5–6; DISH Reply at 4–5; WCB Letter 12/10/10, Attach. at 22–23, *Online Video Goes Mainstream*, EMARKETER, Apr. 28, 2010, www.emarketer.com/Article.aspx?R=1007664 (estimating that 29% of Internet users younger than 25 say they watch all or most of their TV online, that as of April 2010 67% of U.S. Internet users watch online video each month, and that this figure will increase to 77% by 2014); WCB Letter 12/10/10, Attach. at 20–21, Chris Nuttall, *Web TVs bigger for manufacturers than 3D*, FINANCIAL TIMES, Aug. 29, 2010, www.ft.com/cms/s/2/0b34043a-9fe3-11df-8cc5-00144feabdc0.html (stating that 28 million Internet-enabled TV sets are expected to be sold in 2010, an increase of 125% from 2009); WCB Letter 12/13/10, Attach. at 291–92, Sandvine, News and Events: Press Releases, www.sandvine.com/news/pr_detail.asp?ID=288 (estimating that Netflix represents more than 20% of peak downstream Internet traffic). Cisco expects online viewing to exert significant influence on future demand for broadband capacity, ranking as the top source of Internet traffic by the end of 2010 and accounting for 91% of global Internet traffic by 2014. WCB Letter 12/10/10, Attach. at 40–42, Press Release, Cisco, Annual Cisco Visual Networking Index Forecast Projects Global IP Traffic To Increase More than Fourfold by 2014 (June 10,2010), www.cisco.com/web/MT/news/10/news_100610.html.

[42] *Open Internet NPRM*, 24 FCC Rcd at 13098, para. 82.

[43] *See* PEW INTERNET & AM. LIFE PROJECT, HOME BROADBAND ADOPTION (June 2009). Approximately 14 to 24 million Americans remain without broadband access capable of meeting the requirements set forth in section 706 of the Telecommunications Act of 1996, as amended. *Inquiry Concerning the Deployment of Advanced Telecommunications Capability to All Americans in a Reasonable and Timely Fashion, and Possible Steps to Accelerate Such Deployment Pursuant to Section 706 of the Telecommunications Act of 1996, as Amended by the Broadband Data Improvement Act et al.*, Sixth Broadband Deployment Report, 25 FCC Rcd 9556, 9557, para. 1 (2010) (*Sixth Broadband Deployment Report*).

[44] For example, Jonathan Moore founded Rowdy Orbit IPTV, an online platform featuring original programming for minority audiences, because he was frustrated by the lack of representation of people of color in traditional media. Dec. 15, 2009 Workshop Tr. at 39–40, *video available at* www.openinternet.gov/workshops/speech-democratic-engagement-and-the-open-internet.html. The Internet's openness—and the low costs of online entry—enables businesses like Rowdy Orbit to launch without having to gain approval from traditional media gatekeepers. *Id.* We will closely monitor the effects of the open Internet rules we adopt today on the digital divide and on minority and disadvantaged consumers. *See generally* ColorOfChange Comments; Dec. 15, 2009 Workshop Tr. at 52–60 (remarks of Ruth Livier, YLSE); 100 Black Men of America et al. Comments at 1–2; Free Press Comments at 134–36; Center for Media Justice et al. Comments at 7–9.

[45] *See, e.g.*, Letter from Alan Davidson, Google, & Thomas J. Tauke, Verizon, to Chairman Genachowski et al., GN Docket No. 09-191 at 2 (filed Jan. 14, 2010) ("It is essential that the Internet remains an unrestricted and open platform, where people can access the lawful content, services, and applications of their choice."); Verizon Comments at 1 ("Everyone agrees the Internet should be open . . . ."); Comcast Reply at i (noting the "near-universal acceptance that . . . the Internet must remain an unrestricted and open platform").

[46] *See, e.g.*, DISH Comments at 2 ("Vertically-integrated broadband providers have the incentive and ability to discriminate against competitors."); Google Comments at 35 ("Broadband providers will have a natural incentive to use prioritization to favor their own services."); *see also* The Ad Hoc Telecommunications Users Committee (Ad Hoc) Comments at 8–9; ALA Comments at 2; Free Press Comments at 3–4, 22–23; IFTA Comments at 10–12; Netflix Comments at 3, 5; Skype Comments at 2, 10–11; Vonage Comments at 19; Google Reply at 16–17; Vonage Reply at 4.

[47] *See* WIRELINE COMPETITION BUREAU, FCC, HIGH-SPEED SERVICES FOR INTERNET ACCESS 3 (July 2009), *available at* hraunfoss.fcc.gov/edocs_public/attachmatch/DOC-292191A1.pdf; WCB Letter 12/10/10, Attach. at 43–44, Press Release, Leichtman Research Group, Under 350,000 add Broadband in the Second Quarter of 2010: Top Telephone Companies Report a Cumulative Net Loss of Broadband Subscribers (Aug. 11, 2010), *available at* www.leichtmanresearch.com/press/081110release.html (reporting that the nineteen largest providers of broadband Internet access service in the U.S. are all cable and telephone companies and serve approximately 73.5 million subscribers, or approximately 93% of all broadband subscribers).

[48] The Commission's rules define interconnected VoIP as "a service that: (1) enables real-time, two-way voice communications; (2) requires a broadband connection from the user's location; (3) requires Internet protocol-compatible customer premises equipment (CPE); and (4) permits users generally to receive calls that originate on the public switched telephone network and to terminate calls to the public switched telephone network." 47 C.F.R. § 9.3. Over-the-top VoIP services require the end user to obtain broadband transmission from a third-party provider, and providers of over-the-top VoIP can vary in terms of the extent to which they rely on their own facilities. *See SBC Commc'ns Inc. and AT&T Corp. Applications for Approval of Transfer of Control*, WC Docket No, 05-65, Memorandum Opinion and Order, 20 FCC Rcd 18290, 18337-38, para. 86 (2005).

[49] *Tel. Number Requirements for IP-Enabled Servs. Providers*, Report and Order, Declaratory Ruling, Order on Remand, and NPRM, 22 FCC Rcd 19531, 19547, para. 28 (2007); *see also* Vonage Comments at 3–4. In merger reviews and forbearance petitions, the Commission has found the record "inconclusive regarding the extent to which various over-the-top VoIP services should be included in the relevant product market for [mass market] local services." *See, e.g., Verizon Commc'ns Inc. and MCI, Inc. Application for Approval of Transfer of Control*, Memorandum Opinion and Order, 20 FCC Rcd 18433, 18480, para. 89 (2005); *see also Petition of Qwest Corp. for Forbearance Pursuant to 47 U.S.C. § 160(c) in the Phoenix, Arizona Metropolitan Statistical Area*, Memorandum Opinion and Order, 25 FCC Rcd 8622, 8650, para. 54 (2010) (*Qwest Phoenix Order*). In contrast to those proceedings, we are not performing a market power analysis in this proceeding, so we need not and do not here determine with specificity whether, and to what extent, particular over-the-top VoIP services constrain particular practices and/or rates of services governed by section 201. *Cf. Qwest Phoenix Order*, 25 FCC Rcd at 8647–48, paras. 46–47 (discussing the general approach to product market definition); *id.* at 8651–52, paras. 55–56 (discussing the need for evidence that one service constrains the price of another service to include them in the same product market for purposes of a market power analysis).

[50] *See, e.g.*, WCB Letter 12/10/10, Attach. at 45–52, PriMetrica, Inc., Executive Summary to TeleGeography Report 6–7 (2009), *available at* telecomblogs.in/wp-content/uploads/2010/05/TG10_Exec_Sum.pdf ("In the span of 6 years, Skype [an over-the-top VoIP provider] has emerged as the largest provider of cross-border communications in the world, by far. . . . Given these immense traffic volumes, it's difficult not to conclude that at least some of Skype's growth is coming at the expense of traditional carriers.").

[51] *See supra* para. 0.

[52] *See, e.g.*, WCB Letter 12/10/10, Attach. at 54–56, Press Release, Comcast Corp., Time Warner Inc. Announces Widespread Distribution of Cable TV Content Online, (June 24, 2009), *available at* www.comcast.com/About/PressRelease/PressReleaseDetail.ashx?PRID=883 (announcing a partnership between Comcast and Time Warner to develop a "TV Everywhere" model for the MVPD industry); *see also* WCB Letter 12/13/10, Attach. at 247–49, John Moulding, *TV Everywhere: More than One Authentication Model*, VIDEONET, Nov. 16, 2010, www.v-net.tv/NewsDisplay.aspx?id=594&title=tv-everywhere-more-than-one-aggregation-model; DISH Reply at 5–8 (noting that AT&T, Cablevision, Comcast, DirecTV, Dish, Time Warner Cable, and Verizon all offer online video services, but that unlike their competitors, neither DirecTV nor Dish are vertically integrated with broadband providers).

[53] *See supra* para. 0.

[54] *E.g.*, AT&T PN Comments at 55–56 and 56, n.115 (wireless providers permit the use of Hulu, YouTube, and other applications that "compete with their video services"); *Annual Assessment of the Status of Competition in the Market for the Delivery of Video Programming*, Supplemental Notice of Inquiry, 24 FCC Rcd 4401, 4417 n.82 (2009) (noting that in 2009, TWC President and CEO Glenn Britt stated that "the reality is we are starting to see the beginnings of cord cutting where people, particularly young people, are saying all I need is broadband, I don't need video"); WCB Letter 12/13/10, Attach. at 89, TWC, *Caution Concerning Forward-Looking Statements* (Aug. 2010), www.timewarnercable.com/Corporate/investor_relations/caution_forward_statements.html ("companies that deliver programming over broadband Internet connections" identified as a source of "increased competition"); WCB Letter 12/13/10, Attach. at 93–189, DirecTV, Inc. SEC Form 10-K, filed Feb. 26, 2010, at 11 (stating that "we face substantial competition in the MVPD industry from emerging digital media distribution providers" and listing Hulu, Apple, AOL, Amazon, and Netflix among its "Video via the Internet" competitors); WCB Letter 12/13/10, Attach. at 1–13, Transcript, Discussion with Ivan G. Seidenberg, Chairman and Chief Executive Officer, Verizon Communications, Inc., Goldman Sachs 19th Annual Communicopia Conference, Sept. 23, 2010 at 8, 11, *available at* investor.verizon.com/news/20100923; *see also* OIC Comments at 15.

[55] *See, e.g.*, WCB Letter 12/10/10, Attach. at 5763, Ryan Fleming, *New Report Shows More People Dropping Cable TV for Web Broadcasts*, DIGITAL TRENDS, Apr. 16, 2010, *available at* www.digitaltrends.com/computing/new-report-shows-that-more-and-more-people-are-dropping-cable-tv-in-favor-of-web-broadcasts.Congress recently recognized these developments by expanding disabilities access requirements to include advanced communications services. *See* Twenty-First Century Communications and Video Accessibility Act, Pub. L. No. 111-260; *see also* 156 CONG. REC. 6005 (daily ed. July 26, 2010) (remarks of Rep. Waxman) (this legislation before us . . . ensur[es] that Americans with disabilities can access the latest communications technology.); *id.* at 6004 (remarks of Rep. Markey) ("[T]he bill we are considering today significantly increases accessibility for Americans with disabilities to the indispensable telecommunications . . . tools of the 21st century."); Letter from Rick Chessen, NCTA, to Marlene H. Dortch, Secretary, FCC, GN Docket No. 09-191 at 2 n.6 (filed Dec. 10, 2010).

[56] *See, e.g.*, Vonage Comments at 3–4; WCB Letter 12/10/10, Attach. at 64–102, MICHAEL D. PELCOVITS AND DANIEL E. HAAR, MICRA, CONSUMER BENEFITS FROM CABLE-TELCO COMPETITION 15–16, 21 (2007), *available at* www.micradc.com/news/publications/pdfs/Updated_MiCRA_Report_FINAL.pdf (finding "compelling evidence" that telephone companies face increasing competition from over-the-top VoIP offerings and estimating that over the next five years consumers will save over $6 billion from the lower prices offered by these services as well as billions more from the competitive response of the telephone incumbents).

[57] *See, e.g.*, DISH Comments at 3–5; Google Comments at 35.

[58] *See, e.g.*, Free Press Comments at 3.

[59] *See generally* WCB Letter 12/10/10, Attach. at 23–27, Steven C. Salop & David Scheffman, *Raising Rivals' Cost*, 73 AM. ECON. REV. 267–71 (1983); WCB Letter 12/10/10, Attach. at 1–23, Steven C. Salop & Thomas Krattenmaker, *Anticompetitive Exclusion: Raising Rivals' Costs to Achieve Power over Price*, 96 YALE L.J. 214 (1986). *See also* Andrew I. Gavil et al., ANTITRUST LAW IN PERSPECTIVE: CASES, CONCEPTS AND PROBLEMS IN COMPETITION POLICY 1153–92 (2d ed. 2008) (describing how policies fostering competition spur innovation). To similar effect, a broadband provider may raise access fees to disfavored edge providers, reducing their ability to profit by raising their costs and limiting their ability to compete with favored edge providers.

[60] *See* Google Comments at 30–31; Netflix Comments at 7 n.10; Vonage Reply at 4; WCB Letter 12/10/10, Attach. at 28–78, Austan Goolsbee, *Vertical Integration and the Market for Broadcast and Cable Television Programming*, Paper for the Federal Communications Commission 31–32 (Sept. 5, 2007) (Goolsbee Study) (finding that MVPDs excluded networks that were rivals of affiliated channels for anticompetitive reasons). *Cf.* WCB Letter 12/10/10, Attach. at 85–87, DAVID WATERMAN & ANDREW WEISS, VERTICAL INTEGRATION IN CABLE TELEVISION 142–143 (1997) (MVPD exclusion of unaffiliated content during an earlier time period); *see also* H.R. Rep. 102-628 (2d Sess.) at 41 (1992) ("The Committee received testimony that vertically integrated companies reduce diversity in programming by threatening the viability of rival cable programming services."). See *infra* Part 0 for other examples of broadband providers blocking access to content and services that pose an actual or potential competitive threat. In addition to the examples of actual misconduct that we provide, *see infra* Part 0, the Goolsbee Study provides empirical evidence that cable providers have acted in the past on anticompetitive incentives to foreclose rivals, supporting our concern that these and other broadband providers would act on analogous incentives in the future. We thus disagree that we rely on "speculative harms alone" or have failed to adduce "empirical evidence." Baker Statement at *1, *4 (citing AT&T Reply Exh. 2 at 45 (J. Gregory Sidak & David J. Teece, *Innovation Spillovers and the "Dirt Road" Fallacy: The Intellectual Bankruptcy of Banning Optional Transactions for Enhanced Delivery over the Internet*, 6 J. COMPETITION L. & ECON. 521, 571-72 (2010)). To the contrary, the empirical evidence and the misconduct that we describe below validate the economic theories that inform our decision today. Moreover, as we explain below, by comparison to the benefits of the prophylactic measures we adopt, the costs associated with these open Internet rules are likely small. *See infra* para. 0.

[61] *See, e.g.*, Letter from Barbara van Schewick to Marlene Dortch, Secretary, FCC, GN Docket No. 09-191 (filed Jan. 19, 2010) (van Schewick Jan. 19, 2010 *Ex Parte* Letter), Opening Statement at 4–7 (highlighting the risk that—in the absence of Internet openness norms—gatekeeper control and pay-for-prioritization would have prevented Skype and YouTube from surviving because of the threats they presented to the legacy business of telephone-based network providers and Google Video, respectively); Letter from M. Chris Riley, Free Press, to Marlene Dortch, Secretary, FCC, GN Docket No. 09-191 (filed Nov. 24, 2010), Attach., M. Chris Riley and Robb Topolski, "The Hidden Harms of Application Bias," at 3 n.7 and 7 (similar with respect to YouTube's threat to RealVideo).

[62] *See* Free Press Comments at 17 n.8; OIC Comments at 27; Vonage Reply at 53.

[63] *See, e.g.*, Free Press Comments at 3; Google Comments at 34; Red Hat Comments at 2; Google Reply at 36; IPI Reply at 4; Vonage Reply at 4.

[64] *See, e.g.*, AT&T Comments at 108–137; Comcast Comments at 38–39; TWC Comments at 54–55; Verizon Comments at 71–77.

[65] Some end users can be reached through more than one broadband connection, sometimes via the same device (*e.g.*, a smartphone that has Wi-Fi and cellular connectivity). Even so, the end user, not the edge provider, chooses which broadband provider the edge provider must rely on to reach the end user.

[66] Also known as a "terminating monopolist." *See, e.g.*, CCIA Comments at 7; Skype Comments at 10–11; Vonage Comments at 9–10; Google Reply at 8–14. A broadband provider can act as a gatekeeper even if some edge providers would have bargaining power in negotiations with broadband providers over access or prioritization fees.

[67] *See* Google Comments at 35, 59–61; OIC Comments at 20–30; IPI Reply at 2; Ad Hoc Comments at 7, 15–17; ALA Comments at 2; Google Comments at 34; IFTA Comments at 14; Netflix Comments at 3–4; PAETEC Comments at 24–25; PIC Comments at 50–51; Google Reply at 37–38; IPI Reply at 4; WCB Letter 12/10/10, Attach. at 115–130, Robin S. Lee & Tim Wu, *Subsidizing Creativity through Network Design: Zero Pricing and Net Neutrality*, 23 J. ECON. PERSPECTIVES, 61–76 (2009); WCB Letter 12/13/10, Attach. at 201–225, Nicholas Economides, *"Net Neutrality," Non-Discrimination and Digital Distribution of Content Through the Internet,* 4 I/S: J.L. & POL'Y FOR INFO. SOCIETY 209, 232 (2008); WCB Letter 12/13/10, Attach. at 14–77, Barbara van Schewick, *Towards an Economic Framework for Network Neutrality Regulation*, 5 J. ON TELECOMM. & HIGH TECH. L. 329, 378–80 (2007).

[68] A broadband provider may hesitate to impose costs on its own subscribers, but it will typically not take into account the effect that reduced edge provider investment and innovation has on the attractiveness of the Internet to end users that rely on other broadband providers—and will therefore ignore a significant fraction of

the cost of foregone innovation. *See, e.g.*, OIC Comments at 20–24. If the total number of broadband subscribers shrinks, moreover, the social costs unaccounted for by the broadband provider could also include the lost ability of the remaining end users to connect with the subscribers that departed (foregone direct network effects) and a smaller potential audience for edge providers. *See, e.g.*, *id.* at 23. Broadband providers are also unlikely to fully account for the open Internet's power to enhance civic discourse through news and information, or for its ability to enable innovations that help address key national challenges such as education, public safety, energy efficiency, and health care. *See* ARL et al. Comments at 3; Google Reply at 39; American Recovery and Reinvestment Act of 2009, Pub. L. No. 111-5, 123 Stat. 115 (2009).

[69] *See, e.g.*, OIC Comments at 29; Google Reply at 40.

[70] *See, e.g.*, ALA Comments at 3–4; ColorOfChange Comments at 3; Free Press Comments at 69; Google Comments at 34; Netflix Comments at 4; OIC Comments at 29–30; DISH Reply at 10. Such fees could also reduce an edge provider's incentive to invest in existing offerings, assuming the fees would be expected to increase to the extent improvements increased usage of the edge provider's offerings.

[71] Ad Hoc Comments at 15–16; ADTRAN Comments at 17–18; American Composers Forum et al. (ACF) Comments at 3–6; ColorOfChange Comments at 3–4; Debra Brown Comments at 1; Google Comments at 12; Philadelphia Comments at 3; Red Hat Comments at 2.

[72] *See, e.g.*, Google Comments at 59–61; Union Square Ventures Comments at 1; Vonage Comments at 18; OIC Reply at 3–4.

[73] Negotiations impose direct expenses and delay. *See* Google Comments at 34. There may also be significant costs associated with the possibility that the negotiating parties would reach an impasse. *See* ALA Comments at 2 ("The cable TV industry offers a telling example of the 'pay to play' environment where some cable companies do not offer their customers access to certain content because the company has not successfully negotiated financial compensation with the content provider."). Edge providers may also bear costs arising from their need to monitor the extent to which they actually receive prioritized delivery.

[74] *See, e.g.*, Google Comments at 34–35; Shane Greenstein Notice of Ex Parte, GN Docket No. 09-191, *Transaction Cost, Transparency, and Innovation for the Internet* at 19, *available at* www.openinternet.gov/workshops/innovation-investment-and-the-open-internet.html; van Schewick Jan. 19, 2010 *Ex Parte* Letter, Opening Statement at 7 (arguing that the low costs of innovation not only make many more applications worth pursuing, but also allow a large and diverse group of people to become innovators, which in turn increases the overall amount and quality of innovation). There are approximately 1,500 broadband providers in the United States. *See* WIRELINE COMPETITION BUREAU, FCC, INTERNET ACCESS SERVICES: STATUS AS OF DECEMBER 31, 2009 at 7, tbl. 13 (Dec. 2010) (FCC Internet Status Report), *available at* www.fcc.gov/Daily_Releases/Daily_Business/2010/db1208/DOC-303405A1.pdf. The innovative process frequently generates a large number of attempts, only a few of which turn out to be highly successful. Given the likelihood of failure, and that financing is not always readily available to support research and development, the innovation process in many sectors of the Internet's edge is likely to be highly sensitive to the upfront costs of developing and introducing new products. PIC Comments at 50 ("[I]t is unlikely that new entrants will have the ability (both financially and with regard to information) to negotiate with every ISP that serves the markets that they are interested in.").

[75] *See, e.g.*, Verizon Comments at 33.

[76] *See infra* paras. 0–0.

[77] *See* Skype Comments at 11; *see also supra* paras. 0–0.

[78] *See* Skype Comments at 11-12; *see also infra* para. 0.

[79] *See* AT&T Comments at 114, 135–37; TWC Comments at 57-58; Verizon Comments at 47–48, 70–74.

[80] Economics literature recognizes that access charges could be harmful under some circumstances and beneficial under others. *See, e.g.*, WCB Letter 12/10/10, Attach. at 1–62, E. Glen Weyl, *A Price Theory of Multi-Sided Platforms*, 100 AM. ECON. REV. 1642, 1642–72 (2010) (the effects of allowing broadband providers to charge terminating rates to content providers are ambiguous); *see also* WCB Letter 12/10/10, Attach. at 180–215, John Musacchio et al., *A Two-Sided Market Analysis of Provider Investment Incentives with an Application to the Net-Neutrality Issue*, 8 REV. OF NETWORK ECON. 22, 22–39 (2009) (noting that there are conditions under which "a zero termination price is socially beneficial"). Moreover, the economic literature on two-sided markets is at an early stage of development. AT&T Comments, Exh. 3, Schwartz Decl. at 16; Jeffrey A. Eisenach (Eisenach) Reply at 11–12; *cf., e.g.*, WCB Letter 12/10/10, Attach. at 156– 79, Mark Armstrong, *Competition inTtwo-Sided Markets*, 37 RAND J. OF ECON. 668 (2006); WCB Letter 12/10/10, Attach. at 216–302, Jean-Charles Rochet & Jean Tirole, *Platform Competition in Two-Sided Markets*, 1 J. EUR. ECON. ASS'N 990 (2003).

[81] *See* Google Reply at 37.

[82] Indeed, demand for broadband Internet access service might decline even if subscriber fees fell, if the conduct of broadband providers discouraged demand by blocking end user access to preferred edge providers, slowing non-prioritized transmission, and breaking the virtuous circle of innovation.

[83] *See e.g.*, ALA Comments at 2; Google Comments at 35; OIC Comments at 31; DISH Reply at 11; WCB Letter 12/10/10, Attach. at 131–55, Jon Peha, *The Benefits and Risks of Mandating Network Neutrality, and the*

Quest for a Balanced Policy, 1 INTER. J. OF COMM. 644, 653 (2007). *Cf.* WCB Letter 12/10/10, Attach. at 89–114, Raymond J. Deneckere & R. Preston McAfee, *Damaged Goods*, 5 J. OF ECON. & MGMT. STRATEGY 149 (Summer 1996) (sellers may find it profitable to degrade the quality of their lowest tier of service); Netflix PN Comments at 3 ("The Commission should ensure that specialized services do not unreasonably erode capacity devoted to broadband Internet access services.").

[84] *See, e.g.*, CDT Comments at 28–29; Free Press Comments at 4, 22, 29–30, 37–43, 143–44; Google Comments at 35–36; OIC Comments at 31, 46; PIC Comments at 29–30; Free Press Reply at 38; IPI Reply at 16; Letter from Matthew F. Wood et al., Public Interest Commenters, to Marlene Dortch, Secretary, FCC, GN Docket No. 09-51, 09-191, WC Docket No. 07-52 at 3 (filed Aug. 6, 2010); Letter from S. Derek Turner, Free Press, to Chairman Genachowski et al., FCC, GN Docket No. 09-191, WC Docket No. 07-52 at 4–5 (filed Aug. 3, 2010); WCB Letter 12/10/10, Attach. at 63–88, Jay Pil Choi & Byung-Cheol Kim, *Net Neutrality and Investment Incentives*, 41 RAND J. OF ECON. 446, 464–65 (Autumn 2010) (broadband providers have an incentive to limit capacity expansion in order to charge a greater premium for priority service, though other factors may also affect investment incentives).

[85] *See* OIC Comments at 24; Free Press Comments at 45. The transparency and reasonable network management guidelines we adopt today, in particular, should reduce the likelihood of such fragmentation of the Internet.

[86] *See* CCIA/CEA Comments at 4; Free Press Comments at 29–30, 143–46; Google Comments at 32–34; Netflix Comments at 3; OIC Comments at 14, 79–82; DISH Reply at 8–9; IPI Reply at 9; Vonage Reply at 5. For examples of network management tools, see, for example, WCB Letter 12/10/10, Attach. at 1–8, Allot Service Gateway, Pushing the DPI Envelope: An Introduction, at 2 (June 2007), *available at* www.sysob.com/download/AllotServiceGateway.pdf ("Reduce the performance of applications with negative influence on revenues (*e.g.* competitive VoIP services)."); WCB Letter 12/13/10, Attach. at 289–90, Procera Networks, PLR, www.proceranetworks.com/customproperties/tag/Products-PLR.html; WCB Letter 12/13/10, Attach. at 283–88,
Cisco, www.cisco.com/en/US/prod/collateral/ps7045/ps6129/ps6133/ps6150/prod_brochure0900aecd8025258e.pdf (marketing the ability of equipment to identify VoIP, video, and other traffic types). Vendors market their offerings as enabling broadband providers to "make only modest incremental infrastructure investments and to control operating costs." WCB Letter 12/13/10, Attach. at 283, Cisco.

[87] *See supra* paras. 24-26. Because broadband providers have the ability to act as gatekeepers even in the absence of market power with respect to end users, we need not conduct a market power analysis.

[88] *See, e.g.*, FCC Internet Status Report at 49, tbl. 24; National Broadband Plan at 37; Google Comments at 19–20; IFTA Comments at 10–11; Netflix Comments at 5; Vonage Comments at 7–8; Broadband Institute of California (BBIC) Reply at 21; Google Reply at 3–7; IPI Reply at 14; OIC Reply at 14–15.

[89] *See* FCC Internet Status Report at 7, fig. 3(a). A broadband provider's presence in a census tract does not mean it offers service to all potential customers within that tract. And the data reflect subscriptions, not network capability.

[90] *Sixth Broadband Deployment Report*, 25 FCC Rcd at 9559, 9570, paras. 5, 21 (2010).

[91] *See* FCC Internet Status Report at 7, fig. 3(a).

[92] *Id.*

[93] In December 2009, nearly 60% of households lived in census tracts where no more than two broadband providers offered service with 3 Mbps down and 768 Kbps up, while no mobile broadband providers offered service with 10 Mbps down and 1.5 Mbps up. *Id.* at 8, fig. 3(b). Mobile broadband providers generally have offered bandwidths lower than those available from fixed providers. *See* Yottabyte at 13–14.

[94] *See* National Broadband Plan at 40–42. A number of commenters discuss impediments to increased competition. *See, e.g.*, Ad Hoc Comments at 9; Google Comments, at 18–22; IFTA Comments at 10–11; *see also* WCB Letter 12/10/10, Attach. at 9–16, Thomas Monath et al., *Economics of Fixed Broadband Network Strategies*, 41 IEEE COMM. MAG. 132, 132–39 (Sept. 2003).

[95] National Association of Telecommunications Office & Advisors (NATOA) Comments, Attach. 5, Andrew Afflerback & Matthew DeHaven, *A Technical Strategy for Evolution*, at 31 (Jan. 13, 2010); Qualcomm Comments at 7.

[96] *See supra* note 93; Ad Hoc Comments at 9; Google Comments at 21; Vonage Comments at 8; IPI Reply at 14; WCB Letter 12/10/10, Attach. at 56–65, Vikram Chandrasekhar & Jeffrey G. Andrews, *Femtocell Networks: A Survey*, 46 IEEE COMM. MAG., Sept. 2008, 59, at 59–60 (explaining mobile spectrum alone cannot compete with wireless connections to fixed networks). We also do not know how offers by a single wireless broadband provider for both fixed and mobile broadband services will perform in the marketplace.

[97] *See* OIC Comments at 71–72. Large cable companies that provide fixed broadband also have substantial ownership interests in Clear, the 4G wireless venture in which Sprint has a majority ownership interest.

[98] OIC Comments at 71–72; Skype Comments at 10. In cellular telephony, multimarket conduct has been found to dampen competition. *See* WCB Letter 12/10/10, Attach. at 1–24, P.M. Parker and L.H. Röller, *Collusive conduct in duopolies: Multimarket contact and cross ownership in the mobile telephone industry*, 28 RAND J. OF ECON. 304, 304–322 (Summer 1997); WCB Letter 12/10/10, Attach. at 25–58, Meghan R. Busse, *Multimarket contact and price coordination in the cellular telephone industry*, 9 J. OF ECON. & MGMT.

STRATEGY 287, 287–320 (Fall 2000). Moreover, some fixed broadband providers also provide necessary inputs to some mobile providers' offerings, such as backhaul transport to wireline facilities.

[99] ARL et al. Comments at 5; Google Comments at 21–22; Netflix Comments at 5; New Jersey Rate Counsel (NJRC) Comments at 17; OIC Comments at 40, 73; PIC Comments at 23; Skype Comments at 12; OIC Reply at 20–21; Paul Misener (Amazon.com) Comments at 2; *see also* WCB Letter 12/10/10, Attach. at 59–76, Patrick Xavier & Dimitri Ypsilanti, *Switching Costs and Consumer Behavior: Implications for Telecommunications Regulation*, 10(4) INFO 2008, 13, 13–29 (2008). Churn is a function of many factors. *See, e.g.*, WCB Letter 12/10/10, Attach. at 1–53, 97–153, AT&T Comments, WT Docket No. 10-133, at 51 (Aug. 2, 2010). The evidence in the record, *e.g.*, AT&T Comments at 83, is not probative as to the extent of competition among broadband providers because it does not appropriately isolate a connection between churn levels and the extent of competition.

[100] Google Comments at 21–22. Of broadband end users with a choice of broadband providers, 32% said paying termination fees to their current provider was a major reason why they have not switched service. FCC, BROADBAND DECISION: WHAT DRIVES CONSUMERS TO SWITCH—OR STICK WITH—THEIR BROADBAND INTERNET PROVIDER 8 (Dec. 2010) (FCC Internet Survey), *available at* hraunfoss.fcc.gov/edocs_public/attachmatch/DOC-303264A1.pdf.

[101] Google Comments at 22; NJRC Comments at 17.

[102] NJRC Comments at 17.

[103] *See* FCC Internet Survey at 7 (finding that 34% of broadband end users with a choice of providers said giving up their current email address was a major reason for not changing service); Google Comments at 22; NJRC Comments at 17.

[104] *See Madison River Communications, LLC and affiliated companies*, File No. EB-05-IH-0110; Acct. No.; FRN: 0004334082, Consent Decree, 20 FCC Rcd 4295 (EB 2005) (*Madison River Consent Decree*).

[105] *Comcast Network Management Practices Order*, 23 FCC Rcd 13028, 13028, 13055–56, paras. 1, 47–48 (2008) (*Comcast Order*); *see also* WCB Letter 12/13/10, Attach. at 1–15, Comcast Corporation, Description of Current Network Management Practices, downloads.comcast.net/docs/Attachment_A_Current_Practices.pdf.

[106] ACLU PN Comments at 8.

[107] *See, e.g.*, Letter from James W. Cicconi, AT&T Services, Inc., to Ruth Milkman, Chief, Wireless Telecommunications Bureau, FCC, RM-11361, RM-11497 at 6–9 (filed Aug. 21, 2009) ("AT&T indicated to Apple that it does not object to Apple enabling VoIP applications for the iPhone that use Wi-Fi connectivity . . . rather than AT&T's 2G or 3G wireless data services"); Sling Comments at 4–11; DISH PN Reply at 7 ("In reality, it took nine months of regulatory scrutiny and pressure from the public and DISH for AT&T to 'work with' DISH so that AT&T subscribers could access their Slingbox offerings over the wireless network. Other third-party application providers have experienced similar restrictions. VoIP operators such as Skype have faced significant difficulty in gaining access across wireless Internet connections.").

[108] *See* WCB Letter 12/10/10, Attach. at 74, Amy Schatz, *Cox About to Feel Wrath of Net Neutrality Activists*, WASHINGTON WIRE, May 15, 2008, blogs.wsj.com/washwire/2008/05/15/cox-about-to-feel-wrath-of-net-neutrality-activists.

[109] *Chin v. RCN Corp.*, No. 08 Civ. 7349, §3.2 (S.D.N.Y. July 31, 2009) (RCN Settlement Agreement), *available at* www.rcn.com/lehigh-valley/images/pdfs/legal/02-class-action-settlement-agreement.pdf.

[110] *See* RCN Settlement Agreement § 3.2. RCN denied any wrongdoing, but it acknowledges that in order to ease network congestion, it targeted specific P2P applications. *See* Letter from Jean L. Kiddo, RCN, to Marlene Dortch, Secretary, FCC, GN Docket No. 09-191, WC Docket No. 07-52, at 2–5 (filed May 7, 2010).

[111] A 2008 study by the Max Planck Institute revealed significant blocking of BitTorrent applications in the United States. Comcast and Cox were both cited as examples of providers blocking traffic. *See generally* WCB Letter 12/10/10, Attach. at 75–80, MARCEL DISCHINGER ET AL., MAX PLANCK INSTITUTE, DETECTING BITTORRENT BLOCKING (2008), *available at* broadband.mpi-sws.org/transparency/results/08_imc_blocking.pdf; *see also* WCB Letter 12/13/10, Attach. at 235–39, Max Planck Institute for Software Systems, Glasnost: Results from Tests for BitTorrent Traffic Blocking, broadband.mpi-sws.org/transparency/results; WCB Letter 12/13/10, Attach. at 298–315, CHRISTIAN KREIBICH ET AL., NETALYZR: ILLUMINATING EDGE NETWORK NEUTRALITY, SECURITY, AND PERFORMANCE 15 (2010), *available at* www.icsi.berkeley.edu/pubs/techreports/TR-10-006.pdf.

[112] *See generally* Sandoval Reply at 43–54.

[113] WCB Letter 12/10/10, Attach. at 81–92, Cox Communications, Cox High-Speed Internet Acceptable Use Policy, ww2.cox.com/aboutus/policies.cox.

[114] WCB Letter 12/10/10, Attach. at 30–34, MetroPCS, MetroWEB Terms of Use, www.metropcs.com/products/metroweb/terms_of_use.aspx.

[115] *See Zoom Telephonics, Inc. v. Comcast Cable Communications, LLC*, Complaint (Nov. 29, 2010).

[116] *See supra* para. 0.

[117] *See supra* note 3.

[118] *See, e.g.*, Qwest PN Comments at 2 ("Qwest and virtually all major broadband providers have supported the FCC Internet Policy Principles and voluntarily abide by those principles as good policy."); Letter from Kyle E.

McSlarrow, NCTA et al. to Julius Genachowski, Chairman, FCC et al. at 1–2 n.4 (dated Apr. 29, 2010) *attached to* Letter from Robert W. Quinn, Jr., AT&T, to Marlene Dortch, Secretary, FCC at Attach A. (filed April 30, 2010), ("AT&T made a commitment to abide by the FCC's Open Internet Principles when they were first formulated in 2005 and we will continue to do so."); *see also* CenturyLink Comments at 15; TIA Comments at ii, 3, 20–22; Comcast Reply at ii; Qwest Reply at 2–3; Shane Greenstein Notice of Ex Parte, GN Docket No. 09-191, *Transaction Cost, Transparency, and Innovation for the Internet* at 13, *available at* www.openinternet.gov/workshops/innovation-investment-and-the-open-internet.htm.

[119] *See* CDT Reply at 6 ("Unraveling a web of discriminatory deals after significant investments have been made and business plans built would be a difficult and complicated undertaking both logistically and politically."); *see also* Google Comments at 29–36.

[120] As one example, Comcast's transition to a protocol-agnostic network management practice took almost nine months to complete. *See* Letter from Kathryn A. Zachem, V.P., Regulatory Affairs, Comcast Corp., to Marlene Dortch, Secretary, FCC, WC Docket No. 07-52 at 2 (filed July 10, 2008); Letter from Kathryn A. Zachem, V.P., Regulatory Affairs, Comcast Corp., to Marlene Dortch, Secretary, FCC, WC Docket No. 07-52 at Attach. B at 3, 9 (filed Sept. 19, 2008) (noting that the transition required "lab tests, technical trials, customer feedback, vendor evaluations, and a third-party consulting analysis," as well as trials in five markets).

[121] *See* CDT Comments at 6; Vonage Comments at 18.

[122] *See* CDT Comments at 6; Vonage Reply at 5; *cf. United States v. Microsoft Corp.*, 253 F.3d 34, 79 (D.C. Cir. 2001) (court "may infer causation where exclusionary conduct is aimed at producers of nascent competitive technologies," notwithstanding uncertainty of proof).

[123] *See, e.g.*, ALA Comments at 2; IFTA Comments at 14. Even some who generally oppose open Internet rules agree that extracting access fees from entities that produce content or services without the anticipation of financial reward would have significant adverse effects. *See* WCB Letter 12/10/10, Attach. at 35–80, C. Scott Hemphill, *Network Neutrality and the False Promise of Zero-Price Regulation*, 25 YALE J. ON REG. 135, 161–62 (2008) ("[S]ocial production has distinctive features that make it unusually valuable, but also unusually vulnerable, to a particular form of exclusion. That mechanism of exclusion is not subject to the prohibitions of antitrust law, moreover, presenting a relatively stronger argument for regulation."), *cited in* Prof. Tim Wu Comments at 9 n.22.

[124] *See* Free Press Comments at 76.

[125] *See supra* para.11; *infra* note 137. We note that many broadband providers are, or soon will be, subject to open Internet requirements in connection with grants under the Broadband Technology Opportunities Program (BTOP). The American Recovery and Reinvestment Act of 2009 required that nondiscrimination and network interconnection obligations be "contractual conditions" of all BTOP grants. Pub. L. No. 111-5, § 6001(j), 123 Stat. 115 (codified at 47 U.S.C. § 1305). These nondiscrimination and interconnection conditions require BTOP grantees, among other things, to adhere to the principles in the *Internet Policy Statement*; to display any network management policies in a prominent location on the service provider's website; and to offer interconnection where technically feasible.

[126] *See infra* para. 57.

[127] *See infra* Part III.G.

[128] *See, e.g.*, TWC Comments at 33; Verizon Reply at 42–43.

[129] *See, e.g.*, Free Press Comments at 4, 23–25; Google Comments at 38–39; XO Comments at 12. In making prior investment decisions, broadband providers could not have reasonably assumed that the Commission would abstain from regulating in this area, as the Commission's decisions classifying cable modem service and wireline broadband Internet access service as information services included notices of proposed rulemaking seeking comment on whether the Commission should adopt rules to protect consumers. *See Appropriate Framework for Broadband Access to the Internet Over Wireline Facilities et al.*, Report and Order and NPRM, 20 FCC Rcd 14853, 14929–35, paras. 146–59 (2005); *Inquiry Concerning High-Speed Access to the Internet Over Cable & Other Facilities et al.*, Declaratory Ruling and NPRM, 17 FCC Rcd 4798, 4839–48, paras. 72–95 (2002) (seeking comment on whether the Commission should require cable operators to give unaffiliated ISPs access to broadband cable networks); *see also* AT&T Comments at 8 ("[T]he existing principles already address any blocking or degradation of traffic and thus eliminate any theoretical leverage providers may have to impose [unilateral 'tolls']. ").

[130] *See, e.g.*, CCIA/CEA Comments at 7 ("[C]odifying an open Internet access regime is the best solution for guiding existing market forces in a manner that encourages investment, innovation, and subscription."); Clearwire Comments at 7 ("Openness is not merely an important policy issue, it is good business practice."); Free Press Comments at 77; Google Comments at 5–8, 37–39; PAETEC Comments at 21–22; XO Comments at 3–5 (adoption of the proposed rules will increase XO's incentive "to invest further in its broadband facilities"); CDT Reply at 9; SONY Reply at 5–6; XO Reply at 6 & n.13.

[131] *See supra* para. 0.

[132] *See supra* para. 0.

[133] *See, e.g.*, IPI Comments at 11 ("[A]llowing ISPs to price discriminate does not ensure that ISPs will take the additional revenue and reinvest it back in the Internet infrastructure.").

[134] *See Star Wireless, LLC v. FCC*, 522 F.3d 469, 475 (D.C. Cir. 2008) (finding that general bright-line prophylactic measures, such as the anti-collusion rule prohibiting collaborating with competing applicants for licenses, are appropriate when "the probability of abuse in transactions between related organizations is significant enough that it is more efficient to prevent the opportunity for abuse from arising than it is to try to detect actual incidents of abuse"); *see also* IPI Reply at 9; Vonage Reply at ii.

[135] *United States v. Sw. Cable Co.*, 392 U.S. 157, 176–77 (1968) (*Sw. Cable*).

[136] *Telecomms., Inc. and Liberty Media Corp.*, Applications for Consent to Transfer Control of Radio Licenses, 9 FCC Rcd 4783, 4783 para. 21 (Cab. Bur. 1994).

[137] For example, AT&T has recognized that open Internet rules "would reduce regulatory uncertainty, and should encourage investment and innovation in next generation broadband services and technologies." *See* WCB Letter 12/10/10, Attach. at 94, AT&T *Statement on Proposed FCC Rules to Preserve an Open Internet*, AT&T PUBLIC POLICY BLOG, Dec. 1, 2010, attpublicpolicy.com/government-policy/att-statement-on-proposed-fcc-rules-to-preserve-an-open-internet. Similarly, Comcast acknowledged that our proposed rules would strike "a workable balance between the needs of the marketplace and the certainty that carefully-crafted and limited rules can provide to ensure that Internet freedom and openness are preserved." *See* David L. Cohen, *FCC Proposes Rules to Preserve an Open Internet*, COMCASTVOICES, Dec. 1, 2010, blog.comcast.com/2010/12/fcc-proposes-rules-to-preserve-an-open-internet.html; *see also, e.g.*, Final Brief for Intervenors NCTA and NBC Universal, Inc. at 11–13; 19–22, *Comcast Corp. v. FCC*, 600 F.3d 642 (D.C. Cir. 2010) (No. 08-1291). In addition to broadband providers, an array of industry leaders, venture capitalists, and public interest groups have concluded that our rules will promote investment in the Internet ecosystem by removing regulatory uncertainty. *See* Free Press Comments at 10; Google Comments at 40; PIC Comments at 28; WCB Letter 12/10/10, Attach. at 91 (statement of CALinnovates.org), 96 (statement of Larry Cohen, president of the Communications Workers of America), 98 (statement of Ron Conway, founder of SV Angel), 99 (statement of Craig Newmark, founder of craigslist), 105 (statement of Dean Garfield, president and CEO of the Information Technology Industry Council), 111 (Dec. 8, 2010 letter from Jeremy Liew, Managing Director, Lightspeed Venture Partners to Julius Genachowski, FCC Chairman), 112 (Dec. 1, 2010 letter from Jed Katz, Managing Director, Javelin Venture Partners to Julius Genachowski, FCC Chairman), 127 (statement of Gary Shapiro, president and CEO of the Consumer Electronics Association), 128 (statement of Ram Shriram, founder of Sherpalo Ventures), 132 (statements of Rey Ramsey, President and CEO of TechNet, and John Chambers, Chairman and CEO of Cisco), 133 (statement of John Doerr, Kleiner Perkins Caufield & Byers); XO Reply at 6.

[138] *See, e.g.*, CCIA Comments at 7–8; Google Comments at 37; OIC Comments at 34, 40; Skype Comments at 4–5, 12; Vonage Comments at 5–6; XO Comments at 4, 12, 14–15; PAETEC Comments at 8, 22–24; DISH Reply at 14; XO Reply at 5–6; Clearwire PN Comments at 2.

[139] *See* Dec. 15, 2009 Workshop Tr., *supra* note 40, at 31–71, 90–91, 102–07.

[140] *See, e.g.*, Union Square Ventures Comments at 1 (asserting that without open Internet rules, "the businesses in which Union Square Ventures invests could be singled out and charged a different price for network access based solely on the content they transmit across the network. Such practice would be discriminatory and would endanger innovation on the Internet because it would prevent small companies with little capital from having equal access to the audience of global internet users that larger companies would be capable of accessing"); OIC Comments App. A, Letter from 28 Internet and technology leaders to Chairman Genachowski (dated October 19, 2009) ("An open Internet fuels a competitive and efficient marketplace, where consumers make the ultimate choices about which products succeed and which fail. This allows businesses of all sizes, from the smallest startup to larger corporations, to compete, yielding maximum economic growth and opportunity."); Letter from 30 Venture Capitalists to Chairman Genachowski (dated October 21, 2009) ("Open markets for Internet content will drive investment, entrepreneurship and innovation. For these reasons [open Internet rules are] pro-investment, pro-competition, and pro-consumer."); Free Press Comments at 44–45 (asserting that the absence of nondiscrimination protections will have a large impact on investments made in the application and content markets and that the "potential for discriminatory treatment and nonstandard network management could destroy investor confidence in the applications market, stifling growth in the one segment that drives the information economy").

[141] For this reason, we are not persuaded that alternative approaches, such as rules that lack a formal enforcement mechanism, a transparency rule alone, or reliance entirely on technical advisory groups to resolve disputes, would adequately address the potential harms and be less burdensome than the rules we adopt here. *See, e.g.*, Verizon Comments at 130–34. In particular, we reject the notion that Commission action is unnecessary because the Department of Justice and the Federal Trade Commission (FTC) "are well equipped to cure any market ills." *Id.* at 9. Our statutory responsibilities are broader than preventing antitrust violations or unfair competition. *See, e.g., News Corp. and DIRECTV Group, Inc.*, 23 FCC Rcd 3265, 3277–78, paras. 23–25 (2008). We must, for example, promote deployment of advanced telecommunications capability, ensure that charges in connection with telecommunications services are just and reasonable, ensure the orderly

development of local television broadcasting, and promote the public interest through spectrum licensing. *See infra* Part 0; *see also* CDT Comments at 8–9; Comm'r Jon Liebowitz, FTC, *Concurring Statement of Commissioner Jon Leibowitz Regarding the Staff Report: "Broadband Connectivity Competition Policy"* (2007), *available at* www.ftc.gov/speeches/leibowitz/V070000statement.pdf ("[T]here is little agreement over whether antitrust, with its requirements for *ex post* case by case analysis, is capable of fully and in a timely fashion *resolving* many of the concerns that have animated the net neutrality debate.").

[142] Zittrain Comments at 1.

[143] Contrary to the suggestion of some, neither the Department of Justice nor the FTC has concluded that the broadband market is competitive or that open Internet rules are unnecessary. *See* McDowell Statement at *4; Baker Statement at *3. In the submission in question, the Department observed that: (1) the wireline broadband market is highly concentrated, with most consumers served by at most two providers; (2) the prospects for additional wireline competition are dim due to the high fixed and sunk costs required to provide wireline broadband service; and (3) the extent to which mobile wireless offerings will compete with wireline offerings is unknown. *See* DOJ *Ex Parte* Jan. 4, 2010, GN Dkt. No. 09-51, at 8, 10, 13-14. The Department specifically endorsed requiring greater transparency by broadband providers, *id.* at 25-27, and recognized that in concentrated markets, like the broadband market, it is appropriate for policymakers to limit "business practices that thwart innovation." *Id.* at 11. Finally, although the Department cautioned that care must be taken to avoid stifling infrastructure investment, it expressed particular concern about price regulation, which we are not adopting. *Id.* at 28. In 2007, the FTC issued a staff report on broadband competition policy. *See* FTC, *Broadband Connectivity Competition Policy* (June 2007). Like the Department, the FTC staff did not conclude that the broadband market is competitive. To the contrary, the FTC staff made clear that it had not studied the state of competition in any specific markets. *Id.* at 8, 105, 156. With regard to the merits of open Internet rules, the FTC staff report recited arguments pro and con, *see, e.g., id.* at 82, 105, 147-54, and called for additional study, *id.* at 7, 9-10, 157.

[144] The definition of "broadband Internet access service" proposed in the *Open Internet NPRM* encompassed any "Internet Protocol data transmission between an end user and the Internet." *Open Internet NPRM*, 24 FCC Rcd at 13128, App. A. Some commenters argued that this definition would cover a variety of services that do not constitute broadband Internet access service as end users and broadband providers generally understand that term, but that merely offer data transmission between a discrete set of Internet endpoints (for example, virtual private networks, or videoconferencing services). *See, e.g.*, AT&T Comments at 96–100; Communications Workers of America (CWA) Comments at 10–12; Sprint Reply at 16–17; *see also* CDT Comments at 49–50 (distinguishing managed (or specialized) services from broadband Internet access service by defining the former, in part, as data transmission "between an end user and a *limited* group of parties or endpoints") (emphasis added).

[145] In the *Open Internet NPRM*, we proposed separate definitions of the terms "broadband Internet access," and "broadband Internet access service." *Open Internet NPRM*, 24 FCC Rcd at 13128, App. A § 8.3. For purposes of these rules, we find it simpler to define just the service.

[146] *See, e.g., SBC Commc'ns Inc. and AT&T Corp. Applications for Approval of Transfer of Control*, Memorandum Opinion and Order, 20 FCC Rcd 18290, 18335, para. 82 n.243 (2005) ("The Commission has defined mass market customers as residential and small business customers that purchase standardized offerings of communications services."); *Applications of NYNEX Corp. Transferor, and Bell Atlantic Corp., Transferee*, Memorandum Opinion and Order, 12 FCC Rcd 19985, 20016, para. 53 (1997) ("Residential and small business customers are served primarily through mass marketing techniques including regional advertising and telemarketing.").

[147] *See, e.g., AT&T and BellSouth Corp.*, Memorandum Opinion and Order, 22 FCC Rcd 5662, 5709-10, para. 85 (2007) ("[E]nterprise customers tend to be sophisticated and knowledgeable (often with the assistance of consultants), . . . contracts are typically the result of RFPs and are individually-negotiated (and frequently subject to non-disclosure clauses), . . . contracts are generally for customized service packages, and that the contracts usually remain in effect for a number of years.").

[148] *See, e.g.*, Koshernet, www.koshernet.com.

[149] To the extent these services are provided by broadband providers over last-mile capacity shared with broadband Internet access service, they would be specialized services. *See infra* Part 0.

[150] We also note that our rules apply only as far as the limits of a broadband provider's control over the transmission of data to or from its broadband customers.

[151] This is true notwithstanding the increasing sophistication of network management tools, described above in Part 0. *See* Arthur Callado et al., *A Survey on Internet Traffic Identification*, 11 IEEE COMMNC'NS SURVEYS & TUTORIALS 37, 49 (2009).

[152] *See* IETF, REFLECTIONS ON INTERNET TRANSPARENCY, RFC 4924 at 5 (Jul. 2007) (RFC 4924) ("In practice, filtering intended to block or restrict application usage is difficult to successfully implement without customer consent, since over time developers will tend to re-engineer filtered protocols so as to avoid the filters. Thus over time, filtering is likely to result in interoperability issues or unnecessary complexity. These costs come without the benefit of effective filtering . . . ."); IETF, CONSIDERATIONS ON THE USE OF A SERVICE

IDENTIFIER IN PACKET HEADERS, RFC 3639 at 3 (Oct. 2003) (RFC 3639) ("Attempts by intermediate systems to impose service-based controls on communications against the perceived interests of the end parties to the communication are often circumvented. Services may be tunneled within other services, proxied by a collaborating external host (e.g., an anonymous redirector), or simply run over an alternate port (e.g., port 8080 vs port 80 for HTTP)."). *Cf.* RFC 3639 at 4 ("From this perspective of network and application utility, it is preferable that no action or activity be undertaken by any agency, carrier, service provider, or organization which would cause end-users and protocol designers to generally obscure service identification information from the IP packet header."). Our rules are nationwide and do not vary by geographic area, notwithstanding potential variations across local markets for broadband Internet access service. Uniform national rules create a more predictable policy environment for broadband providers, many of which offer services in multiple geographic areas. *See, e.g.*, Level 3 Comments at 13; Charter Comments at iv. Edge providers will benefit from uniform treatment of their traffic in different localities and by different broadband providers. Broadband end users will also benefit from uniform rules, which protect them regardless of where they are located or which broadband provider they obtain service from.

[153] *See* 47 U.S.C. § 153(34) ("The term 'mobile station' means a radio-communication station capable of being moved and which ordinarily does move.").

[154] We note that Section 337(f)(1) of the Act excludes public safety services from the definition of mobile broadband Internet access service.

[155] *But see* AT&T Comments at 32–34; NCTA Comments at 48–49; MetroPCS Reply at 31–34; TWC PN Reply at 11–12.

[156] *See* 47 U.S.C. § 151.

[157] When the Commission adopted the *Internet Policy Statement*, it promised to incorporate the principles into "ongoing policymaking activities." *Internet Policy Statement*, 20 FCC Rcd at 14988, para. 5.

[158] *See, e.g., Applications for Consent to the Assignment and/or Transfer of Control of Licenses, Adelphia Commc'ns Corp. et al.*, Memorandum Opinion and Order, 21 FCC Rcd 8203, 8299, para. 223 (2006) (the *Internet Policy Statement* "contains principles against which the conduct of Comcast, Time Warner, and other broadband service providers can be measured"); *AT&T and BellSouth Corp.*, Memorandum Opinion and Order, 22 FCC Rcd 5662, 5726, para. 119 (2007) (similar).

[159] *See, e.g., Appropriate Framework for Broadband Access to the Internet over Wireline Facilities*, Report and Order and Notice of Proposed Rulemaking, 20 FCC Rcd 14853, 14976 (2005) (*Wireline Broadband Order*) (separate statement of Chairman Martin); *id.* at 14980 (Statement of Commissioner Copps, concurring); *id.* at 14983 (Statement of Commissioner Adelstein, concurring); Verizon June 8, 2009 Comments, GN Docket No. 09-51, at 86 ("These principles have helped to guide wireline providers' practices and to ensure that consumers' expectations for their public Internet access services are met."). The Commission has conditioned wireline broadband provider merger approvals on the merged entity's compliance with these obligations. *See, e.g., SBC Commc'ns Inc. and AT&T Corp. Applications for Approval of Transfer of Control*, Memorandum Opinion and Order, 20 FCC Rcd 18290, 18392, para. 211 (2005).

[160] *See supra* Part 0. We thus find broadband providers distinguishable from other participants in the Internet marketplace. *See, e.g.*, Verizon Comments at 36–39 (discussing a variety of other participants in the Internet ecosystem); Verizon Reply at 36–37 (same); NCTA Comments at 47–49 (same); NCTA Reply at 22 (same).

[161] *See Open Internet NPRM*, 24 FCC Rcd at 13101, para. 91 n.209.

[162] *See Communications Assistance for Law Enforcement Act and Broadband Access and Services*, First Report and Order and Further Notice of Proposed Rulemaking, 20 FCC Rcd 14989, 15006–07, para. 36, n.99 (2005) (*CALEA Order*). Consistent with the Commission's approach in the *CALEA Order*, "[w]e note . . . that the provider of underlying [broadband service] facilities to such an establishment would be subject to [the rules]." *Id.* at 15007, para. 36.

[163] We note that the premise operator that purchases the Internet service remains the end user for purposes of our rules, however. *See infra* Part 0 (discussing the application of our definition of "reasonable network management" in the context of traffic unwanted by premise operators). Moreover, although not bound by our rules, we encourage premise operators to disclose relevant restrictions on broadband service they make available to their patrons.

[164] *See infra* Part 0. We also do not include within the rules free access to individuals' wireless networks, even if those networks are intentionally made available to others. *See* Electronic Frontier Foundation (EFF) Comments at 25–28. No commenter argued that open Internet rules should apply to individual operators of wireless networks in these circumstances.

[165] Broadband providers may have an incentive not to provide such information to end users, as doing so can lessen switching costs for end users. Third-party information sources such as Consumer Reports and the trade press do not routinely provide such information. *See* CDT Comments at 31; CWA Comments at 21; DISH Comments at 2; Google Comments at ii, 64–66; Level 3 Comments at 13; Sandoval Reply at 60. Economic literature in this area also confirms that policies requiring firms to disclose information generally benefit competition and consumers. *See, e.g.*, Mark Armstrong, *Interactions Between Competition and Consumer Policy*, 4 COMPETITION POLICY INT'L 97 113–16 (Spring 2008), eprints.ucl.ac.uk/7634/1/7634.pdf.

[166] *See* PIC Reply at 16–18; Free Press Comments at 43–45; Ad Hoc Comments at ii; CDT Comments at 5–7; ALA Comments at 3; National Hispanic Media Coalition (NHMC) Comments at 8; National Broadband Plan at 168, 174 (lack of trust in Internet is significant factor preventing non-adopters from subscribing to broadband services); 47 U.S.C. §§ 151, 230, 254, 1302. A recent FCC survey found that among non-broadband end users, 46% believed that the Internet is dangerous for kids, and 57% believed that it was too easy for personal information to be stolen online. JOHN B. HORRIGAN, FCC SURVEY: BROADBAND ADOPTION & USE IN AMERICA 17 (Mar. 2010), *available at* www.fcc.gov/DiversityFAC/032410/consumer-survey-horrigan.pdf.

[167] *See, e.g.*, OIC Comments at 89–91 (disclosure requirements would likely increase the speed of innovation, especially in the wireless space); Google Comments at 66–67 (failure to provide information to developers inhibits innovation and investment); Data Foundry Comments at 10; CDT Comments at 31, 33.

[168] On a number of occasions, broadband providers have blocked lawful traffic without informing end users or edge providers. In addition to the Madison River and Comcast-BitTorrent incidents described above, broadband providers appear to have covertly blocked thousands of BitTorrent uploads in the United States throughout early 2008. *See* Marcel Dischinger et al., *supra* note 111; Catherine Sandoval, *Disclosure, Deception, and Deep-Packet Inspection*, 78 FORDHAM L. REV. 641, 666–84 (2009).

[169] *See* 47 U.S.C. §§ 154(k), 218.

[170] *See, e.g.*, CDT Comments at 31; CWA Comments at 21; DISH Comments at 2; Google Comments at ii, 64; Level 3 Comments at 13; Prof. Catherine Sandoval Reply at 30. Other commenters support a transparency rule but oppose codification of other principles. *See, e.g.*, LARIAT Comments at 3–4; NTCA Comments at 2; NTT Comments at 2.

[171] *See Open Internet NPRM*, 24 FCC Rcd at 13110–11, paras. 125–29; *Further Inquiry into Two Under-Developed Issues in the Open Internet Proceeding*, Public Notice, 25 FCC Rcd 12637, 12641 (2010) (*Open Internet PN*).

[172] For purposes of these rules, "consumer" includes any subscriber to the broadband provider's broadband Internet access service, and "person" includes any "individual, group of individuals, corporation, partnership, association, unit of government or legal entity, however organized," *cf.* 47 C.F.R. § 54.8(a)(6). We also expect broadband providers to disclose information about the impact of "specialized services," if any, on last-mile capacity available for, and the performance of, broadband Internet access service. *See infra* Part 0.

[173] Commenters disagree on the risks of requiring disclosure of information regarding technical, proprietary, and security-related management practices. *Compare, e.g.*, American Cable Association (ACA) Comments at 17; AFTRA et al. Comments at ii, 16; Cox Comments at 11; Fiber-to-the-Home Council (FTTH) Comments at 3, 27; Libove Comments at 4; Sprint Comments at 16; T-Mobile Comments at 39, *with, e.g.*, Free Press Comments at 117–18; Free Press Reply at 17–19; Digital Education Coalition (DEC) Comments at 14; NJRC Comments at 20–21. We may subsequently require disclosure of such information to the Commission; to the extent we do, we will ensure that such information is protected consistent with existing Commission procedures for treatment of confidential information.

[174] *Compare, e.g.*, AT&T Comments at 191, 193; Bright House Comments at 11 (high-level disclosure is adequate) *with, e.g.*, CDT Comments at 31; Google Comments at 66; Center for Media Justice et al. Comments at 64; NJRC Comments at 23; Vonage Comments at ii, 23.

[175] In setting forth the following categories of information subject to the transparency principle, we assume that the broadband provider has chosen to offer its services on standardized terms, although providers of "information services" are not obligated to do so. *See generally* paras. 0, 0. If the provider tailors its terms of service to meet the requirements of an individual end user, those terms must at a minimum be disclosed to the end user in accordance with the transparency principle.

[176] *See* CCIA/CEA Comments at 33; DEC Comments at 11–12; Free Press Comments at 112–13, 115–16 n.232; Google Comments at 65–66; Information Technology Industry Council (ITIC) Comments at 10–12; PIC Comments at 63–65; RNK Comments at 7–8; Software & Information Industry Association (SIIA) Comments at 8.

[177] We note that the description of congestion management practices provided by Comcast in the wake of the Comcast-BitTorrent incident likely satisfies the transparency rule with respect to congestion management practices. *See* Comcast, Network Management Update, www.comcast.net/terms/network/update; Comcast, Comcast Corporation Description of Planned Network Management Practices to be Deployed Following the Termination of Current Practices, downloads.comcast.net/docs/Attachment_B_Future_Practices.pdf.

[178] *But see infra* para. 0.

[179] *See* CCIA/CEA Comments at 33; Free Press Comments at 112–13, 115–16 n.232; Google Comments at 65–66; ITIC Comments at 10–12; Nokia Siemens Comments at 12; PIC Comments at 63–65; SIIA Comments at 8.

[180] *See* CCIA/CEA Comments at 33; Free Press Comments at 112–13, 115–16 n.232; Google Comments at 65–66; PIC Comments at 63–65; SIIA Comments at 8.

[181] *Open Internet NPRM*, 24 FCC Rcd at 13110, para. 126.

[182] *See, e.g.*, CDT Comments at 36; Charter Comments at 21; DEC Comments at 3, 14; DISH Comments at 6; NHMC Comments at 9; OIC Comments at 90; PIA Comments at 65.

[183] *See, e.g.*, ACA Comments at iv, 16; Bright House Comments at 11.

[184] *See, e.g.*, Netflix Comments at 8; PIA Comments at 64; NJRC Comments at 19–20, 24; NHMC Comments at 9; BBIC/BRC Comments at 7.

[185] *See infra* Part 0.

[186] But we expect that broadband providers will make disclosures in a manner accessible by people with disabilities.

[187] Some commenters advocate for a standard disclosure format. *See, e.g.*, Adam Candeub et al. Reply at 7; Level 3 Comments at 13; Sprint Comments at 17. Others support a plain language requirement. *See, e.g.*, NATOA Comments at 7; NJRC Comments at 19; IFTA Comments at 16. Other commenters, however, argue against the imposition of a standard format as inflexible and difficult to implement. *See, e.g.*, Cox Comments at 10; National Telecommunications Cooperative Association (NTCA) Comments at 9; Qwest Comments at 11. The approach we adopt is similar to the approach adopted in the Commission's *Truth-in-Billing Proceeding*, where we set out basic guidelines. *Truth-in-Billing and Billing Format*, First Report and Order and Further NPRM, 14 FCC Rcd 7492, 7495–96, paras. 3–5 (1999).

[188] We may address this issue as part of a separate, ongoing proceeding regarding transparency for communications services more generally. *Consumer Information and Disclosure*, Notice of Inquiry, FCC 09-68 (rel. Aug. 28, 2010). Relatedly, the Commission has begun an effort, in partnership with broadband providers, to measure the actual speed and performance of broadband service, and we expect that the data generated by this effort will inform Commission efforts regarding disclosure. *See Comment Sought on Residential Fixed Broadband Services Testing and Measurement Solution, Pleading Cycle Established*, Public Notice, 25 FCC Rcd 3836 (2010) (SamKnows project); *Comment Sought on Measurement of Mobile Broadband Network Performance and Coverage*, Public Notice, 25 FCC Rcd 7069 (2010) (same).

[189] *See, e.g.*, NTCA Comments at 9, 43–44; US Telecom Comments at 52; ADTRAN Comments at i, 9, 11; Texas Public Policy Foundation (TPPF) Comments at 99; Telecommunications Industry Association (TIA) Comments at 31–32.

[190] In a separate proceeding, the Commission has determined that the costs of making disclosure materials available on a service provider's website are outweighed by the public benefits where the disclosure requirement applies only to entities already using the Internet for other purposes. *See Standardized and Enhanced Disclosure Requirements for Television Broadcast Licensee Public Interest Obligations*, Report and Order, 23 FCC Rcd 1274, 1277–78, paras. 7–10 (2008).

[191] *See* Sandoval Comments at 4–5. For example, the Max Planck Institute analyzed data collected by the *Glasnost* tool from thousands of end user, and found that broadband providers were discriminating against application-specific traffic. *See* WCB Letter 12/13/10, Attach. at 235–39, Max Planck Institute for Software Systems, Glasnost: Results from Tests for BitTorrent Traffic Blocking, broadband.mpi-sws.org/transparency/results. *Netalyzr* is a National Science Foundation-funded project that tests a wide range of network characteristics. *See* International Computer Science Institute, Netalyzer, netalyzr.icsi.berkeley.edu. Similar tools are being developed for mobile broadband services. *See, e.g.*, WindRider, Mobile Network Neutrality Monitoring System, www.cs.northwestern.edu/~ict992/mobile.htm.

[192] For an example of a public-private partnership that could encourage the development of new tools to assess network management practices, see FCC Open Internet Apps Challenge, www.openinternet.gov/challenge.

[193] *See, e.g.*, Qwest Comments at 44–45.

[194] *See, e.g.*, Barbara van Schewick, *Network Neutrality: What a Non-Discrimination Rule Should Look Like* at 22 (Dec. 14, 2010) ("In order for disclosure to have a disciplining effect, customers need to be able to switch to another provider that does not impose a similar restriction, and they need to be able to do so at low costs.") (van Schewick Dec. 14, 2010 White Paper), *attached to* Letter from Barbara van Schewick, to Marlene Dortch, Secretary, FCC, GN Docket No. 09-191 at Attach. A (filed Dec. 14, 2010); CCIA/CEA Comments at 32; Frischmann Comments at 5; ARL et al. Comments at 5; Netflix Comments at 5; NJRC Comments at 16–17; OIC Reply at 16; Amazon.com Comments at 2.

[195] *See* CDT Comments at 22–23; National Association of Realtors (NAR) Comments at 1–2; Netflix Comments at 3–4; Red Hat Comments at 2–3; SIIA Comments at 5–6; AOL Reply at 3–4; Google Reply at 16–18; Skype Reply at 1, 5–6; Letter from Ernesto Falcon, PK, to Marlene H. Dortch, Secretary, FCC, GN Docket Nos. 09-191, 10-127, WC Docket No. 07-52 (Oct. 28, 2010).

[196] The Commission has long protected end users' rights to attach lawful devices that do not harm communications networks. *See, e.g., Use of the Carterfone Device in Message Toll Telephone Service*, 13 FCC 2d 420, 424 (1968); *Amendment of Section 64.702 of the Commission's Rules and Regulations (Second Computer Inquiry)*, Final Decision, 77 FCC 2d 384, 388 (1980); *see also* Michael T. Hoeker, *From Carterfone to the iPhone: Consumer Choice in the Wireless Telecommunications Marketplace*, 17 COMMLAW CONSPECTUS 187, 192 (2008); Kevin Werbach, *The Federal Computer Commission*, 84 N.C. L. REV. 1, 21 (2005).

[197] As Qwest states, "Qwest and virtually all major broadband providers have supported the FCC Internet Policy Principles and voluntarily abide by those principles as good policy." Qwest PN Comments at 2–3, 5; *see also, e.g.*, Comcast Comments at 27; Clearwire Comments at 1; Margaret Boles, *AT&T on Comcast v. FCC Decision*, AT&T PUB. POL'Y BLOG (Apr. 6, 2010), attpublicpolicy.com/broadband-policy/att-statement-on-comcast-v-fcc-decision.

[198] *Open Internet NPRM*, 24 FCC Rcd at 13100–03, paras. 88–98.

[199] As described below, we adopt a tailored version of this rule for mobile broadband providers. *See infra* Part 0.

[200] *See* William Lehr et al. Comments at 27 ("While the proposed rules of the FCC appear to make a clear distinction between applications and services on the one hand (rule 3) and content (rule 1), we believe that there will be some activities that do not fit cleanly into these two categories"); PIC Comments at 39; RFC 4924 at 5. For this reason the rule may prohibit the blocking of a port or particular protocol used by an application, without blocking the application completely, unless such practice is reasonable network management. *See* Distributed Computing Industry Ass'n (DCIA) Comments at 7 (discussing work-arounds by P2P companies facing port blocking or other practices); Sandvine Reply at 3; RFC 4924. The rule also is neutral with respect to where in the protocol stack or in the network blocking could occur. *See infra* note 235.

[201] The "no blocking" rule does not impose any independent legal obligation on broadband Internet access service providers to be the arbiter of what is lawful. *See, e.g.*, WISPA Comments at 12–13; *see also infra* Part 0.

[202] We note that MVPDs, pursuant to section 629 and the Commission's implementing regulations, are already subject to similar requirements that give end users the right to attach devices to an MVPD system provided that the attached equipment does not cause electronic or physical harm or assist in the unauthorized receipt of service. *See Implementation of Section 304 of the Telecommunications Act of 1996, Commercial Availibility of Navigation Devices*, Report and Order, 13 FCC Rcd 14775 (1998); 47 U.S.C. § 549; 47 C.F.R. §§ 76.1201–03. Nothing in this Order is intended to alter those existing rules.

[203] For example, a DOCSIS-based broadband provider is not required to support a DSL modem. *See* ACA Comments at 13–14; *see also* Satellite Broadband Commenters Comments at 8–9 (noting that an antenna and associated modem must comply with equipment and protocol standards set by satellite companies, but that "consumers can [then] attach . . . any personal computer or wireless router they wish").

[204] We do not find it appropriate to interpret our rule to impose a blanket prohibition on degradation of traffic more generally. Congestion ordinarily results in degradation of traffic, and such an interpretation could effectively prohibit broadband providers from permitting congestion to occur on their networks. Although we expect broadband providers to continue to expand the capacity of their networks—and we believe our rules help ensure that they continue to have incentives to do so—we recognize that some network congestion may be unavoidable. *See, e.g.*, AT&T Comments at 65; TWC Comments at 16–18; Internet Freedom Coalition Reply at 5.

[205] *See, e.g.*, DCIA Comments at 8; William Lehr et al. Comments at 13, 14, 20; Google Comments at 41, 58, 62, 77–78, 81–82; NAR Comments at 2; Red Hat Comments at 3; Vonage Comments at 17; DISH Reply at 8–9; Skype Reply at 13–14.

[206] *See, e.g.*, AT&T Comments at 8; OIC Reply at 9–10.

[207] *Comcast Order*, 23 FCC Rcd at 13053, para. 44.

[208] *See supra* note 63.

[209] We do not intend our rules to affect existing arrangements for network interconnection, including existing paid peering arrangements.

[210] *See supra* Part 0.

[211] *See supra* note 172 (defining "consumer" for purposes of these rules).

[212] *See infra* Part 0. We also make clear that open Internet protections coexist with other legal and regulatory frameworks. *See infra* Part 0. Except as otherwise described in this Order, we do not address the possible application of the no unreasonable discrimination rule to particular circumstances, despite the requests of certain commenters. *See, e.g.*, AT&T Comments at 64–77, 108–12; PAETEC Comments at 13; *see also* AT&T Comments at 56 (arguing that some existing agreements could be at odds with limitations on pay for priority arrangements). Rather, we find it more appropriate to address the application of our rule in the context of an appropriate Commission proceeding with the benefit of a more comprehensive record.

[213] *See Comcast Order*, 23 FCC Rcd at 13058–59, paras. 52–53.

[214] *See, e.g.*, *id.* at 13058-59, para. 52.

[215] "The rapidly developing array of Internet and other interactive computer services . . . offer[] users a great degree of control over the information that they receive, as well as *the potential for even greater control in the future* as technology develops." 47 U.S.C. § 230(a)(1)–(2) (emphasis added).

[216] van Schewick Jan. 19, 2010 *Ex Parte* Letter. *See also id.* at 4 n.6 (observing that: (1) the Internet "does not create value through its existence alone. It creates value by enabling users to do the things they want or need to do;" (2) "[e]nabling widespread experimentation at the application-level and enabling users to choose the applications they prefer is at the heart of the mechanism that enables innovation under uncertainty to be successful;" and (3) "[c]onsumers, not network providers, should continue to choose winners and losers on the Internet").

[217] In these types of arrangements "[t]he broadband provider does not get any particular leverage, because the ability to select which traffic gets priority lies with individual subscribers. Meanwhile, an entity providing content, applications, or services does not need to worry about striking up relationships with various broadband providers to obtain top treatment. All it needs to worry about is building relationships with users and explaining to those users whether and how they may want to select the particular content, application, or

service for priority treatment." CDT Comments at 27; *see also* Amazon Comments at 2–3; SureWest Comments at 32–33.

[218] We note that default settings set by broadband providers would likely be considered more broadband provider-controlled than end-user controlled. *See generally* Jason Scott Johnston, *Strategic Bargaining and the Economic Theory of Contract Default Rules*, 100 YALE L.J. 615 (1990); Daniel Kahneman et al., *Anomalies: The Endowment Effect, Loss Aversion, and Status Quo Bias*, 5 J. ECON. PERSP. 193, 197–99 (1991).

[219] *See, e.g.*, Verizon Comments at 70–71; AT&T Comments at 10506; ALEC Comments at 11; ALU Comments at 8–9; Bright House Comments at 7–8; CBW Comments at 7–9.

[220] *See, e.g.*, CCIA Comments at 14; CDT Comments at 25–26; FTTH Comments at 18 and Attach., *A Network Engineer's Primer* at 20; OPASTCO Comments at 15; T-Mobile Comments at 20; Verizon Comments at 56 & Attach. C, Michael D. Topper Decl. at 57; *but see* Free Press Comments at 54–55, 61–62; NJRC Comments at 15; SONY Comments at 7–8.

[221] *See, e.g.*, van Schewick Dec. 14, 2010 White Paper at 13.

[222] *See* CDT Comments at 40 ("Congestion management practices should be agnostic as to both the content of subscribers' communications and the identities of the parties with whom the subscribers are communicating."); Ad Hoc Comments at 5–6 ("The agnostic Internet has also enabled vigorous competition to develop at the Internet's 'edge' for new applications, equipment, content, and business processes."); Free Press Comments at 56 (noting that protocol-agnostic network management "does not select winners and losers on the Internet by targeting specific application").

[223] 47 U.S.C. § 230(b)(2).

[224] Broadband providers' practices historically have relied on the efforts of such groups, which follow open processes conducive to broad participation. *See, e.g.*, William Lehr et al. Comments at 24; Comcast Comments at 53–59; FTTH Comments at 12; Internet Society (ISOC) Comments at 1–2; OIC Comments at 50–52; Comcast Reply at 5–7. Moreover, Internet community governance groups develop and encourage widespread implementation of best practices, supporting an environment that facilitates innovation. *See supra* Part 0 (discussing the benefits of edge providers having access to a uniform service interface, consisting of a core set of Internet standards and conventions); CDT Comments at 43–44.

[225] *See, e.g.*, CDT Comments at 38; ISOC Comments at 2 (noting "that while open Internet standards processes are invaluable for establishing specifications for best practices, the question of evaluating whether a given practice is implemented in a way that is reasonable or not (compliance) is outside of their scope"); OIC Comments at 52; Comcast Reply at 6 (noting that "the IETF itself demurs on 'policy-making'").

[226] *Cf., e.g.*, Madison River discussion *supra* para. 0.

[227] *Cf., e.g.*, Comcast-BitTorrent discussion *supra* para. 0.

[228] *Cf., e.g.*, CDT Comments at 5 (describing decision by Telus, one of Canada's largest broadband providers, to block a web site created by an employee labor union that displayed information about the union's contract dispute with Telus); *see also* Statement of Andrew Jay Schwartzman, MAP, at FCC Open Internet Workshop: Speech, Democratic Engagement, and the Open Internet, Dec. 15, 2009 (filed Dec. 17, 2009) at 1; ACLU PN Comments at 9; Free Press PN Comments at 24.

[229] The *Open Internet NPRM* proposed a flat ban on discrimination and interpreted that requirement to prohibit broadband providers from "charg[ing] a content, application, or service provider for enhanced or prioritized access to the subscribers of the broadband Internet access service provider." *Open Internet NPRM*, 24 FCC Rcd at 13104–05, paras. 104, 106. In the context of a "no unreasonable discrimination" rule that leaves interpretation to a case-by-case process, we instead adopt the approach to pay for priority described in this paragraph.

[230] *See supra* Part 0; *see also* PIC Comments at 51 (expressing concern about "market entrants [being required] to negotiate separate prioritization deals with the hundreds of ISPs that serve the United States before having an opportunity to be nationally competitive").

[231] *See supra* para. 0.

[232] *See, e.g.*, Prof. Thomas Nachbar Nov. 1, 2010 Comments at 10 (conceding that "allowing network providers to charge for preferred carriage may disadvantage non-commercial content, application, and service providers *relative* to commercial ones"); Statement of Michele Combs, The Christian Coalition of America, GN Docket No. 09-191, WC Docket No. 07-52, at 5 (filed Dec. 22, 2009) (expressing concern about the impact of prioritization arrangements on political advocacy organizations such as theirs); ALA Comments at 2 (same for libraries); DEC Comments at 7–12 (same for digital education).

[233] *See, e.g.*, Hemphill, *supra* note 123, at 161–62.

[234] *See supra* para. 0.

[235] We reject arguments that our approach to pay-for-priority arrangements is inconsistent with allowing content-delivery networks (CDNs). *See, e.g.*, Cisco Comments at 11–12; TWC Comments at 21–22, 65, 89–90; AT&T Reply at 49–53; Bright House Reply at 9. CDN services are designed to reduce the capacity requirements and costs of the CDN's edge provider clients by hosting the content for those clients closer to end users. Unlike broadband providers, third-party CDN providers do not control the last-mile connection to the end user. And CDNs that do not deploy within an edge provider's network may still reach an end user via

the user's broadband connection. *See* CDT Comments at 25 n.84; George Ou Comments (Preserving the Open and Competitive Bandwidth Market) at 3; *see also* Cisco Comments at 11; FTTH Comments at 23–24. Moreover, CDNs typically provide a benefit to the sender and recipient of traffic without causing harm to third-party traffic. Though we note disagreement regarding the impact of CDNs on other traffic, the record does not demonstrate that the use of CDNs has any material adverse effect on broadband end users' experience of traffic that is not delivered via a CDN. *Compare* Letter from S. Derek Turner, Free Press, to Chairman Genachowski et al., FCC, GN Docket No. 09-191, WC Docket No. 07-52, at 1–2 (filed July 29, 2010) *with* Letter from Richard Bennett, ITIF, to Chairman Genachowski et al., FCC, GN Docket No. 09-191, WC Docket No. 07-52, Attach. at 12 (filed Aug. 9, 2010). Indeed, the same benefits derived from using CDNs can be achieved if an edge provider's own servers happen to be located in close proximity to end users. Everything on the Internet that is accessible to an end user is not, and cannot be, in equal proximity from that end user. *See* John Staurulakis Inc. Comments at 5; Bret T. Swanson Reply at 4. Finally, CDN providers unaffiliated with broadband providers generally do not compete with edge providers and thus generally lack economic incentives (or the ability) to discriminate against edge providers. *See* Akamai Comments at 12; NASUCA Reply at 7; NCTA Reply at 25; *see also supra* Part 0. We likewise reject proposals to limit our rules to actions taken at or below the "network layer." *See, e.g.*, Google Comments at 24–26; Vonage Reply at 2; CDT Reply at 18; Prof. Scott Jordan (Jordan) Comments at 3; *see also* Scott Jordan, *A Layered Network Approach to Net Neutrality*, INT'L J. OF COMMC'N 427, 432–33 (2007) (describing the OSI layers model and the actions of routers at and below the network layer) *attached to* Letter from Scott Jordan, Professor, University of California–Irvine, to Office of the Secretary, FCC, GN Docket No. 09-191, WC Docket No. 07-52 (filed Mar. 22, 2010). We are not persuaded that the proposed limitation is necessary or appropriate in this context.

[236] *See, e.g.*, CWA Comments at 14–16; Nokia Comments at 10–11; TWC Comments at 55, 58–61; TDS Comments at 7. A few parties argued that such an approach would be inadequate. *See, e.g.*, Nickolaus E. Leggett Jan. 5, 2010 Comments at 3; Free Press Comments at 79–80; OIC Comments at 15–16, 35–36.

[237] *See* Broadcast Music Inc. (BMI) Comments at 3–4; Internet Freedom Coalition Comments at 3; Qwest Comments at 34–36; AFTRA et al. Reply at 6–7.

[238] *See, e.g.*, ACLJ Comments at 5–7 (suggesting that ISPs cannot know what the agency will consider "reasonable" network management or "discriminatory" treatment); Free Press Comments at 85; Thomas D. Sydnor II Comments at 6–9; Texas Office of Public Utility Counsel Comments at 6–7.

[239] As recently as 1995, Congress adopted the venerable "reasonableness" standard when it recodified provisions of the Interstate Commerce Act. ICC Termination Act of 1995, Pub. L. No. 104-88, § 106(a) (now codified at 49 U.S.C. § 15501).

[240] AT&T Reply at 33–34 ("And no one has seriously suggested that Section 202 should itself be amended to remove the 'unreasonable' qualifier on the ground that the qualifier is too 'murky' or 'complex.' Seventy-five years of experience have shown that qualifier to be both administrable and indispensable to the sound administration of the nation's telecommunications laws."); *see also* Comcast Reply at 26 ("[T]he Commission should embrace the strong guidance against an overbroad rule and, instead, develop a standard based on 'unreasonable and anticompetitive discrimination.'"); Sprint Reply at 23 ("The unreasonable discrimination standard contained in Section 202(a) of the Act contains the very flexibility the Commission needs to distinguish desirable from improper discrimination."); *Thomas v. Chicago Park District*, 534 U.S. 316, 324 (2002) (holding that denial of a permit "when the intended use would present an unreasonable danger to the health and safety of park users or Park District employees" is a standard that is "reasonably specific and objective, and do[es] not leave the decision 'to the whim of the administrator'") (citation omitted); *Cameron v. Johnson*, 390 U.S. 611, 615–16 (1968) (stating that "unreasonably" "is a widely used and well understood word, and clearly so when juxtaposed with 'obstruct' and 'interfere'").

[241] *See, e.g.*, Cisco Comments at 8 n.14; Corning Comments at 16; Comcast Reply at 23–25; TIA Reply at 13–17.

[242] *See, e.g.*, Letter from Barbara van Schewick, Stanford Law School, to Marlene H. Dortch, Secretary, FCC, GN Docket No. 09-191, at 1–2 (filed Dec. 10, 2010) (noting that concerns about discrimination go beyond "anticompetitive" behavior or harms to competition, as those terms are understood in antitrust law); *United States v. FCC*, 652 F.2d 72, (D.C. Cir. 1980) ("The agency's determination about the proper role of competitive forces in an industry must therefore be based, not exclusively on the letter of the antitrust laws, but also on the 'special considerations' of the particular industry. As the Supreme Court has said, resolution of the sometimes-conflicting public interest considerations 'is a complex task which requires extensive facilities, expert judgment and considerable knowledge of the . . . industry. Congress left that task to the Commission . . . .' (quoting *McLean Trucking Co. v. United States*, 321 U.S. 67, 87 (1944)) (footnotes omitted).

[243] *See supra* Parts 0 and 0; Letter from Prof. Barbara van Schewick, Professor, Stanford Law School, to Marlene H. Dortch, Secretary, FCC, GN Docket No. 09-191, WC Docket No. 07-52, Attach. at 4 (filed Aug. 2, 2010) (van Schewick Aug. 2, 2010 *Ex Parte* Letter) (observing that such a rule would "make[] it impossible to consider the potential impact of discriminatory conduct on the Internet's ability to realize its social, cultural and political potential—important aspects that the open Internet rules are intended to protect").

[244] *See* van Schewick Aug. 2, 2010 *Ex Parte* Letter, Attach. at 2–3. *See also, e.g.*, Letter from Chris Riley, Policy Counsel, Free Press, to Marlene H. Dortch, Secretary, FCC, GN Docket No. 09-191, WC Docket No. 07-52, Attach. (filed Nov. 24, 2009) (arguing that certain types of prioritization are harmful, regardless of any underlying anticompetitive motive on the part of the broadband provider).

[245] For example, slowing BitTorrent packets might only affect a few end users, but it would harm BitTorrent. More significantly, it would raise concerns among other end users and edge providers that their traffic could be slowed for any reason—or no reason at all—which could in turn reduce incentives to innovate and invest, and change the fundamental nature of the Internet as an open platform. *See supra* Part 0.

[246] *See, e.g.*, AT&T Comments at 209–11; Verizon Comments at 93–95; CTIA PN Reply at 20–21. We do not read the Supreme Court's decision in *FCC v. Midwest Video Corp.* as addressing rules like the rules we adopt today. 440 U.S. 689 (1979). There, the Court held that obligations on cable providers to "hold out dedicated channels on a first-come, nondiscriminatory basis . . . relegated cable systems, *pro tanto*, to common-carrier status." *Id.* at 700–01. None of the rules adopted in this Order requires a broadband provider to "hold out" any capacity for the exclusive use of third parties or make a public offering of its service.

[247] 47 U.S.C. § 153(51). Section 332(c)(2) contains a restriction similar to that of § 3(51): "A person engaged in the provision of a service that is a private mobile service shall not, insofar as such person is so engaged, be treated as a common carrier for any purpose under this Act." *Id.* § 332(c)(2). Because we are not imposing any common carrier obligations on any broadband provider, including providers of "private mobile service" as defined in § 332(d)(3), our requirements do not violate the limitation in § 332(c)(2).

[248] Courts have acknowledged that the Commission is entitled to deference in interpreting the definition of "common carrier." *See AT&T v. FCC*, 572 F.2d 17, 24 (2d Cir. 1978) (citing *Red Lion Broad. Co. v. FCC*, 395 U.S. 367, 381 (1969)). In adopting the rule against unreasonable discrimination, we rely, in part, on our authority under section 706, which is not part of the Communications Act. Congress enacted section 706 as part of the Telecommunications Act of 1996 and more recently codified the provision in Chapter 12 of Title 47, at 47 U.S.C. § 1302. The seven titles that comprise the Communications Act appear in Chapter 5 of Title 47. Consequently, even if the rule against unreasonable discrimination were interpreted to require common carriage in a particular case, that result would not run afoul of section 3(51) because a network operator would be treated as a common carrier pursuant to section 706, not "under" the Communications Act.

[249] *Nat'l Ass'n of Reg. Util. Comm'rs v. FCC*, 525 F.2d 630, 641 (D.C. Cir. 1976) (*NARUC I*) (quoting *Semon v. Royal Indemnity Co.*, 279 F.2d 737, 739 (5th Cir. 1960) and other cases); *see also* Verizon Comments at 93 ("'[T]he primary sine qua non of common carrier status is a quasi-public character, which arises out of the undertaking 'to carry for all people indifferently . . . .'" (quoting *Nat'l Ass'n of Reg. Util. Comm'rs v. FCC*, 533 F.2d 601, 608 (D.C. Cir. 1976) (*NARUC II*)). *But see* CTIA Reply at 57 (suggesting that nondiscrimination is the *sine qua non* of common carrier regulation referred to in *NARUC II*).

[250] *NARUC I*, 525 F.2d at 641 (citing *Semon*, 279 F.2d at 739–40). Commenters assert that any obligation that is similar to an obligation that appears in Title II of the Act is a "common carrier" obligation. *See, e.g.*, AT&T Comments at 210–11. We disagree. Just because an obligation appears within Title II does not mean that the imposition of that obligation or a similar one results in "treating" an entity as a common carrier. For the meaning of common carriage treatment, which is not defined in the Act, we look to caselaw as discussed in the text.

[251] Even if edge providers were considered "customers" of the broadband provider, the broadband provider would not be a common carrier with regard to the role it plays in transmitting edge providers' traffic. Our rules permit broadband providers to engage in reasonable network management and, under certain circumstances, block traffic and devices, engage in reasonable discrimination, and prioritize traffic at subscribers' request. Blocking or deprioritizing certain traffic is far from "undertak[ing] to carry for all [edge providers] indifferently." *See NARUC I*, 525 F.2d at 641.

[252] *See Sw. Bell Tel. Co. v. FCC*, 19 F.3d 1475, 1481 (D.C. Cir. 1994) ("If the carrier chooses its clients on an individual basis and determines in each particular case whether and on what terms to serve and there is no specific regulatory compulsion to serve all indifferently, the entity is a private carrier for that particular service and the Commission is not at liberty to subject the entity to regulation as a common carrier.") (internal quotation marks omitted). Although promoting competition throughout the Internet ecosystem is a central purpose of these rules, we decline to adopt as a rule the *Internet Policy Statement* principle regarding consumers' entitlement to competition. We agree with those commenters that argue that the principle is too vague to be reduced to a rule and that the proposed rule as stated failed to provide any meaningful guidance regarding what conduct is and is not permissible. *See, e.g.*, Verizon Comments at 4, 53; TPPF Comments at 7. A rule barring broadband providers from depriving end users of their entitlement to competition does not appear to be a viable method of promoting competition. We also do not wish to duplicate competitive analyses carried out by the Department of Justice, the FTC, or the Commission's merger review process.

[253] *Open Internet NPRM*, 24 FCC Rcd at 13112–15, paras. 133–41.

[254] *Id.*

[255] *See, e.g.*, CCIA/CEA Comments at 21–23, 26–27; CDT Comments at 41; OIC Comments at 67; EFF Comments at 5, 10–18; Google Comments at 72–73; PIC Comments at 39, 41–44, 53–63. *See also infra* Part 0.

[256] *See, e.g.*, AT&T Comments at 75–78; CenturyLink Comments at 8; Cisco Comments at 4; CWA Comments at 24; TIA Comments at 13–14.

[257] *See, e.g.*, Cisco Comments at 4; CCIA Comments at 18–19; GSM Comments at 20–21; TIA Comments at 13–14, 34.

[258] *See, e.g.*, CCIA Comments at 12–17; Cox Comments at 21–23, 30–33; TIA Comments at 34.

[259] *Open Internet NPRM*, 24 FCC Rcd at 13112, para. 134. Several commenters support this approach. *See, e.g.*, CDT Comments at 38; Skype Comments at 15; AOL Reply at 3.

[260] *Open Internet NPRM*, 24 FCC Rcd at 13112, para. 134 (citing *Comcast Order*, 23 FCC Rcd at 13045–46, paras. 29–32).

[261] Some parties contend that there will be uncertainty associated with open Internet rules, subject to reasonable network management, which will limit provider flexibility, stifle innovation, and slow providers' response time in managing their networks. *See, e.g.*, ADTRAN Comments at 11–13; Barbara Esbin (Esbin) Comments at 7. For example, some parties express concern that that the definition proposed in the *Open Internet NPRM* provided insufficient guidance regarding what standard will be used to determine whether a given practice is "reasonable." *See, e.g.*, ADTRAN Comments at 13; AT&T Comments at 13; CDT Comments at 38; PIC Comments at 35–36, 39; Texas PUC Comments at 6–7; Verizon Reply at 8, 75, 78. Others contend that although clarity is needed, the Commission should not list categories of activities considered reasonable. *See, e.g.*, Free Press Comments at 82, 85–86. We seek to balance these interests through general rules designed to give providers sufficient flexibility to implement necessary network management practices, coupled with guidance regarding certain principles and considerations that will inform the Commission's case-by-case analysis.

[262] *See* 47 C.F.R. § 1.2 (providing for "a declaratory ruling terminating a controversy or removing uncertainty").

[263] *See, e.g.*, AT&T Comments at 183–87; ITIF Comments at 26–27.

[264] *See, e.g.*, Free Press Comments at 83–94; PIC Comments at 37–51.

[265] *See Comcast Network Management Practices Order*, 23 FCC Rcd at 13055–56, para. 47 (stating that, to be considered "reasonable" a network management practice "should further a critically important interest and be narrowly or carefully tailored to serve that interest"); *see also* AT&T Comments at 186–87 (arguing that the *Comcast* standard is too narrow); Level 3 Comments at 14; PAETEC Comments at 17–18. *But see* Free Press Comments at 91–92 (stating that the Commission should not retreat from the fundamental framework of the *Comcast* standard). A "reasonableness" standard also has the advantage of being administrable and familiar. *See supra* para. 0.

[266] *See, e.g.*, Level 3 Comments at 14 (asserting that setting a restrictive standard may make operators less willing to take prophylactic actions when problems occur).

[267] *See* AT&T Comments at 187; Google Comments at 68; Hughes Network Systems PN Comment at 3.

[268] *See, e.g.*, LARIAT Comments at 2–3.

[269] *See* Appendix A, § 8.11. We recognize that the standards for fourth-generation (4G) wireless networks include the capability to prioritize particular types of traffic, and that other broadband Internet access services may incorporate similar features. Whether particular uses of these technologies constitute reasonable network management will depend on whether they are appropriate and tailored to achieving a legitimate network management purpose.

[270] *See, e.g.*, RNK Comments at 7 (arguing that transparency will help prevent improper practices from masquerading as reasonable network management); CCIA/CEA Comments at 30–33.

[271] *See* 47 U.S.C. § 230(b)(3).

[272] *See supra* para. 0.

[273] In the context of broadband Internet access service, techniques to ensure network security and integrity are designed to protect the access network and the Internet against actions by malicious or compromised end systems. Examples include spam, botnets, and distributed denial of service attacks. Unwanted traffic includes worms, malware, and viruses that exploit end-user system vulnerabilities; denial of service attacks; and spam. *See* IETF, REPORT FROM THE IAB WORKSHOP ON UNWANTED TRAFFIC MARCH 9–10, 2006, RFC 4948, at 31 (Aug. 2007), *available at* www.rfc-editor.org/rfc/rfc4948.txt.

[274] *See, e.g.*, AT&T Comments at 75, 184–86; Amazon Comments at 3; Comcast Comments at 51, 58–59; Messaging Anti-Abuse Working Group Comments at 2–5; Verizon Comments at 82; SIIA Comments at 7.

[275] *See* Free Press Comments at 5, 78.

[276] *See, e.g.*, Google Comments at 72; NCTA Comments at 30–31; Mobile Future PN Comments at 5; Letter from Most Reverend George H. Niederauer, Archbishop of San Francisco, Chairman, Communications Committee, United States Conference of Catholic Bishops, to Chairman Genachowski et al., FCC, GN Docket No. 09-191, WC Docket No. 07-52 (filed Oct. 23, 2009).

[277] *See, e.g.*, TWC Reply at 25 (hypothesizing about a "broadband Internet access service provider [that] emulated Apple's practices of limiting access to certain types of sites (such as those involving pornography)").

[278] *See* EFF Comments at 26–27. *See generally supra* Part 0.

[279] *See* 47 U.S.C. § 230(c)(2) (no provider of an interactive computer service shall be held liable on account of "(A) any action voluntarily taken in good faith to restrict access to or availability of material that the provider or

user considers to be obscene, lewd, lascivious, filthy, excessively violent, harassing, or otherwise objectionable, whether or not such material is constitutionally protected; or (B) any action taken to enable or make available to information content providers or others the technical means to restrict access to material described in [subparagraph (A)]").

[280] For example, a network provider might be able to assess a network endpoint's posture—see IETF, NETWORK ENDPOINT ASSESSMENT (NEA): OVERVIEW AND REQUIREMENTS, RFC 5209 (Jun. 2008); INTERNET ENGINEERING TASK FORCE, PA-TNC: A POSTURE ATTRIBUTE (PA) PROTOCOL COMPATIBLE WITH TRUSTED NETWORK CONNECT (TNC), RFC 5792 (Mar. 2010)—and tailor port blocking accordingly. With the posture assessment, an end user might then opt out of the network management mechanism by upgrading the operating system or installing a suitable firewall.

[281] *See, e.g.*, ACA Comments at iv, 10–11; Ad Hoc Comments at 24–25; Covad Comments at 6; Google Comments at 68; DISH Reply at 19–21; Vonage Reply at 46–47.

[282] *See, e.g.*, Comcast Corporation, Description of Current Network Management Practices, downloads.comcast.net/docs/Attachment_A_Current_Practices.pdf.

[283] *Open Internet NPRM*, 24 FCC Rcd at 13114, para. 140.

[284] *See, e.g.*, T-Mobile Comments at 1 ("[T]he [mobile wireless] market itself is driving openness and supporting all of the goals articulated by the NPRM."), 12–13; Verizon Comments at 61; Verizon PN Comments at 4 ("[T]he wireless broadband marketplace is moving toward greater openness, as exemplified by Verizon's Open Development program . . . ."), 15.

[285] *See* New America Foundation Comments at 2–3, App. A at 16; Sling Comments at 5–11; Vonage Comments at 9; Skype Reply at 6; Testimony of Jeffrey Glueck, CEO, Skyfire, FCC Workshop on Innovation, Investment and the Open Internet, FCC (Jan. 13, 2010), reboot.fcc.gov/video-archives. *See supra* paras. 0-0.

[286] *See* Clearwire Comments at 10–11; Sprint Comments at 18–19; *cf.* ITIF PN Comments at 7.

[287] *See Open Internet NPRM*, 24 FCC Rcd at 13117–24, paras. 154–74; *Open Internet PN*.

[288] *Implementation of Section 6002(b) of the Omnibus Budget Reconciliation Act of 1993 et al.*, Fourteenth Report, 25 FCC Rcd 11407, 11502–03, para 148 (2010) (*Fourteenth Wireless Competition Report*).

[289] *See, e.g.*, Latinos for Internet Freedom, et al. PN Comments at i ("Lower barriers to adoption have facilitated the widespread use of the mobile Internet in communities of color and low-income areas, where many individuals would otherwise go without Internet access altogether. . . . [M]any of our constituents rely exclusively on mobile wireless Internet access as their onramp to the web."); Free Press PN Reply at 6.

[290] *See, e.g.*, SANDVINE, FALL 2010 GLOBAL INTERNET PHENOMENA REPORT 12 (2010), www.sandvine.com/downloads/documents/2010%20Global%20Internet%20Phenomena%20Report.pdf.

[291] Mobile Future PN Reply at 2 ("In less than three years, a mobile applications market has emerged with annualized growth rates exceeding 500%, giving consumers access to well over 300,000 apps from at least 10 stores."); *see also* Press Release, AT&T, AT&T Announces New Lower-Priced Wireless Data Plans to Make Mobile Internet More Affordable to More People (June 2, 2010), www.att.com/gen/press-room?pid=17991&cdvn=news&newsarticleid=30854 (announcing new usage-based pricing plans). *See generally Fourteenth Wireless Competition Report*.

[292] *Compare* National Broadband Plan at 37 (Exh. 4-A) *with* 39-40 (Exh. 4-E); *see also supra* paras. 0-0. However, in many areas of the country, particularly in rural areas, there are fewer options for mobile broadband. *See Fourteenth Wireless Competition Report* at para. 355, tbl. 39 & chart 48. This may result in some consumers having fewer options for mobile broadband than for fixed.

[293] *See* FCC Internet Status Report, at 30, tbl. 12.

[294] Some fixed broadband providers contend that current mobile broadband offerings directly compete with their offerings. *See* Letter from Michael D. Saperstein, Jr., Director of Regulatory Affairs, Frontier Communications, to Marlene Dortch, Secretary, FCC, GN Docket No. 09-191 (filed Dec. 15, 2010) (discussing entry of wireless service into the broadband market and its effect on wireline broadband subscribership) and Attach. at 1 (citing reports that LTE is "a very practical and encouraging substitution for DSL, particularly when you look at rural markets"); Letter from Malena F. Barzilai, Federal Government Affairs, Windstream Communications, Inc., to Marlene Dortch, Secretary, FCC, GN Docket No. 09-191 (filed Dec. 15, 2010). As part of our ongoing monitoring, we will track such competition and any impact these rules may have on it. *See infra* para. 0.

[295] *See, e.g.*, AT&T Comments at 156–61; CCIA Comments at 15–16; Verizon Comments at 61–63; Leap Reply at 6–8; T-Mobile Reply at 16–23; TIA Reply at 8; CTIA PN Comments at 2–3 ("[W]ireless networks and the devices that operate on them have become increasingly intertwined . . . ."), 9–12; ITIF PN Comments at 16. *But see, e.g.*, Free Press Reply at 29; PIC PN Comments at 13–16.

[296] *See, e.g.*, IFTA Comments at 20; OIC Comments at 37; Skype Comments at 5–7; NCTA PN Comments at 11–12; Free Press PN Reply at 8; OIC PN Reply at 3.

[297] The first network using spectrum subject to these rules has recently started offering service. *See* Press Release, Verizon Wireless, Blazingly Fast: Verizon Wireless Launches The World's Largest 4G LTE Wireless Network On Sunday, Dec. 5 (Dec. 5, 2010), *available at* news.vzw.com/news/2010/12/pr2010-12-03.html. Specifically, licensees subject to the rule must provide an open platform for third-party applications and

devices. *See 700 MHz Second Report and Order*, 22 FCC Rcd 15289; 47 C.F.R. § 27.16. The rules we adopt today are independent of those open platform requirements. We expect our observations of how the 700 MHz open platform rules affect the mobile broadband sector to inform our ongoing analysis of the application of openness rules to mobile broadband generally. *700 MHz Second Report and Order*, 22 FCC Rcd at 15364–65, 15374, paras. 205, 229. A number of commenters support the Commission's waiting to determine whether to apply openness rules to mobile wireless until the effects of the C Block openness requirement can be observed. *See, e.g.*, AT&T PN Reply, at 32–37; Cricket PN Reply at 11. We also note that some providers tout openness as a competitive advantage. *See, e.g.*, Clearwire Comments at 7; Verizon Reply at 47–52.

[298] *Fourteenth Wireless Competition Report*, 25 FCC Rcd at 11442, para. 31.

[299] We note that section 332(a) requires us, "[i]n taking actions to manage the spectrum to be made available for use by the private mobile service," to consider various factors, including whether our actions will "improve the efficiency of spectrum use and reduce the regulatory burden," and "encourage competition." 47 U.S.C. § 332(a)(2), (3). To the extent section 332(a) applies to our actions today, we note that we have considered these factors. *See, e.g., supra* at paras. 0–0, 0–0.

[300] *See, e.g.*, Cricket Comments at 4 (a principle of transparency will protect consumers and counterbalance abuses of network management discretion, thereby fostering an open marketplace that promotes innovation and competition); Leap Comments at 22–24; MetroPCS Comments at 64; Qwest Comments at 11; CWA Comments at 12–13; CDT Comments at 31; Bright House Comments at 10–11; PIC PN Comments at 12; Google Comments at iii, 4, 77; NJRC Comments at 25; NATOA Comments at 11; Texas PUC Comments at 8–9; NASUCA Comments at 24; IFTA Comments at 20.

[301] *See, e.g.*, CTIA Comments at 11, 47; GSM Association (GSM) Comments at 25; Entertainment Software Association (ESA) Comments at 2, 4; Telecom Italia Comments at 12; Verizon Comments, Attach. B at 49; AT&T PN Comments at 70; Verizon PN Comments at 40–42.

[302] *See supra* at paras. 0–0.

[303] *700 MHz Second Report and Order*, 22 FCC Rcd at 15371–72, para. 224 ("[A] C Block licensee must publish [for example, by posting on the provider's website] standards no later than the time at which it makes such standards available to any preferred vendors (*i.e.*, vendors with whom the provider has a relationship to design products for the provider's network). We also require the C Block licensee to provide to potential customers notice of the customers' rights to request the attachment of a device or application to the licensee's network, and notice of the licensee's process for customers to make such requests, including the relevant network criteria.").

[304] *See* 47 C.F.R. 27.16(d) ("Access requests. (1) Licensees shall establish and publish clear and reasonable procedures for parties to seek approval to use devices or applications on the licensees' networks. A licensee must also provide to potential customers notice of the customers' rights to request the attachment of a device or application to the licensee's network, and notice of the licensee's process for customers to make such requests, including the relevant network criteria. (2) If a licensee determines that a request for access would violate its technical standards or regulatory requirements, the licensee shall expeditiously provide a written response to the requester specifying the basis for denying access and providing an opportunity for the requester to modify its request to satisfy the licensee's concerns.").

[305] For the purposes of these rules, an attributable interest includes equity ownership interest in or *de facto* control of, or by, the entity that provides the voice or video telephony service. An attributable interest also includes any exclusive arrangement for such voice or video telephony service, including *de facto* exclusive arrangements.

[306] *See supra* para. 0; *see also supra* para. 0.

[307] ALLOT COMMUNICATIONS, ALLOT MOBILETRENDS - GLOBAL MOBILE BROADBAND TRAFFIC REPORT H2/2009 at 9 (2010), www.allot.com/mobiletrends.html.

[308] *See, e.g.*, Letter from James W. Cicconi, AT&T Services, Inc., to Ruth Milkman, Chief, Wireless Telecommunications Bureau, FCC, RM-11361, RM-11497 at 6–8 (filed Aug. 21, 2009); DISH PN Reply at 7 ("VoIP operators such as Skype have faced significant difficulty in gaining access across wireless Internet connections."). Mobile providers blocking VoIP services is an issue not only in the United States, but worldwide. In Europe, the Body of European Regulators for Electronic Communications reported, among other issues, a number of cases of blocking or charging extra for VoIP services by certain European mobile operators. *See* EUROPEAN COMMISSION, INFORMATION SOCIETY AND MEDIA DIRECTORATE-GENERAL REPORT ON THE PUBLIC CONSULTATION ON "THE OPEN INTERNET AND NET NEUTRALITY IN EUROPE" 2, (Nov. 9, 2010), ec.europa.eu/information_society.

[309] *See, e.g.*, Skype Comments at 8–9; Skype Feb. 20, 2007 Petition, RM-11361, at 13–16.

[310] *See, e.g.*, ITIC PN Comments at 6; PIC PN Comments at 20–21.

[311] LARIAT Comments at 3; Skype Comments at 9; ITIC PN Comments at 6–7; Public Interest Commenters PN Comments at 20–21.

[312] Skype PN Reply at 6; *see also* Sling Media Comments at 1–2; DISH PN Comments at 22–23 (any limits or caps should apply equally to all application providers to ensure fairness and promote competition); OIC PN Comments at 8–9.

[313] Clearwire Comments at 11.

[314] *See, e.g.*, Free Press Comments at 121; OIC Comments at 36–40; DISH PN Comments at 22–24; Skype Comments at 8–9; Free Press PN Comments at 21–23; PIC PN Comments at 13–16; Skype PN Reply at 6. Other commenters support our more targeted rule. *See, e.g.*, CWA PN Comments at 5

[315] *See* Letter from Jonathan Spalter, Chairman, Mobile Future, to Marlene H. Dortch, Secretary, FCC, GN Docket Nos. 09-191 & 10-127, at 3 n.16 (filed Dec. 13, 2010) (supporting tailored prohibition on blocking applications), *citing* AT&T Comments at 65; T-Mobile Comments, Declaration of Grant Castle at 4. The no blocking rule that we adopt for mobile broadband involves distinct treatment of applications that compete with the provider's voice and video telephony services, whereas we have adopted a broader traffic-based approach for fixed broadband. *See supra* para. 0. We acknowledge that this rule for mobile broadband may lead in some limited measure to the traffic-identification difficulties discussed with respect to fixed broadband. We find, however, that the reasons for taking our cautious approach to mobile broadband outweigh this concern, particularly in light of our intent to monitor developments involving mobile broadband, including this and other aspects of the practical implementation of our rules.

[316] For example, app stores are operated by manufacturers and operating system developers such as Nokia, Apple, RIM, Google, Microsoft, and third parties such as GetJar. *See also* AT&T PN Comments at 63–66 (emphasizing the competitiveness of the market for mobile apps, including the variety of sources from which consumers may obtain applications); T-Mobile PN Comments at 21 ("The competitive wireless marketplace will continue to discipline app store owners . . . that exclude third-party apps from their app stores entirely, eliminating the need for Commission action."). We note, however, that for a few devices, such as Apple's iPhone, there may be fewer options for accessing and distributing apps.

[317] *See supra* at para. 0; *see also* OIC PN Comments at 9–10 (while consumers have a meaningful choice with respect to applications and the ability to download and use applications on a carrier's network, app stores should not be subject to nondiscrimination or other open Internet principles).

[318] *See, e.g,* Free Press Comments at 125–26; OIC Comments at 36–39. *See also, e.g.*, Leap Comments at 17–22; Sprint Reply at 24–26. A number of commenters suggest that openness rules should be applied identically to all broadband platforms. *See, e.g.*, CenturyLink Comments at 22–23; Comcast Comments at 32; DISH Network PN Comments at 17; NCTA PN Comments at 11; Qwest PN Comments at 12–19; SureWest PN Comments at 18–20; TWC PN Comments at 33–35; Vonage PN Comments at 10–18; Windstream PN Comments at 6–19.

[319] We note that mobile broadband is the only or primary broadband Internet access platform used by many Americans. *See, e.g., supra* note 289.

[320] *See 700 MHz Second Report and Order*, 22 FCC Rcd at 15374–75, paras. 229–30.

[321] *See* Press Release, Verizon Wireless, Blazingly Fast: Verizon Wireless Launches The World's Largest 4G LTE Wireless Network On Sunday, Dec. 5 (Dec. 5, 2010), *available at* news.vzw.com/news/2010/12/pr2010-12-03.html; Press Release, Verizon, Verizon Launches 4G LTE In 38 Major Metropolitan Areas By The End Of The Year, Oct. 6, 2010, *available at* news.vzw.com/news/2010/10/pr2010-10-01c.html.

[322] *See, e.g.*, Intrado Comments at 1, 3.

[323] *See* 47 U.S.C. § 1002(a).

[324] *See* 50 U.S.C. §§ 1802(a)(4), 1804, 1805(c)(2).

[325] *See* 18 U.S.C. §§ 2518, 2705.

[326] *Open Internet NPRM*, 24 FCC Rcd at 13115–16, para 145.

[327] *Open Internet NPRM*, 24 FCC Rcd at 13115–16, paras. 143, 146.

[328] *See* PIC Comments at 42–44. We intend the term "national security authorities" to include homeland security authorities.

[329] *See* PIC Comments at 52–53; CCIA/CEA Comments at 27–29; EFF Comments at 19–23.

[330] *See, e.g.*, EFF Comments at 11; CDT Reply at 33.

[331] *See* EFF Comments at 21; OIC Comments at 64–66.

[332] *See* EFF Comments at 20–22; CCIA/CEA Comments at 23, 30; PIC Comments at 43–44.

[333] *See* EFF Comments at 20–22. EFF would require a pre-deployment waiver from the Commission if the needs of law enforcement would require broadband providers to act inconsistently with open Internet rules. *Id.* at 22.

[334] *See* 47 C.F.R., Part 64, App.B.

[335] The National Emergency Number Association (NENA) would encourage or require network managers to provide public safety users with advance notice of changes in network management that could affect emergency services. *See* NENA Comments at 5–6. Although we do not adopt such a requirement, we encourage broadband providers to be mindful of the potential impact on emergency services when implementing network management policies, and to coordinate major changes with providers of emergency services when appropriate.

[336] *See, e.g.*, Stanford University—DMCA Complaint Resolution Center; User Generated Content Principles, www.ugcprinciples.com (cited in Letter from Linda Kinney, MPAA, to Marlene H. Dortch, Secretary, FCC, GN Docket Nos. 09-191, 10-137, WC Docket No. 07-52 at 1 (filed Nov. 29, 2010)). Open Internet rules are not intended to affect the legal status of cooperative efforts by broadband Internet access service providers and

other service providers that are designed to curtail infringement in response to information provided by rights holders in a manner that is timely, effective, and accommodates the legitimate interests of providers, rights holders, and end users.

337 *Open Internet NPRM*, 24 FCC Rcd at 13116–17, paras. 148–53.

338 *See, e.g.*, Comcast Comments at 60–61, 64–66; Motorola Comments at 14–16; Sprint Reply at 2–5; Verizon PN Comments at 48.

339 *See Open Internet PN*, 25 FCC Rcd at 12638–39; *Open Internet NPRM*, 24 FCC Rcd at 13116, para. 149; CCIA/CEA PN Comments at 3–4; CDT PN Comments at 1–2; Various Advocates for the Open Internet PN Reply at 5.

340 *See, e.g.*, Netflix Comments at 9–10; CDT Comments at 46–48; Vonage Comments at 27; Dish Network Reply at 12; XO Reply at 20–21.

341 *See, e.g.*, CDT Comments at 46–49; IFTA Comments at 18–19; Sony Reply at 6–7.

342 *See supra* paras. 0–0; *see also* Free Press Comments at 14; Vonage Comments at 7–8; OIC Comments at 71–73.

343 *See, e.g., FCC v. Fox Television Stations, Inc.*, 129 S.Ct. 1800, 1815 (2009) ("Nothing prohibits federal agencies from moving in an incremental manner."); *Nat'l Cable & Telecomms. Ass'n v. Brand X Internet Servs.*, 545 U.S. 967, 1002 (2005) (*Brand X*) ("The Commission need not immediately apply the policy reasoning" underlying its classification of broadband Internet services to other categories of providers to which that reasoning might apply).

344 *See, e.g.*, Free Press Comments at 111; OIC Comments at 92; PIC Comments at 32; Frontier PN Comments at 4; OIC PN Comments at 5; PAETEC PN Comments at 2–3; PIC PN Comments at 6–7.

345 Our decision not to adopt rules regarding specialized services at this time involves an issue distinct from the regulatory classification of services such as VoIP and IPTV under the Communications Act, a subject we do not address in this Order. Likewise, the Commission's actions here do not affect any existing obligation to provide interconnection, unbundled network elements, or special access or other wholesale access under §§ 201, 251, 256, and 271 of the Act. 47 U.S.C. §§ 201, 251, 256, 271.

346 *See supra* 0. Some commenters, including Internet engineering experts and analysts, emphasize the importance of distinguishing between the open Internet and specialized services and state that "this distinction must continue as a most appropriate and constructive basis for pursuing your policy goals." Various Advocates for the Open Internet PN Reply at 3; *see also id.* at 2.

347 *See Consumer Information and Disclosure et al.*, Notice of Inquiry, 24 FCC Rcd 11380 (2009).

348 *See, e.g.*, AICC PN Reply at 2 (noting concerns regarding potential exclusive arrangements between broadband providers and third parties for the provision of specialized services); Clearwire PN Comments at 13 (noting the risk of anticompetitive conduct from specialized services that involve arrangements between broadband providers and affiliates and arguing "that those types of arrangements should be subject to particular scrutiny").

349 47 U.S.C. § 151.

350 *Id.* § 152(a).

351 *Nat'l Broad. Co., Inc. v. United States*, 319 U.S. 190, 219–20 (1943) (Congress did not "attempt[] an itemized catalogue of the specific manifestations of the general problems" that it entrusted to the Commission); *see also FCC v. Pottsville Broad. Co.*, 309 U.S. 134, 137, 138 (1940) (the Commission's statutory responsibilities and authority amount to "a unified and comprehensive regulatory system" for the communications industry that allows a single agency to "maintain, through appropriate administrative control, a grip on the dynamic aspects" of that ever-changing industry).

352 *See Comcast Corp. v. FCC*, 600 F.3d 642, 646–47 (D.C. Cir. 2010).

353 47 U.S.C. § 230(b).

354 47 U.S.C. § 254(b)(2), (6).

355 47 U.S.C. § 1302(a), (b).

356 *Ad Hoc Telecomms. Users Comm. v. FCC*, 572 F.3d 903, 906–07 (D.C. Cir. 2009).

357 S. Rep. No. 104-23, at 51 (1995) ("The goal is to accelerate deployment of an advanced capability that will enable subscribers in all parts of the United States to send and receive information in all its forms—voice, data, graphics, and video—over a high-speed switched, interactive, broadband, transmission capability.").

358 47 U.S.C. § 1302.

359 47 U.S.C. § 1302(d)(1) (defining "advanced telecommunications capability" as "high-speed, switched, broadband telecommunications capability that enables users to originate and receive high-quality voice, data, graphics, and video telecommunications using any technology"). *See National Broadband Plan for our Future*, Notice of Inquiry, 24 FCC Rcd 4342, 4309, App. para. 13 (2009) ("advanced telecommunications capability" includes broadband Internet access); *Inquiry Concerning the Deployment of Advanced Telecomms. Capability to All Americans in a Reasonable and Timely Fashion*, 14 FCC Rcd 2398, 2400, para. 1 (Section 706 addresses "the deployment of broadband capability"), 2406 para. 20 (same). Even when broadband Internet access is provided as an "information service" rather than a "telecommunications service," *see Nat'l Cable & Telecomm. Ass'n v. Brand X Internet Servs.*, 545 U.S. 967, 977–78 (2005), it involves "telecommunications." 47 U.S.C. § 153(24). Given Section 706's explicit focus on deployment of broadband

access to voice, data, and video communications, it is not important that the statute does not use the exact phrase "Internet network management."

[360] 47 U.S.C. § 1302(a).

[361] *See Comcast*, 600 F.3d at 658; *see also* 47 U.S.C. § 1302(a) ("The Commission . . . shall encourage the deployment on a reasonable and timely basis of advanced telecommunications capability to all Americans . . . by utilizing . . . price cap regulation, regulatory forbearance, measures that promote competition in the local telecommunications market, or other regulating methods that remove barriers to infrastructure investment."). Because Section 706 contains a "direct mandate," we reject the argument pressed by some commenters (*see, e.g.*, AT&T Comments at 217–18; Verizon Comments at 100–01; Qwest Comments at 58–59; Letter from Rick Chessen, Senior Vice President, Law and Regulatory Policy, NCTA, to Marlene H. Dortch, Secretary, FCC, GN Docket Nos. 09-191 & 10-127, WC Docket No. 07-52, at 7 (filed Dec. 10, 2010) (NCTA Dec. 10, 2010 *Ex Parte* Letter)) that Section 706 confers no substantive authority.

[362] *Deployment of Wireline Servs. Offering Advanced Telecomms. Capability et al.*, Memorandum Opinion and Order and Notice of Proposed Rulemaking, 13 FCC Rcd 24012 (1998) (*Advanced Services Order*).

[363] *See Comcast*, 600 F.3d at 659.

[364] *See* 47 U.S.C. § 160; *see also Advanced Services Order*, 13 FCC Rcd at 24046, para. 73.

[365] *Advanced Services Order*, 13 FCC Rcd at 24046, para. 73.

[366] Consistent with longstanding Supreme Court precedent, we have understood this authority to include our ancillary jurisdiction to further congressional policy. *See, e.g., Amendment of Section 64.702 of the Commission's Rules and Regulations (Second Computer Inquiry)*, Final Decision, 77 FCC 2d 384, 474 (1980), *aff'd, Computer & Commc'ns Indus. Ass'n v. FCC*, 693 F.2d 198, 211–14 (D.C. Cir. 1982) (*CCIA*).

[367] *Advanced Services Order*, 13 FCC Rcd at 24046-48, paras. 74–77.

[368] *Bloate v. United States*, 130 S. Ct. 1345, 1354 (2010) (citation and internal quotation marks omitted).

[369] *Advanced Services Order*, 13 FCC Rcd at 24046, para. 74.

[370] To the extent the *Advanced Services Order* can be construed as having read Section 706(a) differently, we reject that reading of the statute for the reasons discussed in the text.

[371] 47 U.S.C. § 1302(a).

[372] S. Rep. No. 104-23, at 50–51 (1995).

[373] *See, e.g.*, CenturyLink Comments at 18; Esbin Comments at 72.

[374] 47 U.S.C. §§ 151, 152. The Commission historically has recognized that services carrying Internet traffic are jurisdictionally mixed, but generally subject to federal regulation. *See, e.g., Nat'l Ass'n of Regulatory Util. Comm'rs Petition for Clarification or Declaratory Ruling that No FCC Order or Rule Limits State Authority to Collect Broadband Data*, Memorandum Opinion and Order, 25 FCC Rcd 5051, 5054, paras. 8–9 & n.24 (2010). Where, as here, "it is not possible to separate the interstate and intrastate aspects of the service," the Commission may preempt state regulation where "federal regulation is necessary to further a valid federal regulatory objective, i.e., state regulation would conflict with federal regulatory policies." *Minn. Pub. Utils. Comm'n v. FCC*, 483 F.3d 570, 578 (8th Cir. 2007); *see also La. Pub. Serv. Comm'n v. FCC*, 476 U.S. 355, 375 n.4 (1986). Except to the extent a state requirement conflicts on its face with a Commission decision herein, the Commission will evaluate preemption in light of the fact-specific nature of the relevant inquiry, on a case-by-case basis. We recognize, for example, that states play a vital role in protecting end users from fraud, enforcing fair business practices, and responding to consumer inquiries and complaints. *See, e.g., Vonage Order*, 19 FCC Rcd at 22404–05, para. 1. We have no intention of impairing states' or local governments' ability to carry out these duties unless we find that specific measures conflict with federal law or policy. In determining whether state or local regulations frustrate federal policies, we will, among other things, be guided by the overarching congressional policies described in Section 230 of the Act and Section 706 of the 1996 Act. 47 U.S.C. §§ 230, 1302.

[375] 47 U.S.C. § 1302(a).

[376] *Id.*

[377] *Id.*

[378] *Ad Hoc Telecomms. Users Comm.*, 572 F.3d at 906–07 ("The general and generous phrasing of § 706 means that the FCC possesses significant albeit not unfettered, authority and discretion to settle on the best regulatory or deregulatory approach to broadband.").

[379] *See, e.g.*, 47 U.S.C. §§ 201(b) & 309(a).

[380] *See supra* note 366. In *Comcast*, the court stated that "'[t]he Commission . . . may exercise ancillary jurisdiction only when two conditions are satisfied: (1) the Commission's general jurisdictional grant under Title I [of the Communications Act] covers the regulated subject and (2) the regulations are reasonably ancillary to the Commission's effective performance of its statutorily mandated responsibilities.'" 600 F.3d at 646 (quoting *Am. Library Ass'n v. FCC*, 406 F.3d 689, 691–92 (D.C. Cir. 2005)) (alterations in original). The court further ruled that the second prong of this test requires the Commission to rely on specific delegations of statutory authority. 600 F.3d at 644, 654.

[381] Ignoring that Section 706(a) expressly contemplates the use of "regulating methods" such as price regulation, some commenters read prior Commission orders as suggesting that Section 706 authorizes only deregulatory

actions. *See* AT&T Comments at 216 (citing *Petition for Declaratory Ruling that pulver.com's Free World Dialup is Neither Telecomm. Nor A Telecomms. Serv.*, Memorandum Opinion and Order, 19 FCC Rcd 3307, 3319, para. 19 n.69 (2004) (*Pulver Order*)); Esbin Comments at 52 (citing *Inquiry Concerning High-Speed Access to the Internet Over Cable and Other Facilities et al*, Declaratory Ruling and Notice of Proposed Rulemaking, 17 FCC Rcd 4798, 4801, 4826, 4840, paras. 4, 47, 73, (2002) (*Cable Modem Declaratory Ruling*) and *Appropriate Framework for Broadband Access to the Internet Over Wireline Facilities et al.*, Report and Order and Notice of Proposed Rulemaking, 20 FCC Rcd 14853, 14894 para. 77 (2005) (*Wireline Broadband Report and Order*)). They are mistaken. The *Pulver Order* stated only that Section 706 did not contemplate the application of "economic and entry/exit regulation *inherent in Title II*" to information service Internet applications. *Pulver Order*, 19 FCC Rcd at 3379, para. 19 n.69 (emphasis added). The open Internet rules that we adopt today do not regulate Internet applications, much less impose Title II (*i.e.*, common carrier) regulation on such applications. Moreover, at the same time the Commission determined in the *Cable Modem Declaratory Ruling* and the *Wireline Broadband Report and Order* that cable modem service and wireline broadband services (such as DSL) could be provided as information services not subject to Title II, it proposed new regulations under other sources of authority including Section 706. *See Cable Modem Declaratory Ruling*, 17 FCC Rcd at 4840, para. 73; *Wireline Broadband Report and Order*, 20 FCC Rcd at 14929–30, 14987, para. 146. On the same day the Commission adopted the *Wireline Broadband Report and Order*, it also adopted the *Internet Policy Statement*, which rested in part on Section 706. 20 FCC Rcd 14986, para. 2 (2005). Our prior orders therefore do not construe Section 706 as exclusively deregulatory. And to the extent that any prior order does suggest such a construction, we now reject it. *See Ad Hoc Telecomms. Users Comm.*, 572 F.3d at 908 (Section 706 "direct[s] the FCC to make the major policy decisions and to select *the mix of regulatory and deregulatory tools* the Commission deems most appropriate in the public interest to facilitate broadband deployment and competition") (emphasis added).

382 47 U.S.C. § 1302(b).

383 *Id.* (emphasis added).

384 *Sixth Broadband Deployment Report*, 25 FCC Rcd at 9558, paras. 2–3.

385 *See supra* para. 0. Many broadband providers offer their service on a common carriage basis under Title II of the Act. *See Framework for Broadband Internet Serv.*, Notice of Inquiry, 25 FCC Rcd 7866, 7875, para. 21 (2010). With respect to these providers, the rules we adopt today are additionally supported on that basis. With the possible exception of transparency requirements, however, the open Internet rules are unlikely to create substantial new duties for these providers in practice.

386 *Comcast*, 600 F.3d at 645.

387 47 U.S.C. § 201(b).

388 *Tel. No. Requirements for IP-Enabled Servs. Providers*, Report and Order, Declaratory Ruling, Order on Remand, and NPRM, 22 FCC Rcd 19531, 19547, para. 28 (2007). By definition, interconnected VoIP services allow calls to and from traditional phone networks. *See supra note 48.*

389 *See* NCTA Dec. 10, 2010 *Ex Parte* Letter (arguing that the Commission could exercise authority ancillary to several provisions of Title II of the Act, including Sections 201 and 202, "to ensure that common carrier services continue to be offered on just and reasonable terms and conditions" and to "facilitate consumer access to broadband-based alternatives to common carrier services such as Voice over Internet Protocol"); Vonage Comments at 11–12 ("The Commission's proposed regulations would help preserve the competitive balance between providers electing to operate under Title II and those operating under Title I."); Google Comments at 45–46 ("The widespread use of VoIP and related services as cheaper and more feature-rich alternatives to Title II services has significant effects on traditional telephone providers' practices and pricing, as well [as] on network interconnection between Title II and IP networks that consumers use to reach each other, going to the heart of the Commission's Title II responsibilities.") (footnotes and citations omitted); Letter from Devendra T. Kumar, Counsel to Skype Communications S.A.R.L., to Marlene H. Dortch, Secretary, FCC, GN Docket No. 09-191, WC Docket No. 07-52 (filed Nov. 30, 2010) (arguing that the Commission has authority ancillary to Section 201 to protect international VoIP calling); XO Comments at 20 (noting the impact of, *inter alia*, VoIP on the Commission's "traditional framework" for regulating voice services under Title II); Letter from Alan Inouye et al., on behalf of ALA, ARL and EDUCAUSE, to Chairman Julius Genachowski et al., GN Docket No. 09-191, WC Docket No. 07-52 at 4-5 (filed Dec. 13, 2010) (citing examples of how libraries and higher education institutions are using broadband services, including VoIP, to replace traditional common carrier services). In previous orders, the Commission has embraced the use of VoIP to avoid or constrain high international calling rates. *See Universal Serv. Contribution Methodology et al.*, Report and Order and Notice of Proposed Rulemaking, 21 FCC Rcd 7518, 7546, para. 55 & n.187 (2006) ("[I]nterconnected VoIP service is often marketed as an economical way to make interstate and international calls, as a lower-cost substitute for wireline toll service."), *rev'd in part sub nom. Vonage Holdings Corp. v. FCC*, 489 F.3d 1232 (D.C. Cir. 2007); *Reporting Requirements for U.S. Providers of Int'l Telecomms. Servs.*, Notice of Proposed Rulemaking, 19 FCC Rcd 6460, 6470, para. 22 (2004) ("Improvements in the packet-switched transmission technology underlying the internet now allow providers of VoIP to offer international voice transmission of reasonable quality at a price lower than current IMTS rates.") (footnote omitted); *Int'l Settlements Policy Reform*, Notice

of Proposed Rulemaking, 17 FCC Rcd 19954, 19964, para. 13 (2002) ("This ability to engage in least-cost routing, as well as alternative, non-traditional services such as IP Telephony or Voice-Over-IP, in conjunction with the benchmarks policy have created a market dynamic that is pressuring international settlement rates downward."). In addition, NCTA has explained that, "[b]y enabling consumers to make informed choices regarding broadband Internet access service," the Commission could conclude that transparency requirements "would help promote the competitiveness of VoIP and other broadband-based communications services" and "thereby facilitate the operation of market forces to discipline the charges and other practices of common carriers, in fulfillment of the Commission's obligations under sections 201 and 202" of the Act. NCTA Dec. 10, 2010 *Ex Parte* Letter at 2–3.

390 *See supra* Part II.B.

391 *See CCIA*, 693 F.2d at 212; *see also Orloff v. FCC*, 352 F.3d 415, 418–19 (D.C. Cir. 2003).

392 We reject the argument asserted by some commenters (*see, e.g.*, AT&T Comments at 218–19; Verizon Comments at 98–99) that the various grants of rulemaking authority in the Act, including the express grant of rulemaking authority in Section 201(b) itself, do not authorize the promulgation of rules pursuant to Section 201(b). See AT&T Corp. v. Iowa Utils. Bd., 525 U.S. 366, 378 (1999) ("We think that the grant in § 201(b) means what it says: The FCC has rulemaking authority to carry out the 'provisions of this Act.'").

393 47 U.S.C. § 251(a)(1).

394 *See supra* Part II.B.

395 *See id.*

396 47 U.S.C. § 151.

397 *See also* 47 U.S.C. § 256(b)(1) (directing the Commission to "establish procedures for . . . oversight of coordinated network planning by telecommunications carriers and other providers of telecommunications service for the effective and efficient interconnection of public telecommunications networks used to provide telecommunications service"); *Comcast*, 600 F.3d at 659 (acknowledging Section 256's objective, while adding that Section 256 does not "'expand[] . . . any authority that the Commission' otherwise has under law") (quoting 47 U.S.C. § 256(c)).

398 *See United States v. Sw. Cable Co.*, 392 U.S. 157, 177 (1968); *see also id.* at 174 ("[T]hese obligations require for their satisfaction the creation of a system of local broadcasting stations, such that 'all communities of appreciable size (will) have at least one television station as an outlet for local self-expression.'"); 47 U.S.C. §§ 307(b) (Commission shall "make such distribution of licenses, . . . among the several States and communities as to provide a fair, efficient, and equitable distribution of radio service to each of the same"), 303(f) & (h) (authorizing the Commission to allocate broadcasting zones or areas and to promulgate regulations "as it may deem necessary" to prevent interference among stations) (cited in *Sw. Cable*, 392 U.S. at 173–74).

399 *Nat'l Broad. Co.*, 319 U.S. at 216 (public interest to be served is the "larger and more effective use of radio") (citation and internal quotation marks omitted).

400 *See* 47 U.S.C. § 303(v); *see also N.Y. State Comm'n on Cable Television v. FCC*, 749 F.2d 804, 807–12 (D.C. Cir. 1984) (upholding the Commission's exercise of ancillary authority over satellite master antenna television service); 47 U.S.C. § 548 (discussed below).

401 *See, e.g.*, Google Comments at 45 & n.142; Vonage Comments at 13–15; Vonage Reply Comments at 25; XO Comments at 20–21.

402 *Sw. Cable*, 392 U.S. at 177; *see* 47 U.S.C. § 303(f) & (h) (establishing Commission's authority to allocate broadcasting zones or areas and to promulgate regulations "as it may deem necessary" to prevent interference among stations) (cited in *Sw. Cable*, 392 U.S. at 173–74).

403 *Nat'l Broad. Co.*, 319 U.S. at 216; *see also* 47 U.S.C. §§ 303(g) (establishing Commission's duty to "generally encourage the larger and more effective use of radio in the public interest"), 307(b) ("[T]he Commission shall make such distribution of licenses . . . among the several States and communities as to provide a fair, efficient, and equitable distribution of radio service to each of the same.").

404 *See supra* Parts II.A and II.B.

405 *See supra* Part II.A.

406 *See* Parts II.A. and II.B. NCTA has noted that "[t]he Commission could decide that, based on the growing importance of broadcast programming distributed over broadband networks to both television viewers and the business of broadcasting itself, ensuring that broadcast video content made available over broadband networks is not subject to unreasonable discrimination or anticompetitive treatment is necessary to preserve and strengthen the system of local broadcasting." NCTA Dec. 10, 2010 *Ex Parte* Letter at 3; *see also id.* ("Facilitating the availability of broadcast content on the Internet may also help to foster more efficient and intensive use of spectrum, thereby supporting the Commission's duty in section 303(g) to 'generally encourage the larger and more effective use of radio in the public interest.'") (quoting 47 U.S.C. § 303(g)).

407 *See supra* paras. 0-0, 0-0. The issue whether online-only video programming aggregators are themselves MVPDs under the Communications Act and our regulations has been raised in pending program access complaint proceedings. *See, e.g.*, *VDC Corp. v. Turner Network Sales, Inc.*, Program Access Complaint (Jan.

18, 2007); *Sky Angel U.S., LLC v. Discovery Commc'ns LLC*, Program Access Complaint (Mar. 24, 2010). Nothing in this Order should be read to state or imply any determination on this issue.

[408] 47 U.S.C. § 548(a). The Act defines "video programming" as "programming provided by, or generally considered comparable to programming provided by, a television broadcast station." 47 U.S.C. § 522(20). Although the Commission stated nearly a decade ago that video "'streamed' over the Internet" had "not yet achieved television quality" and therefore did not constitute "video programming" at that time, *see Cable Modem Declaratory Ruling,* 17 FCC Rcd at 4834, para. 63 n.236, intervening improvements in streaming technology and broadband availability enable such programming to be "comparable to programming provided by . . . a television broadcast station," 47 U.S.C. § 522(20). *See supra* Part II.A–II.B. (discussing increasing use of, and end-user demand for, online streaming of video content, including broadcast content). This finding is consistent with our prediction more than five years ago that "[a]s video compression technology improves, data transfer rates increase, and media adapters that link TV to a broadband connection become more widely used, . . . video over the Internet will proliferate and improve in quality." *Ann. Assessment of the Status of Competition in the Mkt. for the Delivery of Video Programming*, Notice of Inquiry, 19 FCC Rcd 10909, 10932, para. 74 (2004) (citation omitted).

[409] *See* Cable Act of 1992, Pub. L. No. 102-385, § 2(a)(5), 106 Stat. 1460, 1461 ("Vertically integrated program suppliers . . . have the incentive and ability to favor their affiliated cable operators over nonaffiliated cable operators and programming distributors using other technologies."); H.R. Rep. No. 102-862, at 93 (1992) (Conf. Rep.), *reprinted in* 1992 U.S.C.C.A.N. 1231, 1275 ("In adopting rules under this section, the conferees expect the Commission to address and resolve the problems of unreasonable cable industry practices, including restricting the availability of programming and charging discriminatory prices to non-cable technologies."); S. Rep. No. 102-92, at 26 (1991), *reprinted in* 1992 U.S.C.C.A.N. 1133, 1159 ("[C]able programmers may simply refuse to sell to potential competitors. Small cable operators, satellite dish owners, and wireless cable operators complain that they are denied access to, or charged more for, programming than large, vertically integrated cable operators.").

[410] *See* 47 U.S.C. § 548(b); *see Nat'l Cable & Telecomms. Ass'n v. FCC*, 567 F.3d 659, 662 (D.C. Cir. 2009) (*NCTA*).

[411] *Review of the Commission's Program Access Rules and Examination of Programming Tying Arrangements*, First Report and Order, 25 FCC Rcd 746, 779, para. 48 & n.190 (2010) (citing *Exclusive Contracts for Provision of Video Serv. in Multiple Dwelling Units and Other Real Estate Devs.*, Report and Order and Further Notice of Proposed Rulemaking, 22 FCC Rcd 20235, 20255, para. 43, *aff'd, NCTA*, 567 F.3d 659); *see also NTCA*, 567 F.3d at 664–65 (referring to "unfair dealing" and "anticompetitive practices").

[412] *See* 47 U.S.C. § 548(b); *NCTA*, 567 F.3d at 664. In *NCTA,* the court held that the Commission reasonably concluded that the "broad and sweeping terms" of Section 628(b) authorized it to ban exclusive agreements between cable operators and building owners that prevented other MVPDs from providing their programming to residents of those buildings. The court observed that "the words Congress chose [in Section 628(b)] focus not on practices that prevent MVPDs from *obtaining* satellite cable or satellite broadcast programming, but on practices that prevent them from 'providing' that programming 'to subscribers or consumers.'" *NCTA*, 567 F.3d at 664 (emphasis in original).

[413] 47 U.S.C. § 548(c)(1).

[414] 47 U.S.C. § 548(j).

[415] DISH Reply at 4–5 ("Pay-TV services continue to evolve at a rapid pace and providers increasingly are integrating their vast offerings of linear channels with online content," while "consumers are adopting online video services as a complement to traditional, linear pay-TV services" and "specifically desire Internet video as a complement to . . . [MVPDs'] traditional TV offerings.") (footnotes and citations omitted). We find unpersuasive the contention that this Order fails to "grapple with the implications of the market forces that are driving MVPDs . . . to add Internet connectivity to their multichannel video offerings." McDowell Statement at *24 (footnote omitted). Our analysis takes account of these developments, which are discussed at length in Part II.A, above.

[416] *Id.* at 5–8 & n.20 (discussing "DishOnline service," which "allows DISH to offer over 3,000 movies and TV shows through its 'DishOnline' Internet video service," and noting that "the success of DishOnline is critically dependent on broadband access provided and controlled by DISH's competitors in the MVPD market"); DISH PN Comments at 2–3; DISH Network, Watch Live TV Online OR Recorded Programs with DishOnline, www.dish-systems.com/products/dish_online.php ("'DISHOnline.com integrates DISH Network's expansive TV programming lineup with the vast amount of online video content, adding another dimension to our 'pay once, take your TV everywhere' product platform.'"); *see also supra* Part II.A. Much of the regular subscription programming that DISH offers online is satellite-delivered programming. *See* DISH Network, Watch Live TV Online OR Recorded Programs with DishOnline, www.dish-systems.com/products/dish_online.php (noting that customers can watch content from cable programmers such as the Discovery Channel and MTV). Thus, we reject NCTA's argument that "[t]here is no basis for asserting that any cable operator or common carrier's practices with respect to Internet-delivered video could . . . 'prevent or

significantly hinder' an MVPD from providing satellite cable programming." NCTA Dec. 10, 2010 *Ex Parte* Letter at 5.

417 DISH Reply at 7.

418 Notwithstanding suggestions to the contrary, the Commission is not required to wait until anticompetitive harms are realized before acting. Rather, the Commission may exercise its ancillary jurisdiction to "plan in advance of foreseeable events, instead of waiting to react to them." *Sw. Cable*, 392 U.S. at 176-77 (citation and internal quotation marks omitted); *see also Star Wireless, LLC v. FCC*, 522 F.3d at 475.

419 *See Open Internet NRPM,* 24 FCC Rcd at 13099, para. 85 (discussing role of the Internet in fostering video programming competition and the Commission's authority to regulate video services).

420 47 U.S.C. § 536(a).

421 *Id.* An MVPD is "a person such as, but not limited to, a cable operator, a multichannel multipoint distribution service, a direct broadcast satellite service, or a television receive-only satellite program distributor, who makes available for purchase, by subscribers or customers, multiple channels of video programming." 47 U.S.C. § 522(13). A "video programming vendor" is any "person engaged in the production, creation, or wholesale distribution of video programming for sale." 47 U.S.C. § 536(b); *see also supra* note 408 (discussing definition of "video programming"). A number of video programming vendors make their programming available online. *See, e.g.*, Hulu.com, www.hulu.com/about; Biography Channel, www.biography.com; Hallmark Channel, www.hallmarkchannel.com. *See also supra* Part II.A.

422 47 U.S.C. § 536(a)(1)–(3); *see also* 47 C.F.R. § 76.1301 (implementing regulations to address practices specified in Section 616(a)(1)–(3)).

423 47 U.S.C. § 536(a)(3).

424 The Act does not define "related practices" as that phrase is used in Section 616(a). Because the term is neither explicitly defined in the statute nor susceptible of only one meaning, we construe it, consistent with dictionary definitions, to cover practices that are "akin" or "connected" to those specifically identified in Section 616(a)(1)–(3). *See Black's Law Dictionary* 1158 (5th ed. 1979); *Webster's Third New Int'l Dictionary* 1916 (1993). The argument that Section 616(a) has no application to Internet access service overlooks that the statute expressly covers these "related practices."

425 *See, e.g.*, NCTA Dec. 10, 2010 *Ex Parte* Letter at 3 (discussing authority ancillary to Title III).

426 47 U.S.C. § 301.

427 47 U.S.C. §§ 304, 316(a)(1). We thus disagree with commenters who suggest in general that there is nothing in Title III to support the imposition of open Internet rules. *See, e.g.*, EFF Comments at 6 n.13.

428 47 U.S.C. § 309(a); *see also* 47 U.S.C. § 307(a) ("The Commission, if public convenience, interest, or necessity will be served thereby, subject to the limitations of this [Act], shall grant to any applicant therefor a station license provided for by this [Act].").

429 47 U.S.C. § 309(j)(3).

430 47 U.S.C. § 316(a)(1).

431 *See WBEN Inc. v. United States*, 396 F.2d 601, 618 (2d Cir. 1968).

432 *See* 47 U.S.C. § 309(j)(6); *Celtronix Telemetry v. FCC*, 272 F.3d 585 (D.C. Cir. 2001).

433 *700 MHz Second Report and Order*, 22 FCC Rcd at 15363, para. 201.

434 *Id.* at 15365, para. 206.

435 *See supra* Part III.E. In addition, the use of mobile VoIP applications is likely to constrain prices for CMRS voice services, similar to what we described earlier with regard to VoIP and traditional phone services. *See supra* para. 0.

436 AT&T PN Reply at 32. AT&T asserts that winners of non-C-Block licenses paid a premium for licenses not subject to the open platform requirements that applied to the upper 700 MHz C Block licenses. *Id.* at 33–34.

437 AT&T Comments at 233–34.

438 *Celtronix*, 272 F.3d at 589.

439 The Commission may act by rulemaking to modify or impose rules applicable to all licensees or licensees in a particular class; in order to modify specific licenses held by particular licensees, however, the Commission generally is required to follow the modification procedure set forth in 47 U.S.C. § 316. *See Comm. for Effective Cellular Rules v. FCC*, 53 F.3d 1309, 1319–20 (D.C. Cir. 1995).

440 *See generally*, *700 MHz Second Report and Order*, 22 FCC Rcd at 15358–65. In the *700 MHz Second Report and Order*, the Commission stated that its decision to limit open-platform requirements to the C Block was based on the record before it "at this time," *id.* at 15361, and noted that openness issues in the wireless industry were being considered more broadly in other proceedings. *Id.* at 15363. The public notice setting procedures for the 2008 auction advised bidders that the rules governing auctioned licenses would be subject to "pending and future proceedings" before the Commission. *See Auction of 700 MHz Band Licenses Scheduled for January 24, 2008*, Public Notice, 22 FCC Rcd 18141, 18156, para. 42 (2007).

441 *See, e.g.*, AT&T PN Reply at 34–35.

442 *See, e.g.*, 47 C.F.R. §§ 27.5(b)–(c), 27.6(b)–(c), 27.14, 27.53(c)–(e).

443 *See supra* Part III.E.

[444] 47 U.S.C. § 154(k). In a similar vein, Section 257 of the Act directs the Commission to report to Congress every three years on "market entry barriers" that the Commission recommends be eliminated, including "barriers for entrepreneurs and other small businesses in the provision and ownership of telecommunications services and information services." 47 U.S.C. § 257(a) & (c); *see also Comcast*, 600 F.3d at 659; NCTA Dec. 10, 2010 *Ex Parte* Letter at 3 ("[S]ection 257's reporting mandate provides a basis for the Commission to require providers of broadband Internet access service to disclose the terms and conditions of service in order to assess whether such terms hamper small business entry and, if so, whether any legislation may be required to address the problem.") (footnote omitted).

[445] *See, e.g.*, *New Part 4 of the Commission's Rules Concerning Disruptions to Commc'ns*, Report and Order and Further Notice of Proposed Rulemaking, 19 FCC Rcd 16830, 16837, paras. 1, 12 (2004) (extending Commission's reporting requirements for communications disruptions to certain providers of non-wireline communications, in part based on Section 4(k)); *DTV Consumer Educ. Initiative*, Report & Order, 23 FCC Rcd 4134, 4147, paras. 1, 2, 28 (2008) (requiring various entities, including broadcasters, to submit quarterly reports to the Commission detailing their consumer education efforts related to the DTV transition, in part based on section 4(k)); *Review of the Commission's Broad. Cable and Equal Emp't Opportunity Rules and Policies*, Second Report and Order and Third Notice of Proposed Rulemaking, 17 FCC Rcd 24018, 24077, paras. 5, 195 (2002) (promulgating recordkeeping and reporting requirements for broadcast licensees and other regulated entities to show compliance with equal opportunities hiring rules, in part based on section 4(k)).

[446] 600 F.3d at 659. All, or nearly all, providers of broadband Internet access service are regulated by the Commission insofar as they operate under certificates to provide common carriage service, or under licenses to use radio spectrum.

[447] 47 U.S.C. § 218.

[448] Cf. US West, Inc. v. FCC, 778 F.2d 23, 26–27 (D.C. Cir. 1985) (acknowledging Commission's authority under Section 218 to impose reporting requirements on holding companies that owned local telephone companies).

[449] *See, e.g.*, AT&T Comments at 235–44; AT&T Reply at 167–73; Verizon Comments at 111–18; Verizon Reply at 108–17; TWC Comments at 44–50; TWC Reply at 51–56.

[450] *See* AT&T Comments at 235; Verizon Comments at 112.

[451] *See, e.g.*, Google Reply at 28; PK Reply at 23; Free Press Comments at 137–38.

[452] AT&T Comments at 235.

[453] *Turner Broad. Sys., Inc. v. FCC*, 512 U.S. 622, 636 (1994) (*Turner I*) (internal quotation marks omitted); *see also Los Angeles v. Preferred Commc'ns, Inc.*, 476 U.S. 488, 494 (1986).

[454] *See, e.g.*, AT&T, AT&T U-verse, www.att-services.net/att-u-verse.html (AT&T U-verse: "Customers can get the information they want, when they want it"); Verizon, FiOS Internet, www22.verizon.com/Residential/FiOSInternet/Overview.htm and Verizon, High Speed Internet, www22.verizon.com/Residential/HighSpeedInternet (Verizon FiOS and High Speed Internet: "Internet, plus all the free extras").

[455] *See* Verizon Comments at 117 ("[B]roadband providers today provide traditional Internet access services that offer subscribers access to *all lawful content* and have strong economic incentives to continue to do so.") (emphasis added).

[456] *See* 17 U.S.C. § 512(a) (a "service provider shall not be liable . . . for infringement of copyright by reason of the provider's transmitting, routing, or providing connections for" material distributed by others on its network); 47 U.S.C. § 230(c)(1) ("[N]o provider or user of an interactive computer service shall be treated as the publisher or speaker of any information provided by another information content provider"); *see also Recording Indus. Ass'n of Am., Inc. v. Verizon Internet Servs., Inc.*, 351 F.3d 1229, 1234 (D.C. Cir. 2003) (discussing in context of subpoena issued to Verizon under the Digital Millennium Copyright Act Section 512(a)'s "four safe harbors, each of which immunizes ISPs from liability from copyright infringement"), *cert. denied,* 543 U.S. 924 (2004). For example "Verizon.net, the home page for Verizon Internet customers, contains a notice explicitly claiming copyright over the contents of the page. In contrast, the terms of service of Verizon Internet access explicitly disclaim any affiliation with content transmitted over the network." PK Reply at 22.

[457] *See, e.g.*, *Charter Commc'ns, Inc., Subpoena Enforcement Matter*, 393 F.3d 771, 777 (8th Cir. 2005) (subpoenas served on Charter were not authorized because "Charter's function" as a broadband provider "was limited to acting as a conduit for the allegedly copyright protected material" at issue); *Verizon Internet Servs.*, 351 F.3d at 1237 (accepting Verizon's argument that federal copyright law "does not authorize the issuance of a subpoena to an ISP acting as a mere conduit for the transmission of information sent by others").

[458] We recognize that in two cases, federal district courts have concluded that the provision of broadband service is "speech" protected by the First Amendment. In *Itasca*, the district court reasoned that broadband providers were analogous to cable and satellite television companies, which are protected by the First Amendment. *Ill. Bell Tel. Co. v. Vill. of Itasca,* 503 F. Supp. 2d 928, 947–49 (N.D. Ill. 2007). And in *Broward County*, the district court determined that the transmission function provided by broadband service could not be separated from the content of the speech being transmitted. *Comcast Cablevision of Broward Cnty., Inc. v. Broward Cnty.*, 124 F. Supp. 2d 685, 691–92 (S.D. Fla. 2000). For the reasons stated, we disagree with the reasoning of those decisions.

[459] *See* TWC Comments at 45; *see also supra* Part III.
[460] AT&T Reply at 170; NCTA Reply at 40.
[461] *See* CWA Reply at 13–14.
[462] *See Turner I*, 512 U.S. at 642. Regulations generally are content neutral if justified without reference to content or viewpoint. *Id.* at 643; *BellSouth Corp. v. FCC*, 144 F.3d 58, 69 (D.C. Cir. 1998); *Time Warner Entm't Co., L.P. v. FCC*, 93 F.3d 957, 966–67 (D.C. Cir. 1996).
[463] Verizon Comments at 115.
[464] *Turner I*, 512 U.S. at 660–61 (quoting *Minneapolis Star & Tribune Co. v. Minn. Comm'r of Revenue*, 460 U.S. 575, 585 (1983)).
[465] *Turner I*, 512 U.S. at 662 (internal quotation marks omitted).
[466] These interests are consistent with the Communications Act's charge to the Commission to make available a "rapid and efficient" national communications infrastructure, 47 U.S.C. § 151; to promote, consistent with a "vibrant and competitive free market," "the continued development of the Internet and other interactive computer services"; and to "encourage the development of technologies which maximize user control over what information is received," 47 U.S.C. § 230(b)(1)–(3). Indeed, AT&T concedes that "[t]here is little doubt that preservation of an open and free Internet is an 'important or substantial government interest.'" AT&T Comments at 237 (quoting *Turner I*, 512 U.S. at 662).
[467] 512 U.S. at 663. The *Turner I* Court continued: "Indeed, it has long been a basic tenet of national communications policy that the widest possible dissemination of information from diverse and antagonistic sources is essential to the welfare of the public." *Id.* (internal quotation marks omitted). *See also FCC v. Nat'l Citizens Comm. for Broad.*, 436 U.S. 775, 795 (1978) (*NCCB*) (quoting *Associated Press v. United States*, 326 U.S. 1, 20 (1945)).
[468] *See* Time Warner Comments at 48; Verizon Comments at 117.
[469] *See NCCB,* 436 U.S. at 814.
[470] AT&T contends (AT&T Comments at 219–20) that our rules would conflict with prohibitions contained in Section 326 of the Act against "censorship" of "radio communications" or interference with "the right of free speech by means of radio communication." 47 U.S.C. § 326. For the same reasons that our rules do not violate the First Amendment, they do not violate Section 326's statutory prohibition.
[471] *See, e.g.*, Verizon Comments at 119–23; AT&T Comments at 244–48.
[472] Verizon contends that "[t]o the extent the proposed rules would prohibit the owner of a broadband network from setting the terms on which other providers can occupy its property, the rule would give those providers the equivalent of a permanent easement on the network – a form of physical occupation." Verizon Comments at 119 (citing *Loretto v. Teleprompter Manhattan CATV Corp.*, 458 U.S. 419, 430 (1982)). Not so. Such transmissions are neither "occupations" nor "permanent." *See Loretto*, 458 U.S. at 435 n.12; *see also Cablevision Sys. Corp. v. FCC*, 570 F.3d 83, 98 (2d Cir. 2009) (upholding Commission's finding that a must-carry obligation did not constitute a physical occupation because "the transmission of WRNN's signal does not involve a physical occupation of Cablevision's equipment or property"). In addition, to the extent broadband providers voluntarily allow any customer to transmit or receive information, the imposition of reasonable non-discrimination requirements would not be a taking under *Loretto*. *See Hilton Washington Corp. v. District of Columbia*, 777 F.2d 47 (D.C. Cir. 1985); *Yee v. City of Escondido*, 503 U.S. 519, 531 (1992).
[473] *Penn Cent. Transp. Co. v. City of N.Y.*, 438 U.S. 104, 124 (1978).
[474] *Lucas v. S.C. Coastal Council*, 505 U.S. 1003, 1027 (1992); *Gen. Tel. Co. of the Sw. v. United States*, 449 F.2d 846, 864 (5th Cir. 1971); *see also Hispanic Info. & Telecomms. Network v. FCC,* 865 F.2d 1289, 1294–95 (D.C. Cir. 1989).
[475] This history likewise refutes the assertion that prior Commission decisions "engendered serious reliance interests" that would be unsettled by our adoption of open Internet rules. Baker Statement at *11 n.41 (citation and internal quotation marks omitted).
[476] *See, e.g.*, Bright House Networks Comments at 10; CCIA Comments at 2, 34; Google-Verizon Joint Comments at 4 ("A robust role for technical and industry groups should be encouraged to address any challenges or problems that may arise and to help guide the practices of all players …."); WISPA Comments at 14–16; DISH Network Reply at 24–26; Qwest Reply at 32.
[477] Providers and other parties may also seek guidance from the Commission on questions about the application of the open Internet rules in particular contexts, for instance by requesting a declaratory ruling. *See* 47 C.F.R. § 1.2.
[478] *See, e.g.*, ACA Comments at v, 19–20; Corning Inc. Comments at 14–15; Ericsson Comments at 24; Google-Verizon Joint Comments at 4; ITIC Comments at 7–8; Netflix Comments at 10–11; Qwest Comments at 50; RCA Comments at 19, 25–26; TIA Comments at 44–46.
[479] *Open Internet NPRM* at 13124–25, paras. 175–76.
[480] *See, e.g.*, ACA Comments at v, 19–20; Ad Hoc Comments at 27; Google Comments at 87–92; OIC Comments at 68; Microsoft Reply at 13–14.
[481] 47 C.F.R. § 1.41.

[482] As with our other complaint rules, the availability of complaint procedures does not bar the Commission from initiating separate and independent enforcement proceedings for potential violations. *See* 47 C.F.R. § 0.111(a)(16).

[483] *See, e.g.*, ACA Comments at 19–20; PIC Comments at 70–71; WISPA Comments at 14–16.

[484] *See* ACA Comments at 19 (advocating for the use of rules governing cable carriage complaints); Google Comments at 87–92 (advocating for the use of rules governing section 208 complaints); Netflix Comments at 10–11 (same); RCA Comments at iii, 19 (same); OIC Comments at 68–70 (advocating for the use of a new set of rules developed specifically for open Internet disputes).

[485] The Commission is authorized to resolve formal complaints—and adopt procedural rules governing the process—pursuant to sections 4(i) and 4(j) of the Act. 47 U.S.C. §§ 154(i), 154(j). In addition, section 403 of the Act enables the Commission to initiate inquiries and enforce orders on its own motion. 47 U.S.C. § 403. Inherent in such authority is the ability to resolve disputes concerning violations of the open Internet rules.

[486] The Part 76 rules were promulgated to address complaints against cable systems. *See 1998 Biennial Regulatory Review – Part 76 – Cable Television Service Pleading and Complaint Rules*, Report and Order, 14 FCC Rcd 418, 420, para. 6 (1999) ("*1998 Biennial Review*"). For example, a local television station may bring a complaint, pursuant to the Part 76 rules, claiming that it was wrongfully denied carriage on a cable system. *See* 47 C.F.R. § 76.61. Some complaints alleging open Internet violations may be analogous, such as those brought by a content or application provider claiming that broadband providers—many of which are cable companies—are unlawfully blocking or degrading access to end users.

[487] *See* 47 C.F.R. § 8.12.

[488] As with other formal complaint procedures, a filing fee will be required. *See* 47 C.F.R. § 1.1106.

[489] *See* 47 C.F.R. §§ 8.14(b), (c).

[490] The rules give the Commission discretion to order other procedures as appropriate, including briefing, status conferences, oral argument, evidentiary hearings, discovery, or referral to an administrative law judge. *See* 47 C.F.R. §§ 8.14(e)–(g).

[491] *See, e.g.*, *Consumer.net, LLC v. Verizon Communications, Inc.*, Memorandum Opinion and Order, 25 FCC Rcd 2737, 2740, para. 10 (Enf. Bur. 2010).

[492] *See, e.g.*, Ad Hoc Comments at 27; Google Comments at 90 ("For example, after a web content or applications provider makes a *prima facie* case that its packets are being degraded or otherwise discriminated against by the broadband provider, the burden should shift to the broadband provider to demonstrate by a preponderance of the evidence that either: (i) it is not engaging in any activity or practice that degrades the web content provider's packets relative to other web sites; or (ii) such practice falls within a reasonable network management practice exception."); Google-Verizon Joint Comments at 4–7; OIC Comments at 48–49; PIC Comments at 70–71; DISH Network Reply at 23; TIA Reply at 18–19.

[493] *See, e.g.*, Ad Hoc Comments at 27; Google Comments at 88; Google-Verizon Joint Comments at 4–7; NJ Rate Counsel Comments at 11–12; PK et al. Comments at 71; Qwest Comments at 51; Microsoft Reply at 13.

[494] *See* 47 C.F.R. § 1.730. Furthermore, for good cause, pursuant to 47 C.F.R. § 1.3, the Commission may shorten the deadlines or otherwise revise the procedures herein to expedite the adjudication of complaints.

[495] The rules adopted today explicitly authorize the Enforcement Bureau to resolve complaints alleging open Internet violations.

[496] *See* 47 U.S.C. §§ 403, 503(b); 47 C.F.R. § 1.80.

[497] *See supra* paras. 0-0, 0-0.

[498] *See* 5 U.S.C. § 603.

[499] *See Open Internet NPRM*, 24 FCC Rcd at 13136–52 (App. C).

[500] *See* Letter from Wireline Competition Bureau, FCC, to Marlene Dortch, Secretary, FCC, GN Docket No. 09-191, WC Docket No. 07-52 (filed Dec. 13, 2010).

[501] This Appendix lists major commenters and the short forms by which they are cited in the Order. The Commission also received tens of thousands of brief comments in this proceeding, which are not listed here but which were considered.

[502] *See* 5 U.S.C. § 603. The RFA, see 5 U.S.C. §§ 601–12, has been amended by the Small Business Regulatory Enforcement Fairness Act of 1996 (SBREFA), Pub. L. No. 104-121, Title II, 110 Stat. 857 (1996).

[503] *See Preserving the Open Internet; Broadband Industry Practices*, Notice of Proposed Rulemaking, 24 FCC Rcd 13064, 13136–52 (2009) (*Open Internet Notice*).

[504] *See* 5 U.S.C. § 604.

[505] National Broadband Plan at xi, 3–5.

[506] *See Appropriate Framework for Broadband Access to the Internet Over Wireline Facilities et al.*, Policy Statement, 20 FCC Rcd 14986 (2005) (*Internet Policy Statement*); *SBC Commc'ns, Inc. and AT&T Corp. Applications for Approval of Transfer of Control*, Memorandum Opinion and Order, 20 FCC Rcd 18290, 18392, para. 211 (2005); *Verizon Commc'ns Inc. and MCI, Inc. Applications for Approval of Transfer of Control*, Memorandum Opinion and Order, 20 FCC Rcd 18433, 18537, para. 221 (2005); *AT&T Inc. and BellSouth Corp. Application for Transfer of Control*, Memorandum Opinion and Order, 22 FCC Rcd 5662, 5663, para. 2 (2007).

507 *Service Rules for the 698–746, 747–762 and 777–792 MHz Bands et al.*, Second Report and Order, 22 FCC Rcd 15289 (2007) (*700 MHz Second Report and Order*); 47 C.F.R. § 27.16.
508 *Broadband Industry Practices*, Notice of Inquiry, 22 FCC Rcd 7894, 7896, para. 8 (2007).
509 Center for Regulatory Effectiveness Jan. 8, 2010 Comments, filed by Jim Tozzi, GN Docket No. 09-191, at 7.
510 *See* Center for Regulatory Effectiveness Jan. 8, 2010 Comments, filed by Jim Tozzi, GN Docket No. 09-191, at 7–8.
511 Center for Regulatory Effectiveness Jan. 8, 2010 Comments, filed by Jim Tozzi, GN Docket No. 09-191, at 8.
512 We also note that we are not sure how openness is improved by guessing at the number of burden hours that a small entity could incur from our rules, without receiving comments from small entities first. We would argue that such systematic guessing would not be regulatorily effective.
513 Smithville Telephone Company Jan. 14, 2010 Comments, GN Docket No. 09-191.
514 *See, e.g.*, NTCA Comments at 9, 43–44; US Telecom Comments at 52; ADTRAN Comments at i, 9, 11; TPPF Foundation Comments at 99; TIA Comments at 32.
515 *See infra* para. 0.
516 ACA Jan. 14, 2010 IRFA Comments, GN Docket No. 09-191, WC Docket No. 07-52, at 4.
517 ACA Jan. 14, 2010 IRFA Comments, GN Docket No. 09-191, WC Docket No. 07-52, at 2–3; ACA Jan. 14, 2010 Comments, GN Docket No. 09-191, WC Docket No. 07-52, at 10–14 (asking the Commission to "make clear the regulations do not impose" various obligations).
518 5 U.S.C. § 604(a)(3).
519 5 U.S.C. § 601(6).
520 5 U.S.C. § 601(3) (incorporating by reference the definition of "small-business concern" in the Small Business Act, 15 U.S.C. § 632). Pursuant to 5 U.S.C. § 601(3), the statutory definition of a small business applies "unless an agency, after consultation with the Office of Advocacy of the Small Business Administration and after opportunity for public comment, establishes one or more definitions of such term which are appropriate to the activities of the agency and publishes such definition(s) in the Federal Register."
521 15 U.S.C. § 632.
522 *See* 5 U.S.C. §§ 601(3)–(6).
523 *See* SBA, Office of Advocacy, "Frequently Asked Questions," web.sba.gov/faqs.
524 5 U.S.C. § 601(4).
525 INDEPENDENT SECTOR, THE NEW NONPROFIT ALMANAC & DESK REFERENCE (2002).
526 5 U.S.C. § 601(5).
527 U.S. CENSUS BUREAU, STATISTICAL ABSTRACT OF THE UNITED STATES: 2006, Section 8, page 272, tbl. 415.
528 We assume that the villages, school districts, and special districts are small, and total 48,558. *See* U.S. CENSUS BUREAU, STATISTICAL ABSTRACT OF THE UNITED STATES: 2006, section 8, page 273, tbl. 417. For 2002, Census Bureau data indicate that the total number of county, municipal, and township governments nationwide was 38,967, of which 35,819 were small. *Id.*
529 U.S. Census Bureau, 2007 NAICS Definitions, "517110 Wired Telecommunications Carriers," www.census.gov/naics/2007/def/ND517110.HTM#N517110.
530 13 C.F.R. § 121.201, NAICS code 517110.
531 U.S. Census Bureau, 2007 NAICS Definitions, "517919 All Other Telecommunications," www.census.gov/naics/2007/def/ND517919.HTM#N517919.
532 13 C.F.R. § 121.201, NAICS code 517919 (updated for inflation in 2008).
533 U.S. Census Bureau, 2007 Economic Census, Subject Series: Information, "Establishment and Firm Size," NAICS code 5171103 (released Nov. 19, 2010) (employment size). The data show only two categories within the whole: the categories for 1-4 employees and for 5-9 employees.
534 U.S. Census Bureau, 2007 Economic Census, Subject Series: Information, "Establishment and Firm Size," NAICS code 5179191 (released Nov. 19, 2010) (receipts size).
535 13 C.F.R. § 121.201, NAICS code 517110.
536 FCC, WIRELINE COMPETITION BUREAU, INDUSTRY ANALYSIS AND TECHNOLOGY DIVISION, TRENDS IN TELEPHONE SERVICE, tbl. 5.3, Page 5-5 (Aug. 2008) (TRENDS IN TELEPHONE SERVICE). This source uses data that are current as of November 1, 2006.
537 13 C.F.R. § 121.201, NAICS code 517110.
538 TRENDS IN TELEPHONE SERVICE, tbl. 5.3.
539 5 U.S.C. § 601(3).
540 Letter from Jere W. Glover, Chief Counsel for Advocacy, SBA, to William E. Kennard, Chairman, FCC (filed May 27, 1999). The Small Business Act contains a definition of "small business concern," which the RFA incorporates into its own definition of "small business." 15 U.S.C. § 632(a); 5 U.S.C. § 601(3). SBA regulations interpret "small business concern" to include the concept of dominance on a national basis. 13 C.F.R. § 121.102(b).
541 13 C.F.R. § 121.201, NAICS code 517110.
542 TRENDS IN TELEPHONE SERVICE, tbl. 5.3.
543 13 C.F.R. § 121.201, NAICS code 517110.

[544] TRENDS IN TELEPHONE SERVICE, tbl. 5.3.

[545] U.S. Census Bureau, 2007 NAICS Definitions, "517210 Wireless Telecommunications Categories (Except Satellite)," www.census.gov/naics/2007/def/ND517210.HTM#N517210.

[546] U.S. Census Bureau, 2002 NAICS Definitions, "517211 Paging"; www.census.gov/epcd/naics02/def/NDEF517.HTM.; U.S. Census Bureau, 2002 NAICS Definitions, "517212 Cellular and Other Wireless Telecommunications," www.census.gov/epcd/naics02/def/NDEF517.HTM.

[547] 13 C.F.R. § 121.201, NAICS code 517210 (2007 NAICS). The now-superseded, pre-2007 C.F.R. citations were 13 C.F.R. § 121.201, NAICS codes 517211 and 517212 (referring to the 2002 NAICS).

[548] U.S. Census Bureau, 2007 Economic Census, Sector 51, EC0751I1 Information: Industry Series: Preliminary Summary Statistics for the United States: 2007, NAICS code 517210 (issued Oct. 20, 2009), factfinder.census.gov/servlet/IBQTable?-fds_name=EC0700A1&-_clearIBQ=Y&-ds_name=EC0751I1&-NAICS2007=51721.

[549] *Id.*

[550] *Amendment of the Commission's Rules to Establish Part 27, the Wireless Communications Service (WCS)*, Report and Order, 12 FCC Rcd 10785, 10879, para. 194 (1997).

[551] *See* Letter from Aida Alvarez, Administrator, SBA, to Amy Zoslov, Chief, Auctions and Industry Analysis Division, Wireless Telecommunications Bureau, FCC (filed Dec. 2, 1998) (*Alvarez Letter 1998*).

[552] 47 C.F.R. § 2.106; *see generally* 47 C.F.R. §§ 27.1–.70.

[553] 13 C.F.R. § 121.201, NAICS code 517210.

[554] *Id.*

[555] TRENDS IN TELEPHONE SERVICE, tbl. 5.3.

[556] *Id.*

[557] *See Amendment of Parts 20 and 24 of the Commission's Rules – Broadband PCS Competitive Bidding and the Commercial Mobile Radio Service Spectrum Cap et al.*, Report and Order, 11 FCC Rcd 7824, 7850–52, paras. 57–60 (1996) ("*PCS Report and Order*"); *see also* 47 C.F.R. § 24.720(b).

[558] *See PCS Report and Order*, 11 FCC Rcd at 7852, para. 60.

[559] *See Alvarez Letter 1998.*

[560] *See Broadband PCS, D, E and F Block Auction Closes*, Public Notice, Doc. No. 89838 (rel. Jan. 14, 1997).

[561] *See C, D, E, and F Block Broadband PCS Auction Closes*, Public Notice, 14 FCC Rcd 6688 (WTB 1999). Before Auction No. 22, the Commission established a very small standard for the C Block to match the standard used for F Block. *Amendment of the Commission's Rules Regarding Installment Payment Financing for Personal Communications Services (PCS) Licensees*, WT Docket No. 97-82, Fourth Report and Order, 13 FCC Rcd 15743, 15768, para. 46 (1998).

[562] *See C and F Block Broadband PCS Auction Closes; Winning Bidders Announced*, Public Notice, 16 FCC Rcd 2339 (2001).

[563] *See Broadband PCS Spectrum Auction Closes; Winning Bidders Announced for Auction No. 58*, Public Notice, 20 FCC Rcd 3703 (2005).

[564] *See Auction of Broadband PCS Spectrum Licenses Closes; Winning Bidders Announced for Auction No. 71*, Public Notice, 22 FCC Rcd 9247 (2007).

[565] *Id.*

[566] *See Auction of AWS-1 and Broadband PCS Licenses Closes; Winning Bidders Announced for Auction 78*, Public Notice, 23 FCC Rcd 12749 (WTB 2008).

[567] *Id.*

[568] 47 C.F.R. § 90.814(b)(1).

[569] 47 C.F.R. § 90.814(b)(1).

[570] *See* Letter from Aida Alvarez, Administrator, SBA, to Thomas Sugrue, Chief, Wireless Telecommunications Bureau, FCC (filed Aug. 10, 1999) (*Alvarez Letter 1999*).

[571] *See Correction to Public Notice DA 96-586 "FCC Announces Winning Bidders in the Auction of 1020 Licenses to Provide 900 MHz SMR in Major Trading Areas,"* Public Notice, 18 FCC Rcd 18367 (WTB 1996).

[572] *See Multi-Radio Service Auction Closes*, Public Notice, 17 FCC Rcd 1446 (WTB 2002).

[573] *See 800 MHz Specialized Mobile Radio (SMR) Service General Category (851–854 MHz) and Upper Band (861–865 MHz) Auction Closes; Winning Bidders Announced*, Public Notice, 15 FCC Rcd 17162 (2000).

[574] *See 800 MHz SMR Service Lower 80 Channels Auction Closes; Winning Bidders Announced*, Public Notice, 16 FCC Rcd 1736 (2000).

[575] *See generally* 13 C.F.R. § 121.201, NAICS code 517210.

[576] *See Reallocation and Service Rules for the 698–746 MHz Spectrum Band (Television Channels 52–59)*, Report and Order, 17 FCC Rcd 1022 (2002) (*Channels 52–59 Report and Order*).

[577] *See Channels 52–59 Report and Order*, 17 FCC Rcd at 1087–88, para. 172.

[578] *See id.*

[579] *See id.*, 17 FCC Rcd at 1088, para. 173.

[580] *See Alvarez Letter 1999.*

[581] *See Lower 700 MHz Band Auction Closes*, Public Notice, 17 FCC Rcd 17272 (WTB 2002).
[582] *See Lower 700 MHz Band Auction Closes*, Public Notice, 18 FCC Rcd 11873 (WTB 2003).
[583] *See id.*
[584] *700 MHz Second Report and Order*, Second Report and Order, 22 FCC Rcd 15289, 15359 n. 434 (2007).
[585] *See Auction of 700 MHz Band Licenses Closes*, Public Notice, 23 FCC Rcd 4572 (WTB 2008).
[586] *700 MHz Second Report and Order*, 22 FCC Rcd 15289.
[587] *See Auction of 700 MHz Band Licenses Closes*, Public Notice, 23 FCC Rcd 4572 (WTB 2008).
[588] *See Service Rules for the 746–764 MHz Bands, and Revisions to Part 27 of the Commission's Rules*, Second Report and Order, 15 FCC Rcd 5299 (2000) (*746–764 MHz Band Second Report and Order*).
[589] *See 746–764 MHz Band Second Report and Order*, 15 FCC Rcd at 5343, para. 108.
[590] *See id.*
[591] *See id.* at 5343, para. 108 n.246 (for the 746–764 MHz and 776–794 MHz bands, the Commission is exempt from 15 U.S.C. § 632, which requires Federal agencies to obtain SBA approval before adopting small business size standards).
[592] *See 700 MHz Guard Bands Auction Closes: Winning Bidders Announced*, Public Notice, 15 FCC Rcd 18026 (WTB 2000).
[593] *See 700 MHz Guard Bands Auction Closes: Winning Bidders Announced*, Public Notice, 16 FCC Rcd 4590 (WTB 2001).
[594] 13 C.F.R. § 121.201, NAICS codes 517210.
[595] *Amendment of Part 22 of the Commission's Rules to Benefit the Consumers of Air-Ground Telecommunications Services et al.*, Order on Reconsideration and Report and Order, 20 FCC Rcd 19663, paras. 28–42 (2005).
[596] *Id.*
[597] *See* Letter from Hector V. Barreto, Administrator, SBA, to Gary D. Michaels, Deputy Chief, Auctions and Spectrum Access Division, Wireless Telecommunications Bureau, FCC (filed Sept. 19, 2005).
[598] *See Service Rules for Advanced Wireless Services in the 1.7 GHz and 2.1 GHz Bands*, Report and Order, 18 FCC Rcd 25162, App. B (2003), *modified by Service Rules for Advanced Wireless Services In the 1.7 GHz and 2.1 GHz Bands*, Order on Reconsideration, 20 FCC Rcd 14058, App. C (2005).
[599] *Service Rules for Advanced Wireless Services in the 1915–1920 MHz, 1995–2000 MHz, 2020–2025 MHz and 2175–2180 MHz Bands et al.*, Notice of Proposed Rulemaking, 19 FCC Rcd 19263, App. B (2005); *Service Rules for Advanced Wireless Services in the 2155–2175 MHz Band*, Notice of Proposed Rulemaking, 22 FCC Rcd 17035, App. (2007); *Service Rules for Advanced Wireless Services in the 2155-2175 MHz Band*, Further Notice of Proposed Rulemaking, 23 FCC Rcd 9859, App. B (2008).
[600] The service is defined in section 90.1301 *et seq.* of the Commission's Rules, 47 C.F.R. § 90.1301 *et seq.*
[601] *See* 47 C.F.R. Part 101, Subparts C and I.
[602] *See* 47 C.F.R. Part 101, Subparts C and H.
[603] Auxiliary Microwave Service is governed by Part 74 of Title 47 of the Commission's Rules. *See* 47 C.F.R. Part 74. Available to licensees of broadcast stations and to broadcast and cable network entities, broadcast auxiliary microwave stations are used for relaying broadcast television signals from the studio to the transmitter, or between two points such as a main studio and an auxiliary studio. The service also includes mobile TV pickups, which relay signals from a remote location back to the studio.
[604] *See* 47 C.F.R. Part 101, Subpart L.
[605] *See* 47 C.F.R. Part 101, Subpart G.
[606] *See id.*
[607] *See* 47 C.F.R. §§ 101.533, 101.1017.
[608] 13 C.F.R. § 121.201, NAICS code 517210.
[609] 13 C.F.R. § 121.201, NAICS code 517210 (2007 NAICS). The now-superseded, pre-2007 C.F.R. citations were 13 C.F.R. § 121.201, NAICS codes 517211 and 517212 (referring to the 2002 NAICS).
[610] U.S. Census Bureau, 2007 Economic Census, Sector 51, EC0751I1 Information: Industry Series: Preliminary Summary Statistics for the United States: 2007, NAICS code 517210 (rel. Oct. 20, 2009), factfinder.census.gov/servlet/IBQTable?_bm=y&-fds_name=EC0700A1&-_clearIBQ=Y&-ds_name=EC0751I1&-NAICS2007=51721&-_lang=en.
[611] *Id.*
[612] *Amendment of Parts 21 and 74 of the Commission's Rules with Regard to Filing Procedures in the Multipoint Distribution Service and in the Instructional Television Fixed Service and Implementation of Section 309(j) of the Communications Act—Competitive Bidding*, MM Docket No. 94-131, PP Docket No. 93-253, Report and Order, 10 FCC Rcd 9589, 9593, para. 7 (1995).
[613] 47 C.F.R. § 21.961(b)(1).
[614] 47 U.S.C. § 309(j). Hundreds of stations were licensed to incumbent MDS licensees prior to implementation of Section 309(j) of the Communications Act of 1934, 47 U.S.C. § 309(j). For these pre-auction licenses, the applicable standard is SBA's small business size standard of 1500 or fewer employees.

[615] *Auction of Broadband Radio Service (BRS) Licenses, Scheduled for October 27, 2009, Notice and Filing Requirements, Minimum Opening Bids, Upfront Payments, and Other Procedures for Auction 86*, Public Notice, 24 FCC Rcd 8277 (2009).
[616] *Id.* at 8296.
[617] *Auction of Broadband Radio Service Licenses Closes, Winning Bidders Announced for Auction 86, Down Payments Due November 23, 2009, Final Payments Due December 8, 2009, Ten-Day Petition to Deny Period*, Public Notice, 24 FCC Rcd 13572 (2009).
[618] The term "small entity" within SBREFA applies to small organizations (nonprofits) and to small governmental jurisdictions (cities, counties, towns, townships, villages, school districts, and special districts with populations of less than 50,000). 5 U.S.C. §§ 601(4)–(6). We do not collect annual revenue data on EBS licensees.
[619] U.S. Census Bureau, 2007 NAICS Definitions, "517110 Wired Telecommunications Carriers," (partial definition), www.census.gov/naics/2007/def/ND517110.HTM#N517110.
[620] 13 C.F.R. § 121.201, NAICS code 517110.
[621] U.S. Census Bureau, 2002 Economic Census, Subject Series: Information, tbl. 4, Receipts Size of Firms for the United States: 2002, NAICS code 517510 (rel. November 2005).
[622] *Id.* An additional 61 firms had annual receipts of $25 million or more.
[621] 13 C.F.R. § 121.201, NAICS code 517410.
[622] 13 C.F.R. § 121.201, NAICS code 517919.
[623] 13 C.F.R. § 121.201, NAICS codes 517410 and 517910 (2002).
[624] U.S. Census Bureau, 2007 NAICS Definitions, "517410 Satellite Telecommunications," www.census.gov/naics/2007/def/ND517410.HTM.
[625] U.S. Census Bureau, 2002 Economic Census, Subject Series: Information, "Establishment and Firm Size (Including Legal Form of Organization)," tbl. 4, NAICS code 517410 (rel. Nov. 2005).
[626] *Id.* An additional 38 firms had annual receipts of $25 million or more.
[627] U.S. Census Bureau, 2007 NAICS Definitions, "517919 All Other Telecommunications," www.census.gov/naics/2007/def/ND517919.HTM#N517919.
[628] U.S. Census Bureau, 2002 Economic Census, Subject Series: Information, "Establishment and Firm Size (Including Legal Form of Organization)," tbl. 4, NAICS code 517910 (issued Nov. 2005).
[629] *Id.* An additional 14 firms had annual receipts of $25 million or more.
[630] U.S. Census Bureau, 2007 NAICS Definitions, "517110 Wired Telecommunications Carriers," (partial definition), www.census.gov/naics/2007/def/ND517110.HTM#N517110.
[631] 13 C.F.R. § 121.201, NAICS code 517110.
[632] U.S. Census Bureau, 2002 Economic Census, Subject Series: Information, tbl. 4, Receipts Size of Firms for the United States: 2002, NAICS code 517510 (rel. Nov. 2005).
[633] *Id.* An additional 61 firms had annual receipts of $25 million or more.
[634] 47 C.F.R. § 76.901(e). The Commission determined that this size standard equates approximately to a size standard of $100 million or less in annual revenues. *Implementation of Sections of the 1992 Cable Act: Rate Regulation,* Sixth Report and Order and Eleventh Order on Reconsideration, 10 FCC Rcd 7393, 7408 (1995).
[635] *See* BROADCASTING & CABLE YEARBOOK 2006, at A-8, C-2 (Harry A. Jessell ed., 2005) (data current as of June 30, 2005); TELEVISION & CABLE FACTBOOK 2006, at D-805 to D-1857 (Albert Warren ed., 2005).
[636] 47 C.F.R. § 76.901(c).
[637] TELEVISION & CABLE FACTBOOK 2006, at F-2 (Albert Warren ed., 2005) (data current as of Oct. 2005). The data do not include 718 systems for which classifying data were not available.
[638] 47 U.S.C. § 543(m)(2); *see* 47 C.F.R. § 76.901(f) & nn. 1–3.
[639] 47 C.F.R. § 76.901(f); *see FCC Announces New Subscriber Count for the Definition of Small Cable Operator*, Public Notice, 16 FCC Rcd 2225 (Cable Services Bureau 2001).
[640] *See* BROADCASTING & CABLE YEARBOOK 2006, at A-8, C-2 (Harry A. Jessell ed., 2005) (data current as of June 30, 2005); TELEVISION & CABLE FACTBOOK 2006, at D-805 to D-1857 (Albert Warren ed., 2005).
[641] The Commission does receive such information on a case-by-case basis if a cable operator appeals a local franchise authority's finding that the operator does not qualify as a small cable operator pursuant to § 76.901(f) of the Commission's rules. *See* 47 C.F.R. § 76.909(b).
[642] U.S. Census Bureau, 2002 NAICS Definitions, "2211 Electric Power Generation, Transmission and Distribution," www.census.gov/epcd/naics02/def/NDEF221.HTM.
[643] 13 C.F.R. § 121.201, NAICS codes 221111, 221112, 221113, 221119, 221121, 221122, n. 1.
[644] U.S. Census Bureau, 2002 Economic Census, Subject Series: Utilities, "Establishment and Firm Size (Including Legal Form of Organization)," tbl. 4, NAICS codes 221111, 221112, 221113, 221119, 221121, 221122 (rel. Nov. 2005).
[645] 5 U.S.C. § 603(c).
[646] *See* 5 U.S.C. § 801(a)(1)(A).
[647] *See* 5 U.S.C. § 604(b).
[648] John Hilvert, *UN Mulls Internet Regulation Options*, ITNEWS, Dec. 17, 2010, http://www.itnews.com.au/News/242051,un-mulls-internet-regulation-options.aspx.

[649] And at this juncture, I need to dispel a pervasive myth that broadband was once regulated like a phone company. The FCC's 2002 cable modem order did not move broadband from Title II. It formalized an effort to insulate broadband from antiquated regulations, like those adopted today, that started under then-FCC Chairman Bill Kennard. Furthermore, after the Supreme Court's *Brand X* decision, all of the FCC votes to classify broadband technologies as information services were bipartisan. A more thorough history is attached to this dissent as "Attachment A".

[650] *See* Aaron Smith, Pew Internet & American Life Project, *Americans and their gadgets* (Oct. 14, 2010) at 2, 5, 9 (76 percent of Americans own either a desktop or laptop computer; 4 percent of Americans have "tablet computers").

[651] Roger Entner, Nielsenwire, *Smartphones to Overtake Feature Phones in U.S. by 2011* (Mar. 26, 2010).

[652] *See* Distimo, GigaOm, Softpedia (links at: http://www.distimo.com/appstores/stores/index/country:226; http://gigaom.com/2010/10/25/android-market-clears-100000-apps-milestone/; and http://news.softpedia.com/news/4-000-Apps-in-Windows-Phone-Marketplace-171764.shtml).

[653] *See* Chetan Sharma, *Sizing Up the Global Mobile Apps Market* (2010) at 3, 9.

[654] Federal Communications Commission, *Connecting America: The National Broadband Plan* at 20 (rel. Mar. 16, 2010) (*National Broadband Plan*).

[655] Federal Trade Commission, Internet Access Task Force, Broadband Connectivity Competition Policy FTC Staff Report (rel. June 27, 2007) at 157.

[656] *See Ex Parte* Submission of the U.S. Dept. of Justice, GN Docket No. 09-51 (dated Jan. 4, 2010).

[657] *Id.* at 28.

[658] *Comcast Corp. v. FCC*, 600 F.3d 642 (D.C. Cir. 2010).

[659] Order, ¶ 118.

[660] While it is true that an agency may reverse its position, "the agency must show that there are good reasons." *FCC v. Fox Television Stations, Inc.*, 129 S. Ct. 1800, 1811 (2009). Moreover, while *Fox* held that "[t]he agency need not always provide a more detailed justification than what would suffice for a new policy created on a blank slate," the Court noted that "[s]ometimes it must – when, for example, its new policy rests upon factual findings that contradict those which underlay its prior policy; or when its prior policy has engendered serious reliance interest that must be taken into account." *Id.* (internal citations omitted).

[661] The D.C. Circuit in *Comcast* set forth this framework in very plain English:

Through the Communications Act of 1934, ch. 652, 48 Stat. 1064, as amended over the decades, 47 U.S.C. § 151 *et seq.*, Congress has given the Commission express and expansive authority to regulate common carrier services, including landline telephony, *id.* § 201 *et seq.* (Title II of the Act); radio transmissions, including broadcast television, radio, and cellular telephony, *id.* § 301 *et seq.* (Title III); and "cable services," including cable television, *id.* § 521 *et seq.* (Title VI). In this case, the Commission does not claim that Congress has given it express authority to regulate Comcast's Internet service. Indeed, in its still-binding 2002 *Cable Modem Order*, the Commission ruled that cable Internet service is neither a "telecommunications service" covered by Title II of the Communications Act nor a "cable service" covered by Title VI. *In re High-Speed Access to the Internet Over Cable and Other Facilities*, 17 F.C.C.R. 4798, 4802, P 7 (2002), *aff'd Nat'l Cable & Telecomms. Ass'n v. Brand X Internet Servs.*, 545 U.S. 967, 125 S. Ct. 2688, 162 L. Ed. 2d 820 (2005).

600 F.3d at 645.

[662] *See, e.g., id.; FCC v. Midwest Video Corp*, 440 U.S. 689 (1979) (*Midwest II*).

[663] For example, in the *Comcast* case, FCC counsel conceded at oral argument that the ancillary jurisdiction argument there could even encompass rate regulation, if the Commission chose to pursue that path. *Id.* at 655 (referring to Oral Arg. Tr. 58-59).

[664] *Id.*

[665] *Id.* (quoting *Midwest Video II*, 440 U.S. at 706).

[666] Order, ¶ 52.

[667] Howard Buskirk, *Investors, Analysts Uneasy About FCC Direction on Net Neutrality*, COMM. DAILY, Oct. 2, 2009, at 2; *see also* National Cable & Telecommunications Association Comments at 19; Verizon and Verizon Wireless Reply Comments at 17–18.

[668] *Comcast,* 600 F.3d at 655 (referring to Oral Arg. Tr. 58-59).

[669] *See, e.g.*, Order, ¶ 76.

[670] *See Formal Complaint of Free Press and Public Knowledge Against Comcast Corporation for Secretly Degrading Peer-to-Peer Applications*, File No. EB-08-IH-1518, Memorandum Opinion and Order, 23 FCC Rcd. 13,028 (2008) (*Comcast Order*). Comcast and BitTorrent settled their dispute, in the absence of net neutrality rules, four months before the Commission issued its legally flawed order. *See, e.g.*, David Kirkpatrick, *Comcast-BitTorrent: The Net's Finally Growing Up*, CNN.COM, Mar. 28, 2008, at http://money.cnn.com/2008/03/27/technology/comcast.fortune/index.htm

[671] Furthermore, as Commissioner Baker has noted, with this Order the Commission is inviting parties to file petitions for declaratory rulings, which will likely result in competitors asking the government to regulate their rivals in advance of market action. I am hard pressed to find a better example of a "mother-may-I" paternalistic industrial policy making apparatus.

[672] Neelie Kroes, Vice President for the Digital Age, European Commission, Net Neutrality – The Way Forward: European Commission and European Parliament Summit on "The Open Internet and Net Neutrality in Europe" (Nov. 11, 2010).

[673] LARIAT Comments at 2-3.

[674] *Id.* at 3.

[675] *Id.* at 5 (emphasis added).

[676] Letter from Brett Glass, d/b/a LARIAT, to Julius Genachowski, Chairman, FCC, *et al.*, at 2 (Dec. 9, 2010) (LARIAT Dec. 9 Letter).

[677] *See, e.g.*, Letter from Paul Conlin, President, Blaze Broadband, to Marlene H. Dortch, Secretary (Dec. 14, 2010) (Blaze Broadband Dec. 14 Letter).

[678] Section 2 of the Sherman Act, 15 U.S.C. § 2, prohibits conduct that would lead to monopolization. In the event of abuse of market power, this is the main statute that enforcers would use. In the context of potential abuses by broadband Internet access service providers, this statute would forbid: (1) Exclusive dealing – for example, the only way a consumer could obtain streaming video is from a broadband provider's preferred partner site; (2) Refusals to deal (the other side of the exclusive dealing coin) – *i.e.*, if a cable company were to assert that the only way a content delivery network could interconnect with it to stream unaffiliated video content to its customers would be to pay $1 million/port/month, such action could constitute a "constructive" refusal to deal if any other content delivery network could deliver any other traffic for a $1,000/port/month price; and (3) Raising rivals' costs – achieving essentially the same results using different techniques.

Section 5 of the Federal Trade Commission Act, 15 U.S.C. § 45, essentially accomplishes the same curative result, only through the FTC. It generally forbids "unfair competition." This is an effective statute to empower FTC enforcement as long as Internet access service is considered an "information service." The FTC Act explicitly does not apply to "common carriers."

See also, 15 U.S.C. §13(a), *et seq.*

[679] ABA Comment on Federal Trade Commission Workshop: Broadband Connectivity Competition Policy, 195 Project No. V070000 (2007).

[680] *Comcast Corp. v. FCC*, 600 F.3d 642 (D.C. Cir. 2010).

[681] The D.C. Circuit in *Comcast* set forth this framework in very plain English:

> Through the Communications Act of 1934, ch. 652, 48 Stat. 1064, as amended over the decades, 47 U.S.C. § 151 *et seq.*, Congress has given the Commission express and expansive authority to regulate common carrier services, including landline telephony, *id.* § 201 *et seq.* (Title II of the Act); radio transmissions, including broadcast television, radio, and cellular telephony, *id.* § 301 *et seq.* (Title III); and "cable services," including cable television, *id.* § 521 *et seq.* (Title VI). In this case, the Commission does not claim that Congress has given it express authority to regulate Comcast's Internet service. Indeed, in its still-binding 2002 *Cable Modem Order*, the Commission ruled that cable Internet service is neither a "telecommunications service" covered by Title II of the Communications Act nor a "cable service" covered by Title VI. *In re High-Speed Access to the Internet Over Cable and Other Facilities*, 17 F.C.C.R. 4798, 4802, P 7 (2002), *aff'd Nat'l Cable & Telecomms. Ass'n v. Brand X Internet Servs.*, 545 U.S. 967, 125 S. Ct. 2688, 162 L. Ed. 2d 820 (2005).

600 F.3d at 645.

[682] *Id.* at 655.

[683] *Id.* at 644.

[684] The scattered references to the Internet and advanced services in a few provisions of the 1996 Act, *see, e.g.*, 47 U.S.C. §§ 230, 254, do not constitute a congressional effort to systemically regulate the management of the new medium. A better reading of the 1996 Act in this regard is that Congress recognized that the emergence of the Internet meant that something new, exciting, and yet still amorphous was coming. Rather than act prematurely by establishing a detailed new regulatory scheme for the Net, Congress chose to leave the Net unregulated at that time.

[685] *Inquiry Concerning High-Speed Access to the Internet Over Cable & Other Facilities; Internet Over Cable Declaratory Ruling; Appropriate Regulatory Treatment for Broadband Access to the Internet Over Cable Facilities*, GN Docket No. 00-185, CS Docket No. 02-52, Declaratory Ruling and Notice of Proposed Rulemaking, 17 FCC Rcd. 4,798 (2002) (*Cable Modem Declaratory Ruling*); *Appropriate Framework for Broadband Access to the Internet Over Wireline Facilities et al.*, CC Docket Nos. 02-33, 01-337, 95-20, 98-10, WC Docket Nos. 04-242, 05-271, Report and Order and Notice of Proposed Rulemaking, 20 FCC Rcd. 14,853 (2005) (*Wireline Broadband Order*); *Appropriate Regulatory Treatment for Broadband Access to the Internet Over Wireless Networks*, WT Docket No. 07-53, Declaratory Ruling, 22 FCC Rcd. 5,901 (2007) (*Wireless Broadband Order*).

[686] Order, ¶¶ 121-23.

[687] *See, e.g.*, *Marsh v. Oregon Natural Res. Council*, 490 U.S. 360, 378 (1989) ("in the context of reviewing a decision ... courts should not automatically defer to the agency's express reliance on an interest in finality without carefully reviewing the record and satisfying themselves that the agency has made a reasoned decision based on its evaluation of the significance – or lack of significance – of the new information.").

688 To the degree that the Order suggests that other sections in the Act provide it with direct authority to impose new Internet network management rules, such arguments are not legally sustainable. For the reasons set forth in Section B of this extended legal analysis, *infra*, the claimed bases for extending even ancillary authority are unconvincing, which renders contentions about direct authority untenable.

689 47 U.S.C. §§ 1302 (a), (b).

690 The National Broadband Plan even noted that, "[d]ue in large part to private investment and market-driven innovation, broadband in America has improved considerably in the last decade." Federal Communications Commission, *Connecting America: The National Broadband Plan* at 3 (rel. Mar. 16, 2010) (*National Broadband Plan*). Note that during this same time period of investment, no network management rules existed.

691 The Commission has been warned about this consequence many times in the recent past. For example, during the Commission's October 2009 Capital Formation Workshop, several investment professionals raised red flags about a Title I approach to Internet regulation. Trade press accounts reported Chris King, an analyst at Stifel Nicolaus, as saying that "[w]hen you look at the telecom sector or cable sector, one of the things that scares them to death is net neutrality.... Any regulation that would limit severely [Verizon's and AT&T's] ability to control their own networks to manage traffic of their own networks could certainly have a negative role in their levels of investment going forward." Howard Buskirk, *Investors, Analysts Uneasy About FCC Direction on Net Neutrality*, COMM. DAILY, Oct. 2, 2009, at 1. Similarly, Tom Aust, a senior analyst at GE Asset Management, stated that regulatory risk is "ultimately unknowable because it's so broad and it can be so quick. For a company it means that they can't predict their revenues and cash flows as well, near or long term." *Id.* at 2.

692 Network management regulations will affect the investment outlook for transmission providers large and small. In the latter category, Brett Glass, the sole proprietor of LARIAT, a wireless Internet service provider in Wyoming, has filed comments expressing concern that the imposition of network management rules will impede his ability to obtain investment and will limit his "ability to deploy new service to currently unserved and underserved areas." LARIAT Comments at 2–3. He stated that "[t]he imposition of regulations that would drive up costs or hamper innovation would further deter future outside investment in our company and others like it." *Id.* at 3. Specifically, he argues that "[t]o mandate overly [burdensome] network management policies would foster lower quality of service, raise operating costs (which in turn would raise prices for all subscribers), and/or create a large backlog of adjudicative proceedings at the Commission (in which it would be prohibitively expensive for small and competitive ISPs to participate). *Id.* at 5. "Due to immediate deleterious impacts upon investment, these damaging effects would be likely to occur even if the Commission's Order was later invalidated, nullified, or effectively modified by a court challenge or Congressional action." Letter from Brett Glass, d/b/a LARIAT, to Julius Genachowski, Chairman, FCC, *et al.*, at 2 (Dec. 9, 2010) (Glass Dec. 9 Letter). *See also* Letter from Paul Conlin, President, Blaze Broadband, to Marlene H. Dortch, Secretary (Dec. 14, 2010) (Blaze Broadband Dec. 14 Letter).

693 47 U.S.C. § 1302(a).

694 *Comcast,* 600 F.3d at 644.

695 *Id.* at 654.

696 In support of its jurisdictional arguments, the Order cites to language in *Ad Hoc Telecomms. Users Comm. v. FCC*, 572 F.3d 903 (D.C. Cir. 2009). In that case, the D.C. Circuit does, in fact, state that "[t]he general and generous phrasing of § 706 means that the FCC possesses significant albeit not unfettered, authority and discretion to settle on the best regulatory or deregulatory approach to broadband – a statutory reality that assumes great importance when parties implore courts to overrule FCC decisions on this topic." *Ad Hoc Telecomms.,* 572 F.3d at 906–07. But, there are several reasons why that statement in *Ad Hoc Telecomms.* cannot be used for the proposition that Section 706 provides the FCC with the authority to impose network management rules. First, it is notable that the petitioners in *Ad Hoc Telecomms.* were challenging one of the FCC's forbearance decisions. As such, the FCC was not relying on Section 706 authority *alone* in that case, it was also relying on it's forbearance authority which is specifically delegated to the FCC pursuant to Section 10. The D.C. Circuit made this point in *Comcast,* when it rejected the FCC's use of *Ad Hoc Telecomms.* for its Section 706 authority arguments. *Comcast*, 600 F.3d at 659 ("In [*Ad Hoc Telecomms.*], however, we cited section 706 merely to support the Commission's choice between regulatory approaches clearly within its *statutory authority under other sections of the Act*.") (emphasis added). Second, the text of Section 706(a) actually lists "regulatory forbearance" as an example of one of the tools that the FCC may employ in order to "encourage the deployment on a reasonable and timely basis of advanced telecommunications capability to all Americans." 47 U.S.C. § 1302(a). By contrast, network management regulations are not listed in Section 706 or anywhere else in the Act. Finally, as the D.C. Court reiterated in *Comcast,* 600 F.3d at 659, the central issue that it focused on in *Ad Hoc Telecomms.* was not jurisdictional; rather it was whether the FCC's underlying forbearance decision had been arbitrary and capricious, specifically "when and how much" can the FCC forbear from Title II obligations. *Ad Hoc Telecomms.,* 572 F.3d at 904. Moreover, the court was very clear in noting that such authority was "not unfettered." *Id.* at 907.

[697] On that note, the Order even highlights the fact that "706(a) expressly contemplates the use of "regulating methods" such as price regulation." *See* Order, n. 381. This aside is an unsettling foreshadow of how these rules could be used to regulate broadband rates in the future, through either *ad hoc* enforcement cases or declaratory rulings.

[698] 47 U.S.C. § 1302(a) (emphasis added). This focus on infrastructure investment makes sense in light of Congress' express concern that broadband facilities quickly reach "elementary and secondary schools and classrooms," *id*., which in 1996 may have lacked the economic appeal of business and residential districts as early targets for infrastructure upgrades.

[699] 47 U.S.C. § 1302(b).

[700] Order, ¶ 120.

[701] While it is true that an agency may reverse its position, "the agency must show that there are good reasons." *FCC v. Fox Television Stations, Inc.*, 129 S. Ct. 1800, 1811 (2009). Moreover, while *Fox* held that "[t]he agency need not always provide a more detailed justification than what would suffice for a new policy created on a blank slate," the Court noted that "[s]ometimes it must – when, for example, its new policy rests upon factual findings that contradict those which underlay its prior policy; or when its prior policy has engendered serious reliance interest that must be taken into account." *Id.* (internal citations omitted). This warning is thrown into sharp focus by the billions of dollars invested in broadband infrastructure since the Commission first began enunciating its decisions against Title II classification of broadband Internet networks. *See, e.g.*, AT&T Comments at 19; Verizon Comments at 22.

[702] *See* Order, ¶ 122; *see also Comcast Corp. v. FCC*, 600 F.3d 642, 658 (D.C. Cir. 2010) (noting that "[i]n an earlier, still binding order, however, the Commission ruled that section 706 'does not constitute an independent grant of authority.'" (quoting *Deployment of Wireline Servs. Offering Advanced Telecomms. Capability,* CC Docket No. 98-147, Memorandum Opinion and Order, 13 FCC Rcd. 24,012, 24,047 ¶ 77 (1988)).

[703] *Comcast*, 600 F.3d at 659.

[704] 47 U.S.C. § 1302(b).

[705] *Id.*

[706] *Inquiry Concerning the Deployment of Advanced Telecommunications Capability to All Americans in a Reasonable and Timely Fashion, and Possible Steps to Accelerate Such Deployment Pursuant to Section 706 of the Telecommunications Act of 1996,* GN Docket No. 09-137, Sixth Broadband Deployment Report, *25 FCC Rcd. 9,556,* 9,558 ¶¶ 2–3 (2010). Commissioner Baker and I dissented from the July 2010 adoption of the latest Section 706 Report.

[707] *National Broadband Plan* at 20.

[708] *See* John Horrigan, Pew Internet and American Life Project, *Home Broadband Adoption 2009*, 11 (2009).

[709] *National Broadband Plan* at 20.

[710] 47 U.S.C. § 1302(b).

[711] If the Commission is successful with this assertion of authority, the agency could use Section 706 as an essentially unfettered mandate to impose not only new regulations but to pick winners and losers – all without any grant of authority from Congress to intervene in the marketplace in such a comprehensive manner. In fact, this Order has already done so. For example, it decides that these new network management rules will apply to broadband Internet service providers but not to edge providers. *See* Order, ¶ 50. The Order makes an interesting attempt to justify this line-drawing. It rationalizes, *inter alia,* that because the new regulatory scheme is putatively an outgrowth of the Commission's *Internet Policy Statement*, which was not aimed at edge providers, the Order's new mandates should not apply to those entities either. This argument is irrationally selective at best and arbitrary and capricious at worst. If the Commission's *Internet Policy Statement* was the "template" for the rules, why isn't the substance of the rules the same as the previous principles? In particular, why does the Order add nondiscrimination to the regulations when that concept was never part of the previous principles?

[712] *Comcast*, 600 F.3d at 654.

[713] *Id.* at 647.

[714] *Id.* at 644 (citing *Library Ass'n v. FCC*, 406 F.3d 689, 692 (D.C. Cir. 2005).

[715] *Id.* at 653 (emphasis in original) (citing *Nat'l Ass'n of Regulatory Util. Comm'rs v. FCC*, 533 F.2d 601, 612 (D.C. Cir. 1976) (*NARUC II*)).

[716] *Compare* Order, ¶ 133 (opining that Open Internet rules for wireless services are supported by Title III of the Communications Act pursuant to the Commission's authority "to protect the public interest through spectrum licensing") *with Comcast*, 600 F.3d at 651 ("each and every assertion of jurisdiction ... must be *independently justified* as reasonably ancillary to the Commission's power") (emphasis in original).

[717] *See Comcast*, 600 F.3d. at 653 (discussing how the *NARUC II* court "found it 'difficult to see how any action which the Commission might take concerning *two-way cable* communications could have as its primary impact the furtherance of any *broadcast* purpose.'") (emphasis added); *id* at 654 (discussing the *Midwest Video II* court's recognition that the Communications Act bars common carrier regulation of broadcasting and

therefore rejecting the imposition of public access obligations on cable because the rules would "relegate[ ] cable systems ... to common-carrier status.").

[718] The fact that some regulated services may be mixed on the same transmission platform with unregulated traffic does not afford the Commission scope to impose legal obligations on all data streams being distributed via that system. For example, the D.C. Circuit also has rejected other past Commission efforts to extend its ancillary reach over all services offered via a transmission platform merely because the platform provider uses it to provide one type of regulated service along with other services not subject to the same regulatory framework. *See id.* at 653 (citing *NARUC II*, 533 F.2d at 615–16, that overturned a series of Commission orders that preempted state regulation of non-video uses of cable systems, including precursors to modern cable modem service); *NARUC II*, 533 F.2d at 616 ("[T]he point-to-point communications ... involve one computer talking to another...."). The Order appears to be silent on this issue.

[719] *Comcast*, 600 F.3d at 651. As the Comcast decision explained, although "the Commission's ancillary authority may allow it to impose some kinds of obligations on cable Internet providers," it does not follow that the agency may claim "plenary authority over such providers." *Id.* at 650. To do so, would "run[ ] afoul" of the Supreme Court precedent set forth in *Southwestern Cable* and *Midwest Video I*." *Id. See also id.* ("Nothing in *Midwest Video I* even hints that *Southwestern Cable*'s recognition of ancillary authority over one aspect of cable television meant that the Commission had plenary authority over all aspects of cable.").

[720] *Id.* at 651. It follows that the potential for years of litigation over individual enforcement cases is high, thereby leading to a period of prolonged uncertainty that likely will discourage further investment in broadband infrastructure, contrary to the directives of Sec. 706.

[721] *See, e.g., id.* at 651, 653. For example, the court untangled the Commission's arguments about the implications of language in *Brand X* for the agency's assertion of authority over Internet network management by explaining that:

[n]othing in *Brand X*, however, suggests that the Court was abandoning the fundamental approach to ancillary authority set forth in *Southwestern Cable*, *Midwest Video I*, and *Midwest Video II*. Accordingly, the Commission cannot justify regulating the network management practices of cable Internet providers simply by citing *Brand X's* recognition that it may have ancillary authority to require such providers to unbundle the components of their services. These are altogether different regulatory requirements. *Brand X* no more dictates the result of this case than *Southwestern Cable* dictated the results of *Midwest Video I*, *NARUC II*, and *Midwest Video II*. The Commission's exercise of ancillary authority over Comcast's network management practices must, *to repeat*, "be independently justified." (emphasis added) (internal citation omitted).

[722] *Id.* at 653–54.

[723] It is curious that in reciting several provisions of Title II as potential bases for ancillary jurisdiction, the Order avoids the most obvious one: Section 202(a), which explicitly authorizes the nondiscrimination mandate imposed on Title II common carriers. This oversight is especially curious given the Order's reliance on the statutory canon of "the specific trumps the general" in revising the agency's interpretation of Section 706. *See* Order, ¶¶ 117-23 (distinguishing *Deployment of Wireline Services Offering Advanced Telecommunications Capability*, CC Docket No. 98-147, Memorandum Opinion and Order and Notice of Proposed Rulemaking, 13 FCC Rcd. 24,012 (1998) (*Advanced Services Order*) as limited only to the determination that the general provisions of Section 706 did not control the specific forbearance provisions of Section 10). That canon would seem to apply here as well, given that Section 202(a) certainly is more specific about nondiscrimination than is Section 706. Perhaps reliance on Section 202(a) as a basis for ancillary authority was omitted here in order to avoid reopening divisions over potential Title II reclassification? Of course, any effort to classify broadband Internet access as a common carrier service would confront a different set of serious legal and policy problems, see, *e.g.*, *Cable Modem Declaratory Ruling*, GN Docket No. 00-185, CS Docket No. 02-52, Declaratory Ruling and Notice of Proposed Rulemaking, 17 FCC Rcd. 4,798 (2002); *Wireline Broadband Order*, CC Docket Nos. 02-33, 01-337, 95-20, 98-10, WC Docket Nos. 04-242, 05-271, Report and Order and Notice of Proposed Rulemaking, 20 FCC Rcd. 14,853 (2005); *Wireless Broadband Order*, WT Docket No. 07-53, Declaratory Ruling, 22 FCC Rcd. 5,901 (2007), but violation of this basic canon of statutory construction would not be among them.

[724] Section 202(a)'s prohibition against "unjust or unreasonable discrimination" carries with it decades of agency and court interpretation which is much different from the Order's "nondiscrimination" mandate. For instance, the Order questions the reasonableness of tiered pricing and paid prioritization. Under the case history of Section 202, tiered pricing and concepts similar to paid prioritization are not presumed to constitute "unjust or unreasonable discrimination." *See, e.g.*, *Nat'l Ass'n of Regulatory Util. Comm'rs v. FCC*, 737 F.2d 1095, 1133 (D.C. Cir. 1984) ("But when there is a neutral, rational basis underlying apparently disparate charges, the rates need not be unlawful. For instance, when charges are grounded in relative use, a single rate can produce a wide variety of charges for a single service, depending on the amount of the service used. Yet there is no discrimination among customers, since each pays equally according to the volume of service used."); *Competitive Telecomm. Ass'n v. FCC*, 998 F.2d 1058, 1064 (D.C. Cir. 1993) ("By its nature, § 202(a) is not concerned with the price differentials between qualitatively different services or service packages. In other

words, so far as 'unreasonable discrimination' is concerned, an apple does not have to be priced the same as an orange.'").

725 *See, e.g.*, 47 U.S.C. § 153(11); *FCC v. Midwest Video Corp*, 440 U.S. 689, 705 (1979) (*Midwest II*) (construing the statute to prohibit treating broadcasters – and, by extension, cable operators – as common carriers). *See also infra* pp. 21-25. With respect to those Title III services that are subject to some common carriage regulation, mobile voice service providers bear obligations pursuant to explicit provisions of Title II of the Act, including but not limited to the provision of automatic voice roaming (Sections 201 and 202); maintainance of privacy of customer information, including call location information explicitly (Section 222); interconnection directly or indirectly with the facilities and equipment of other telecommunications carriers (Section 251); contribution to universal service subsidies (Section 254); and obligation to ensure that service is accessible to and usable by persons with disabilities (Section 255).

726 For example, in the *Comcast* case, the FCC counsel conceded at oral argument that the ancillary jurisdiction argument there could even encompass rate regulation, if the Commission chose to pursue that path. *Comcast*, 600 F.3d at 655.

727 *Id.* at 655 (emphasis added).

728 *Id.* at 657–58 (discussing *Nat'l Ass'n of Regulatory Util. Comm'rs v. FCC*, 880 F.2d 422, 425 (D.C. Cir. 1989) (*NARUC III*) and noting that "the Commission had emphasized that '[o]ur prior preemption decisions have generally been limited to activities that are closely related to the provision of services and which affect the provision of interstate services.' The term 'services' referred to 'common carrier communication services' within the scope of the Commission's Title II jurisdiction. 'In short,' the Commission explained, 'the interstate telephone network will not function as efficiently as possible without the preemptive detariffing of inside wiring installation and maintenance.' The Commission's pre-emption of state regulation of inside wiring was thus ancillary to its regulation of interstate phone service, precisely the kind of link to express delegated authority that is absent in this case." (quoting *Detariffing the Installation and Maintenance of Inside Wiring*, CC Docket No. 79-105, Memorandum Opinion and Order, 1 FCC Rcd. 1,190, 1,192, ¶ 17 (1986)).

729 Order, ¶ 125 (quoting *Comcast,* 600 F.3d at 645).

730 47 U.S.C. § 201(b).

731 *Id.*

732 The term "discrimination" in the context of communications networks is not a synonym for "anticompetitive behavior." While the word "discriminate" has carried negative connotations, network engineers consider it "network management" – because in the real world the Internet is able to function only if engineers may discriminate among different types of traffic. For example, in order to ensure a consumer can view online video without distortion or interruption, certain bits need to be given priority over other bits, such as individual emails. This type of activity is not necessarily anticompetitive.

733 *Comcast*, 600 F.3d at 645 (citing to Section 201).

734 47 U.S.C. 251(a)(1).

735 *See Vonage Holdings Corporation Petition for Declaratory Ruling Concerning an Order of the Minnesota Public Utilities Commission*, WC Docket No. 03-211, Memorandum Opinion and Order, 27 FCC Rcd. 22,404 ¶¶ 14, 20–22 (2004).

736 *See Comcast*, 600 F.3d at 654.

737 47 U.S.C. § 153(11).

738 *See Comcast*, 600 F.3d at 654 (citing *Midwest Video II*, 440 U.S. 689, 700–01) (Commission could not "relegate[ ] cable systems ... to common-carrier status"). Although the *Midwest Video II* case predated congressional enactment of cable regulation, none of the statutory amendments of the Communications Act since that time – the 1984 Cable Act, the Cable Consumer Protection and Competition Act of 1992, and the Telecommunications Act of 1996 – have imposed any form of Title II-style nondiscrimination mandates on the multichannel video services regulated pursuant to Title VI. To the contrary, the court has recognized that by its nature MVPD service involves a degree of editorial discretion that places it outside the Title II orbit. *See, e.g.*, *Denver Area Educ. Telecomm. Consortium, Inc., v. FCC*, 518 U.S. 727 (1996) (*DAETC*) (upholding § 10(a) of the 1992 Cable Act, which permitted cable operators to restrict indecency on leased access channels).

739 Order, ¶ 128.

740 *Id.*

741 *United States v. Southwestern Cable*, 392 U.S. 157 (1968) (upholding a limit on cable operators' importation of out-of-market broadcast signals); *United States v. Midwest Video Corp.*, 406 U.S. 649 (1972) (*Midwest Video I*) (plurality opinion upholding FCC rule requiring cable provision of local origination programming); *id.* at 676 (Burger, C.J., concurring) ("Candor requires acknowledgment, for me, at least, that the Commission's position strains the outer limits of even the open-ended and pervasive jurisdiction that has evolved by decisions of the Commission and the courts."). With respect to the local origination programming mandate at issue in *Midwest Video I*, the Commission reportedly "stepped back from its position during the course of the ... litigation" by "suspend[ing] the ... rule and never reinstat[ing] it." T. BARRON CARTER, JULIET L. DEE & HARVEY L. ZUCKMAN, MASS COMMUNICATIONS LAW 522–23 (West Group 2000).

[742] *Midwest Video II*, 440 U.S. at 694–95 (rejecting rules mandating cable provision of public access channels, which the FCC claimed were justified by "longstanding communications regulatory objectives" to "increas[e] outlets for local self-expression and augment[ ] the public's choice of programs").

[743] One therefore must wonder whether by this argument the Order seeks to pave the way for future regulation of mobile broadband Internet services. The Order has taken great pains to explain that today's treatment of mobile broadband Internet access service providers is in consumers' best interest. History suggests that the Order may merely be postponing the inevitable. In fact, the new rule (Section 8.7) need only be amended by omitting one word: "fixed." The Commission will be poised to do just that when it reviews the new regulations in two years.

[744] Taking the Order at its apparent word that it is not (yet) applying all new mandates on wireless broadband Internet service providers, it must be that the Order invokes the Commission's Title III licensing authority to impose the rules on fixed broadband Internet access service providers – that is, cable service providers, common carriers, or both. If so, this is curious on its face because these services are regulated under Titles VI and II, respectively, and as a legal matter the Commission does not "license" either cable service providers or common carriers.

[745] *See Truth-in-Billing and Billing Format*, CC Docket No. 98-170, Notice of Inquiry, *24 FCC Rcd. 11,380 (rel Aug. 28, 2009) (Aug. 2009 Truth-in-Billing NOI)*.

[746] *See* Service *Rules for the 698-746, 747-762 and 777-792 MHz Bands*, WT Docket No. 06-150, Report & Order, 22 FCC Rcd 15289 (2007).

[747] *See Review of the Commission's Program Access Rules and Examination of Programming Tying Arrangements*, MB Docket No. 07-198, First Report and Order, 25 FCC Rcd. 746 (2010) (*Terrestrial Loophole Order*); *id.* at 822 (McDowell, Comm'r dissenting) ("Section 628 refers to 'satellite'-delivered programming 36 times throughout the length of the provision, including 14 references in the subsections most at issue here. The plain language of Section 628 bars the FCC from establishing rules governing disputes involving terrestrially delivered programming, whether we like that outcome or not."). This FCC decision currently is under challenge before the D.C. Circuit. *See Cablevision Systems Corporation v. FCC*, No. 10-1062 (D.C. Cir. filed March 15, 2010).

[748] *See* 47 U.S.C. § 522(13) (defining "multichannel video programming distributor"). Some of the transmission systems used by such distributors, such as satellites, also are regulated under Title III.

[749] Order, ¶ 130 (citing 47 U.S.C. § 548(b)).

[750] The D.C. Circuit has upheld the Commission's reliance on Section 628(b) to help drive the provision of competitive Title VI multichannel video programming services into apartment buildings and similar "multi-dwelling unit" developments, *see Nat'l Cable & Telcoms. Ass'n v. FCC*, 567 F.3d 659 (D.C. Cir. 2009), but the policy thrust of that case unquestionably concerned Title VI video services. As the Order acknowledges, it is an open question as to whether OTT video providers might someday be made subject to Title VI, with all of the attendant legal rights and obligations that come with that classification. Order at n. 417. But it is misleading in suggesting that the regulatory classification of OTT video providers has been pending only since 2007. *Id.* On the contrary, it has been pending before the Commission since at least 2004 in the IP Enabled Services docket, WCB Docket 04-36, and the agency has consistently avoided answering the question ever since. While I do not prejudge the outcome of that issue, I question the selective invocation of sections of Title VI here as a basis for ancillary jurisdiction. Such overreaching seems to operate as a way of prolonging our avoidance of an increasingly important, albeit complex, matter.

[751] *See, e.g.*, Letter from William M. Wiltshire, Counsel for DIRECTV, to Marlene H. Dortch, Secretary, FCC, at 1 (Oct. 1, 2010) (DIRECTV Oct. 1 *Ex Parte* Letter) (outlining the wealth of innovative devices currently available in the market, including AppleTV, Boxee, and Roku); Adam Satariano & Andy Fixmer, *ESPN to Web Simulcast, Make Pay TV Online Gatekeeper*, BLOOMBERG, Oct. 15, 2010, at http://www.bloomberg.com/news/2010-10-15/espn-to-stream-channels-to-time-warner-cable-users-to-combat-web (explaining ESPN's plan to begin streaming its sports channels online to Time Warner Cable Inc. customers as part of the pay-TV industry's strategy to fend off Internet competitors); Walter S. Mossberg, *Google TV: No Need To Tune In Just Yet*, WALL ST. J., Nov. 18, 2010, at D1 (comparing Google TV technology to its rivals Apple TV and Roku); Louis Trager, *Netflix Plans Rapid World Spread of Streaming Service*, COMM. DAILY, Nov. 19, 2010, at 7 (examining Netflix's plans to offer a streaming-only service in competition with Hulu Plus, as well as its plans for expansion worldwide).

[752] 47 U.S.C. § 536.

[753] For example, Section 616(a)(1) bars cable operators from linking carriage to the acquisition of a financial interest in the independent programmers' channel – a restraint borrowed from antitrust principles that is readily understandable in the context of a traditional cable system with a limited amount of so-called "linear channel" space. The construct does not conform easily to the Internet setting, which is characterized by a considerably more flexible network architecture that allows end users to make the content choices – and which affords them access to literally millions of choices that do not resemble "video programming" as it is defined in Title VI, *see* 47 U.S.C. §522(20), including but not limited to simple, text-heavy websites, video shorts and all manner of personalized exchanges of data.

754 The federal government first involved itself in setting basic rates, terms, and conditions in the context of service agreements between railroads and their customers, but at least one historian (and former FCC commissioner) traced the "'ancient law' of common carriers" back to the development of stage coaches and canal boats. *See* GLEN O. ROBINSON, "THE FEDERAL COMMUNICATIONS ACT: AN ESSAY ON ORIGINS AND REGULATORY PURPOSE," IN A LEGISLATIVE HISTORY OF THE COMMUNICATIONS ACT OF 1934, 26 (Max D. Paglin, ed. 1989) (noting that a 19th Century Supreme Court case identified the concept emerging as far back as the reign of William and Mary).

755 In *Midwest Video II*, the Supreme Court invalidated FCC rules that would have required cable operators to provide public access channels. The Court reasoned that, in the absence of explicit statutory authority for such mandates, the public access rules amounted to an indirect effort to impose Title II common carriage obligations – and that, in turn, conflicted with the Title III basis for the agency's ancillary jurisdiction claim. *See* 440 U.S. at 699-02.

756 *Comcast*, 600 F.3d at 654.

757 *Comcast*, 600 F.3d at 661 (internal citations omitted).

758 The Order incorrectly asserts that the new network management rules raise no serious questions about a Fifth Amendment taking of an Internet transmission platform provider's property. At the outset, the Order too quickly dismisses the possibility that these rules may constitute a *per se* permanent occupation of broadband networks. Under *Loretto v. Teleprompter Manhattan CATV Corp*., a taking occurs when the government authorizes a "permanent physical occupation" of property "even if they occupy only relatively insubstantial amounts of space and do not seriously interfere with the [owner's] use of the rest of his [property]." 458 U.S. 419, 430 (1982). Here, the new regulatory regime effectively authorizes third-party occupation of some portion of a broadband ISP's transmission facilities by constraining the facility owner's ability to decide how to best manage the traffic running over the broadband platform. The new strictures have parallels to the Commission's decision to grant competitive access providers the right to the exclusive use of a portion of local telephone company's central office facilities – an action which the D.C. Circuit held constituted a physical taking. *Bell Atlantic Tel. Cos. v. FCC*, 24 F.3d 1441, 1445 (D.C. Cir. 1994).

But even assuming *arguendo* that the regulations may not constitute a physical taking, they still trigger serious "regulatory takings" concerns. Today's situation differs from the one at issue in *Cablevision Systems Corp. v FCC*, where the court held that Cablevision had failed "to show that the regulation had an economic impact that interfered with 'distinct investment backed expectations.'" 570 F.3d 83, 98–99 (2d Cir. 2009). Here, many obvious investment-backed expectations are at stake: Network operators have raised, borrowed, and spent billions of dollars to build, maintain, and modernize their broadband plant – based at least in part on the expectation that they would recoup their investment over future years under the deregulatory approach to broadband that the Commission first adopted for cable in 2002 and quickly extended to other types of facilities. Moreover, today's action could result in significant economic hardships for platform providers even if they have no debt load to pay off. For example, the Order announces the government's "expectation" that platform providers will build-out additional capacity for Internet access service before or in tandem with expanding capacity to accommodate specialized services. Order, ¶ 114. Although property owners may not be able to expect existing legal requirements regarding their property to remain *entirely* unchanged, today's vague "expectation" places a notable burden on platform providers – heavy enough, given their legitimate investment-backed expectations since 2002, to amount to a regulatory taking under *Penn Central Transp. Co. v. City of New York*, 438 U.S. 104 (1978).

759 Order, ¶ 144 (citing CWA Reply at 13-14, which cites to *Turner Broadcasting System, Inc. v. FCC*, 512 U.S. 622 (1994) and *Time Warner Entertainment, L.P. v. FCC*, 93 F.3d 957 (D.C. Cir. 1996)).

760 The Supreme Court has never directly addressed the First Amendment issues that would be associated with a government compulsion to serve as a common carrier in a marketplace that offers consumers alternatives to a monopoly provider. This is not surprising, for the courts have had no opportunity to pass on the issue; the FCC in the modern era has found that it served the public interest to waive common carrier status on numerous occasions. *See, e.g., In re Australia-Japan Cable (Guam) Limited*, 15 FCC Rcd. 24,057 (2000) (finding that the public interest would be served by allowing a submarine cable operator to offer services on a non-common carrier basis because AJC Guam was unable to exercise market power in light of ample alternative facilities); *In re Tycom Networks Inc., et al.*, 15 FCC Rcd, 24,078 (2000) (examining the public interest prong of the *NARUC I* test, and determining that TyCom US and TyCom Pacific lacked sufficient market power given the abundant alternative facilities present). In fact, in the more than 85 reported cases in which the FCC has addressed common carrier waivers in the past 30 years, it has only imposed common carriage on an unwilling carrier once – and in that instance the agency later reversed course and granted the requested non-common carrier status upon receiving the required information that the applicant previously omitted. *In re Applications of Martin Marietta Communications Systems, Inc.; For Authority to Construct, Launch and Operate Space Stations in the Domestic Fixed-Satellite Service*, 60 Rad. Reg. 2d (P & F) 779 (1986).

761 The Order is flatly wrong in asserting that "no court has ever *suggested* that regulation of common carriage arrangements triggers First Amendment scrutiny." Order, ¶ 144 (emphasis added). In *Midwest Video II*, the Court stated that the question of whether the imposition of common carriage would violate the First

Amendment rights of cable operators was "not frivolous." 440 U.S. 689 (1979), 709 n.19. In *DAETC*, 518 U.S. 727 (1996), the plurality opinion appeared split on, among other things, the constitutional validity of mandated leased access channels. Justice Kennedy reasoned that mandating common carriage would be "functional[ly] equivalent[t]" to designating a public forum and that both government acts therefore should be subject to the same level of First Amendment scrutiny. *Id.* at 798 (Kennedy, J., concurring in part, concurring in the judgment in part, and dissenting in part). Justice Thomas' analysis went even further in questioning the old [dicta] about common carriers' speech rights. *See id.* at 824–26 (Thomas, J., concurring in the judgment in part and dissenting in part) (stating that "Common carriers are private entities and may, consistent with the First Amendment, exercise editorial discretion in the absence of a specific statutory prohibition").

[762] Order, ¶ 140 (citing, *e.g.*, *Turner Broadcast Systems, Inc v. FCC*, 512 U.S. 622, 636 (1994) (*Turner I*)).

[763] *Illinois Bell Telephone Co. v. Village of Itasca*, 503 F. Supp. 2d 928 (N.D. Ill. 2007) (analogizing broadband network providers to cable and DBS providers); *Comcast Cablevision of Broward County, Inc. v. Broward County*, 124 F. Supp. 2d 685 (S.D. Fla. 2000) (relying on Supreme Court precedent in *Ex parte Jackson*, 96 U.S. 727, 733 (1878) and *Lovell v. Griffin*, 303 U.S. 444, 452 (1938), the court concluded that the message, as well as the messenger, receives constitutional protection because the transmission function provided by broadband services could not be separated from the content of the speech being transmitted).

[764] Order, n. 458.

[765] Order, ¶ 143.

[766] In addition, the Order's citation to a Copyright Act provision, U.S.C. § 230(c)(1), to support the proposition that broadband providers serve no editorial function, see Order, ¶ 142, ignores the fact that broadband ISPs engage in editorial discretion – as permitted under another provision of the Copyright Act, 17 U.S.C. § 230(c)(2) – to block malicious content and to restrict pornography. *See Batzel v. Smith*, 333 F.3d 1018, 1030 n.14 (9th Cir. 2003) (noting that § 230(c)(2) "encourages good Samaritans by protecting service providers and users from liability for claims arising out of the removal of potentially 'objectionable' material from their services.... This provision insulates service providers from claims premised on the taking down of a customer's posting such as breach of contract or unfair business practices.").

[767] Nor does the availability of alternative venues for speech undercut the platform owner's First Amendment rights to be able to effectively use its own regulated platform for the speech it wishes to disseminate. *See, e.g.*, *Nat'l Cable Television Ass'n v. FCC*, 33 F.3d 66 (D.C. Cir. 1994).

[768] *See, e.g.*, McInnis & Associates, "The Basics of Selling Newspaper Advertising," Newspaper Print and Online ad Sales Training, at http://www.ads-on-line.com/samples/Your_Publication/chapterone2.html (visited 12/7/10). This ratio has remained relatively constant for decades. *See* Robert L. Jones & Roy E. Carter Jr., "Some Procedures for Estimating 'News Hole' in Content Analysis," The Public Opinion Quarterly, Vol. 23, No. 3 (Autumn, 1959), pp. 399-403, pin cite to p. 400 (noting measurements of non-advertising newsholes as low as 30 percent, with an average around 40 percent) (available at http://www.jstor.org/stable/2746391?seq=2) (visited 12/7/10).

[769] Alan Mutter, "Robust ad recovery bypassed newspapers," Reflections of a Newsosaur (Dec. 3, 2010) (available at http://newsosaur.blogspot.com/) (visited 12/7/10).

[770] Order, ¶¶ 145-46.

[771] Order, ¶¶ 112-14.

[772] Although the Order addresses only intermediate scrutiny, the potential for application of strict scrutiny should not be disregarded completely. Although the Court in *Turner I* declined to apply strict scrutiny to the statutorily mandated must-carry rules, the network management mandates established by today's Order may be distinguishable. For example, while rules governing the act of routing data packets might arguably be content neutral regulations, application of the rules in the real world may effectively dictate antecedent speaker-based and content-based choices about which data packets to carry and how best to present the speech that they embody.

[773] *American Library Ass'n v. Reno*, 33 F.3d 78 (D.C. Cir. 1994).

[774] Under First Amendment jurisprudence, it typically is not difficult for the government to convince a court that the agency's interest is important or substantial. *See, e.g.*, *Carey v. Brown*, 447 U.S. 455, 464–65 (1980) ("even the most legitimate goal may not be advanced in a constitutionally impermissible manner"); *Simon & Schuster, Inc. v. Members of the N.Y. State Crime Victims Bd.*, 502 U.S. 105 (1991) (finding that the state interest was compelling, but the Son of Sam law was not narrowly tailored to advance that objective). But I question whether the Order will survive even this prong of the test because the Commission lacks evidence of a real problem here to be solved. Two examples plus some economic theorizing may be insufficient to demonstrate that the asserted harms to be addressed are, in fact, real and systemic. *See Century Communications Corp. v. FCC*, 835 F.2d 292, 300 (D.C. Cir. 1987) (suggesting that to establish a real harm the Commission has the burden of producing empirical evidence such as studies or surveys). The Commission's most recent Section 706 Report, which – over the dissent of Commissioner Baker and me – reversed course on 11 years' worth of consistent findings that advanced services are being deployed on a timely basis, is no foundation on which this part of the argument can securely rest. *See supra* Section A.

[775] *Turner I*, 512 U.S. at 662.

[776] *See* Order, ¶ 114 ("We fully expect that broadband providers will increase capacity offered for broadband Internet access service if they expand network capacity to accommodate specialized services. We would be concerned if capacity for broadband Internet access service did not keep pace.").

[778] *See Fox v. FCC,* 613 F.3d 317 (2d Cir. 2010) (holding that the FCC's indecency policy "violates the First Amendment because it is unconstitutionally vague, creating a chilling effect").

[779] *See, e.g.*, Order, ¶¶ 146-48.

[780] *Oversight of the Federal Communications Commission: The National Broadband Plan: Hearing Before the Subcomm. on Communications, Technology, and the Internet of the House Comm. on Energy and Commerce,* 111th Cong., 2d Sess. (March 25, 2010).

[781] Some who are advocating that broadband Internet access service should be regulated under Title II cite to the Commission's 1998 *GTEADSL Order* to support their assertion. *See GTE Telephone Operating Cos.,* CC Docket No. 98-79, Memorandum Opinion and Order, 13 FCC Red. 22,466 (1998) *{GTEADSL Order).* The *GTE ADSL Order,* however, is not on point, because in that order the Commission determined that GTE-ADSL service was an interstate service for the purpose of resolving a tariff question.

[782] Departments of Commerce, Justice, and State, the Judiciary, and Related Agencies Appropriations Act, 1998, Pub. L. No. 105-119,111 Stat. 2440,2521-2522, § 623.

[783] *Federal-State Board on Universal Service,* CC Docket No. 96-45, Report to Congress, 13 FCC Red. 11501, K 73 (1998) *{Report to Congress).*

[784] *Id.* at 180 (emphasis added).

[785] *Id.* at Tj 82 ("Our findings in this regard are reinforced by the negative policy consequences of a conclusion that Internet access services should be classed as 'telecommunications.'").

[786] As Seth P. Waxman, former Solicitor General under President Clinton, wrote in an April 28,2010 letter to the Commission, "[t]he Commission has *never* classified any form of broadband Internet access as a Title II 'telecommunications service* in whole or in part, and it has classified all forms of that retail service as integrated 'information services' subject only to a light-touch regulatory approach under Title I. These statutory determinations are one reason why the Clinton Administration rejected proposals to impose 'open access' obligations on cable companies when they began providing broadband Internet access in the late 1990s, even though they then held a commanding share of the market. The Internet has thrived under this approach." (Emphasis in the original.)

[787] *Inquiry Concerning High-Speed Access to the Internet Over Cable and Other Facilities,* GN Docket No. 00-185, Notice of Inquiry, 15 FCC Red 19287 (2000) *(Cable Modem NOI).*

[788] *Inquiry Concerning High- Speed Access to the Internet Over Cable and Other Facilities; Internet Over Cable Declaratory Ruling; Appropriate Regulatory Treatment for Broadband Access to the Internet Over Cable Facilities,* GN Docket No. 00-185, CS Docket No. 02-52, Declaratory Ruling and Notice of Proposed Rulemaking, 17 FCC Red 4798 (2002) *(Cable Modem Declaratory Ruling), aff'd, Nat'I. Cable & Telecomms. Ass'n* v. *Brand X Internet Servs.,* 545 U.S. 967 (2005) *(Brand X).*

[789] *Id.* at H 2.

[790] *Appropriate Framework for Broadband Access to the Internet over Wireline Facilities, Universal Service Obligations of Broadband Providers,* CC Docket No. 02-33, Notice of Proposed Rulemaking, 17 FCC Red 3019 (2002) (*Wireline Broadband NPRM).*

[791] *Brand X,* 545 U.S. 967.

[792] *Id.* at 977 (emphasis added, internal citations to the Commission's *Computer Inquiry II* decision omitted).

[793] *Appropriate Framework for Broadband Access to the Internet over Wireline Facilities; Universal Service Obligations of Broadband Providers; Review of Regulatory Requirements for Incumbent LEC Broadband Telecommunications Services; Computer III Further Remand Proceedings: Bell Operating Company Provision of Enhanced Services; 1998 Biennial Regulatory Review—Review of Computer III and ONA Safeguards and Requirements; Conditional Petition of the Verizon Telephone Companies for Forbearance Under 47 U.S.C. § I60(c)with Regard to Broadband Services Provided Via Fiber to the Premises; Petition of the Verizon Telephone Companies for Declaratory Ruling or, Alternatively, for Interim Waiver with Regard to Broadband Services Provided Via Fiber to the Premises; Consumer Protection in the Broadband Era,* CC Docket Nos. 02-33, 95-20, 98-10,01-337, WC Docket Nos. 04-242, 05-271, Report and Order and Notice of Proposed Rulemaking, 20 FCC Red 14853 (2005) *{Wireline Broadband Order), affd, Time Warner Telecom, Inc. v. FCC,* 507 F.3d 205 (3d Cir. 2007).

[794] *United Power Line Council's Petition for Declaratory Ruling Regarding the Classification of Broadband over Power Line Internet Access Service as an Information Service,* WC Docket No. 06-10, Memorandum Opinion and Order, 21 FCC Red 13281 (2006).

[795] *Appropriate Regulatory Treatment for Broadband Access to the Internet Over Wireless Networks,* WT Docket No. 07-53, Declaratory Ruling, 22 FCC Red 5901 (2007).

[796] *Comcast Corp. v. FCC,* 600 F.3d 642 (D.C. Cir. 2010)("*Comcast*").

[797] USTelecom Comments at 5 (detailing that "cumulative capital expenditures by broadband providers from 2000-2008 were over half a trillion dollars, and private investment in broadband infrastructure has grown consistently from 2003 through 2008.").

[798] CONNECTING AMERICA: THE NATIONAL BROADBAND PLAN, The Federal Communications Commission, GN Docket No. 09-51, 20 (2010).

[799] *Id.*

[800] FCC Working Paper, "Broadband satisfaction: What consumers report about their broadband Internet provider," at 3 (Dec. 2010) (finding that 93 percent of users are satisfied, or somewhat satisfied, with their broadband service).

[801] Jeffry Bartash, *Comcast, Cablevision Stocks Decline on Cloudy Outlook,* Wall Street Journal, May 10, 2010; David Barden, Bank of America – Merrill Lynch, *Internet Regulation Back on the Front Burner* (May 5, 2010) (noting that Title II regulation could "threaten" both "jobs and investment" across the Internet ecosystem.); Craig Moffett, *Quick Take—U.S. Telecommunications, U.S. Cable & Satellite Broadcasting: The FCC Goes Nuclear,* Bernstein Research, May 5, 2010 (noting that "[m]arkets abhor uncertainty" and that he expects "a profoundly negative impact on capital investment" from the proposed rules.").

[802] If regulatory certainty is one of the majority's priorities, they should have also closed the Title II docket today, slamming shut the door on proposals to apply highly intrusive monopoly-era common carrier restrictions on competitive broadband platforms.

[803] The Order states that the Commission will "review all of the rules in this Order no later than two years from their effective, and will adjust its open Internet framework as appropriate." To promote regulatory certainty, this future proceeding should mirror our biennial review process under which the Commission's task is limited to determining whether any rule is no longer in the public interest as a result of meaningful competition. *See* 47 U.S.C. **§ 161.** It would be hard to suggest that this Order provides any certainty if the Commission intends to conduct an open-ended review in 2013.

[804] *Appropriate Framework for Broadband Access to the Internet over Wireline Facilities,* Policy Statement, Separate Statement of Chairman Kevin Martin, FCC 05-150 (2005).

[805] Federal Trade Commission, "Broadband Connectivity Competition Policy," at 11 (June 2007) ("*FTC Report*").

[806] *Id.*

[807] *Nat'l Fuel Gas Supply Corp. v. FERC,* 468 F.3d 831, 843, 844 (D.C. Cir. 2006)(finding that "if [an agency] chooses to rely solely on a theoretical threat, it will need to explain how the potential danger …unsupported by a record of abuse, justifies such costly prophylactic rules."); *see also BellSouth Telecommunications Inc. v. FCC,* 469 F.3d 1052, 1060 (D.C. Cir. 2006)(finding that "the agencies' predictive judgment gives [it] no license to ignore the past when the past relates directly to the question at issue,").

[808] J. Gregory Sidak and David J. Teece, "Innovation Spillovers and the 'Dirt Road' Fallacy: The Intellectual Bankruptcy of Banning Optional Transactions for Enhanced Delivery over the Internet," at 46. Forthcoming in 6 *Journal of Competition Law & Economics* (2010) (attached as Exhibit 2 to AT&T Reply Comments); *see also id.* at 45 (explaining that "[u]ntil empirical evidence is presented that network providers in fact have a substantial – and not merely theoretical – incentive to foreclose competing content and applications and that this incentive is likely to outweigh *countervailing* incentives, we believe that … appropriate support for such regulation is lacking."); *see also* Declaration of Gary S. Becker and Dennis W. Carlton at 5 (attached as Attachment A to Verizon Comments)(concluding that "[t]he absence of widespread complaints about anticompetitive discrimination indicates that the FCC's competitive concerns are overstate in the current Internet environment."); Declaration of Marius Schwartz at 39 (attached as Exhibit 3 to AT&T Comments) (contending that "[g]eneralized references to future irreversible harm should not suffice to justify intrusive regulation in advance of clear evidence of a problem, especially when similar alarms have consistently been proven wrong.").

[809] FCC Working Paper, "Broadband decisions: What drives consumers to switch – or stick with – their broadband Internet provider," at 1-2, 5 (Dec. 2010)(finding that "63% of broadband adopters with a choice of multiple providers said it would be easy to switch providers," and that "37% of home broadband users had switched Internet service providers (ISPs) in the last three years.").

[810] *2007 FTC Report* at 11.

[811] *Id.*

[812] *See* Declaration of Michael D. Topper at 54 (attached as Attachment C to Verizon Comments) (arguing that "[c]ontractual pricing arrangements between broadband providers and application and content providers may result in the provision of new and better services. A two-sided pricing model where both consumers and content providers pay fees may also be a more efficient way for network providers to recover the substantial fixed costs of building, improving, and maintaining broadband access networks."). The Order acknowledges this economic theory, yet discounts its import suggesting "no broadband provider has stated in this proceeding that it actually would use any revenue from edge provider charges to offset subscriber charges." There is considerable expert testimony on the record regarding the potential of two-sided markets to reduce end-user pricing and benefit consumers, and the majority should have addressed the pro-consumer potential in a more forthright manner. *See, e.g.,* Declaration of Michael L. Katz, "Economic Arguments in the Network Neutrality Proceeding" at 30 (attached as Attachment B to Verizon Reply Comments) (explaining that "strategies such as two-sided pricing and offering of menus of service options can promote increased adoption. Specifically, network operators might use revenue from arrangements with online service or application providers to

subsidize the costs of consumer access, which would increase adoption."); Declaration of Marius Schwartz at 18 (attached as Exhibit 3 to AT&T Comments) (describing that "if broadband providers were to charge fees to content providers (and, indirectly, online advertisers), the likely result would be lower prices or other improved terms to consumers.").

813 Robert C. Atkinson and Ivy E. Schultz, "Broadband in America," Columbia Institute for Tele-Information, 68 (Nov. 11, 2009) ("*CITI Report*").

814 The focus on networks as the solitary challenge with respect to Internet transparency strains credibility. In the text of the Order, the majority references privacy and other considerations that seem more applicable to concerns consumers have primarily about applications and websites, not underlying broadband networks. This only underscore that these issues are best left to Congress or cross-industry groups working towards best practices and a more holistic and consistent approach. Given the Commission's overall lack of authority to act in this area, it is regrettable the majority is willing to draw artificial lines within the Internet economy, anoint certain players as gatekeepers, and cherry pick the type of player and conduct it wishes to regulate in an arbitrary manner.

815 *Consumer Information and Disclosure Truth-in-Billing Format IP-Enabled Services,* Notice of Proposed Rulemaking, CG Docket No. 09-158, FCC 10-180 (2010).

816 Equally unconvincing is the claim that new entrepreneurs—the next Google, the next Yahoo!—are the beneficiaries of the rules. The majority has crafted rules that will provide a regulatory advantage for those companies that benefit the most from today's business models. In particular, those edge companies with their own multi-million dollar—if not multi-billion dollar—infrastructures comprised of private networks, server farms, and content delivery networks will benefit. For new ventures, the Order may dissuade networks and new entrants from experimenting in new ways to reach consumers, to compete with better financed and established Internet companies, and to formulate pro-consumer, pro-competition business models that do not yet exist.

817 Cisco Visual Networking Index: Forecast and Methodology, 2009-2014 (June 2, 2010) (available at http://www.cisco.com/en/US/solutions/collateral/ns341/ns525/ns537/ns705/ns827/white_paper_c11-481360_ns827_Networking_Solutions_White_Paper.html).

818 *CITI Report* at 68.

819 Remarks of Neelie Kroes, "Net Neutrality in Europe," Address at ARCEP Conference (Apr. 13, 2010) (available at http://europa.eu/rapid/pressReleasesAction.do?reference=SPEECH/10/153); *see also* Remarks of Neelie Kroes, "Net Neutrality, the Way Forward," European Commission and European Parliament Summit on The Open Internet and Net Neutrality in Europe (Nov. 11, 2010) (available at http://europa.eu/rapid/pressReleasesAction.do?reference=SPEECH/10/643) (advocating that regulators "avoid regulation that might deter investment.").

820 Craig Moffett, "Weekend Media Blast: Building Networks is Hard ... Earning a Return on Them is Even Harder," Bernstein Research (Dec. 17, 2010).

821 *See* 3rd Generation Partnership Project (3GPP), "Technical Specification Group Services and System Aspects; Policy and charging control architecture (Release 9)" December 2009 (available at: http://ofdm.jp/3GPP/Specs/23203-930.pdf).

822 By naming itself Internet referee, the Commission has also introduced a new strategic option into every commercial dispute in the Internet sector. Parties will have the ability to try to manipulate our procedures for their commercial gain, or as simple leverage to extract concessions in private deals. This is not conjecture. In the buildup to this Order, we have seen countless different disputes across the Internet sector be labeled as Net Neutrality issues. I fear actual engineering issues will be subsumed by commercial and political considerations.

823 BITAG is an independent non-profit organization, "whose mission is to bring together engineers and other similar technical experts to develop consensus on broadband network management practices or other related technical issues that can affect users' Internet experience, including the impact to and from applications, content and devices that utilize the Internet." (available at http://members.bitag.org/kwspub/home/).

824 *American Library Ass'n v. FCC,* 406 F.3d 689, 691, 698 (D.C. Cir. 2005) ("*ALA*") (citing *Louisiana Public Service Commission v. FCC,* 476 U.S. 355, 374 (1986)).

825 *MCI Telecommunications Corp. v. AT&T Co.,* 512 U.S. 218, 234 (1994) ("*MCI*").

826 *See* Remarks of Chairman Julius Genachowski, "Preserving Internet Freedom and Openness" (Dec. 1, 2010) (explaining that "this proposal would build upon the strong and balanced framework developed by Chairman Henry Waxman").

827 *ALA,* 406 F.3d at 704.

828 *United States v. Southwestern Cable Co.,* 392 U.S. 157, 178 (1968).

829 *Deployment of Wireline Servs. Offering Advanced Telecomms. Capability*, Memorandum Opinion and Order and Notice of Proposed Rulemaking, 13 FCC Rcd 24012, ¶ 74 (1998) ("*Advanced Services Order*").

830 *Review of the Section 251 Unbundling Obligations of Incumbent Local Exchange Carriers,* Report and Order on Remand and Further Notice of Proposed Rulemaking, 18 FCC Rcd 16978, ¶ 278 (2003).

831 *Advanced Services Order,* ¶ 77.

[832] *Qwest Petition for Forbearance Under 47 U.S.C. § 160(c) from Title II and Computer Inquiry Rules with Respect to Broadband Services*, Memorandum Opinion and Order, 23 FCC Rcd 12260, ¶ 52 (2008); *see also Appropriate Framework for Broadband Access to the Internet Over Wireline Facilities*, Report and Order and Notice of Proposed Rulemaking, 20 FCC Rcd 14853,¶ 19 (2005) ("*Wireline Broadband Order*") (finding that "the directives of section 706 of the 1996 Act require that we ensure that our broadband policies promote infrastructure investment, consistent with our other statutory obligations under the Act.").

[833] Even if the *Advanced Services Order* interpretation were limited to the "regulatory forbearance" language as the majority now claims, there is no reasonable reading under which that interpretation would not be controlling on section 706(a) as a whole. Specifically, the term "regulatory forbearance" appears in the middle of a list, and every item on the list is prefaced by the same language, the language authorizing the Commission to "utiliz[e] in a manner consistent with the public interest, convenience, and necessity," the various tools listed. Thus, if the Commission found no independent authority to forbear, there could then be no independent authority to take any other action mentioned in section 706(a). It would be illogical to suggest that some of the items on the list convey independent authority while others do not.

[834] *Comcast,* 600 F.3d at 658-59. The majority's expansive reading of the 2008 *Ad Hoc* decision is equally misplaced. *Ad Hoc Telecom. Users Committee v. FCC,* 572 F.3d 903 (D.C. Cir. 2009). In that case, the court upheld a deregulatory measure (special access relief) that was pursuant to the Commission's section 10 forbearance authority, not section 706(a). *Id.,* 572 F.3d at 907. The *Comcast* court already rejected the majority's claim, explaining that the court in *Ad Hoc* "cited section 706 merely to support the Commission's choice between regulatory approaches clearly within its statutory authority under other sections of the Act." *Comcast*, 600 F.3d at 659. The *Comcast* court concluded explicitly that, "[n]owhere did [the D.C. Circuit] question the Commission's determination that section 706 does not delegate any regulatory authority. The Commission's reliance on section 706 thus fails." *Id.* Tellingly, the Commission's own brief in that case characterized section 706 in the manner it has always been understood: "Guided by the deregulatory mandate of section 706, the Commission - in a series of decisions affirmed by the courts - has taken measures designed to ease regulatory burdens on providers of broadband services." Brief for Respondents at 8, *Ad Hoc Telecom. Users Committee v. FCC*, 572 F.3d 903 (D.C. Cir. 2009) (No. 07-1426). This is a deregulatory power.

[835] *Framework for Broadband Internet Service*, Notice of Inquiry 25 FCC Rcd 7866, ¶ 36 (2010).

[836] By attempting to manipulate our prior interpretation, the majority has also failed to provide procedurally an adequate justification to change the interpretation of section 706(a) from policy statement to direct authority. The Supreme Court recently emphasized that when an agency changes its position it "must show that there are good reasons for the new policy." *FCC v. Fox Television Stations*, 129 S.Ct. 1800, 1811 (2009). There is a heightened burden here because the "prior policy has engendered serious reliance interests." *Id.* Network operators have invested billions into their infrastructure relying on the deregulatory approach to broadband networks best evidenced, until now, by the section 706 deregulatory policy statement. The Commission, therefore, must provide "a more detailed justification than would suffice for a new policy created on a blank slate." *Id.*, at 1811. Not only does the Commission fail to offer any justification, it also failed to establish a factual record on this question. In another proceeding, the Commission asked the right questions about "revisit[ing] and chang[ing] its conclusion that section 706(a) is not an independent grant of authority." *Framework for Broadband Internet Service*, Notice of Inquiry 25 FCC Rcd 7866, ¶ 36 (2010). We further asked what "findings would be necessary to reverse that interpretation." *Id.* The Commission failed to properly justify a change in interpretation, and is, therefore, not entitled to do so in this proceeding.

[837] 47 U.S.C. § 1302(a).

[838] *United States Telecom Ass'n v. FCC, 359 F.3d* 554, 579 (D.C. Cir. 2004).

[839] *See, e.g., Wireline Broadband Order,* ¶ 19.

[840] The cursory attempt to use section 706(b) as direct authority suffers a similar fate. That provision directs the Commission to evaluate the deployment of advanced services. The majority's action bears no logical connection with Congress's directive to "take immediate action to accelerate deployment of such capability by removing barriers to infrastructure investment and by promoting competition in the telecommunications market." 47 U.S.C. § 1302(b). The majority raises barriers here, not lowers them, and takes steps that will not accelerate broadband deployment. Further, it making the negative finding triggering this authority, the Commission outlined the "immediate" steps it intended to take, noting "several [active] proceedings" related to implementing recommendations to the National Broadband Plan and "other[proceedings] still be to be commenced." *Inquiry Concerning the Deployment of Advanced Telecommunications Capability to All Americans in a Reasonable and Timely Fashion, and Possible Steps to Accelerate Such Deployment Pursuant to Section 706 of the Telecommunications Act of 1996, Amended by the Broadband Data Improvement Act*, Order, FCC 10-129, ¶ 29 (2010). The Net Neutrality proceeding—initiated prior to that finding—was never mentioned as one of the steps required by section 706(b). I also have institutional concerns in the lack of discussion of how the section 706(b) power functions, given it has never been evoked before. We sidestep the question of what happens if a subsequent section 706 report finds broadband deployment to be timely again. The attempt to use this power so broadly here also underscores the need for a more searching and analytically sound approach to the section 706 reports. The Commission's finding of nationwide untimely and

unreasonable deployment was, among other defects, overly broad. The analysis should have been significantly more granular to identify particular geographic areas or communities for which deployment has lagged, and I hope we correct that error in future reports.

[841] *Comcast,* 600 F.3d at 655.

[842] Section 706 was ultimately codified at section 1302, twelve years after it was enacted.

[843] *FDA v. Brown & Williamson*, 529 U.S. 120, 160 (2000).

[844] *Id.,* 529 U.S. at 121; *see also, MCI,* 512 U.S. at 231 ("It is highly unlikely that Congress would leave the determination of whether an industry will be entirely, or even substantially, rate regulated to agency discretion and even more unlikely that it would achieve that through such a subtle device…").

[845] *Board of Governors of Fed. Reserve Sys. v. Dimension Fin. Corp.,* 474 U.S. 361, 374 (1986).

[846] *See e.g.,* Letter from Ranking Member Joe Barton *et al* to Honorable Julius Genachowski (Nov. 19, 2010); Sara Jerome, "Hutchinson pans net-neutrality proposal," The Hill (Dec. 1, 2010); Press Release, "Upon Urges FCC to Cease and Desist on Net Neutrality" (Dec. 1, 2010).

[847] *See e.g.,* Press Release, "Kerry, Dorgan, Wyden Urge FCC to Act This Year on Open Internet," (Nov. 30, 2010).

[848] Letter from Senator John Ensign *et al* to Honorable Julius Genachowski (Dec. 15, 2010).

[849] *Id.*

[850] Letter from Chairman Fred Upton *et al* to Honorable Julius Genachowski (Dec. 16, 2010).

[851] *Joint Statement on Broadband,* FCC 10-42, ¶ 3 (Mar. 16, 2010).

CHAPTER SOURCES

The following chapters have been previously published:

Chapter 1 – This is an edited reformatted and augmented version of a Congressional Research Service Publication, report R40234, dated December 2, 2010.

Chapter 2 – This is an edited reformatted and augmented version of a Federal Communications Commission publication, report FCC 10-201, dated December 23, 2010.

INDEX

#

21st century, 100, 139
4G wireless offerings, 125

A

abuse, 63, 145, 172, 181
access charges, 141
access device, 27
accessibility, 139
accommodations, 59
accounting, 138
ACF, 141
Activists, 143
Administrative Procedure Act, 52
adverse effects, 127, 144
advertisements, 137
advocacy, 16, 35, 82, 151
affirmative action, 66
affirming, 5
age, 101, 102
agencies, 19, 58, 63, 85, 109, 111, 131, 158, 169, 181
aggregation, 19, 139
ALEC, 69, 75, 151
America Online, 20
American Cable Association (ACA), 84, 148
American Library Assn. v. FCC, 5, 6
American Recovery and Reinvestment Act, 141, 144
American Recovery and Reinvestment Act of 2009, 141, 144
annual rate, 107
Anti-Defamation League, 69
antithesis, 36, 128
antitrust, 108, 111, 144, 145, 152, 177
appointees, 106
Appropriations Act, 180
arbitrage, 106
Asia, 129
assessment, 3, 113, 130, 155
Associated Press, vii, 1, 2, 4, 11, 165
AT&T, 12, 52, 53, 54, 69, 75, 78, 80, 101, 135, 137, 138, 139, 140, 141, 143, 144, 145, 146, 147, 148, 149, 150, 151, 152, 153, 154, 155, 156, 157, 159, 160, 161, 163, 164, 165, 166, 173, 174, 181, 182
attachment, 102, 156
authorities, 42, 43, 61, 63, 108, 157
authority, vii, 1, 2, 3, 5, 6, 7, 8, 9, 10, 12, 34, 43, 44, 45, 46, 47, 48, 49, 50, 51, 52, 57, 63, 65, 66, 68, 98, 103, 106, 107, 108, 109, 112, 113, 114, 115, 116, 117, 118, 124, 125, 130, 131, 132, 133, 134, 153, 158, 159, 160, 161, 163, 164, 166, 170, 171, 172, 173, 174, 175, 176, 177, 182, 183
avoidance, 177
awareness, 45

B

ban, 98, 103, 151, 162
bandwidth, 34, 38, 129
bargaining, 140
barriers, 17, 19, 20, 21, 34, 46, 47, 48, 83, 107, 108, 113, 114, 132, 155, 159, 164, 183
barriers to entry, 17, 20, 34, 83
base, 1, 125, 133
BEA, 89
Bell Atlantic, 146, 178

BellSouth, 135, 146, 147, 165, 166, 181
benchmarks, 5, 161
beneficiaries, 123, 182
benefits, 16, 18, 21, 23, 25, 26, 29, 31, 43, 44, 45, 49, 82, 96, 98, 101, 102, 136, 140, 149, 151, 152
BitTorrentTM, vii, 1, 2, 4
blogger, 34
blogs, 20, 143
BMI, 70, 76, 152
bounds, 103
Broadband Internet Technical Advisory Group (BITAG), 130
browser, 41
browsing, 41
business costs, 110
business model, 16, 26, 39, 82, 97, 98, 117, 125, 128, 129, 130, 182
business processes, 135, 151
businesses, vii, 16, 18, 19, 21, 82, 87, 89, 90, 92, 98, 110, 126, 129, 138, 145

C

cable programming service, 140
cable service, 93, 94, 115, 171, 172, 177
cable system, 51, 94, 117, 153, 166, 175, 176, 177
cable television, 53, 171, 172, 175
capital expenditure, 180
capital markets, 110
Capitol Hill, 106
case law, 84, 113, 119, 131
cash, 109, 173
cash flow, 109, 173
causation, 144
CCR, 69, 78
censorship, 165
Census, 85, 87, 92, 93, 94, 95, 167, 168, 169, 170
Center for Regulatory Effectiveness (CRE), 83
certificate, 63
certification, 5, 17, 40, 83
challenges, 18, 37, 39, 112, 118, 120, 129, 134, 141, 165
Chamber of Commerce, 69, 70, 71, 72, 73, 74, 75, 78
Chicago, 73, 137, 152
China, 107
circus, 110
cities, 85, 104, 137, 170
citizens, 103, 105
City, 12, 70, 73, 165, 178
civic life, 16, 18, 82, 127
civil rights, 100
clarity, vii, 15, 16, 36, 37, 81, 82, 96, 128, 154
classes, 12, 20, 30, 34, 51, 95, 109, 111, 129
classification, 7, 9, 112, 121, 122, 158, 174, 177
clients, 151, 153
Clinton Administration, 121, 180
CNN, 171
coaches, 178
Code of Federal Regulations, 4, 60
coffee, 28, 109, 124, 133
collaboration, 107, 111, 123
collateral, 142, 182
collusion, 145
color, 138, 155
Comcast, v, vii, 1, 2, 3, 4, 5, 6, 8, 11, 12, 13, 23, 24, 25, 37, 46, 48, 52, 70, 76, 102, 108, 109, 110, 111, 112, 113, 114, 115, 116, 118, 131, 132, 135, 136, 138, 139, 140, 143, 144, 145, 147, 148, 149, 150, 151, 152, 154, 155, 157, 158, 159, 160, 161, 164, 171, 172, 173, 174, 175, 176, 178, 179, 180, 181, 183, 184
Comcast Network Management Practices Order, 25, 37, 143, 154
commerce, 45, 47
commercial, 18, 24, 28, 29, 34, 40, 59, 61, 87, 91, 98, 130, 151, 182
common carriers, 52, 54, 102, 116, 119, 121, 161, 172, 175, 176, 177, 178, 179
common sense, 133
communication, 16, 18, 28, 45, 47, 52, 82, 116, 147, 165, 176
Communications Act, 1, 2, 3, 6, 7, 8, 10, 12, 17, 28, 33, 35, 45, 47, 48, 49, 51, 52, 59, 65, 83, 94, 109, 111, 112, 117, 121, 131, 153, 158, 159, 161, 165, 169, 171, 172, 174, 176, 178
Communications Act of 1934, 3, 59, 94, 169, 171, 172, 178
communities, 104, 110, 123, 155, 161, 184
community, 19, 29, 126, 127, 134, 136, 151
compensation, 128, 134, 141
competition, vii, 3, 15, 16, 17, 18, 23, 24, 25, 28, 32, 33, 34, 35, 38, 42, 44, 45, 46, 47, 48, 50, 54, 60, 81, 82, 83, 98, 101, 102, 107, 108, 113, 114, 117, 118, 123, 125, 126, 127, 129, 130, 134, 138, 139, 140, 142, 143, 145, 146, 147, 151, 152, 153, 155, 156, 159, 160, 163, 172, 177, 181, 182, 183

competition policy, 146
Competitive Access Providers (CAPs, 86
competitive advantage, 106, 156
Competitive Local Exchange Carriers (Competitive LECs, 86
competitiveness, 15, 81, 97, 102, 129, 157, 161
competitors, 23, 49, 116, 138, 139, 162, 171, 177
complement, 162
complexity, 146
compliance, 5, 25, 31, 39, 40, 59, 84, 95, 96, 147, 151, 164
compression, 162
compulsion, 153, 178
computer, 6, 18, 27, 46, 107, 150, 154, 164, 165, 171, 175
computing, 7, 139
conference, 65, 66
confidentiality, 67
conflict, 114, 118, 159, 165
conformity, 34
Congress, 2, 3, 6, 13, 19, 33, 34, 45, 47, 49, 50, 51, 52, 53, 59, 96, 100, 102, 106, 108, 109, 111, 112, 113, 120, 121, 131, 133, 139, 152, 153, 158, 162, 164, 171, 172, 174, 180, 182, 183, 184
connectivity, 8, 9, 12, 27, 107, 118, 140, 143, 162
consensus, 10, 41, 105, 106, 133, 182
consent, 146
consolidation, 96
constituents, 155
constitutional law, 37
constitutional principles, 120
construction, 107, 160, 175
consulting, 136, 144
consumer advocates, 58
consumer choice, 17, 35, 51, 54, 60, 83, 106, 107, 125, 128, 129, 134
consumer education, 164
consumer protection, 44, 102, 107, 111
consumers, 2, 3, 4, 9, 10, 15, 16, 19, 29, 35, 38, 39, 40, 44, 50, 51, 61, 81, 82, 97, 98, 99, 100, 102, 103, 104, 105, 107, 108, 110, 113, 123, 124, 125, 126, 127, 128, 129, 130, 134, 136, 137, 138, 139, 144, 145, 146, 147, 150, 153, 155, 156, 157, 160, 162, 177, 178, 181, 182
consumption, 50, 119
controversial, 126, 133
conversations, 2
cooperation, 111
coordination, 142
copyright, 43, 44, 53, 61, 164, 179
cost, 19, 21, 23, 31, 47, 56, 59, 84, 96, 125, 128, 130, 134, 141, 160
costs of compliance, 16, 18, 25, 31, 82, 84, 96
counsel, 66, 115, 171, 176
counterbalance, 156
Court of Appeals, vii, 1, 3, 12
cracks, 126
creativity, 95
cure, 111, 145
cures, 111
customers, 4, 23, 24, 26, 31, 33, 36, 49, 50, 52, 53, 96, 102, 103, 116, 127, 128, 136, 141, 142, 146, 149, 153, 156, 162, 163, 164, 172, 175, 177, 178

D

danger, 152, 181
data processing, 8
data rates, 33
data transfer, 162
defects, 184
deficiencies, 127
degradation, 24, 37, 144, 150
delegates, 49
democracy, 19, 97, 101
denial, 38, 64, 152, 154
denial of service attack, 154
Department of Justice, 108, 111, 145, 146, 153
deposits, 23
depth, 105
designers, 147
differential treatment, 33
digital divide, 19, 138
direct broadcast satellite service, 163
direct-broadcast satellite (DBS), 49
directives, 4, 112, 115, 118, 131, 175, 183
disaster, 43
disaster relief, 43
disclosure, 17, 25, 28, 29, 31, 32, 39, 40, 45, 52, 53, 58, 59, 67, 83, 84, 85, 95, 96, 104, 146, 148, 149
discrimination, 9, 10, 15, 17, 25, 26, 27, 31, 33, 34, 35, 37, 42, 61, 81, 83, 98, 101, 103, 116, 150, 151, 152, 153, 161, 165, 175, 176, 181
disposition, 66
distribution, 19, 49, 51, 53, 95, 137, 139, 161, 163
district courts, 119, 164

District of Columbia, 165
diversity, 19, 50, 138, 140
DOC, 12, 13, 138, 141, 143
DOJ, 109, 146
dominance, 86, 167
draft, 107, 133
drawing, 130, 174
duopoly, 101

E

e-commerce, 18, 19, 135
economic development, 95
economic growth, vii, 15, 81, 97, 101, 106, 145
economic incentives, 20, 152, 164
economic theory, 127, 181
ecosystem, 28, 39, 97, 132, 145, 147, 153, 181
education, 18, 25, 124, 141, 151
educational institutions, 92, 103
election, 66
electricity, 18, 95, 104
electronic communications, 109, 111
Electronic Communications Privacy Act, 43
Electronic Frontier Foundation, 4, 71, 76, 147
e-mail, 27, 59
emergency, 42, 43, 61, 157
emergency communications, 42, 43, 61
emergency response, 43
employees, 59, 67, 84, 85, 86, 87, 88, 89, 92, 93, 94, 152, 167, 169
employment, 88, 92, 167
encoding, 2
end-users, 101, 128, 147
energy, 18, 27, 95, 104, 141
energy consumption, 27
energy efficiency, 18, 141
enforcement, vii, 1, 9, 11, 23, 24, 25, 31, 43, 55, 56, 57, 96, 97, 103, 110, 145, 166, 172, 174, 175
engineering, 30, 34, 37, 55, 57, 58, 124, 128, 130, 131, 158, 182
enhanced service, 121, 122
entrepreneurs, 21, 97, 98, 99, 100, 103, 104, 128, 164, 182
environment, 25, 104, 128, 134, 141, 147, 151, 181
equipment, 18, 23, 27, 36, 58, 61, 136, 138, 142, 150, 151, 165, 176
equity, 156
e-readers, 27, 39
erosion, 24
Europe, 129, 156, 172, 182
European Commission, 110, 129, 156, 172, 182
European Parliament, 172, 182
evidence, 4, 17, 24, 25, 34, 57, 65, 67, 68, 108, 109, 110, 113, 114, 123, 126, 127, 129, 133, 134, 139, 140, 143, 166, 179, 181
evolution, 39, 40, 51, 99
exclusion, 140, 144
exercise, 6, 44, 51, 53, 101, 112, 114, 118, 119, 131, 159, 160, 161, 163, 175, 178, 179
externalities, 21

F

Facebook, 20
fairness, 156
faith, 62, 64, 67, 154
families, 6, 46, 100, 105
family life, 105
farms, 182
faster delivery, 50
FDA, 184
fear, 32, 107, 130, 134, 182
fears, 110, 114
Federal Communications Act, 178
Federal Communications Commission, vii, 1, 2, 12, 13, 15, 120, 133, 140, 171, 173, 180, 181
federal government, 19, 178
Federal Government, 155
federal law, 159
Federal Register, 31, 58, 60, 84, 96, 167
Federal Trade Commission, 126
Federal Trade Commission Act, 172
fiber, 19, 37, 134
Fifth Amendment, 53, 55, 109, 178
file sharing programs, vii, 1, 2
filters, 119, 146
financial, 16, 82, 141, 144, 177
First Amendment, 53, 54, 118, 119, 120, 164, 165, 178, 179, 180
Fixed broadband providers, 15, 81
fixed costs, 181
flavor, 118
flaws, 116
flexibility, 17, 25, 29, 31, 35, 36, 37, 38, 41, 46, 55, 59, 83, 84, 96, 98, 99, 152, 154
fluid, 45
FMC, 79
force, 2, 9, 21, 34, 132

formation, 134
formula, 130
franchise, 170
fraud, 159
freedom, vii, 15, 16, 17, 32, 38, 54, 58, 60, 81, 82, 83, 97, 98, 99, 101, 102, 104, 105, 107, 118, 119, 145
funding, 19, 137

G

GDP, 135
Georgia, 71
global markets, 18
governance, 34, 106, 107, 111, 151
government intervention, 111, 125
governments, 85, 107, 167
grants, 6, 45, 144, 161
grassroots, 106
grounding, 118
growth, 23, 25, 39, 45, 97, 107, 108, 134, 137, 139, 145, 155
growth rate, 155
guessing, 167
guidance, 3, 4, 29, 33, 37, 40, 55, 123, 152, 153, 154, 165
guidelines, 142, 149

H

harbors, 164
harmful effects, 45, 123, 124
health, 18, 19, 25, 46, 104, 141, 152
health care, 18, 46, 141
higher education, 160
highways, 106
hiring, 164
history, 39, 46, 55, 100, 101, 104, 106, 107, 114, 121, 131, 132, 165, 171, 175
Hmong, 71
homeland security, 43, 157
host, 147
House, 70, 71, 76, 77, 78, 120, 134, 136, 148, 151, 156, 165, 180
House of Representatives, 120
housing, 114

I

ICC, 152
identification, 147, 157
ideology, 97
images, 143
immunity, 53
improvements, 16, 18, 82, 103, 104, 128, 141, 162
income, 155
increased competition, 139, 142
incumbent local exchange carrier, 113
Incumbent Local Exchange Carriers (Incumbent LECs), 86
incumbents, 91, 139
indecency, 176, 180
individuals, 6, 20, 46, 120, 147, 148, 155
industrial policy, 171
industries, 93
industry, 4, 7, 10, 16, 18, 50, 82, 85, 86, 93, 94, 95, 96, 100, 111, 118, 122, 123, 125, 126, 127, 129, 134, 136, 139, 141, 142, 145, 152, 158, 162, 163, 165, 177, 182, 184
inflation, 167
information economy, 145
infrastructure, 19, 25, 29, 35, 38, 46, 47, 48, 54, 93, 94, 97, 101, 104, 108, 113, 114, 125, 126, 132, 134, 136, 142, 145, 146, 159, 165, 174, 175, 180, 183
injury, 55
institutions, 92, 160
integrity, 36, 37, 154
interest groups, 110, 128
interface, 151
interference, 24, 49, 50, 55, 161, 165
interoperability, 104, 146
intervention, 53, 111, 129
investment, vii, 15, 16, 17, 18, 24, 25, 29, 33, 34, 35, 42, 44, 46, 47, 48, 52, 54, 55, 81, 82, 83, 97, 98, 99, 100, 101, 108, 109, 110, 113, 114, 124, 126, 128, 132, 134, 136, 140, 141, 142, 144, 145, 146, 148, 159, 173, 174, 175, 178, 181, 182, 183
investment incentive, 142
investments, 24, 52, 108, 142, 144, 145
investors, 22, 26, 58, 97, 98, 100, 101, 109, 126
Iowa, 161
IP networks, 160

issues, 9, 16, 41, 42, 45, 55, 58, 64, 65, 66, 82, 84, 87, 91, 98, 99, 100, 106, 107, 123, 127, 128, 130, 133, 146, 156, 163, 178, 182
IXCs, 87

J

Japan, 178
job creation, vii, 15, 81, 97, 100, 101, 129
Jordan, 74, 79, 152
journalists, 19
jurisdiction, 1, 2, 3, 5, 6, 7, 8, 9, 17, 45, 47, 48, 49, 83, 85, 109, 115, 116, 117, 118, 132, 159, 163, 171, 174, 175, 176, 177, 178
Justice Scalia, 7
justification, 9, 23, 171, 174, 183

K

kill, 125

L

laptop, 171
latency, 22, 30, 39, 129
Latin America, 72, 77
Latinos, 77, 79, 155
law enforcement, 3, 42, 43, 61, 157
lawful Internet content, 3
lawful network traffic, 15, 33, 61, 81, 87
laws, 29, 35, 42, 46, 106, 111, 152
lawyers, 106, 124
lead, 16, 18, 21, 82, 112, 114, 121, 157, 172
leadership, 97, 121, 134
learning, 23, 111
legislation, 52, 109, 133, 139, 164
legislative authority, 48
liberty, 153
light, 8, 9, 16, 30, 35, 39, 58, 82, 97, 98, 107, 111, 157, 159, 174, 178, 180
Lion, 153
litigation, 53, 175, 176
lobbying, 110
local government, 85, 159
location information, 176
Louisiana, 77, 182
lower prices, 136, 139, 182

M

magnitude, 20, 25, 126, 133
majority, 86, 87, 88, 91, 92, 93, 94, 104, 106, 108, 109, 110, 111, 119, 124, 125, 126, 127, 128, 129, 130, 131, 132, 133, 134, 136, 142, 181, 182, 183
malware, 154
man, 77
mania, 101
market economy, 96
market failure, 107, 111, 124, 126
market segment, 21
market structure, 99
marketing, 45, 142, 146
marketplace, 42, 49, 98, 100, 119, 123, 142, 145, 147, 155, 156, 157, 174, 178
Maryland, 78
mass, 26, 27, 34, 61, 139, 146
materials, 31, 54, 59, 66, 67, 68, 130, 149
matter, 35, 45, 47, 55, 64, 68, 87, 103, 112, 116, 128, 134, 177
measurements, 179
media, vii, 1, 2, 4, 77, 94, 101, 136, 137, 138, 139, 162
membership, 136
messages, 39
metaphor, 126
Miami, 137
Microsoft, 77, 144, 157, 165, 166
Minneapolis, 165
minorities, 19, 104
mission, 123, 125, 182
mobile device, 39
mobile phone, 24, 39, 124
models, 29, 128, 182
monopoly, 101, 178, 181
multichannel video programming service, 27, 109, 111, 119, 177
multimedia, 136
music, 77
music technology, 77

N

naming, 182
National Association of Manufacturers, 73, 77

National Broadband Plan, 15, 81, 110, 114, 121, 134, 135, 136, 142, 148, 155, 158, 166, 171, 173, 174, 180, 183
national security, 42, 43, 61, 157
negotiating, 141
network congestion, 22, 35, 143, 150
network elements, 158
network providers, 3, 33, 97, 113, 118, 120, 140, 150, 151, 179, 181
neutral, 3, 54, 96, 130, 150, 165, 175, 179
next generation, 23, 134, 145
North America, 71
NRP, 163

O

obstacles, 132
Office of Management and Budget, 31, 58, 59, 60, 84, 96
officials, 133
omission, 115
online advertising, 18
Open Internet NPRM, 16, 17, 19, 29, 31, 32, 35, 36, 37, 38, 39, 43, 44, 55, 58, 81, 82, 83, 135, 136, 138, 146, 147, 148, 149, 151, 153, 154, 155, 157, 158, 165, 166
openness, vii, 15, 16, 17, 18, 19, 20, 22, 23, 24, 25, 26, 32, 34, 38, 39, 40, 41, 42, 52, 58, 81, 82, 83, 84, 95, 97, 98, 99, 101, 102, 103, 104, 123, 135, 138, 140, 145, 155, 156, 157, 163, 167
operating costs, 110, 142, 173
operating system, 41, 155, 157
operations, 91, 92
Operator Service Providers (OSPs), 87
opportunities, 19, 55, 92, 102, 104, 105, 124, 164
opt out, 155
orbit, 176
oversight, 29, 161, 175
ownership, 142, 156, 164
oxygen, 134

P

P2P applications, vii, 1, 2, 3, 4, 143
Pacific, 178
parental control, 36, 38
parity, 103, 104
participants, 4, 147
pay television services, 16, 82
peer-to-peer (P2P), vii, 1, 2, 23
penalties, 57
permission, vii, 16, 17, 18, 37, 38, 54, 60, 82, 83, 101, 107, 130
permit, 46, 56, 101, 102, 139, 152, 153
personal communication, 88, 91
personal computers, 20
persons with disabilities, 95, 176
Peru, 73
Philadelphia, 70, 141
platform, vii, 15, 16, 17, 18, 19, 20, 26, 35, 38, 39, 40, 42, 44, 60, 81, 82, 83, 97, 99, 100, 104, 111, 117, 118, 119, 120, 127, 138, 153, 155, 157, 162, 163, 175, 178, 179
playing, 16, 82, 98
police, 109
policy, vii, 1, 3, 4, 6, 9, 11, 12, 33, 37, 45, 48, 55, 99, 101, 102, 103, 105, 111, 113, 115, 116, 120, 121, 123, 124, 125, 126, 131, 132, 133, 134, 143, 144, 145, 147, 149, 151, 158, 159, 160, 161, 165, 171, 174, 175, 177, 180, 183
policy issues, 123
policy making, 105
policy problems, 175
policymakers, 146
poor performance, 33
population, 85, 114, 137
portfolio, 133
precedent, 106, 115, 116, 119, 120, 131, 159, 175, 179
predictability, 26, 97
prejudice, 64
preparation, iv
preservation, 165
president, 145
President, 74, 76, 79, 121, 125, 139, 145, 172, 173, 180
President Clinton, 121, 180
price cap regulation, 47, 48, 113, 159
prima facie, 57, 166
principles, 1, 3, 4, 10, 11, 16, 17, 24, 25, 26, 28, 29, 32, 33, 37, 42, 43, 48, 51, 52, 82, 84, 97, 98, 123, 125, 135, 143, 144, 147, 148, 149, 154, 157, 174, 177
private investment, 15, 44, 81, 98, 134, 173, 180
privatization, 121
probability, 145
procedural rule, 56, 166
producers, 144

product market, 139
professionals, 173
profit, 4, 21, 85, 124, 140, 182
programming, 19, 20, 32, 50, 51, 53, 117, 137, 138, 139, 140, 161, 162, 163, 176, 177
project, 105, 129, 149
prophylactic, 16, 17, 18, 25, 41, 82, 140, 145, 154, 181
prophylactic rules, 16, 17, 18, 25, 82, 181
proposed regulations, 10, 160
proposition, 35, 173, 179
protection, 9, 27, 41, 119, 179
protocol-agnostic network management, 5, 11, 144, 151
public interest, vii, 1, 9, 35, 42, 46, 48, 49, 51, 52, 54, 55, 63, 124, 133, 145, 146, 152, 160, 161, 174, 178, 181, 183
public policy, 101, 103, 106
public safety, 42, 43, 61, 134, 141, 147, 157
publishing, 12
purity, 97

Q

QoS, 119
quality of service, 35, 110, 119, 129, 173
questioning, 126, 179
Qwest, 74, 77, 79, 80, 136, 139, 143, 149, 152, 156, 157, 159, 165, 166, 183

R

race, 21, 105
radar, 93
radio, 17, 19, 26, 28, 45, 47, 49, 51, 52, 61, 83, 88, 91, 102, 117, 137, 147, 161, 164, 165, 171, 172
ramp, 137
reading, 47, 84, 113, 118, 131, 132, 159, 172, 183
reality, 139, 143, 173
reasoning, 119, 158, 164
recognition, 35, 112, 119, 123, 174, 175
recommendations, 52, 58, 183
recovery, 179
reform, 4, 126, 134
Reform, 69, 75, 78, 80, 160
regulations, 2, 3, 5, 6, 7, 9, 10, 13, 51, 52, 54, 97, 110, 112, 113, 115, 119, 120, 150, 159, 160, 161, 163, 167, 171, 173, 174, 177, 178, 179
regulatory framework, 150, 175
regulatory requirements, 52, 156, 175
reliability, 33
relief, 62, 63, 65, 183
repair, 105
reporters, 67
requirements, 31, 42, 45, 46, 52, 53, 55, 57, 58, 60, 62, 63, 64, 65, 67, 84, 91, 95, 96, 104, 138, 139, 144, 146, 148, 150, 151, 153, 156, 160, 161, 163, 164, 165, 178
reserves, 24
resolution, 63, 65, 66, 152
resources, 56, 57, 84, 96, 126, 129, 131
response, vii, 1, 3, 5, 85, 119, 121, 136, 139, 154, 156, 158
response time, 154
restrictions, 30, 38, 40, 134, 143, 147, 181
retail, 26, 34, 61, 121, 180
revenue, 20, 22, 145, 170, 181
rights, 2, 3, 10, 24, 42, 53, 54, 101, 103, 119, 120, 126, 149, 156, 158, 177, 179
risk, 17, 18, 20, 22, 23, 25, 29, 83, 97, 101, 128, 129, 130, 134, 140, 148, 158, 173
rural areas, 155

S

safety, 42, 43, 45, 102, 152
sanctions, 63
satellite service, 61
Saudi Arabia, 107
scale economies, 102
school, 6, 26, 35, 46, 85, 104, 124, 167, 170
science, 97
scope, 27, 37, 43, 44, 65, 86, 133, 151, 175, 176
secondary schools, 46, 174
security, 29, 30, 31, 36, 37, 38, 42, 43, 96, 99, 148, 154
self-expression, 161, 177
self-interest, 50, 117
sellers, 142
Senate, 47
sensors, 27
servers, 152
service provider, 3, 4, 10, 24, 33, 35, 37, 58, 59, 84, 86, 87, 94, 97, 101, 110, 112, 115, 116,

118, 136, 144, 147, 149, 150, 151, 154, 157, 164, 172, 173, 174, 176, 177, 179, 181
Shared-Tenant Service Providers, 86
Sherman Act, 172
showing, 57, 64, 67, 114, 137
signals, 93, 102, 169, 176
signs, 45
small businesses, 18, 26, 59, 84, 85, 86, 87, 88, 89, 90, 91, 92, 93, 103, 110, 113, 124, 135, 164
Smithville Telephone Company (Smithville), 84
social costs, 141
social network, 19
society, 33, 156
software, 31
sole proprietor, 173
Solicitor General, 180
solution, 134, 144
spam, 29, 53, 119, 154
specifications, 151
speech, 10, 17, 19, 53, 54, 83, 101, 119, 120, 137, 138, 164, 165, 179
Spring, 126, 134, 147
Sprint, 74, 77, 79, 142, 146, 148, 149, 152, 155, 157, 158
stability, 102
stakeholders, 18, 28, 55, 99, 123
state, 19, 38, 39, 42, 43, 46, 47, 58, 62, 63, 64, 84, 99, 106, 120, 146, 158, 159, 162, 173, 175, 176, 179
states, 6, 12, 84, 99, 113, 149, 159, 181
statutes, 43, 48, 83
statutory authority, 12, 46, 47, 48, 51, 52, 63, 109, 112, 118, 125, 131, 159, 173, 178, 183
statutory foundation, 113
statutory provisions, 6, 48, 131
storage, 27
stress, 18
strictures, 178
structure, 25
style, 115, 117, 118, 176
subpoena, 164
subscribers, 4, 20, 21, 22, 23, 28, 33, 34, 38, 50, 92, 94, 110, 125, 138, 140, 143, 150, 151, 153, 158, 162, 163, 164, 173
substitutes, 44
substitution, 103, 155
suppliers, 58, 107, 162
supply chain, 107
suppression, 54
Supreme Court, 6, 7, 9, 12, 25, 45, 53, 113, 114, 116, 117, 122, 131, 133, 152, 153, 159, 171, 175, 178, 179, 183

T

tactics, 106
takeover, 97
target, 127
tariff, 9, 121, 180
taxonomy, 20
technical assistance, 57
techniques, 125, 146, 154, 172
Technological Advisory Process, 16, 82
technological change, 118
technologies, 6, 16, 18, 24, 26, 27, 37, 38, 46, 58, 82, 104, 154, 165, 171
technology, 17, 18, 21, 24, 26, 30, 36, 37, 38, 41, 62, 83, 93, 94, 97, 100, 104, 107, 114, 136, 139, 145, 150, 158, 160, 162, 171, 177
telecommunications, 2, 3, 5, 7, 8, 9, 12, 35, 46, 47, 48, 49, 85, 93, 94, 101, 102, 103, 113, 116, 121, 122, 139, 145, 152, 158, 159, 161, 164, 171, 172, 173, 176, 180, 183
Telecommunications Act, 7, 9, 10, 17, 45, 59, 83, 102, 112, 121, 138, 150, 153, 174, 176, 183
telecommunications services, 7, 8, 9, 35, 49, 93, 116, 121, 122, 145, 164
telemarketing, 146
telephone, 5, 20, 23, 28, 34, 49, 50, 62, 66, 86, 94, 102, 104, 116, 119, 124, 138, 139, 140, 142, 160, 164, 176, 178
telephone companies, 20, 49, 50, 102, 119, 138, 139, 164
television stations, 137
tension, 35
thoughts, 97, 104, 109
threats, 16, 18, 20, 23, 82, 130, 140
Title I, 2, 3, 5, 6, 7, 8, 9, 13, 28, 49, 51, 103, 108, 109, 112, 114, 115, 116, 117, 119, 121, 122, 126, 132, 153, 159, 160, 163, 166, 171, 172, 173, 174, 175, 176, 177, 178, 180, 181, 183
Title II, 2, 3, 5, 7, 8, 9, 13, 28, 49, 51, 103, 109, 112, 114, 115, 116, 117, 119, 121, 122, 126, 132, 153, 160, 163, 166, 171, 172, 173, 174, 175, 176, 177, 178, 180, 181, 183
Title V, 50, 109, 115, 117, 118, 171, 172, 176, 177
trade, 23, 147
trade-off, 23

transaction costs, 22, 34
transactions, 145
transition period, 5
transmission, 1, 7, 8, 20, 21, 22, 23, 50, 51, 53, 54, 93, 94, 95, 102, 118, 121, 122, 138, 141, 146, 158, 160, 164, 165, 173, 175, 177, 178, 179
transparency, 4, 10, 17, 24, 25, 26, 29, 31, 32, 37, 39, 40, 45, 46, 52, 53, 55, 58, 83, 84, 95, 96, 98, 99, 104, 117, 128, 142, 143, 145, 146, 148, 149, 154, 156, 160, 161, 182
transport, 121, 143
treatment, 5, 33, 34, 37, 47, 55, 57, 104, 122, 129, 145, 147, 148, 150, 152, 153, 157, 161, 177
triggers, 54, 178
twist, 131

U

uniform, 40, 147, 151
United, 6, 12, 15, 45, 51, 70, 75, 77, 78, 79, 81, 85, 94, 100, 106, 120, 129, 130, 141, 143, 144, 145, 148, 151, 152, 154, 156, 158, 159, 161, 163, 165, 167, 168, 169, 170, 176, 180, 182, 183
United Nations (UN), 107, 170
United States, 6, 12, 15, 45, 51, 75, 78, 79, 81, 85, 94, 100, 106, 120, 129, 130, 141, 143, 144, 145, 148, 151, 152, 154, 156, 158, 159, 161, 163, 165, 167, 168, 169, 170, 176, 182, 183
universe, 86
unreasonable discrimination, 9, 10, 15, 25, 26, 27, 33, 34, 35, 37, 42, 61, 81, 98, 103, 150, 151, 152, 153, 161, 175
USA, 75, 78, 79, 81

V

variables, 129
variations, 147
vein, 164
venture capital, 97, 100, 145
Verizon, 39, 54, 75, 78, 79, 81, 135, 138, 139, 140, 141, 144, 145, 147, 151, 153, 154, 155, 156, 157, 158, 159, 161, 164, 165, 166, 171, 173, 174, 180, 181
Vice President, 11, 77, 159, 172
video programming, 19, 50, 51, 92, 117, 118, 161, 162, 163, 177
videos, 137
viruses, 154
vision, 100, 125
voice over Internet Protocol (VoIP), 85
VoIP services, 5, 20, 49, 116, 138, 139, 142, 156, 160
vote, 97, 100, 104, 114
voting, 104
vulnerability, 38

W

waiver, 66, 157
war, 120
Washington, 70, 75, 105, 120, 143, 165
wealth, 177
web, 40, 41, 137, 138, 139, 144, 151, 155, 166, 167, 177
web sites, 166
webpages, 54
websites, 15, 17, 19, 27, 31, 38, 39, 40, 41, 55, 61, 81, 83, 87, 96, 99, 117, 137, 177, 182
welfare, 127, 165
wholesale, 158, 163
Wi-Fi, 140, 143
Wired Telecommunications Carriers., 86, 87
wireless networks, 43, 129, 147, 154
wires, 122
Wisconsin, 69, 72
witnesses, 67
World Wide Web, 18, 27, 96, 136
worldwide, 156, 177
worms, 154
worry, 124, 150
wrongdoing, 130, 143

Y

young people, 139